BETWEEN DEVELOPMENT AND DESTRUCTION

Between Development and Destruction

An Enquiry into the Causes of Conflict in Post-Colonial States

Edited by

Luc van de Goor

Kumar Rupesinghe

Paul Sciarone

The Netherlands Ministry of Foreign Affairs (DGIS)
in association with
The Netherlands Institute of International Relations, CLINGENDAEL
The Hague

First published in Great Britain 1996 by
MACMILLAN PRESS LTD
Houndmills, Basingstoke, Hampshire RG21 6XS
and London
Companies and representatives throughout the world

A catalogue record for this book is available
from the British Library.

ISBN 0–333–65037–9 hardcover
ISBN 0–333–65038–7 paperback

First published in the United States of America 1996 by
ST. MARTIN'S PRESS, INC.,
Scholarly and Reference Division,
175 Fifth Avenue,
New York, N.Y. 10010

ISBN 0–312–16264–2

Library of Congress Cataloging-in-Publication Data
Between development and destruction : an enquiry into the causes of
conflict in post-colonial states / edited by Luc van de Goor, Kumar
Rupesinghe, Paul Sciarone ; [authors, Shrin Akiner . . . et al.].
p. cm.
Includes bibliographical references and index.
ISBN 0–312–16264–2
1. Civil war. 2. Regionalism (International organization)
3. Security, International. 4. International economic relations.
I. Goor, Luc L. P. van de. II. Rupesinghe, Kumar. III. Sciarone,
Paul.
JX4541.B48 1996
303.6'4—dc20   96–16522
                                                        CIP

10   9   8   7   6   5   4   3   2   1
05   04   03   02   01   00   99   98   97   96

Printed and bound in Great Britain by
Mackays of Chatham PLC, Chatham, Kent

This publication was financed by the Netherlands Ministry of Foreign Affairs, which
also shares copyright. Responsibility for the contents and for the opinions expressed
rests solely with the author; publication does not constitute an endorsement by the
Netherlands Minister for Development Cooperation.

Contents

Part II State-Formation

Part III Ethnicity and Nationalism

About the Authors

Shirin Akiner is Director of the Central Asia Research Forum at the School of Oriental and African Studies, the University of London.

Abdul-Monem Al-Mashat was Professor of Political Science at Cairo University. He is now Cultural Counselor and Director of the Cultural and Educational Bureau of the Egyptian Embassy in Washington, DC. He has published a book on *National Security in the Third World* (1985) and several articles on security issues in the Arab World.

Mohammed Ayoob is Professor of International Relations, James Madison College, Michigan State University. His most recent publications include *The Third World Predicament: State-Making, Regional Conflict, and the International System*; *India and Southeast Asia: Indian Perceptions and Policies*; two edited volumes, *Regional Security in the Third World* and *Leadership Perceptions and National Security: The Southeast Asian Experience*; and articles in *Foreign Policy, Asian Survey, International Affairs, International Studies Quarterly, World Politics*, and *Alternatives*.

Francis M. Deng is Senior Fellow of the Brookings Institution and Special Representative of the United Nations Secretary-General on Internally Displaced Persons. His recent publications include *Protecting the Disposessed: A Challenge for the International Community*; several co-edited volumes, *Conflict Resolution in Africa* (co-edited with I. William Zartman) and *The Search for Peace and Unity in the Sudan* (with Prosser Gifford); and articles in the *Middle East Journal* and *Africa Today* and chapters in books on security issues in Africa.

Jan Eliasson was Permanent Representative of Sweden to the United Nations in New York. He was Under Secretary-General for Humanitarian Affairs at the United Nations from 1992-1994. He is Director of the International Peace Acadamy.

Luc L.P. van de Goor studied History at the University of Utrecht. He is a researcher at the Netherlands Institute of International Relations, 'Clingendael' in the framework of the project *Causes of Conflict in the Third World*. He has written the survey on causes of conflict in the Third World which formed the basis for this book. Additionally, he has published several articles on the subject.

Makram Haluani is Director of the Graduate School of Political Science, Simon Bolivar University, Caracas, Venezuela. His recent publications include *Introduction to Political Science* (1990) and *Protest or Migrate: Strategies and Problems of Social Protest Movements* (1991).

Henk W. Houweling is Associate Professor of International Relations, University of Amsterdam. His publications concentrate on the study of war. His recent publications include articles in *International Interactions*, *Journal of Conflict Resolution* and the *Journal of Conflict Research*, and chapters in books on conflict research, security issues and international politics.

Dietrich Jung studied Political Science and Islamic Studies at the University of Hamburg and is Research Associate at the Unit for the Study of War, Armament and Development, University of Hamburg. His recent publications include articles and chapters in books on conflicts in the Middle East.

Omari H. Kokole is Associate Director at the Institute of Global Cultural Studies, State University of New York at Binghamton. His recent publications include chapters in books, and articles on African security issues in *Third World Quarterly*, and articles in *India Quarterly*.

Keith Krause is Deputy Director of the Center for International and Strategic Studies and Assistant Professor at the Department of Political Science at York University. He is also Professor at the Graduate Institute of International Studies in Geneva. His major research has been in the area of arms production and arms trade involving the Third World. He has written for the Canadian Institute for International Peace and Security, the *International Studies Quarterly* and the *International Journal* on this subject. His recent publications include *Arms and the State: Patterns of Military Production and Trade in Historical Perspective* (1994), and chapters in books on security issues and armament.

Joel S. Migdal is Professor at the Henry M. Jackson School of International Studies, University of Washington. His recent publications include *Strong Societies and Weak States: State-Society Relations and State Capabilities in the Third World*; and articles in *World Politics, International Journal of Group Tensions, Comparative Studies in Society and History, International Political Science Review* and *Perspectives on War and Peace*.

S.D. Muni is Professor at the Centre for South, Central & South-East Asian and South-West Pacific Studies, School of International Studies, Jawaharlal Nehru University. His recent publications include articles in the *Bulletin of Peace Proposals*, and chapters in books on the security problematic of Third World states.

Jan P. Pronk is The Netherlands Minister for Development Cooperation. The Global Coalition for Africa came into being on his initiative. He was also Deputy Secretary-General of UNCTAD and is a member of the Commission on Global Governance (the Carlsson Commission).

Kumar Rupesinghe is Secretary-General of International Alert and Chair of the International Peace Research Association's Commission on Internal Conflicts and their Resolution (ICON). He has published and edited many articles and books on the issues of ethnicity, identity and governance in relation to international conflict, as well as the role of non-governmental and intergovernmental organizations in conflict transformation.

Klaus Schlichte studied Political Science, Philosophy, Economics and African Studies at the University of Hamburg. He is Research Associate at the Unit for the Study of War, Armament and Development, University of Hamburg. His recent publications include articles and chapters in books on conflicts in West Africa.

Paul Sciarone is a member of the Policy Planning Staff at the Netherlands Ministry of Foreign Affairs (Directorate-General of International Cooperation, DGIS). He has been active in the field of Development Cooperation since 1977. His current work focuses on military expenditures of developing countries, humanitarian aid, and conflict and development.

Jens Siegelberg is Researcher at the Unit for the Study of War, Armament and Development, University of Hamburg. His recent publications include *Die Kriege 1985 bis 1990, Analysen ihrer Ursachen* (ed.), and several articles in books and journals. His current work focuses on the causes of conflict.

Kingsley M. de Silva is Foundation Professor of History at the University of Peradeniya, Sri Lanka. He is also director of the International Centre for Ethnic Studies (ICES), Kandy, Sri Lanka. He has written many articles and chapters in books in Sri Lankan, British and American journals. His recent publications include *Managing Ethnic Tensions in Multi-Ethnic Societies: Sri Lanka 1880-1985* (1986) and *Sri Lanka: The Problem of Governance* (1993).

J. David Singer is Professor of Political Science at the Department of Political Science, University of Michigan, Ann Arbor. His publications include several books and standards such as *The Wages of War, Resort to Arms* and *To Auger Well: Early Warning Indicators in World Politics*; chapters in books and several articles in the *Journal of Conflict Resolution, International Studies Quarterly, American Political Science Review* and *World Politics*.

Conflict and Development:
A General Introduction

The twentieth century has been the bloodiest in all human history. Two world wars incurred the toll of many millions of deaths and immeasurable human suffering, and although the subsequent Cold War fortunately never turned into a hot war, many bloody conflicts were bitterly fought in its shadow. These conflicts often occurred in the so-called 'Third World', and while these were initially mainly wars of colonial liberation, they increasingly became struggles for the control over power, territory and resources. More often than not they are conflicts within, rather than between, states; civil war, not international conflict, has become the normal pattern.

This is certainly the case since the end of the Cold War, when the world took notice of an upsurge in armed conflicts which had been going on for a long time. In the former communist world, such conflicts seem to accompany the breaking up of empire: old feuds have been reignited there in the search for new identities. Meanwhile, in the developing world the growing demands for legitimate government are reinforcing the growing pressures of demography, ecology and poverty. In Africa, in particular, 'failed states' have been engulfed by civil strife, ethnic conflict, and even genocide.

This is a matter of grave concern, particularly for humanitarian reasons. As cruel as they are complex, these conflicts entail human suffering of a staggering scale. On top of the many people killed, there are now tens of millions of homeless, displaced persons and refugees, putting serious strains on the international capacity for emergency assistance.

It is also of great concern for international security. A multitude of localized 'low-intensity' conflicts scattered around the world may look much less dangerous than the possibility of one deadly and annihilating explosion on a global scale, but local conflicts do not make the world a safe place, and with nuclear arms and technology still in circulation, the opposite may in fact be nearer to the truth. In recent years the United Nations has developed an ambitious *Agenda for Peace*, precisely to try and control this type of violent internal conflict. The apparent intractability of internal conflicts has, however, seriously tempered hopes that the United Nations could easily perform its mission for peace. As a result, emphasis is increasingly put on conflict prevention and early intervention, as opposed to peace enforcement.

A third, but no less important reason for concern is the impact of conflict on chances for development. Given the uprooting nature of the development process, it is certainly only natural for conflict to emerge in developing societies. It is, however, equally true that violent conflict is highly disruptive for development prospects. The costs in human potential, social and productive capital and physical infrastructure can be such that decades of development effort are lost. This obviously has very destabilizing effects, both for the country and the surrounding region. Peace and political stability are thus preconditions for development, an insight that is rapidly gaining ground among developing countries and aid donors alike.

For various reasons, therefore, there is an urgent need to increase our knowledge and understanding of the nature and causes of conflicts in developing countries. This is in the interest of both the people and societies directly affected, and the world as a whole, and could be put to use not only in situations of actual conflict, but preferably also as a means of preventing conflicts from breaking out, or at least to prevent violence from escalating. It could help build structures, at the national and international levels, which facilitate the long-term 'domestication' of violence and conflict. It could strengthen the peace-promoting potential of the development process.

Consequently, and also with a view to helping shed the dominant East-West bias in the study of conflict resolution, the Dutch Minister for Development Cooperation, *Jan Pronk*, commissioned an extensive research project into the causes of conflict in developing countries. Since 1993, the Netherlands Institute of International Relations 'Clingendael' in The Hague, in close cooperation with researchers and institutes from developing countries, has been engaged in this project. A literature survey was conducted by *Luc van de Goor* and a two-day international seminar was held in March 1994 in order to make an inventory of the present research on the subject. This volume, *Between Development and Destruction. An Enquiry into the Causes of Conflict in Post-Colonial States*, presents the project to date, and, in fact, reflects the state of the art in research on the relationship between conflict and development.

The book distinguishes between four different categories of causes of violent or armed conflict and tries to establish their relevance for developing countries. The first category pertains more or less to the political domain, as it deals with state-formation and nation-building as factors for the outbreak of civil war. *Mohammed Ayoob* argues that the majority of conflicts that have taken place since 1945 are related to the birth, formation and fragmentation of 'Third World' states. Drawing a parallel with the history of European state-formation, he foresees continued violence in developing countries as long as their states have not grown more stable. Democratization may be of little avail. Meanwhile, *Joel Migdal* draws attention to the relationship between state and society and to its relevance for understanding the causes of conflicts in developing countries.

The second category can be seen as cultural factors, although they can become highly politicized: ethnicity, language, and religion. The number of violent conflicts with these cultural connotations have risen dramatically in recent years, and the term 'ethnic conflict', although often used, may raise more questions than it answers. What is, for instance, the relationship between ethnicity and nationalism, and how are both connected with political processes such as the formation or disintegration of states? *Kingsley de Silva* stresses the importance of ethnicity in the outbreak of conflicts, on the condition that it is manipulated for political purposes in the context of a multi-ethnic society. Meanwhile, *Omari Kokole* regards ethnic pluralism as a major element in the vulnerability of African societies to violent conflict, especially given the colonial heritage of state-formation in the African continent.

The third category pertains to socio-economic factors like poverty and inequality, often considered to be at the heart of armed conflicts in developing countries. In his essay, *Henk Houweling* deals with both the external and domestic aspects of the relationship between socio-economic factors and conflict. Average levels of economic development do not as such seem to have much impact on the degree of political stability, but he sees, however, a relevant connection between income inequality, on the one hand, and the breakdown of democratization processes, on the other.

The fourth and final category builds on a long-standing question: is there a direct relationship between the availability of weapons and the outbreak of armed conflict? According to *Keith Krause*, such a direct relationship does not exist, although armaments can, however, act as catalysts of armed conflict. Beyond armaments, he sees the often intrusive role of military establishments in developing countries as a more important factor, and this role can be understood in the context of 'Third World' state-formation. *S.D. Muni* also sees a catalytic role of weapons in violent conflict, especially at the intra-state level. He argues that post-Cold War security is challenged by the massive availability of small arms and by the proliferation of weapons of mass destruction. He calls for a universal and non-discriminatory approach towards non-proliferation.

This treatment of the causes of conflicts in developing countries is preceded by a general section on the classification of conflicts and is followed by chapters on specific regional causes of conflicts.

As to the first, there are various methods of classifying armed conflicts, each having both strengths and weaknesses. By counting the number of battle-related deaths, the relative intensity of a conflict can be measured, although statistical problems can easily confuse the issue. Conflicts could also be classified by distinguishing between their causes, although rarely can a single factor be identified as the root cause of a conflict. A third method differentiates between the kind of actors involved in a conflict – states (inter-state) or parties within a state (intra-state) – although internal conflicts without external involvement are, however, relatively rare. *J. David Singer* argues that the conventional methods of classification, which have mainly been applied to the analysis of European inter-state wars, may not necessarily be applicable to armed conflicts in developing countries. He warns against labelling conflicts in anything other than a strictly neutral way, as long as they have not been thoroughly studied. In their contribution, *Dietrich Jung, Klaus Schlichte* and *Jens Siegelberg* do not consider typologies of conflict as explanatory theories, but merely as tools for their orderly description. Their approach towards classification focuses on the relationship between conflicts and processes of state-formation and democratization, also giving particular attention to the role played by nationalism and ethnicity.

Trends in various regions are investigated in the chapters following the general treatment of the causes of conflict in developing countries. Is there a pattern for developing countries as a whole, or are there regional variations? The regions selected for specific treatment in this volume are sub-Saharan Africa, the Middle East, the Central Asian republics, South Asia and Latin America.

In his contribution on sub-Saharan Africa, *Francis Deng* stresses the effects of the colonial heritage on post-colonial African states. As a result of the way in which African states were created and peoples were separated, the states are now confronted with a crisis of nation-building. The ethnically highly heterogenous states are now challenged by competition for state power and national resources, often escalating to crisis and armed conflicts (in which the legitimacy of the state and the controlling authorities falls into question).

According to *Abdul Monem Al-Mashat*, current relations between the Middle Eastern countries are no longer dominated by the Arab-Israeli conflict. Since 1978 – and especially since 1993 – old patterns of alliances have faded, while economic and technical cooperation between countries has become more important than strategic concerns. New issues, such as human rights, environmental matters and rights of minorities, have appeared on the region's political agenda. In his contribution, Al-Mashat highlights the effects of political and socio-economic discontent among large groups of society on internal conflicts, discontent which in some countries has resulted in the rise of Islamic fundamentalism.

Shirin Akiner argues that although Central Asia has experienced some fundamental changes during the twentieth century – the creation of the five republics and transformation of society under Soviet rule – a significant degree of continuity still persists. The sudden transition from colonial status to independence, however, has created an intense sense of exposure and insecurity at every level. Among the potential conflict-causing factors in the region, clan rivalry (in the case of Tadjikistan), the management of natural resources (water), economic inequality and the marginalization of people stand out. On a regional level, she sees a new cause in the competition for political supremacy. She also cautions that Western aid might act as a destabilizing factor if it is not properly identified and implemented.

In his analyses of the causes of conflict in South Asia, *Kingsley de Silva* differentiates between three levels: international, national and sub-national. He also argues that the causes of conflict in South Asia mainly have their roots in the colonial past and the manner in which independence was attained. The overwhelming dominance of India in the South Asian political system constitutes a main issue: the asymmetry of military power. At the national and sub-national level, most South Asian countries are confronted with separatist agitation and politicized religion.

For the Latin American region, *Makram Haluani* shows that inter-state wars are not the main issue: full-fledged wars have occurred only sporadically, and other inter-state conflicts have concerned relatively unimportant border and territorial disputes. Latin America, however, has plenty of ingredients for intra-state conflicts. As the main causes, Haluani identifies political dissidence and the role of the military in politics, armed insurgency as part of the history of most Latin American countries, and the issue of ethnicity. Drug cartels might also become important with regard to conflicts in the future.

The chapters on regional causes of conflict are followed by a section dealing with policy perspectives on conflict and development. Two views are presented.

Jan Eliasson deals with the United Nations' perspective, first addressing the theme of conflict and changes in the international environment. As a result of the vitalization of the UN Security Council and the high number of armed conflicts, the UN has become increasingly involved in conflicts around the world. Eliasson argues that in order not to become overburdened, the United Nations has to adapt to this new security environment, and especially to dealing with crises within states. He also stresses the dynamic relationship between peace-making, peace-keeping and peace-building, processes that should be dealt with simultaneously. He finally draws attention to what he regards as the future aim of the United Nations: the prevention of conflicts, and shows how the UN could get rid of its 'fireman syndrome'.

A policy perspective from the Netherlands' Ministry for Development Cooperation is then presented. *Jan Pronk* and *Paul Sciarone* look into the requirements for more efficient development policies directed towards conflict prevention in conflict-prone developing countries for the 1990s. Two policy perspectives are highlighted – the socio-economic and the political dimension (that is, good governance) – and they then focus on specific issues which they regard as relating to both policy perspectives: the effect on development of military expenditure, and, more particularly, the proliferation of small armaments.

The volume opens with a bibliographical essay by the editors. This essay, based on the above-mentioned literature survey by *Luc van de Goor*, is included in the book as a general introduction to the themes, and serves as an inventory on the present research and literature on the subject.

Finally, while reflecting upon the contents of this book, the editors realize that a complex world confronts us, a world in which politics are infinitely more intricate and diverse than just conflicts. The editors are thus aware that while the focus is on conflicts, this is at the expense of more positive developments in developing countries. However, since developing countries and complete regions of the 'Third World' are increasingly related to violent conflicts, and since the world is becoming a smaller place, developments on a global scale will in future become more and more affected by each other. The editors are therefore convinced that it is crucial to understand the nature and dynamics of relationships causing these conflicts.

This book argues that this is not a simple matter which can easily be solved. A recent analyses of the costs of conflict shows that their impact on human lives, economic development and the environment is devastating. However, before the international community can take more effective action, it needs clearer criteria to determine when and how such action should be taken. Since ad hoc responses are unsatisfactory – as often can be observed – more consistent and effective policies for preventing and managing conflict should be developed. The development of a coherent policy framework has to rely on capabilities to identify the causes of conflict. This volume attempts to make a valuable contribution to constructing more effective early conflict management and conflict prevention policies.

Introduction to the Themes

THE QUEST FOR A TYPOLOGY OF CONFLICTS

The bipolar structure of the global political system has rapidly disappeared since 1989. On a positive level, this has helped to bring a number of protracted conflicts to an end; on a negative level, however, the end of the Cold War has created scope for new eruptions of violence, some of which have already happened and others which may occur in the near future. These conflicts are partly new or, if they existed previously, had little or no chance of escalating during the era of East-West rivalry, as, for example, with ethnic and religious differences. But there also seems to be a new, or perhaps long-forgotten type: conflicts connected with the structural transformation of societies. These conflicts concern the long-term processes of state-formation and nation-building, and are primarily located in developing countries.

As long as the global political system was characterized by the East-West divide, most armed conflicts could be successfully explained by the tension between the superpowers. Now that the global situation has changed, it may be questioned whether traditional research on issues of war and peace can still provide adequate explanations for violence and conflicts in developing countries. Do armed conflicts in developing countries indeed constitute a new type of conflict? Can existing typologies of armed conflict be usefully applied to these conflicts?

Studying Conflict

No consensus exists among scholars about the criteria to be applied for defining conflicts. Roughly speaking, conflict occurs where there is interaction between at least two individuals or groups whose ultimate objectives differ (Nicholson, 1972). In this connection, Miall lists four criteria which may be useful in distinguishing conflict from other situations: (1) a conflict can only exist where the participants perceive it as such; (2) a clear difference of opinion regarding values, interests, aims or relations must lie at the root of a conflict; (3) the parties in a conflict may be either states or 'significant elements of the population' within the state; (4) the outcome of the conflict must be considered extremely important by the parties. In addition, in the case of internal conflicts, the outcome must be of great importance to the whole of society and political or legal solutions must be impossible, so

1

that violence becomes a last resort (Miall, 1992). When two or more conflicting parties become engaged in overt mutually opposing and violent
interactions, aimed at destroying, injuring or controlling their opponents,
such an interaction is called an armed conflict.

Looking at armed conflicts from the perspective of the inter-state system,
a distinction can be made between inter-state conflicts, intra-state conflicts,
and mixed forms. Intra-state conflicts are defined as those conflicts that
occur within the boundaries of a state. They manifest themselves according
to two modalities. First, conflicts between government forces and secessionist groups seeking either political autonomy within the state or a separate
state. Second, conflicts with regard to the composition and form of government, and often with the involvement of civilian groups (Edmonds, 1972).
Boundary problems within a state – for example, between different ethnic
groups, languages, religions, cultures – may constitute a source of potential
conflicts. If these boundaries overlap the borders between states, such
disputes may escalate into inter-state conflicts.

During the five decades following the Second World War, intra-state
wars largely outnumbered inter-state wars and overt military interventions
(Tillema, 1989). Conflict research remained traditional, however, and was
almost exclusively devoted to inter-state wars. Data on armed conflicts show
that the shift from inter-state armed conflicts to intra-state armed conflicts
started after the Second World War, and persisted during the period from
1989-93 (Gantzel, 1995). Strikingly, not one inter-state armed conflict was
going on in 1993 (Wallensteen and Axell, 1994). A similar shift in conflict
research towards intra-state armed conflicts is now happening. This implies
that one should be careful in applying the traditional theories on conflict and
international relations to this type of armed conflict.

Looking at conflicts from the perspective of the use of violence, different
stages of violence may be distinguished. On a continuous scale, the intensity
of violence moves from a dispute with no violence or force, to stages in
which minor or major violence is used by at least one party. The intensity of
violence is generally measured in terms of numbers of battle-related deaths
during the course of the conflict.

Finally, a differentiation between conflicts is possible on the basis of
their causes. This typology, however, is controversial because of the complex and dynamic nature of most conflicts. A factor can rarely be singled out
as the root cause of a specific armed conflict.

An Increasing Number of Low-Intensity Conflicts?

An important issue in the debate on the analysis of armed conflicts is the casualty criterion which is used in most definitions of conflict. The classical inter-state war was defined as an armed conflict with military casualties exceeding a minimum of 1,000 deaths during one year (Correlates of War Project) or during the course of the conflict (AKUF and SIPRI). But, how should armed conflicts with less than 1,000 battle-related deaths per year or per dispute be described? The call for a *more precise* differentiation based on intensity of violence has been answered by Peter Wallensteen and Karen Axell. Their focus is on *armed conflicts* where the use of armed force by two parties, of which at least one is the government of a state, results in at least 25 battle-related deaths per year. The armed conflicts recorded are grouped into three categories:

1. *Minor armed conflicts*, where the battle-related deaths during the course of the conflict are below 1000;
2. *Intermediate conflicts*, where there are more than 1,000 battle-related deaths recorded during the course of the conflict, and where 25 but less than 1,000 deaths have occurred during a particular year;
3. *Wars*, where there are more than 1,000 battle-related deaths during one particular year.

For convenience, the two latter categories are sometimes referred to as *major armed conflicts*.

According to Wallensteen and Axell, the total number of armed conflicts during the period 1989-1993 amounted to 90. These conflicts took place in 61 locations around the world, so about one-third of UN member states were involved in armed conflict. In the period 1988-1993 Wallensteen and Axell counted only four inter-state armed conflicts. Consequently, a considerable number of non-governmental forces or sub-state groups were active in armed conflict (Wallensteen and Axell, 1994).

From the fact that intra-state conflicts have become the rule rather than the exception, it would be incorrect to conclude that the casualty criterion loses its significance because of a lower intensity of violence. Out of the 47 armed conflicts that were active in 1993, 15 were wars. Of the 32 other active armed conflicts, 17 were intermediate conflicts and 15 were minor armed conflicts.

Throughout the period 1989-1993, the total number of armed conflicts per year remained on a very high level, averaging 50 with small variations. The total number of armed conflicts grew gradually in 1991 to 50, then increased in 1992 to 55 but decreased in 1993 to 47, thus breaking the upward trend since the end of the Cold War.

A regional breakdown of these data shows a stark contrast between Europe and the other regions. In Europe, we witness a gradual increase in the number of armed conflicts: from 2 in 1989 to 10 conflicts in 1993. The Americas show the reverse pattern, with 3 conflicts recorded in 1993 compared to 8 in 1989. Asia has the most variation with a large reduction in 1991, an upsurge in 1992 and again a reduction in 1993. Notwithstanding the general image, conflicts in Africa continue to decline in numbers (from 17 in 1990 to 12 in 1993) as well as in intensity (5 wars in 1993 compared to 9 in 1990). However, these data only cover armed conflicts, not the repression or massacre of civilians, such as events in Burundi in 1993 and those in Rwanda in 1994.

A Nomothetic Versus an Idiographic Approach and the Issue of Classification

Every scholar who wants to construct a typology of armed conflicts has to make a choice between a more generalizing and a more individualistic approach, a choice between a nomothetic, universal approach – based on the presumption that a general, universal applicable theory on conflicts does exist – and a more idiographic, individualistic approach which focuses primarily on the regional or local context. Is it possible to combine both approaches so that local variables are integrated into universal theories? According to Ted Robert Gurr: '... general theories of violence are in principle relevant to African cases, but only in so far as they incorporate whatever concepts and variables are needed to make sense of distinctly African conditions. What may be assumed constant in other world cultural settings is not necessarily constant in Africa and vice versa' (Gurr, 1991).

Kalevi Holsti argues that research on armed conflict is characterized by a twofold Euro-centric distortion. Most scholars come from industrialized countries and, in addition, they study inter-state conflicts. This explains why the history of militarized disputes in the modern international system mostly takes the year 1648 as a starting point. With the Treaty of Westphalia, the state made its entrance as the primary actor in most armed conflicts, and it is only recently that a reverse trend away from the state as the primary actor in armed conflict has revealed itself in developing countries and, particularly, in Africa. Parties at sub-state level – be they nations, ethnic groups, religious groups or tribes – are becoming more and more important. In general, the states in Africa have no long history of independent statehood and are considered in most analyses as a security liability in so far that sub-state groups dispute their sovereignty. Holsti concludes that we should differ between two distinct international systems, a mature system in the North and a new one in the South, each with its own principal causes of conflict. Traditionally, studies into the causes of armed conflict relate to the mature system. According to Holsti, however, armed conflicts in the new system are of an entirely different order:

> The players are not well established in the sense of having a long history of statehood, secure boundaries, an absence of secession movements, and generally impermeable societies and government structures. Regimes ... tend to face more internal threats in the form of attempted *coups d'état*, secession, ethnic, language, and religious violence, and subversion, than external threats ... The stakes of politics for them are primarily sovereignty-related: establishing some reasonably well-defined national identity, creating stable borders, controlling a permanent population, and in general trying to keep themselves together as something akin to a modern state (Holsti, 1991).

Typology Revisited

How conflicts should be labelled is still an issue of debate. Most of the existing typologies of conflict show weaknesses in the field of logical exhaustiveness, mutual exclusiveness of categories, semantic consistency, and neutrality. These weaknesses especially apply for attempts to construct a typology according to causes of conflict. Firstly, the causes of conflict are hardly ever monocausal. It would thus be wrong to speak of, for example, ethnic, religious or civilizational conflict. Secondly, the causes of armed conflict cannot be known prior to serious investigation. Labelling conflicts wrongfully beforehand could thus result in inadequate measures in the field of conflict management or resolution. One way to solve this problem is to aim for a neutral typology, as is, for example, done by the Correlates of War Project (COW). They strongly recommend a juridical typology that characterizes armed conflicts according to the parties in dispute.

The question remains, however, as to whether such a neutral typology meets the other requirements. It also shows certain shortcomings. Any juridical typology, the COW typology included, is neither logically nor empirically exhaustive. As can be learned from history, every historical period presents new types of actors in a dispute. This implies that every time such a new actor emerges, a new category has to be invented and added to this typology. Recently this has been the case with the conflicts occurring in failed states, such as Somalia. Here neither of the parties in dispute is the government. This implies that we are dealing with a new type of conflict that cannot be accommodated in the present juridical typology. It could thus be stated that, like other theories, the search for typologies must evolve in accordance with our knowledge and understanding, since we cannot prophesy what kinds of conflict will happen in the future.

STATE-FORMATION AND NATION-BUILDING

Introduction

Developing countries are confronted with numerous security problems and concerns – often of an internal kind – which frequently escalate into overt violent conflicts. When studying theories of 'Third World' security, the emphasis on state-formation as a tool for the analyses of security and conflict is most striking. This state-centric approach is based on the historical record of states in Europe. State-formation in Europe was a violent process, but this process, however, was unintended. Modern European states are most likely the result of an *evolutionary* process involving infinite political, social and economic changes, and this process has had its effects on the states, as well as on the inter-state system, as can be learned from the trend towards globalization and regional cooperation. The present inter-state system can no longer be compared with the emerging system of states in sixteenth-century Europe, so the question of whether state-making in the contemporary situation – that is, in developing countries – can take place along the historical lines of the European example. How should the state-formation predicament in the 'Third World' be interpreted?

The Process of State-Formation: A Comparison Between Europe and the 'Third World'

Both Charles Tilly (1990) and Mohammed Ayoob (1992) feel that a better understanding of state-building in Europe would help to shed light on the problems facing non-European states:

> State-making is a process that can be compared over time and space, and its main elements ... are of universal significance [and] can be isolated for analytical purposes (Ayoob, 1992).

The European model of state-building shows that 'with the possible exception of the Balkans, the emergence of the modern state was the precondition for the formation of the nation' (Ayoob, 1992); the modern states of Europe were states before they became nations. The European process of state-formation can initially also be described as a struggle between local leaders and the centralizing power. Any attempt by the centralizing power to impose central authority throughout the territory of the state naturally met with resistance. Ultimately, however, Europe's numerous little kingdoms and counties produced a far smaller number of states. Yet, it would be a mistake to think that this happened without the use of force. The fact is that none of these rulers was prepared to surrender power without a fight.

Next to this *internal pacification* and *domination* aspect of state-formation, there was also an external stimulus to create compact, stable and largely homogeneous states. Since there were neither internationally accepted norms of sovereignty nor internationally recognized borders, the erstwhile emergent states of north-west Europe posed a serious threat to one another. Not losing a war against a main power became the test of a state's viability. This geopolitical pressure on the leaders of these new states necessitated them to mobilize their societies against external threats. This meant raising an army for the survival of the state, as well as acquiring resources to maintain these armies, and this need for revenue in the form of taxes fostered the realization that economic growth was vital for the survival of the state (Thomas, 1991). Since the development process in Europe depended on external threats, it is also characterized as a 'pessimistic' model of development. According to Mullins, it can be described as follows: '... to the extent that a military force is a necessity, development is a necessity, and just as development permits acquisition of force, so the acquisition of force permits development' (Mullins, 1987).

The situation in most 'Third World' countries contrasts strongly with the erstwhile emergent European states. First, the internal aspect of state-building differs. Most 'Third World' states have not evolved gradually over a period of time but were (geographically) designed and created by outsiders. In comparison with European states, there has been no opportunity for binding factors to take root. As a result, in most developing countries traditional structures have remained intact, which means that they lack the unifying force of nationalism at state level. In this connection, Ali Mazrui refers to the effects of 'multiple structures of authority' under colonial regimes, when particular groups functioned as mediators between the colonizers and their subjects, the outcome being that some groups came to regard others as interlopers, rivals or even enemies (Mazrui, 1986). These feelings did not change fundamentally at the time of independence.

Second, the international context differs from the European development model. The law of the jungle which governed international affairs a few centuries ago has now vanished without trace. In the contemporary situation, states are in principle protected by the internationally accepted norm of sovereignty and recognized national borders. State leaders no longer need to mobilize their societies against external threats, and the absence of a hostile international environment removed the incentive for integration. The result has been a reversed process of state-formation, since the creation of the state preceded that of a national army. The military assistance that many 'Third World' states received during the Cold War amplified this effect and made it possible for *quasi states* to emerge (Jackson and Rosberg, 1982), states that lack both the legitimacy and the capacity to govern. It could be said that in comparison with European state-formation, the new values of sovereignty, territorial integrity and non-intervention may be seen as handicaps to the process of state-making. The common weakness of many 'Third World' states, and their vulnerability to internal turmoil or the challenging of borders, thus creates a common interest in international rules and institutions. In his contribution to this book, Ayoob observes that most interventions in the past were mainly for the purpose of maintaining the *status quo* and the territorial integrity of the quasi-state in question (Somalia is the most recent example of this). An exception to this rule, of course, is the Indian intervention in Pakistan, resulting in the emergence of a new state, Bangladesh.

The Creation of States, Violence and Development

From the history of state-formation in Europe we can learn that it can lead to strong states. State-formation in the 'Third World' has until now, however, resulted in weak states. A most important question concerning the process of state-formation is thus whether conflicts in the process of state-formation should be interpreted as a mark of development or as a sign of political decay.

The high value that the North attaches to progress and modernization appears to rule out a paradoxical evolutionary link between development and violence. Moreover, the history of the organizational stability and legitimacy of government in the North seems almost never to be held up to question. The North sees economic development, the rise of the 'trading state' (Rosecrance, 1984), and democratic forms of government – the substitution of other forms of behaviour for violence – as the marks of progress (see Rosecrance, 1984; Ullman, 1990; Singer and Wildavsky, 1993). Violence and warfare as ways of achieving political goals are dismissed as archaic, undemocratic and indicative of political decay. Nevertheless, this could well be a way of denying the background against which the states of Europe came into being. Our current mode of thinking emphasizes political and economic conditions for stability – 'good governance' – with complete disregard for the processes of change which produced them. However, to argue that democracy is an ideal political system or that democratic elections are some kind of final stage is not the same as agreeing to the fact that democratization is part of a historical process. If confrontation and violence are banished as instruments in the processes leading to state-building, then state-building is equated with a linear process leading to more order and stability. Instability and conflict then become synonyms for decline, yet comparison with the European history of state-formation illustrates that this conclusion would be wrong.

With regard to the intra-state anarchy in many 'Third World' countries, however, the observation can be made that instability and conflict can be both instrumental in the process of state-building as well as signs of decline. Since states in the current inter-state system are no longer put to the test of fighting a war against a main power, the vitality of a state will mainly depend on its ability to create intra-state stability. The phenomenon of weak or failed states in the 'Third World' should thus be related to the intra-state relations and the capacity of the state – the central government – to keep to the path of state-formation.

Mention has already been made of the difference between weak and strong states. Strong states can be defined as those in which central author-ities have the ability to use the agencies of the state to get people in the state to do what they want. This does not imply that the use of violence or des-potic power – as in a police state – can or should be related to strong states. Referring to a strong state and a strong central authority is not the same as referring to regimes that control the instruments of violence. This would imply that states in which regimes do not transcend the use of violence can also be defined as strong states. Many states in the 'Third World' could than be defined as strong states, although they are not. The problems of weak states are more complex, but should also be related to the lack of legitimacy and efficiency. The question, however, is what can be done about them and how this can be related to state-formation.

Some authors, like Joel Migdal, look for an answer in capacity-building processes: the solution for the problem would be the strengthening of the penetrative capability of weak states. These authors often refer to Michael Mann's concept of *infrastructural power* (Mann, 1986). Infrastructural power can be seen as the institutional capacity which provides the means for running the state, and essential capabilities are penetration, participation, distribution and legitimation. Legitimation, in particular, can be seen as an important aspect, since formulating and implementing policy depends on a certain level of agreement. Limited legitimacy and insufficient institutional-ization of central governments in developing countries are a precondition for not being successful. If a central government is lacking legitimacy, fragmentation of power within the state and an increase of conflict can be the result.

Other authors, such as Mohammed Ayoob, explain the security predicament of weak 'Third World' states by stressing their problems as intrinsic to the ongoing process of state-making. The aim of this process should be to achieve the goal of what Nettle has defined as *stateness*: 'a balanced combination of the coercive capacity and infrastructural power of the state with a degree of identification on the part of the citizenry with the idea of the state that encompasses them territorially' (Nettle, 1968). State-makers, however, are challenged by innumerable internal and external problems in their efforts to create a state in as short a period as possible. Authors like Ayoob, therefore, feel that a better understanding of state-building in Europe would help to shed light on the problems facing non-European states, so accordingly conflicts and political instability in developing countries can be interpreted as marks of an ongoing process of development.

Charles Tilly also adheres to the view that state-building is a violent process, and the same conclusion can be drawn from Cohen, Brown and Organski's analysis. They all conclude that violence in new states is not *per se* a sign of decline, but that it can be part of what they call the 'process of primitive accumulation of power'. It would, however, be wrong to conclude that the processes of development and state-formation can be characterized as inherently and permanently of a violent nature.

Samuel Huntington concludes the opposite: that the process of state-formation tends to suppress violence. His view is based on the fact that the developed countries have reached a level of political and economic stability which is characterized by stability. It seems that both views are correct as long as the process is seen as a series of phases. Tilly's argument of state-building as a violent process applies to the first stage of accumulation of power by the state. This stage is followed by a second phase, which confirms Huntington's view that the state exercises its influence to suppress the use of force.

The relationship between development and (political) violence can thus be characterized as *curvilinear*; violence will decrease only once a certain level of development has been reached. It is not yet clear, however, what this level is or whether economic and political development (in the form of more democracy) are sufficient in themselves to prevent conflict. It can be plausibly argued, however, that the state's response to any internal threat would be to increase its capacity and flexibility. A strong state is in a position to make concessions if necessary or to suppress uprisings without any real loss of power. A weaker state, on the other hand, has to consider the risk to its national sovereignty and integrity when faced with any danger. Under such circumstances violence will not remain a means of last resort for long.

NATIONALISM AND ETHNICITY

Introduction

Because of the system- and state-oriented focus in theories of international relations, domestic variables have for a long time been looked upon as an insignificant source of inter-state conflict. As a result, conflict research has mainly concentrated on states as actors. Developments within the borders of a state – be they ethnic, religious or otherwise cultural – were, in the Weberian tradition, considered of only marginal importance. Thus, ethnicity and religious fundamentalism were long considered as merely cultural phenomena that would disappear in the process of state-building.

Since the beginning of this decade, however, feelings about these issues have been changing rapidly. Several authors have been writing about them in rather alarming terms (Mearsheimer, 1990; Huntington, 1993). Maynes even wrote that 'animosity among ethnic groups is beginning to rival the spread of nuclear weapons as the most serious threat to peace that the world faces' (Maynes, 1993). From recent developments in Rwanda, Burundi, the former Yugoslavia and former Soviet Union, we can learn that ethnicity and nationalism are universal phenomena. It even seems as if the end of the Cold War has taken the lid off many old hostilities. As a result, some conflicts that were formerly regarded as dead and buried are, once again, manifesting themselves.

How alarming is the situation? According to some estimates there are over 5,000 ethnic minorities in the world (Boulding, 1987), and only 9 per cent to 11 per cent of the over 180 states in the international system are ethnically 'homogeneous' in the sense that ethnic minorities comprise less than 5 per cent of the total population (Connor, 1972; Welsh, 1993). Recent assessments by the Minorities at Risk Project indicate that ethnic groups have been involved in over 70 protracted conflicts all over the world. Most of these so-called 'ethno-political conflicts' – conflicts in which groups that define themselves using ethnic criteria make claims on behalf of their collective interests against the state, or against other political actors – occurred in Asia (28) and Africa (23), followed by Europe (10), the Middle East (6) and Latin America (3). The risk of ethnicity as a cause of conflict thus seems not to be restricted to merely a few countries.

How should we account for ethnicity as a cause of conflict? Is ethnic conflict a short-term response to the process of state-building and therefore restricted to the 'Third World' or decaying empires? Or does it concern more permanent factors of identity? What theories have been developed?

A Framework of Analysis

The literature on the subject reveals three schools of thought: the primordialists, the instrumentalists and the constructivists (Young, 1993). The primordialist and instrumentalist schools try to explain what motivates ethnic groups. The primordialists, building on anthropological theories, emphasize that members of the same ethnic group have a common primordial bond that determines their personal identity and turns the group into a natural community of a type that is older than the modern nation-state or modern class-systems. The elements of shared culture have been transmitted over generations and created a sort of historical continuity, about which Anthony Smith speaks of a 'quartet' of characteristics: myths, memories, values, and symbols (Smith, 1986). These characteristics change only very slowly, so ethnicity thus also changes either very slowly or hardly at all, and accordingly, ethnic identity can lie dormant for long periods. However, although the attitude of 'us against them' is sometimes subdued, it remains permanently present.

Instrumentalists, in contrast, do not think in terms of psychological bonding. They perceive ethnicity as one of the many means or resources available to elites to be used to achieve political or economic goals. The primordialist and instrumentalist approaches, however, are not mutually exclusive. As Solomon Gashaw put it: 'The primordialist emphasis on ethnicity as a quasi-ontological object does not preclude it from being used as a manipulative instrument by elites' (Gashaw, 1993). Indeed, the primordialist approach can produce markers for purposes of political mobilization. According to Barth, six such markers can be distinguished: race, kinship, religion, language, identity, customary mode of livelihood and regionalism (Barth, 1969).

The third school of thought, the constructivist, adheres to a different approach. Constructivists try to explain the existence of group instead of what drives it. They see ethnicity as a social construction, manufactured rather than given. According to Franz Ansprenger, there are cases in Africa in which the historic roots of ethnic groups and tribes are of a recent character. In some cases they were even created during the colonial period (Ansprenger, 1994). This means that more historical research is needed to explain the origins and the temporal fluctuations of ethnic and nationalist movements and sentiments. Interesting in this regard is the observation made by Daniel Horowitz that boundaries between groups are not fixed, and that the size of ethnic groups may grow and shrink as their situations change. Horowitz refers to processes of assimilation (amalgamation and incorporation) and differentiation (division and proliferation) (Horowitz, 1985). These processes indicate that the boundaries between groups can indeed be manipulated, although the extent to which this can be done remains a matter of discussion. It would, however, be incorrect to suggest that ethnic groups can be called into being by political leaders whenever it is convenient to do so in the quest for competitive advantage or in the service of economic interest, that is, that the mutability of their boundaries is merely 'strategic'.

The various approaches to ethnicity complicate the task of determining which are the necessary and sufficient conditions for conflict escalation, since it is obvious that the way in which ethnicity is perceived largely determines the causal factors for ethnic conflict. Most theories consider a combination of factors – political, economic, psychological, cultural – to be necessary for generating hostility between groups. At least as important, however, are the reciprocity and the levels of animosity and violence between groups. Here the psycho-cultural primordialist approach can explain the emotional potency of conflict, its disposition to arouse deep-seated anxieties, fears, and insecurities, or the degree of aggressiveness. When ethnicity is involved in conflicts, they are often protracted, bloody, and inimitable in degree of violence. These characteristics cannot be explained in terms of objective interest, since material issues are always open to some sort of compromise. Meanwhile, the reverse is true for highly symbolic cultural and moral values, such as language or religion. These issues cannot be compromised easily, but arrangements can be made with regard to freedom of religion and bilingualism. There are some cases, however, when such arrangements have not been sufficient to solve the problems, as can be learned from Northern Ireland with regard to religious issues, as well as from Belgium and Canada – though on a less violent scale – with regard to linguistic issues.

Since conflicts involving ethnicity mainly take place within states, it is interesting to look for domestic elements, thus linking ethnic issues to the main issues of state-building and the political issue of who will rule.

Nationalism, Ethnicity and Failing State-Formation

The term modern state usually corresponds to a term often used in political science: the nation-state. The two components of this term, nation and state, often appear to have become interchangeable (as, for example, the United

Nations or national security). On careful reflection, however, nation and state are in fact different concepts. The definition of state differs from definitions of nation. In international relations, both entities are often defined in different terms of sovereignty. States are defined in terms of the territories over which institutional authorities exercise legitimate control. Nations, however, are defined in terms of 'communities of sentiment'. Buzan, for example, defines a nation as 'a large group of people sharing the same cultural and possibly the same ethnic or racial heritage' (Buzan, 1991). In this context, the term 'nation-state' refers to a situation in which the territorial boundaries of ethnic identity, or nation, coincide with those of the state, and in which the people basically identify themselves with the state. Yet this is seldom the case. This indicates, according to Welsh, that 'nation-building ... is a project that failed' (Welsh, 1993). The failing of state-building was neither obvious nor foreseeable. Crawford Young admits that after having had high expectations himself, he now regards the transforming relationship between cultural pluralism and the nation state as a central drama of our times (Young, 1993). The few states that have succeeded in the process of nation-building and are ethnically homogeneous are mainly to be found in Western Europe. Most 'Third World' countries, however, are of a multi-ethnic character, consisting of several nations, yet the nation-state was to be the goal of each and every newly independent (developing) country. It was regarded a sign of progress, and therefore imperative. Crawford Young cites Rupert Emerson, who captured the mood of the period in which statehood that was won by anti-colonial struggle required completion with the construction of nationality:

> Since the state is in modern times the most significant form of organization of men and embodies the greatest concentration of power, it is inevitable that there should have been, and should still be, a great and revolutionary struggle to secure a coincidence between state and nation. The nation seeks to take over the state as the political instrument through which it can protect and assert itself ... the nation has in fact become the body which legitimizes the state ... Where the state is based on any principle other than the national one, as is by definition the case in any imperial system, its foundations are immediately suspect in a nationalist age (Young, 1993).[1]

During the period immediately following decolonization, many developing countries tried to follow the example of state- and nation-building set by the colonial powers and characterized by the integrative power of the national idea. However, the new independent states were not able to create the requirements of assimilative or integrative nationhood, and their govern-ments failed to convince their populations that they shared a common culture or a common goal. The nationalist sentiments which made themselves felt at the time of independence turned out to be only temporary and superficial. Buzan characterized this temporary nationalism as a negative group unity and a 'bond of xenophobia' which disintegrated once the euphoria of inde-pendence had subsided (Buzan, 1991).

The issue now arises as to whether attempts to promulgate the idea of a common culture were either doomed to fail because the populations within these states shared neither common norms and values, nor common myths and symbols. Or does it concern a temporary problem, as in the history of European states? Problems in the newly independent countries have also arisen from attempts to bring about cultural homogenization. This process was an essential component of the historical European state-to-nation route as well. The process, however, involved problems and conflicts resulting from the modernization attempts to assimilate or homogenize. The problem-atic nature of this process can best be understood by citing Walker Connor:

> Since most of the less developed states contain a number of nations, and since the transfer of primary allegiance from these nations to the state is generally considered the *sine qua non* of successful integration, the true goal is not 'nation-building' but 'nation destroying' (Connor, 1972).

The process of nation-destroying and attempts to create situations of cultural dominance are both major factors in the emergence of conflicts based on ethnicity. Where the state attempts to impose new values on one or more ethnic groups, and where certain opportunities and freedoms are denied – or taken away from – certain groups, resistance will ensue. This argument does not even consider the fact 'the state' as such need not be a neutral actor. The assumption that the state is neutral has been invalidated in the 'Third World', as elsewhere. Myron Weiner observes more of a 'mono-ethnic tendency'. He states that:

> In country after country, a single ethnic group has taken control over the state and used its powers to exercise control over the state and used its powers to exercise control over others ... In retrospect there has been far less 'nation-building' than many analysts had expected or hoped, for the process of state-building has rendered many ethnic groups devoid of power or influence (Weiner, 1987).

Or, as Samuel Huntington has put it: 'Ethnic or religious groups which have lived peacefully side by side in traditional society become aroused to violent conflict as a result of the interaction, the tension, the inequalities generated by social and economic modernization' (Huntington, 1968).

In addition to the view that modernization and development of a state act as a catalyst for ethnic problems, there is also the commonly held assumption that ethnicity will disappear with the development of nation-states and the accompanying processes of integration and modernization. The second assumption attributes special importance to the link between state- or nation-building and modernization. In the Marxist view, for example, modernization should lead to a society in which ethnic identities no longer play a role because of the far-reaching division of labour and the development of economic classes. This view has not been backed up by events. Nor indeed has the 'strain theory' (Newman, 1991), which sees the process of modernization as one marked by intermittent periods in which societies find themselves in a state of uncertainty during which there is a desire to revert to old certainties such as ethnic identity. The shortcomings of both theories are evident from the fact that 'ethnic conflicts' break out throughout the globe, in developing countries as well as in modern industrialized countries (for example, in Spain, Northern Ireland, Canada and Belgium).

The Internationalization of 'Ethnic' and 'Nationalist' Conflict: The Doctrine of Self-Determination

Another area lacking consensus is the international dimension of ethnic conflict. Several types of armed ethnic conflict can be distinguished. Some relate almost exclusively to intra-state issues: nativism, ethnic corporatism and demands of interest groups concerning autonomy in certain fields (economics, religion, language). Other types will certainly influence relations with other states: irredentism, the strive for autonomy, and the strive for separatism. How does ethnic conflict become internationalized?

Recent developments concerning ethnic and nationalist groups and their aspirations to autonomy and separatism focus attention on a legal aspect: the right to self-determination. Barkin and Cronin argue in this regard that 'there has been a historical tension between state sovereignty, which stresses the link between sovereign authority and a defined territory, and national sovereignty, which emphasizes a link between sovereign authority and a defined population' (1994). Modern nationalism, based on the idea of self-determination, claims that nations should be politically self-determining and that group sentiment should serve as the sole criterion in defining the nation (Gellner, 1983; Hobsbawm, 1990; Anderson, 1994; Smith, 1983).

Since the idea of self-determination entered the world, it has always been considered a potential threat to central governments and states, during the nineteenth as well as the twentieth century. The importance of self-determination was boosted when it was accepted as a right in Articles 1 and 73 of the United Nations Charter. The discrepancy of the right of self-determination with the right of states to self-defence and to the preservation of territorial integrity has never been clearly resolved since both rights were accepted. The application of the doctrine to the struggle of the colonized countries in Africa, Asia and the Caribbean during the 1960s can be seen as an attempt to settle this discrepancy. The problems with the doctrine, however, seem to have reappeared now with the new impulse given by that ethnicity and nationalism. The right to self-determination should thus again be viewed with suspicion. In this connection, Walker Connor wrote that:

> In its pristine form, the doctrine (of the right of self-determination) makes ethnicity the ultimate measure of political legitimacy, by holding that any self-differentiating people, simply because it *is* a people, has the right, should it desire, to rule itself ... It has therefore been more than a justification for ethnic movements: it has been a catalyst for them (Connor, 1972).

Separatism is not the only alternative for such groups; a number of options are open to them. At first they may attempt to acquire influence by political means, although this, however, requires a democratic system in which they are represented and have a certain amount of influence (the absence of any such representation is often, in itself, a cause of conflict). Other options include invoking the rights of minorities or international human rights, although these options also require a cooperative attitude on the part of the central government. If the government is utterly unwilling to cooperate, the ethnic and nationalist groups have no option other than to strive for more autonomy (internal self-determination) or, in extreme cases, for a state of their own (internal and external self-determination and separatism).

During the Cold War, Bangladesh was the only example of an ethnic group succeeding in creating an independent state (after intervention by India). Since 1991 this situation has changed fundamentally. The breakup of the former Soviet Union and former Yugoslavia, as well as the independence of Eritrea and the unification of the two German states set the stage for new attempts. The successful achievement of independence on the part of states in their former empires may serve as an example to ethnic and nationalist groups striving for independence elsewhere. Abkhazia and Chechnya are the latest examples on the territory of the former Soviet Union. In addition, it is becoming increasingly difficult for central governments of states to take action against secessionist movements. The use of force to suppress such movements (as in Turkey against the Kurds and in Russia against the Chechens) tends to arouse criticism from the international community. In this connection, Cutler speaks of a tendency in which 'self-determination ... is rapidly moving into the category of internationally recognized human rights, upon which no state can infringe without objection – and sometimes intervention – by the international community' (Halperin, 1992).

In the end, however, it is questionable whether separatism and redrawing borders are solutions for the problems of ethnic and nationalist groups. The number of ethnic groups is too great. According to Etzioni:

> It is simply impossible to sustain the notion that every ethnic group can find its expression in a full-blown nation-state, fly its flag at the United Nations, and have its ambassadors accredited by other nation-states; the process of ethnic separation and the breakdown of existing states will then never be exhausted ... Subtle differences in geography, religion, culture, and loyalty can be fanned into new separatist movements, each seeking their own symbols and powers of statehood (Etzioni, 1992).

The ultimate result of any accession to demands for self-determination could be a United Nations with more than a thousand members (Helman and Ratner, 1993; Hamburg, 1993). In this regard, Halperin, *et al.*, compiled a list of states world-wide that were confronted with one or more self-determination movement (Halperin, 1992): 19 were in Africa, 12 in Asia, 4 in Latin America, 4 in the Middle East, 12 in the former Soviet republics, and 17 in Europe (including former Yugoslavia). The desire for self-determination is thus a problem with which we should deal.

ECONOMIC ISSUES AND INTEGRATION IN THE WORLD MARKET

Introduction

The relationship between conflict and economics has interested economists as well as political scientists for many years. However, notwithstanding numerous studies investigating the relationship between economic issues, political instability and conflict, substantial evidence about the nature of this relationship is still lacking. The issue at stake seems to be one of a two-way causality problem: political instability and conflict may be either a result of a disappointing economic record, or discontent with the economic situation may be a result of political circumstances. Moreover, and specifically with regard to developing countries, poverty, inequality, scarcity of (non-)renewable resources and external economic forces are supposed to have a major destabilizing effect on political stability. This view is the corner-stone of theories that try to link economic factors directly to conflicts.

The International Level

Conflict-instigating economic factors can be found at all levels. According to the proponents of the economic-conflict perspective, a destabilizing effect can, for example, be attributed to the inter-state level. Instability and conflict can here be the result of the vulnerability of developing countries to trends in the international markets in capital, goods and raw materials, as the economies of developing countries are strongly affected by fluctuations on the world market. Unexpected shortfalls in export revenues may diminish the ability of the government to satisfy the demands of groups within society, and such shortfalls may lead to forms of inter-group conflict because the state is not able to take redistributive measures. If the negative relationship between the two is indeed strong, this is of importance with regard to the future integration of developing countries in the world market. This process could accordingly boost the destabilizing effects. However, are the problems related to the continuing integration of the developing countries into the world capitalist system a cause for alarm?

According to Jens Siegelberg, these problems are not as unique as they appear. The problems experienced by Europe in the past can also be placed within the framework of integration in a wider market (Siegelberg, 1991). On the one hand, the fact that Europe arrived at a period of prosperity is cause for optimism; on the other hand, certain similarities notwithstanding, the developing countries of today differ from the old European states. This is also the view of Lofchie, and to quote him extensively:

> The political environment of Western society during early industrialization was such as to insulate fledgling state institutions from the social misery generated by an incipient industrial process. A widening of the political franchise and a change of political values from *laissez-faire* to welfare liberalism did not occur until the industrialization process was well advanced and many of its more harsh social consequences had been ameliorated ... The political burden on state institutions was lightened considerably by the fact that the basic dynamism for economic transformation was supplied by an autonomous entrepreneurial class outside the state ... the stimulation of economic growth was not a gov-

ernmental function. In Africa, where autonomous economic elites are largely lacking, the generation of economic growth is a state function. This means that embryonic political institutions have a twofold task to perform. They must be concerned both with economic growth and with alleviation of the human hardships created by economic change (Lofchie, 1971).

Lofchie draws attention to the internal political processes involved. The governments of developing countries have to carry out the developmental tasks in the shortest time possible. In another context, Ayoob talks of 'telescoping' the processes of state-making and nation-building (Ayoob, 1990). The accomplishment of the tasks mentioned by Lofchie seems to request a similar principle, in this case with regard to limiting the time-frame of economic development and poverty alleviation.

The economic problems of developing countries cannot be dealt with in a strict economic sense. The problems related to economic growth and inequality should also be treated from a political-economy point of view. Economic growth and income distribution are largely the result of economic policy choices, and therefore of the organization of the polity (democratic or authoritarian). The entitlements of people to resources (natural or political), or to services (health care) and facilities (education) – and inequality with regard to these entitlements – should also be treated from the political-economy point of view. Political struggles within the institutional structure of the state should thus also be analysed, as will be done. First, however, some of the theories on economic conflict that have been developed will be introduced.

Theories on Economic Conflict

The interrelationship of economic issues and violent conflict, however complex, is often linked to a single factor: poverty. Theories on revolution, in particular, stress this link. In a situation where a large group of people living in poverty faces a small and very rich group of individuals in their own country or their own community, they are expected to demand radical changes or to revolt. Theories which are of importance when discussing economic factors – and especially poverty – in relation to conflict, concern the *frustration-aggression theory* and the *relative deprivation theory*.

These theories are based on psychological analysis of collective violence. They suggest that individuals become aggressive when they feel something or someone is blocking them from fulfilling a strong and perceived as fair economic desire. The relative deprivation approach concentrates especially on an economic interpretation of feelings of dissatisfaction. Since it concerns economic factors, it could be said that the feelings of dissatisfaction concern rational calculations.

Ted Gurr has attempted to demonstrate the connection between the probability of collective violence and the degree of relative deprivation. He concludes that the most important – although certainly not the only – factor must be sought in an increasing discrepancy between what people expect and what they themselves consider possible or actually get (Gurr, 1970). It is reasonable to expect people to become frustrated and aggressive if, in their own eyes, they feel undervalued. This also applies to the more general frustration-aggression approach, which argues that individuals may become aggressive if they feel frustrated. Perceptions, however, may mean very little, and are liable to change depending on the situation or the individual, so the question remains as to whether and to what extent perceptions are applicable at the level of organized groups, as well as how they relate to large-scale political conflicts. From developments in the past it can be learned that economic factors such as food shortages, waves of inflation and the abolishment of subsidies can instigate riots and disturbances.

The literature reveals a number of connections between economic inequality and political conflict. The first is that an increase in economic inequality is followed by an increase in the number of participants in the conflict (both rich and poor). Research into this hypothesis has produced positive results with regard to the Philippines, South Vietnam and Africa (Lichbach, 1989).

The opposite hypothesis argues that economic inequality in fact reduces the chance of conflict. The underlying idea here is that the 'haves' will do their utmost to maintain the situation as it is, and will thus suppress every form of opposition. Moreover, extreme poverty can lead to conflict as well as to apathy.

Others have attempted to link the two views. Nagel thus talks of a U-shaped relationship in which 'political violence will occur most likely at intermediate levels of economic inequality, least frequently at very low or very high levels' (Lichbach, 1989).

The contradictions in findings have led other researchers to deny any connection between economic inequality and political conflict. They attribute the absence of a direct correlation to the fact that economic inequality changes little or not at all over longer periods of time, whereas political conflicts arise (in)frequently (Jackson, 1986).

As a result, the economic inequality/political conflict nexus approach can be criticized because it does not focus sufficiently on the problem of why economic inequality leads to political conflicts in only a limited number of cases. On the basis of empirical research at a macro level, poverty and economic inequality, both individually and in combination, prove to be at most necessary, but not sufficient preconditions for conflict. Additional assumptions are essential. In the view of the fact that mobilization of groups plays a crucial role, it is profitable to search for answers in the political sphere.

Demography, Democracy, Development and Conflict

Demography and Conflict

From the previous parts of this essay on state-formation and ethnicity, it can be learned that developing and maintaining broad-based public loyalty to the nation-state is not easy for multi-ethnic 'Third World' countries. In developing countries the quality of life is generally not high, and people are often not able to improve their lives. A combination of structural problems related to limited material resources creates a woeful existence for most persons living in these countries: economy-related problems in developing countries include accumulated foreign debt, population growth and its demographic effects, inadequate and badly distributed food supplies, poverty, underdeveloped infrastructures, environmental degradation, and many others. These problems are more severe in some geographical regions and countries than in others. It is important, however, to investigate how these problems relate to violent conflict.

For instance, what is the effect of population growth? This includes factors such as the pace and pattern of population growth, the demographics of the population, the habitation patterns and population movement within and between countries. Related to the issue of population growth is the food-environment nexus, and, again closely related, the issue of access to land and resources. How can people maximize the production of food from a given piece of land without destroying the local ecosystem for themselves and for future generations? The simultaneous and related occurrence of degradation of land, growing population pressure, as well as limited access to land and resources can result in civil strife. This effect can be intensified when a political elite changes property rights, distributing resources in its own favour, thus excluding local or ethnic minorities.

Democracy, Development and Conflict

The remedies which are regarded as most important to reduce inequality, and thus the risk of economic conflict, are democratization and/or socio-economic development. How are these processes interrelated? Does development indeed lead to democracy?

According to some theories, basic material needs must be met before a democratic society can exist (Marks and Diamond, 1992): Taiwan is an example of a country in which economic success acted as a catalyst for democratization. Samarasinghe, however, finds that evidence is too weak to fully support this view. On the one hand India shows that democracy can survive in a country faced with a high unemployment rate and extensive poverty. On the other hand, in countries such as Singapore, economic success has for the time being failed to move the regime towards further democratization. The relationship between socio-economic development and democracy is even more complex if the transformation process in Central and Eastern Europe is taken into account. Here, economic failure of the former communist regimes brought about the change towards democracy (Samarasinghe, 1995).

What about the reverse relationship? Does democracy help development? Here Samarasinghe differentiates between two concepts: governance and development. Additionally, he distinguishes a narrow and a broader interpretation of the concept of governance. The narrow definition refers to the notion of 'good governance' as used by the World Bank: public sector management, a legal framework for development, and information and transparency. The broader definition of governance refers to democratic governance: legitimacy of authority, public responsiveness and public accountability of government (Samarasinghe, 1995; and Boeninger, 1992). Again, the relationship between the two is weak. The East Asian NICs have shown that good governance (in the narrow sense) and economic growth are possible without democracy. Sirowy and Inkeles even note that 'democracy does not widely and directly facilitate more rapid economic growth' (Sirowy and Inkeles, 1990). However, good governance in the narrow sense can help promote the process of democratization by encouraging socio-economic development and gradually introducing practices that enhance the accountability and the responsiveness of government.

Aside from this complex relationship between socio-economic development and democracy, it is also unclear how both processes relate to conflict. According to some views, democratization neither helps in promoting development nor in reducing conflict. It can, for example, be expected that the number of dissident groups, which are able to appeal to (and mobilize) people, increases. The stronger these dissident groups, the greater the risk for political instability and conflict. Countries at the beginning of a democratic political structure may encounter huge pressure to accommodate the conflicting demands and wishes of different groups. If the groups are mobilized along ethnic fault-lines, or when such cleavages are encouraged, development, as well as democratization, are jeopardized. Resource allocation may become distorted by using ethnic criteria, and the risk of violent opposition increases. Fear for such a scenario has led some regimes in the 'Third World' to the conclusion that socio-economic development is preferred before democratization.

It can, however, also be expected that an increase in political participation and influence from poorer groups within society facilitates measures against inequality. This will counteract escalation towards violent opposition (Huntington, 1991; Diamond *et al.*, 1990; Rueschemeyer *et al.*, 1992; O'Donnel and Schmitter, 1986; Healy and Robinson, 1992; and Nelson, 1990). The question remains, however, of whether the absence of a democratic structure automatically results in more inequality and more violent resistance. South-East Asia, for example, is a region with economically successful authoritarian, but stable, political regimes that helped improve equity (Alesina *et al.*, 1992).

The relationship between socio-economic development and political conflict is also in no way fixed. Huntington argues that when poor countries go through a period of rapid economic growth and economic take-off, political discord may increase. This is especially true when institutions designed to structure the social and economic developments are lacking, as is often the case in developing countries. These causes of political unrest are of a socio-political kind: turbulent developments within society related to new demands, urbanization, etc. As a result, and in contrast to the rich industrialized countries, a period of rapid economic growth may therefore destabilize the political situation in poor countries, and when these countries are moreover confronted with 'revolutionary' political developments, such as embryonic democratization, the destabilizing effects may increase further. Economic growth, often thought of as a stabilizing factor, thus also contains conflict-generating factors, so, in this regard, economic development can be referred to as a 'double-edged sword'. Apart from an increase in inequality and the development of new economic disparities, a higher standard of living may also lead to new demands in the political sphere by a larger group of (newly) affluent people (Sayigh, 1990; and Al-Mashat, 1985).

In contrast to Huntington's view, Londregan and Poole find that poverty and a low level of growth increase political instability (Londregan and Poole, 1990). Their findings can be related to integration in the world market. The inability of government to accommodate demands from groups within society because of unexpected shortfalls in export revenues, may increase the likelihood of *coups*. Such shortfalls may lead to forms of inter-group conflict because the state is no longer able to take expected and/or necessary redistributive measures.

No Conclusion So Far

Since consensus concerning the relationship between economic issues and political instability and conflict is lacking, more research is needed. In the following chapter on economic issues and conflict, Henk Houweling analyses this relationship in a comprehensive way.

THE ROLE OF ARMAMENTS

Introduction

The 'Third World' has experienced increasing arms build-up and growing militarization since 1945, a process involving both the formation of armed forces and the acquisition of increasing stocks of armaments. During the same period, the 'Third World' has been the stage for most of the conflicts being fought, thus raising the question of the role that military factors have played in the origins of these conflicts.

The problem of arms acquisition in relation to conflicts can be analysed in various ways. A distinction should be made between the inter- and the intra-state level: the inter-state level relates to the external security of states. Here the anarchic character of the inter-state system is still of importance. Recent examples showing why states need to be able to defend themselves against external threats, are Iraq's attempt to sweep Kuwait from the map and the struggle for survival being waged by Bosnia-Herzegovina. Meanwhile, developing countries are mainly faced with internal security problems, so how can armaments and militarization be related to the internal security threats of developing countries? And are small arms and the availability of these weapons the main threat to the internal stability of states?

Theories on Armaments and Conflict

The international community has until now mainly focused on major-weapon systems and the proliferation of nuclear and chemical weapons. The issue of small arms drew much less attention. During the Cold War, interest in major-weapon systems and technologies was obvious because of their military and strategic importance. However, the result of the end of the Cold War has been that major-weapon systems have lost their great significance — although equipment still counts in larger-scale conflicts such as Bosnia-Herzegovina. Protracted intra-state conflicts are mainly being fought with so-called small arms. According to some political analysts the shift towards these new kinds of conflict can also be felt in the arms trade. Aaron Karp observes a 'revolution' that has hit the arms trade since the end of the Cold War:

> [The arms trade] ... no longer serves primarily to influence the international balance of power. Instead it helps to regulate the emergence of new states. Its most important role is not arming the forces of allies and regional powers as in the past, but as a lever for controlling or promoting ethnic violence and the outbreak of war in the near future (Karp, 1994).

This raises the question of whether there is a direct causal relationship between armaments and conflict.

According to Keith Krause, three models can roughly be distinguished: (1) weapons as an independent variable; (2) as a purely dependent variable; and (3) as an intervening variable. In the first model a direct causal link between armaments and conflicts is suggested. Increased armaments can directly exacerbate the security dilemma and/or increase the potential for misperception and thus eventually lead to war. In this regard it is also sometimes suggested that the arms build-up in Iraq resulted in the Gulf War. The partial disarmament of Iraq should also be seen in this perspective. The second model posits that armaments are *not* origins of conflict, but that the reversal is true: armaments follow conflict. In this model armaments can be seen as aggravating factors, which influence the duration and intensity of violent conflict.

The third model concerns an intermediate form and refers to what Karp has called 'promoting'. According to this view, armaments can accelerate the momentum (or tilt the balance) towards conflicts. However, this does *not* imply that the availability of weapons causes conflict. On the contrary, the third model should be interpreted in a broader context in which political, social and economic factors function as providers of 'deeper' problems, and in which armaments can alter the balance of power within a state in favour of the advocates of violent solutions. This raises the question of why the easy availability of weapons influences the pace and direction of conflict in developing countries.

The Impact of Small Arms on Politics and Conflict

The view that small arms influence the pace and direction of conflict corresponds with what is now happening in several 'Third World' countries. Intra-state conflicts are the dominant form of conflict in the 'Third World', and of the 30 conflicts documented in the *SIPRI Yearbook 1993*, it can be concluded that all but four were being fought almost entirely with small arms and light weapons, mostly the cheapest and least advanced kind (Karp, 1993). Martin van Creveld characterizes this trend towards intra-state conflicts as the 'reprimitivization' of wars: a return to a pre-Westphalian world of warrior societies (Van Creveld, 1991). This view means an end to the Clausewitzian concept that war is an instrument of states to serve their political goal by the use of military means – the continuation of politics by other means.

This development towards a pre-Westphalian world can be boosted if the state's monopoly on the means of violence is no longer widely accepted, and if states fail to provide security for their citizens. Ineffective states – characterized by a vacuum of state authority – are not able to check an unfolding anarchic social order and societal implosion. The central government is no longer the 'manager' of conflict. In such circumstances the proliferation of (small) arms can promote the process of state-breakdown by fuelling conflicts or by accelerating a trend towards insurgency and guerrilla activities. Such a breakdown of the legal monopoly of the armed forces of the state can be observed in several 'Third World' countries (Lebanon, Sri Lanka, Peru, Colombia), as well as in Russia (Chechnya). Kaplan, in his article on 'the coming anarchy', perceives that the same process is taking place on a regional scale in West Africa (Kaplan, 1994).

Arming Sub-State Groups

The breakdown of the legal monopoly of the armed forces of states can also be concluded from the increasing participation of sub-state groups in conflict. On the basis of Wallensteen's and Axell's assessment, we can deduce that almost 175 of such groups were active during the period from 1988-1993. This number, however, may be much larger. According to estimates by the Indian government, for example, there are 180 groups active in Kashmir. Counting sub-state groups, however, is complicated, as a result of the alliances and fronts among these groups. Despite such uncertainties, it can be concluded that armed sub-state groups are challenging state power in weak states. According to Chipman, 'the sophisticated small-arms trade is such that guerrilla groups throughout the world are able to garner for themselves quite impressive inventories' (Chipman, 1991). An important factor in this regard is the permeability of borders, resulting in the easy circulation of arms in states close to conflict zones. This questions the role of the international community, and in particular that of neighbouring countries, in arming sub-state groups.

The other side of the coin, of course, is that if the availability of these weapons is a catalyst to conflict – and intra-state conflict in particular – then they can no longer be regarded as irrelevant to international security. There is always the risk of intra-state conflicts spreading to neighbouring countries and thus becoming destabilizing factors for whole regions. This implies that if we have to deal with the problem of these new intra-state conflicts, attention should also be paid to the issue of (trade in) small arms.

Nevertheless, the impact of small arms and their trade should not be exaggerated. The availability of small-calibre armaments is not a sufficient condition to initiate killings within countries. During the conflicts between Hindus and Muslims caused by the partition of India after the Second World War, millions were killed with knives and other small weapons. Another, more recent, example can be found in Africa: during the genocide in Rwanda, which began in April 1994, hundreds of thousands of people were killed with machetes. Apparently, guns and arms are not necessary to cause large numbers of casualties. The easy availability of small arms, however, should still be regarded as an important factor, and perhaps even a necessary condition with regard to fuelling conflicts. According to Stephen Goose and Frank Smyth, the distribution of firearms to militia members months before the genocide in Rwanda began, illustrates this fact (1994). The same authors also stress the importance of foreign suppliers. This not only applies to the Rwandan conflict, but also to other conflicts, especially those in which conflicting parties draw heavily on military force. In such situations, an (external) supply of arms is necessary to sustain conflict, yet in spite of these facts, the international community has no viable mechanism for monitoring the transfer of light and small weapons. The trade in small arms, especially the pattern of arms sales preceding the outbreak of hostilities and the pattern of arms sales during the conflict itself, should therefore receive more attention from the international community.

NOTE

1. Crawford Young cites Rupert Emerson, *From Empire to Nation: The Rise of Self-Assertion of Asian and African Peoples* (Cambridge, MA: Harvard University Press, 1960).

BIBLIOGRAPHY

A. Alesina, S. Ozler, N. Roubini and P. Swagel, *Political Instability and Economic Growth*, NBER Working Paper 4173 (Cambridge, MA: National Bureau of Economic Research, 1992).

A.M. Al-Mashat, *National Security in the Third World* (Boulder, CO.: Westview, 1985).

B. Anderson, *Imagined Communities: Reflections on the Origins and Spread of Nationalism* (London: Verso, 1994).

F. Ansprenger, 'Konflikte in Afrika', *Europa Archiv*, no. 20, 1994.

M. Ayoob, 'The Security Problematic of The Third World', *World Politics*, vol. 43, January 1991, pp. 257-83; 'The Security Predicament of the Third World State: Reflections on State-Making in a Comparative Perspective', in B.L. Job (ed.), *The Insecurity Dilemma: National Security of Third World States* (Boulder, CO: Lynne Rienner, 1992).

J.S. Barkin and B Cronin, 'The State and the Nation: Changing Norms and the Rules of Sovereignty in International Relations', *International Organization*, vol. 48, no. 1, winter 1994, pp. 107-30.

F. Barth, *Ethnic Groups and Boundaries* (Oslo: Norwegian University Press, 1969).

E. Boeninger, 'Governance and Development: Issues and Constraints', in *Proceedings of the World Bank Annual Conference on Development Economics*, pp. 267-87.

E. Boulding, 'Ethnic Separatism and World Development', *Conflict and Change*, vol. 2, 1979.

B. Buzan, *People, States and Fear: An Agenda for International Security Studies in the Post-Cold War Era* (London: Harvester Wheatsheaf, 1991).

J. Chipman, 'Third World Politics and Security in the 1990s: "The World Forgetting, By the World Forgot"?', *The Washington Quarterly*, vol. 14, no. 1, winter 1991, pp. 151-68.

W. Connor, 'Nation-Building or Nation-Destroying?', *World Politics*, vol. 24, no. 3, 1972, pp. 319-55.

M. van Creveld, *The Transformation of War* (New York: Free Press, 1991).

G. O'Donnel and P.C. Schmitter, *Transitions from Authoritarian Rule: Tentative Conclusions about Uncertain Democracies* (Baltimore, MD: Johns Hopkins University Press, 1986).

M. Edmonds, 'Civil War, Internal War and Intra-Societal Conflict: A Taxonomy and Typology', in R. Higham (ed.), *Civil Wars in the Twentieth Century* (Lexington, KY: University Press of Kentucky, 1972), pp. 11-26.

A. Etzioni, 'The Evils of Self-Determination', *Foreign Policy*, vol. 89, winter 1992-93, pp. 21-35.

K.J. Gantzel and T. Schwinghammer (eds), *Die Kriege nach dem Zweiten Weltkrieg bis 1992: Daten und Tendenzen* (Munich: Lit-Verlag, 1995).

S. Gashaw, 'Nationalism and Ethnic Conflict in Ethiopia', in C. Young (ed.), *The Rising Tide of Cultural Pluralism: The Nation-State at Bay?* (Madison, WI: University of Wisconsin Press, 1993), pp. 138-58.

Introduction to the Themes

S. Gashaw, 'Nationalism and Ethnic Conflict in Ethiopia', in C. Young (ed.), *The Rising Tide of Cultural Pluralism: The Nation-State at Bay?* (Madison, WI: University of Wisconsin Press, 1993), pp. 138-58.

E. Gellner, *Nations and Nationalism* (Ithaca, NY: Cornell University Press, 1983).

S.D. Goose and F. Smyth, 'Arming Genocide in Rwanda', *Foreign Affairs*, vol. 73, no. 5, September/October 1994, pp. 86-96.

T.R. Gurr, *Why Men Rebel* (Princeton, NJ: Princeton University Press, 1970); 'Theories of Political Violence and Revolution in the Third World', in F.M. Deng and I.W. Zartman (eds), *Conflict Resolution in Africa* (Washington, DC: Brookings Institution, 1991).

M.H. Halperin and David J. Scheffer with P.L. Small, *Self-Determination in the New World Order* (Washington, DC: Carnegie Endowment for International Peace, 1992).

J. Healy and M. Robinson, *Democracy, Governance and Economic Policy: Sub-Saharan Africa in Comparative Perspective* (London: Overseas Development Institute, 1992).

G.B. Helman and S.R. Ratner, 'Saving Failed States', *Foreign Policy*, vol. 89, winter 1992-93, pp. 3-20.

E.J. Hobsbawm, *Nations and Nationalism since 1870: Programme, Myth, Reality* (Cambridge: Cambridge University Press, 1990).

K.J. Holsti, *Peace and War: Armed Conflicts and International Order 1648-1989*, Cambridge Studies in International Relations:14 (Cambridge: Cambridge University Press, 1991).

D. Horowitz, *Ethnic Groups in Conflict* (Los Angeles, CA: University of California Press, 1985).

S.P. Huntington, *Political Order in Changing Societies* (New Haven, CT: Yale University Press, 1968); *The Third Wave: Democratization in the Late Twentieth Century* (Norman, OK: University of Oklahoma Press, 1991); 'The Clash of Civilizations?', *Foreign Affairs*, vol. 72, no. 3, summer 1993, pp. 22-49; 'If Not Civilizations, What? Paradigms of the Post-Cold War World', *Foreign Affairs*, vol. 72, no. 5, November/December 1993, pp. 186-94.

K.D. Jackson, 'Post-Colonial Rebellions: Lessons from South-East Asia', in R.A. Scalapino, S. Sato and J. Wanandi (eds), *Internal and External Security Issues in Asia* (Berkeley, CA: University of Berkeley for Institute of East Asian Studies, 1986).

R.H. Jackson and C.G. Rosberg, 'Why Africa's Weak States Persist: The Empirical and Juridical Statehood', *World Politics*, vol. 35, no. 1, October 1982, pp. 1-24.

R.D. Kaplan, 'The Coming Anarchy', *The Atlantic Monthly*, February 1994, pp. 44-76.

A. Karp, 'The Covert Arms Trade and the Future of Intra-National Conflict', in *Resolving Intra-National Conflicts: A Strengthened Role for Intergovernmental Organizations*, Carter Center of Emory University, Conference Report Series, vol. 5, no. 1, 1993; 'Arming Ethnic Conflict', *Arms Control Today*, vol. 23, no.

7, 1993, pp. 8-13; 'The Arms Trade Revolution: The Major Impact of Small Arms', *The Washington Quarterly*, vol. 17, no. 4, 1994, pp. 65-77.

M.I. Lichbach, 'An Evaluation of "Does Economic Inequality Breed Political Conflict?" Studies', *World Politics*, vol. 41, no. 4, 1989, pp. 431-71.

M.F. Lofchie (ed.), *The State of Nations: Constraints on Development in Independent Africa* (Berkeley, CA: University of California Press, 1971).

J.B. Londregan and K.T. Poole, 'Poverty, the Coup Trap, and the Seizure of Executive Power', *World Politics*, vol. 42, no. 2, 1990, pp. 151-83.

M. Mann, 'The Autonomous Power of the State: Its Origins, Mechanisms and Results', in J.A. Hall (ed.), *States in History* (Oxford: Basil Blackwell, 1986), pp. 109-36.

G. Marks and L. Diamond (eds), *Re-examining Democracy* (Newbury Park, CA: Sage, 1992).

C.W. Maynes, 'Containing Ethnic Conflict', in *Foreign Policy*, vol. 90, spring 1993, pp. 3-21.

A.A. Mazrui, 'The Triple Heritage of the State in Africa', in A. Kazancigil (ed.), *The State in Global Perspective* (Aldershot: Gower, 1986).

H. Miall, *The Peace-makers: Peaceful Settlement of Disputes since 1945* (London: Macmillan, 1992).

J.J. Mearsheimer, 'Back to the Future: Instability in Europe After the Cold War', in S.M. Lynn-Jones (ed.), *The Cold War and After: Prospects for Peace* (Cambridge, MA: MIT Press, 1991), pp. 141-92.

A.F. Mullins, *Born Arming: Development and Military Power in New States* (Stanford, CA: Stanford University Press, 1987).

J.M. Nelson (ed.), *Economic Crisis and Policy Choice: The Politics of Adjustment in the Third World* (Princeton, NJ: Princeton University Press, 1990).

J.P. Nettle, 'The State as a Conceptual Variable', *World Politics*, vol. 20, no. 4, July 1968, pp. 559-92.

S. Newman, 'Does Modernization Breed Ethnic Political Conflict?', *World Politics*, vol. 43, April 1991, pp. 451-78.

M. Nicholson, *Conflict Analysis* (London: English University Press, 1971).

D. Rueschemeyer, E.H. Stephens and J.D. Stephens, *Capitalist Development and Democracy* (Cambridge: Polity Press, 1992).

R. Rosecrance, *The Rise of the Trading State: Commerce and Conquest in the Modern World* (New York: Basic Books, 1984).

S.W.R. de A. Samarasinghe, 'Ethnicity, Democratization and Development: The South and South-East Asian Experience' (Conference Paper).

Y. Sayigh, 'Confronting the 1990s: Security in the Developing Countries', *Adelphi Papers*, no. 251 (London: International Institute of Strategic Studies, 1990).

J. Siegelberg (ed.), *Die Kriege 1985-1990: Analyse ihrer Ursachen*, Reihe Kriege und militante Konflikte Bd. 2 (Munich: Lit-Verlag, 1991).

M. Singer and A. Wildavsky, *The Real World Order: Zones of Peace, Zones of Turmoil* (Chatham: Chatham House Publishers, 1993).

L. Sirowy and A. Inkeles, 'The Effects of Democracy on Economic Growth and Inequality: A Review', *Studies in Comparative International Development*, vol. 25, 1990, pp. 126-57.

A.D. Smith, 'Conflict and Collective Identity: Class, *Ethnie* and Nation', in E.E. Azar and J.W. Burton, *International Conflict Resolution: Theory and Practice* (Sussex: Wheatsheaf Books, 1986), pp. 63-84; *The Ethnic Origins of Nations* (Oxford: Basil lackwell, 1986); 'State-Making and Nation-Building', in J.A. Hall (ed.), *States in History* (Oxford: Basil Blackwell, 1986), pp. 228-73.

C. Thomas, 'New Directions in Thinking about Security in the Third World', in K. Booth (ed.), *New Thinking about Strategy and International Security* (London: HarperCollins Academic, 1991), pp. 267-89.

H.K. Tillema, 'Foreign Overt Military Intervention in the Nuclear Age', *Journal of Peace Research*, vol. 26, no. 2, 1989, pp. 179-95.

C. Tilly, *Coercion, Capital, and European States, AD 990-1990* (Cambridge, MA: Basil Blackwell, 1990).

R.H. Ullman, 'Enlarging the Zone of Peace', *Foreign Policy*, vol. 80, fall 1990, pp. 102-20.

P. Wallensteen and K. Axell, 'Conflict Resolution and the End of the Cold War, 1989-93', *Journal of Peace Research*, vol. 31, no. 3, 1994, pp. 333-49.

D. Welsh, 'Domestic Politics and Ethnic Conflict', *Survival*, vol. 35, no. 1, spring 1993, pp. 63-80.

M. Weiner, 'Political Change: Asia, Africa and the Middle East', in M. Weiner and S.P. Huntington, *Understanding Political Development* (Boston, MA: Little Brown, 1987).

C. Young, 'The Dialectics of Cultural Pluralism: Concept and Reality', in C. Young (ed.), *The Rising Tide of Cultural Pluralism: The Nation-State at Bay?* (Madison, WI: University of Wisconsin Press, 1993), pp. 3-35.

Part I

CLASSIFICATION

1

Armed Conflict in the Former Colonial Regions: From Classification to Explanation

J. David Singer*

INTRODUCTION

As we contemplate the winding down of the Soviet-American armed rivalry and the declining probability of global nuclear war, our attention is increasingly drawn to the frequency and severity of armed conflict in what used to be called the 'Third World'. And while the conventional wisdom sees this level of regional and communal war as something new – permitted, if not catalysed, by the end of superpower confrontation – the evidence suggests otherwise. That is, since the Second World War there has been a dramatic movement in the location of both international war and civil war from the northern part of the globe to the southern regions, to approximately below the 40 degrees north latitude. To put it another way, the only international war in the north between 1945 and 1990 was the three-week Russo-Hungarian war of 1956, killing about 10,000 combatants (three-quarters of them on the Soviet side), whereas there were 45 in the rest of the world; similarly, the only civil war during that period in the northern region was that which raged in Greece from 1944 to 1949, killing 160,000 combatants, while the rest of the world saw 69 such wars, with combat fatalities of approximately six and a half million (Singer, 1991). These figures are cited to help us appreciate that this trend has been with us for nearly half a century, and in no way can be understood as a consequence of the end of the Cold War. It is just that most of us living in the 'First' and 'Second' worlds were too preoccupied with the senselessness of our own confrontation to notice the death and destruction going on elsewhere. Had we stopped and looked, we might have become aware of these tragedies, and furthermore might even have observed that these were largely wars over land, resources, populations, and self-determination, whereas we hovered at the brink of a global

* The author would like to acknowledge the research assistance of J. Scott DeSonia.

holocaust over the matter of some dubious dominance, couched in terms normative and ideological.

Be that as it may, conflict and combat have been part of the former colonial world for a long time, not only causing human grief beyond imagination, but virtually assuring that economic, social, and political development would not occur. But now that there seems to be fast-growing concern over this dreadful state of affairs, it is appropriate that the policy and scholarly communities begin to seek a reversal of these trends. To do so, a major requisite is that we learn more about the factors that lead to communal and regional conflict in the 'peripheral' areas, building on the fact that our knowledge regarding inter-state war in the European regions has gradually begun to accumulate (for example, Vasquez, 1993; Cashman, 1993; Houweling and Siccama, 1988; Midlarsky, 1989), but that the applicability of that knowledge to the rest of the world remains open to question.

TRUTH IN PACKAGING AND SEMANTIC OBFUSCATION

Nothing is as central to the explanation of any phenomenon as the kind of typology we use to identify and discuss it and the factors that allegedly lead to it. Typology and classification make it possible to generalize, to speculate, and ultimately to test alternative explanations. And given the ubiquitousness of armed combat, not to mention its human costs and the difficulty of studying it, one might expect that students of conflict would be especially careful of the language, concepts, and categories currently used. This, unhappily, is far from the case. Although it would not be easy to demonstrate, the strong impression is that social scientists are more careless than biological or physical scientists in their vocabularies, and that within the social sciences, those who specialize in conflict among political entities are even less attentive to semantic precision.

To illustrate, going from the general to the particular, we note the frequency with which 'theory' – which should be a word used only to describe a body of codified knowledge – is applied to all sorts of ideas, idle speculations, casual hunches, plausible arguments, familiar assumptions, and so forth. If the same concept is used to describe our ideas *before* the research is done, how shall we differentiate what we know *after* a major piece of work has been completed? One might even suggest that if the objective of scientific research is to produce a substantiated theory, we need not bother; the theory is there *without* the research! Another embarrassing example is that of the currently popular 'hegemon'. A moment's thought suggests that this is a dichotomous term: a state is either a hegemon or it is not, and there cannot be more than one hegemon in any system, so all the others are non-hegemons. Does this really mean that one state fully and totally controls all the others in the global system, or even in a regional sub-system? As Lasswell and Kaplan (1950) reminded us long ago, the power of an actor can and should be measured in relative terms: over which other actors, regarding which particular activities, and to what extent? The only appropriate expression is to what extent does A influence, control, or dominate actors B...n, and in what area of policy? This leads, in turn, to the widespread confusion between power on the one hand and material strength or capabilities on the other. One actor may have extraordinary military, industrial, or demographic capabilities and might even be able to obliterate others, but, as Thibaut and Kelley (1959) demonstrated, 'fate control' does not always translate into 'behaviour control'. Physical strength is one thing, and the capacity to exercise and to resist influence – that is, power – is quite another.

Returning to simplistic dichotomies, our literature is studded with references to 'totalitarian' regimes (Arendt, 1951, 1963), as if the modern world has ever seen a regime – at the city, province, or state level – that exercised total control over its population. Then there is the familiar, but bizarre, use of the word 'stability'. It is baffling that the admired late Quincy Wright (1954) would introduce and legitimize stability to mean peacefulness or the relative absence of war. While a case can be made for the hypothesis that continuity, stability, and the absence of radical change in the system may contribute to its peacefulness, this is neither well established nor is it synonymous.

This discussion of semantic imprecision, then, will be closed with what is perhaps the classic example of careless verbiage: the widespread use of a vague line of argument under the label of 'hegemonic stability theory'. Presumably, these authors have in mind the plausible suspicion that the global system, or one of its regional or functional subsystems, will experience less conflict, discord, and war when there is one very powerful and dominant state committed to preserving the *status quo*. But since there is no reproducible body of knowledge in support of this contention, it is far from being a theory; and since there can be no such entity as a hegemon and stability may or may not lead to peace, we can see that those scholars (Gilpin, 1981; Keohane, 1980) who have embraced this sonorous-sounding triplet are doing little to enhance 'truth in packaging'!

In addition to the deleterious effects of loaded and imprecise classifications upon scholarly research, we should not overlook the policy implications. That is, if decision-makers look at an incipient or ongoing armed conflict and, in response to some common but ill-founded typology, hasten to treat the problem as if it were purely or largely ethnic or territorial or ideological, when it is in fact more complex and multi-dimensional, they might easily opt for a highly inappropriate policy response. For example, most Western elites interpreted the civil war in Vietnam as an ideological conflict between freedom and democracy on the one hand and the forces of the international communist conspiracy or coalition on the other, when in fact it had begun as a struggle between the Vietminh (later known as Vietcong) and the regime in Saigon. By giving political and military support to the latter, and rejecting the overtures of Ho Chi Minh, the United States converted what might have been a relatively brief period of turbulence into one of the bloodiest wars of this century, with disastrous consequences for both the people of Asia and the United States, and by extension those who are indirect victims of America's 'Vietnam Syndrome'.

EPISTEMOLOGICAL CONSIDERATIONS

In addition to the need for semantic precision as discussed above, there are several other considerations in trying to develop useful typologies for the study of armed conflict in former colonial regions. First, the categories must be mutually exclusive, with clear and operational criteria for distinguishing between and among the cases that are assigned to each category or class of cases. Second, the categories must be logically exhaustive; all possible cases must be included, even though some class of cases might not show up in a given region or period of time.

Beyond these two mechanical requirements there is a more sophisticated issue, revolving around the role of a typology in our search for explanation. That is, while there is no such thing as a typology that is totally free of theory, we need to come as close to that objective as possible. The problem is to avoid a categorization scheme that is theoretically 'loaded', in the sense that it assumes or prejudges the explanation or driving force behind the phenomena that are being described; descriptions must never embrace and foreclose the explanation. For example, a typology that is built around 'wars of expansion' and 'wars of defence' would assign the cases to one or the other category in advance of the research that might illuminate the motives of the protagonists, even though it is known that most international wars are fought between entities whose leadership is not only preoccupied with the preservation and defence of its existing territories, but simultaneously interested in the amount of expansion that might be offered by a buffer zone and thus enhance security. This, after all, is what the 'security dilemma' implies: one side's defensive moves are the rival's provocation; there is almost always a mix of the offence and the defence on both sides in a dispute that escalates to a resort to arms.

Then there is the equally ubiquitous – and ill-founded – concept of 'territorial dispute', as if elites are concerned with the gain or loss of territory regardless of the demographic, strategic, or economic significance of the land in question. If what some students call 'Singer's First Law' is invoked, no political event ever occurs for one reason alone. Not only are there always multiple pushes of the past, there are also multiple pulls of the future, in which those diverse groups and individuals who support a given foreign policy do so for different reasons. And to bring diverse constituencies on board in support of a given policy, the elites need to appeal to their several disparate interests. To put it bluntly, if our purpose is to discover the factors that account for different types of conflict, it would not be adaptive to label them in advance of the research with names that assert or imply the factors that produce the conflicts.

The final example brings us quite a bit closer to the current agenda: that of 'ethnic conflict'. While it would be foolish to deny the role of ethnic and other cultural differences in the onset and escalation of conflicts in the former colonial regions, or any part of the world for that matter, a serious mistake is made in calling them ethnic conflicts, for several reasons. First, in a study now under way at Michigan (Singer and DeSonia, 1995), we find that ethnic, religious, and linguistic differences between states show virtually no correlation with either the onset of rivalries or war between them. Similarly, we find that such cultural cleavages *within* the society have little discernible effect on the frequency of civil war. Then, in an ongoing study of inter-state disputes 'over territory', Huth again finds that ethnic differences play only the most modest role in the onset of these disputes as well as their resolution (Huth, 1995). Moreover, these patterns hold not only for the 175 years since the Congress of Vienna, but also for the more recent period beginning with the establishment of all the newly independent states after 1960. Second, to label the conflicts so within and between these new states is not only to ignore the quantitative historical evidence, but also to manifest an embarrassing degree of cultural provincialism. That is, we recognize that the more developed industrial states get into disputes over such 'reasonable' issues as threats to spheres of influence, control of and access to markets, resources, investment and trade opportunities, and territorial integrity, while suggesting that coloured people do so merely because of long-standing tribal, religious, and ethnic rivalries. Of course 'we' used to do so, but that was before we in the Western world became more 'civilized'; ethnic conflict is, we imply, quite pejorative. And, third – as already suggested – to label disputes, conflicts, and wars as 'ethnic' is to foreclose further investigation and conclude that we already know what these disputes are about. On the basis of what is known and not known at the moment, the more reasonable model would have us assume that most conflicts arise out of a wide – but dimly understood – array of conditions and events, and that cultural differences are often played upon by political elites and counter-elites in order to mobilize support or to pander to 'we-versus-them' emotions in a search for popularity and support. One might say that many conflicts will inevitably have an inter-ethnic dimension and are thus often 'ethnicized' by those who are in power or hope to be.

Having suggested this possible course of events, we might also note that there is also an external factor that helps to convert milder disputes into armed combat, and that of course is the export of weapons to these regions by those societies that are sufficiently advanced industrially to produce fairly sophisticated weapons in large numbers (Krause, 1990). As a matter of fact, Mullins (1987) found in his study of the newly independent states of sub-Saharan Africa that they began to get into disputes early on, but that war was quite infrequent until these societies began to militarize and to import conventional weapons from abroad.

To reiterate, semantic precision, clarity, and continuity must be understood as an essential element in the growth and integration of social scientific knowledge. We need to resist the temptation to be cute, clever, original, or outrageous in our use of language, and this is particularly true of English-speaking scholars, given the dominant role of this language in the world-wide social science community. And nowhere is this carefulness more critical than in developing and refining our typologies, taxonomies, classifications. Reduced to a simple set of rules, our categories need to be logically exhaustive, mutually exclusive, operationally explicit, semantically consistent, and substantively comparable. Moreover, we need to remain as atheoretical as possible, explicitly rejecting the proposition that 'it depends on the specific theoretical question that is being addressed', for such a proposition guarantees the continuing torrent of new typologies and the assurance that we will forever live in the tower of Babel. As a matter of reality, of course, it has to be recognized that no classification scheme can fully avoid the effects of empirical and substantive focus, leading thus to the pragmatic rule that typologies be as catholic as possible and compatible with a maximum number of theoretical predispositions.

SOME COMMON CLASSIFICATIONS OF ARMED CONFLICT

With these general observations in mind, let us turn to the problem at hand, which is limited to armed conflict – or sustained combat – for two reasons. First, it is to emphasize that conflict in general is not only ubiquitous within and between all socially interacting groups, but is just as likely to be adaptive and constructive as it is to be maladaptive and destructive. Our concern is better to understand and diminish those forms of conflict that dehumanize, destroy, and degrade us in the material and spiritual sense of the word. As Kenneth Boulding used to say, our task is to help 'make the world safe for conflict'. Second, and following from the above, is that the range and variety of human conflict is awesome in its complexity and diversity. Any attempt to understand all forms and types of conflict under a single scheme is doomed to failure or to an empty, vague, and fatuous outcome. Consequently, the focus here is on conflicts that have crossed a certain threshold of hostility that is marked by organized, armed violence involving two or more identifiable human groups.

The first task in proposing or evaluating a typology of armed conflict is to settle on the *dimensions* – or classes of variables – by which we hope to differentiate among the different types of armed conflict. Let us consider some of the more popular of these dimensions first. As already suggested above, the most frequently invoked typology is that based on the alleged 'cause', or issue, about which the participants are fighting. Among these, all of the usual suspects are found: territory, ideology, dynastic legitimacy, religion, language, ethnicity, self-determination, resources, markets, dominance, equality, and, of course, revenge. As argued earlier, this is a poor basis for a typology, not only because every armed conflict – in order to escalate to the level of organized combat – needs to mobilize several sectors and strata of the society, and each such group will be mobilized by somewhat different issues. It is also inadequate because it is rarely known, even long after the blood-letting ends, what issues had motivated those who helped to carry the conflict to these levels of destruction. It should be noted further that this long list inevitably assumes that the fighting is fairly rational and purposive, in the sense that it is in order to right some wrong, remedy some inequity, assure some gain, or avoid some loss. It typically ignores the incentives to combat that arise from problems within society or from some cultural or structural conditions of the larger system within which the protagonists are embedded.

Yet a second basis often invoked to differentiate and classify episodes of armed conflict is that of the *capabilities* of the protagonists. Focusing on the differences in military, economic, technological, and demographic capabilities of the opposing parties, this orientation often blends into the issues and motivations at work, resulting in terms like wars of aggression and expansion, imperial wars, wars of self-defence, wars of national liberation, and so forth. The difficulty here is that classification by difference in material capabilities – whether allies are included or not – would put such diverse cases as the Sinai, Russo-Hungarian, Falkland, and Gulf wars in the same category, not to mention the Italo-Ethiopian and Russo-Persian cases, along with the opening stages of the First and Second World Wars.

Another difficulty with this criterion of classification is that it inevitably gets us into the notion that armed conflict is often a consequence of the relative parity or discrepancy of the protagonists' capabilities. Even though measuring relative capabilities is a fairly manageable task, and has been done for all sovereign states since 1816 (Singer, 1988), we are still faced with the important question of the relationship between different ratios and the likelihood that a dispute will escalate to armed conflict. There are four divergent views, the most widely accepted of which is that a clear advantage on one side will frequently propel that side to escalate a dispute and initiate hostilities. A second perspective holds that approximate parity is the most war prone, on the premise that both parties can reasonably predict victory, given the ambiguity of estimates as to superiority and/or victory, while a third view holds that such ambiguity and uncertainty generate caution and prudence. Yet a fourth argument is that while the weaker party initiates combat with surprising frequency (Mack, 1975; Paul, 1994), it is nevertheless a rare event. Regardless of what the evidence will ultimately demonstrate, the point is that such a typology rests upon a dimension that contains far too much unfounded explanatory power. And, to reiterate, the principle being urged here is that classification should be as descriptively unambiguous – and as theoretically neutral – as possible.

Yet a third scheme might be based on the observed or inferred *consequences*. Examples might include hegemonic war in which the outcome is either the maintenance or replacement of the dominant state in the system; for some, the label is world war or systemic war, but, in each case, the classification rests on the resulting distribution or redistribution of power or wealth. Surprisingly enough, we even find that Quincy Wright – certainly one of the pioneers of systematic research into the aetiology of war – uses 'the importance of its legal and political consequences' as one of the bases for identifying what he calls 'wars of modern civilization'. While such a classification dimension may be appropriate to a study of the consequences of war, it offers little research guidance in our search for the explanation of war, and even less guidance if our concern is to head off a conflict before it escalates to all-out hostilities.

While there are many bases for classification, most of them are known, and in my view they run afoul of many of the criteria discussed above. Consequently, the solution that seems most appropriate is to be examined, even while recognizing its shortcomings: the status and class of the social groupings that are protagonists in the armed conflicts under study. Let me begin with the typology utilized in the Correlates of War project, and then go on to those social entities with which we have considerably less experience.

CLASSIFICATION BY POLITICAL STATUS OF PROTAGONISTS

We begin with those entities that constitute, and have constituted, the dominant actors in the global system for the past three or four centuries: the 'sovereign' territorial state. From 23 sovereign states following the Napoleonic Wars and 'the world restored' (Kissinger, 1957) and 66 after the Second World War, the number of such entities is now close to 190 and probably growing, thanks to the renewed pursuit of 'self-determination'. When two or more of these entities – classified as sovereign territorial states if they: a) have a population of 500,000 or more; b) exercise reasonably effective control over the people, resources and facilities within their boundaries; and c) enjoy diplomatic recognition from any two major powers or membership in the League of Nations or the United Nations get into sustained combat culminating in 1,000 or more combatant fatalities, we speak of an inter-state war. These wars, of which there have been 75 world-wide between 1816 and 1992, are the major focus of traditional students of 'international relations', capture most of the historical attention, employ the most advanced technologies, and produce the greatest impact throughout the global system. But they no longer kill as many people as other types of war; for example, since 1946, there have been about 6.62 million battle fatalities from civil wars around the world compared to 4.79 million from inter-state and extra-systemic wars combined.

This leads, then, to this second type of armed conflict. These extra-systemic wars, of which there have been 134 since 1816, involve a member state of the system on one side against the forces of a political entity that has *some* of the characteristics of states, but is usually less developed economically and politically and does not enjoy diplomatic recognition from the requisite two major powers or very many other sovereign states. Almost always, these extra-systemic entities are within a major power's empire, colonial realm, or claimed sphere of influence, and the armed struggle is typically carried on to resist or to overthrow that foreign domination. During this century, they have often been known as 'wars of national liberation', even though such colonies and possessions typically contain people of more than one 'national' group.

For inter-state wars (including major versus major power, minor versus major, and minor versus minor), as well as the extra-systemic wars, it is obvious that we rarely see the abrupt and sudden onset of sustained military combat leading to 1,000 or more battle-connected combatant fatalities. Rather, the historical pattern shows that virtually every such war is preceded by one or more episodes of brief duration known as a 'militarized dispute'. To achieve the level of militarized, the dispute must take one of the following forms: at least one of the parties must issue an explicit threat of war, usually in the context of an ultimatum, or it must mobilize reserve forces, or it must redeploy existing forces, or it must commit an act of military violence short of war. If both or additional parties cross one of those thresholds, we have a reciprocated militarized dispute, and if those acts of violence are reciprocated over more than one or two episodes, we certainly have an international armed conflict, but not yet sufficiently sustained or deadly enough to constitute a war.

As we think about extra-systemic armed conflicts or wars, it is obvious that they are not dramatically different from civil wars or civil armed conflict. The crucial distinction between extra-systemic and civil conflict is that while one protagonist in either class of conflict is the government of a territorial state, the other is a political grouping without full legitimacy but that is nevertheless able to organize a respectable armed force. In the case of civil war or intra-state armed conflict, the protagonist is an insurgent or revolutionary group within the recognized territorial boundaries of the state, and in the extra-systemic case the protagonist group is located outside of the state, and perhaps even on another continent. It might be appropriate here to recognize that at one time or another a territorial state may be so shattered and disorganized that its institutions cease to function, but this is not a sufficient reason to suggest that the state no longer exists. Recent examples might be Liberia, Burundi, Haiti or perhaps Bosnia, and a decade ago Lebanon would have been illustrative. Even though Lebanon is largely a Syrian satellite today, we still recognize it as a state, and if it is legally and effectively annexed by Syria or another state it will then be treated as a province. In other words, states do indeed come and go, but it takes more than civil war or a dramatic breakdown of its political institutions to remove it from the population of states.

To this juncture, the problems of classifying armed conflict and/or war on the basis of the political status of the protagonists is complicated, but nevertheless solvable. However, as we examine armed conflict in the post-Second World War world, we discover new conditions that generate new complications. In the century between the Congress of Vienna and the Treaty of Versailles, things were conceptually (and more or less politically) manageable from the perspective of the political elites and citizens of the territorial states. Human groups were classified on the political and legal dimensions as citizens of the 50 or so territorial states, usually referred to as nation-states despite the fact that few were truly national, many were multinational, and some were merely quasi-national in that many of their conationals lived across the border within another state. But even during that period, a variety of affinity groups were not only scattered around in the states of the inter-state system, but also in the peripheral regions, living in colonies, protectorates, dependencies, and condominiums, for example.

With the end of the First World War, however, the first major challenge to colonialism appeared in full force. The war brought an unambiguous end to the Ottoman, Romanov, and Hapsburg empires, and, with that, a rising demand for self-determination on the part of those groups that had lived under the suzerainty of these empires, and incidentally, were contiguous to the metropole or 'mother country'. Thus, in the Middle East, the Balkans, Africa, and Asia, newly independent states were created, along with a number of League of Nations' mandates. The latter were deemed by the Europeans to be not yet ready for self-government, and the former rulers (usually) were given the mandate to hasten and supervise the process. As a matter of fact, the just anointed sovereign states were also not deemed ready to govern themselves, and largely for the same reasons: boundary lines that ignored ethnic and cultural boundaries (Nicolson, 1933), lop-sided economies designed for foreign exploitation rather than local prosperity, educational systems based on colonial principles, and political bureaucracies of dubious strength and competence.

This 'liquidation of colonialism', which faltered markedly in the 1930s and 1940s, took on new life after the Second World War, marked first by the extra-systemic wars primarily against France, the United Kingdom and the Netherlands, and reaching a peak in the 1960s with the package deal that brought 45 new states into the United Nations organization. Whether these post-1945 states achieved 'independence' by armed struggle or less bloody means, few of them were much more viable then their predecessors.

Consequently, as the century draws to a close, marked by – *inter alia* – the crumbling of the Soviet empire, the drive to 'self-determination' is once again taking on renewed momentum and a powerful salience in world politics. This, of course, poses a major challenge to those concerned with understanding and trying to reduce the frequency and severity of armed conflict in these regions. Without for a moment suggesting that industrialization brings harmony and prosperity, it can nevertheless be agreed that our geographical region of focus is that populated by societies that are clearly not 'modern' and/or 'industrial'. We avoid the word 'pre-industrial' because it implies that these societies are indeed industrializing or developing or modernizing, and for many of them this is just not the case; thus, we should also avoid the 'developing' label. For the moment, then, the regions and societies of concern are generally understood to be those that lie in most cases between the Tropics of Cancer and Capricorn, astride the Equatorial belt, and between the Northern and Southern Temperate Zones. While this crude geographical similarity is already recognized – as well as the approximate similarities along the dimensions of political and economic development, industrialization, and modernity – there is too much variability among these societies to find these labels satisfactory. And, as already noted, the 'Third World' label is not only condescending, but is clearly a product of the Cold War mentality, especially in the 'West', where the enemy was classified as 'Second', and the less relevant was called the 'Third'. As to the suggestion that the 'Third World' (as distinct, of course, from the 'third estate' around the time of the French Revolution) has some sort of historical legitimacy, it seems that one of the earliest uses of the phrase is found in Sauvy (1961), and was given further credence in *The Discovery of the Third World* (Sachs, 1976).

These considerations lead me to propose the label of 'former colonial', as found in the chapter title. To be sure, this label has certain liabilities of its own (such as the fact that Canada, Australia, New Zealand, and the United States are former colonies), the most serious of which is that it carries with it the strong suggestion that the societies of these regions suffer most of their afflictions and problems as a result of colonialism. While one can make a moderately strong case in support of that explanation – and many scholars from Marx and Engels to Fanon (1963) and Frank (1970) have done so – an adequate empirical test still remains to be conducted. On the other hand, this classification has the virtue of being historically accurate, quite precise and operational, while nevertheless recognizing the very real variability among those groups included.

Having digressed for the purpose of identifying the regions and societies within which many of these more recent types of armed conflict occur, it is appropriate to return to the problem of classifying these conflicts. Following the precedent established at the beginning of this section – classification on the basis of the political status of the protagonists – we will now approach the task of identifying the types of entities we need to specify in order to classify the growing numbers of armed conflict protagonists that go beyond territorial states (major or minor powers), civil war insurgents, or those rather large entities that were, or soon became, colonies, possessions, protectorates, mandates, or trusteeships. In general, these entities can be found either entirely within territorial states, across boundaries (such as Kurds in Turkey, Syria, Iran, and Iraq), or even in a diaspora with no clear territorial base (such as gypsies throughout Central Europe, Africans in the Western Hemisphere, or Jews before the establishment of Israel). In empirical fact, most of these will be within the boundaries of a single state, and usually in a fairly well defined territorial region therein.

Whom do we identify as the protagonists in these increasingly complex intra-state wars? The examples above suggest that they will typically be culturally defined groups whose members identify with one another and with the group on the basis of shared racial, ethnic, linguistic, religious, or kinship characteristics. And given the different bases of shared identities, it makes sense to think of them as *affinity* groups or *identity* groups or *communal* groups, rather than the more restricted conventional 'ethnic' groups. If it is then considered that a very large fraction of all of the world's such identity, affinity, or communal groups never have – and perhaps never will – become involved in armed conflict, the next step is to try to identify those that have, or may in the future, become so engaged. These should quite reasonably be labelled as 'politicized communal groups' following Gurr's usage (1993). Our debt to Gurr, however, goes considerably further, for unlike too many of the phrase-makers in the social sciences, he has not only proposed a typology of communal groups and argued for this as a basis for classifying a range of political and military conflicts, but he and his associates have also done the monumental job of identifying and labelling the 227 communal groups who have, since the Second World War, become sufficiently mobilized and politicized to engage in organized conflict *vis-à-vis* other groups, as well as the state itself, in the territorial states of the global system during the closing decades of the twentieth century.

CONCLUSION

It requires little prescience to anticipate that the next few decades will bring untold misery to the human race. It is not only that those who enlisted in one or other armed camp in the Cold War are now claiming victory or lamenting defeat and wrongly speak of the 'end of history'; it is the fact that the half-century of armed rivalry between the Soviet and American coalitions so mobilized – or better still mesmerized – so many of us around the world that we ignored, or acquiesced in, the distinctive misallocation of material and spiritual resources to a tragic extent. By aggregating the needs and necessities of human beings into this alleged confrontation between the forces of light and forces of darkness, we totally neglected the fact that, for most of the human race, the East-West rivalry was utterly beside the point. The people in the former colonial regions were, as before, treated as objects and instruments during the Cold War, whose needs could not be taken seriously. Now their revenge is at hand. Whether in Bosnia or Burundi, Mexico or Morocco, those human beings whose needs and interests were effectively subordinated to an amoral and destructive version of the Thirty Years War are now mobilizing and demanding their rights. Their cases may seem problematic and their leadership as corrupt as those in Washington and Moscow, not to mention London and Warsaw, or Bonn and Budapest, but they are now calling in their chips.

Returning, then, to the title of this chapter, the danger of saying that 'we don't care what you call it as long as you define your terms' should again be emphasized. One need not be a disciple of Benjamin Lee Whorf (1956) to believe that labels do matter, that they carry large amounts of preconception and meaning, and thus impact on problem definition and problem solving for policy-makers as well as scholars. As some historical examples used suggest, by accepting conventional labels of certain armed conflicts, we buy into simplistic interpretations, and ultimately embrace disastrous reactions and responses. It would be a shame to continue that practice in the coming decades, especially since we are now being told that the next epoch will be a 'clash of civilizations' and that Islam will be the next 'evil empire'!

BIBLIOGRAPHY

Hannah Arendt, *The Origins of Totalitarianism* (New York: Harcourt Brace, 1951); *Eichmann in Jerusalem: a Report on the Banality of Evil* (New York: Viking Press, 1963).
Greg Cashman, *What Causes War?* (New York: Lexington, 1993).
Franz Fanon, *The Wretched of the Earth* (New York: Grove Press, 1963).
Andre Gunder Frank, *Latin America: Underdevelopment or Revolution: Essays on the Development of Underdevelopment and the Immediate Enemy* (New York: Monthly Review Press, 1970).
Robert Gilpin, *War and Change in World Politics* (Cambridge: Cambridge University Press, 1981).
Ted R. Gurr, 'Why Minorities Rebel: A Global Analysis of Communal Mobilization and Conflict since 1945', *International Political Science Review*, 1993, 14/2, pp. 161-201; *Minorities at Risk* (Washington, DC: United States Institute for Peace, 1993).
Henk Houweling and Jan G. Siccama, *Studies of War* (Dordrecht, Netherlands: Nijhoff, 1988).

Paul Huth, *Standing Your Ground: Disputed Territory and International Conflict* (Ann Arbor, MI: University of Michigan Press, forthcoming).

Robert Keohane, 'The Theory of Hegemonic Stability', in Holsti *et al.* (eds), *Change in the International System* (Boulder, CO: Westview, 1980).

Keith Krause, 'Controlling the Trade in Conventional Arms', *International Journal*, spring 1990.

Harold Lasswell and Abraham Kaplan, *Power and Society* (New Haven, CT: Yale University Press, 1950).

Andrew Mack, 'Why Big Nations Lose Small Wars: The Politics of Asymmetric Conflict', *World Politics*, 1975, 27, pp. 175-200.

Manus Midlarsky, *Handbook of War Studies* (Boston, MA: Unwin Hyman, 1989).

Alden Mullins, *Born Arming: Development and Military Power in New States* (Stanford, CA: Stanford University Press, 1987).

Harold George Nicolson, *Peacemaking 1919* (London: Constable and Co., 1933).

T.V. Paul, *Asymmetric Conflicts: War Initiation by Weaker Powers* (New York: Cambridge University Press, 1994).

Bruce Russett, Melvin Small and J. David Singer, 'National Political Units in the Twentieth Century: A Standardized List', *American Political Science Review*, 1968, 62/3, pp. 932-51.

Egnacy Sachs, *The Discovery of the Third World* (Cambridge, MA: MIT Press, 1976).

Alfred Sauvy, *Le 'tiers-monde', sous-développement et développement*, in Balandier (ed.), (Paris: Presses Universitaires de France, 1961).

J. David Singer, 'The Global System and its Sub-Systems: A Developmental View', in Rosenau (ed.), *Linkage Politics* (New York: Free Press, 1969); 'Cumulativeness in the Social Sciences: Some Counter-Prescriptions', *Political Science*, 1975, pp. 10-21; 'Reconstructing the Correlates of War Dataset on Material Capabilities of States, 1816-1985', *International Interactions*, 1988, 14/2, pp. 15-32; 'Peace in the Global System: Displacement, Interregnum, or Transformation?', in Kegley (ed.), *The Long Post-War Peace* (New York: Harper-Collins, 1991), pp. 56-84.

J. David Singer and J. Scott DeSonia, 'Cultural Differences and the Onset of Inter-State and Civil War', forthcoming.

John Thibaut and Harold Kelley, *The Social Psychology of Groups* (New York: Wiley, 1959).

John Vasquez, *The War Puzzle* (Cambridge, UK: Cambridge University Press, 1993).

Benjamin Whorf, *Language, thought, and reality: selected writings of Benjamin Lee Whorf* (Cambridge, MA: MIT Press, 1956).

Quincy Wright, *Problems of Stability and Progress in International Relations* (Berkeley, CA: University of California Press, 1954).

2

Ongoing Wars and their Explanation*

Dietrich Jung, Klaus Schlichte and Jens Siegelberg

INTRODUCTION

In 1994, there was a depressing number of ongoing wars and armed conflicts being waged in the world: 43 wars and 18 other major armed conflicts just below the threshold of war. Since the end of the Second World War, the world has experienced only two weeks, in September 1945, without the plagues of war. Since then, the number of wars and major armed conflicts has been steadily increasing.

Scientific efforts to explain this phenomenon have mostly been made by political scientists, and the discipline of 'International Relations', in particular, has laid claim to its competence for the scientific treatment of war, although sociologists, social psychologists and even anthropologists are also keen to undertake this task. Corresponding to the distinction between academic disciplines, three major paths of explanation have developed, but hitherto none of them have reached satisfactory results.

The famous problem of 'levels of analysis' has accompanied scientific explanations of war from the outset.[1] The links and delimitations between explanations, either on the level of the international system, on the level of societies, or finally on the level of individuals, has remained unclear. Apparently none of them alone can deliver a sufficient explanation, either for the geographical patterns of distribution of wars in contemporary world society, or for the increasing number of wars in the period since 1945.

---

* This is a revised version of a paper that has been previously published in *Interdependenz*, Nr. 16, K.J. Gantzel und K. Schlichte (eds), Das Kriegsgeschehen 1993. Daten und Tendenzen der Kriege und bewaffneten Konflikte im Jahr 1993. Dietrich Jung, Klaus Schlichte and Jens Siegelberg, 'Das Kriegsgeschehen 1993 - Analysen und Tendenzen'. Reprinted by permission of Stiftung Entwicklung und Frieden.

In this chapter an attempt will be made to sketch the basic features of ongoing wars, that is, the connection between statehood, democratization and war development in recent years and the role played by fundamentalism and ethnicity within this process. These remarks will be preceded by a brief summary of empirical findings.[2]

DEFINITIONS AND TYPOLOGY

There has been much discussion about the question of how the terms 'war' and 'conflict' should be defined. However, it is surprising to observe that most current data banks show similar results concerning the main trends of conflict development, despite their considerably varying definitions of armed conflict and war. The increasing number of violent internal conflicts, for example, was observed by all data banks,[3] and most scientific observers share the opinion that internal violent conflicts have become much more important than inter-state wars in the classical sense of the term. When it comes to typologies and definitions, however, the approaches are as numerous as the scholars, and their results diverge to such a degree that the state of the discipline can be described as atomistic but not as cumulative. This is due to a considerable lack of theoretical reflections. The theoretical relevance of typologies is often overestimated, for typologies are mere tools for descriptions and for ordering objects. Nevertheless, they are often passed off as theories or are misunderstood as such.[4] The function of definitions and typologies is first and foremost to structure the unordered manifoldness of innumerable information, thus seeking answers to questions which have to be formulated as precisely as possible.

We consequently start with a brief discussion of definition, types and numbers of wars in the period after 1945. More important are the theoretical reflections which try to explain these conflicts by referring to the spread of civil-capitalist patterns of *Vergesellschaftung*[5] in contemporary world society. First and superficial analysis shows that the importance of inter-state wars has decreased during the period. Civil wars during decolonization, and other forms of collective violence involving only one party which could be considered as a state, have been the most frequent forms of violent mass conflict since 1945. Thus, the classical usage of the term 'war', referring only to violent conflicts between states, would cover only a small and decreasing proportion of warlike events. On the other hand, however, the understanding of 'war' for scientific analysis has to be limited in an operational definition, as opposed to other phenomena of collective violence, such as banditry, rebellions, mutinies, *coups d'état*, etc.

The definition of 'war' has hence been determined as follows: a war is a violent mass conflict, fulfilling the following three characteristics:
a. two or more armed forces are involved in the fighting, where at least one of them is the regular armed force of a government in power;
b. both sides show a minimum of centrally directed organization of the fighting, even if this means nothing more than organized armed defence or strategically planned attacks;
c. the armed operations show a certain degree of continuity and are not only spontaneous occasional confrontations, that is to say, both sides are acting according to a recognizable strategy.

This definition still has many disadvantages, but, unlike so many other definitions, it includes the increasing number of intra-state conflicts without relying on questionable indicators such as the number of battle-related deaths, etc. Based on this definition, 186 wars can be counted in the period since 1945, most of them in 'Third World' countries. Ordered on the basis of the typology used in Table 2.1, more conclusions about the main trends of war development during the post-war period can be drawn.

When it comes to quantitative analysis based on these typological distinctions, general lines of the development of wars since 1945 can be sketched. The quantitative analysis delivers at least some insights, of which only a few can be presented here.

More than 90 per cent of the 186 wars between 1945 and 1994 took place in 'Third World' countries. The number of wars per year is steadily increasing; whereas in the 1950s twelve wars per year were waged, the number increased to 22 per year in the 1960s, 32 per year in the 1970s and eventually more than 40 in the 1980s. However, these numbers should be treated with caution, as increasingly intensive observation may have led to a growing number of registered armed conflicts and wars in the two last decades, and the history of most peripheral societies has not yet been examined so painstakingly that one can be sure about the exact number of conflicts. Nevertheless, it is highly improbable that these corrections would reverse the general trend of a growing number of violent mass conflicts since 1945.

The early 1990s have shown a higher amount of violent conflicts than ever seen before in the period since 1945. In the middle of 1994, 43 wars were being waged in the world, all apart from three in developing countries. The other 18 armed conflicts, just below the level of war, also emerged in the so-called developing countries.

However, the developed capitalistic societies were involved in a large number of conflicts as interveners, in particular the former colonial powers, the United States and former USSR. On the other hand, these countries have not waged war against each other directly since 1945.

The share of decolonization wars has steadily decreased during the post-war period. In the mid-1970s the decolonization era neared its close and the peaceful settlement of the war in Namibia in 1988 marked the end of this era. Meanwhile, the number of internal wars has grown consistently over the period whereas the classical inter-state war has become the exception among

TABLE 2.1   *Ongoing Wars and Armed Conflicts and their Typology (May 1994)*

Country	since	type
Europe		
Bosnia-Herzegovina	1991	B-1
Croatia vs Serbia	1991	B-2
Northern Ireland	1969	B-2
Africa		
Algeria	1992	A-2
Angola	1961	A-2
Chad	1966	ABC-1
Djibouti	1991	AB-2
Ethiopia (Oromo)	1976	AB-2
Liberia/Sierra Leone	1989	A-1
Mali/Niger (Tuareg)	1990	B-2
Rep. South Africa	1976	AB-2
Rwanda	1990	A-1
Senegal (Casamance)	1990	B-2
Somalia	1988	AB-1
Sudan	1983	BA-2
The Middle East		
Afghanistan	1978	A-1
Azerbaijan /Nag.-Karabach)	1990	B-2
Georgia (Abkhasia)	1992	B-2
Georgia (Gamsadkurdia)	1991	A-2
Iraq (Kurds)	1976	BA-1
Iraq (Shiites)	1991	A-2
Israel (Palestine)	1968	B-2
Lebanon	1975	ABC-1
Russian Fed. (northern Ossetia)	1992	B-2
Tajikistan	1992	A-1
Turkey (Kurds)	1984	B-2
Yemen	1994	B-2
Asia		
Bangladesh (Chittagong)	1973	B-2

Burma (Myanmar)	1948	AB-2
Cambodia	1975	A-1
India (Kashmir)	1990	B-2
India (Punjab)	1982	B-2
Indonesia (East Timor)	1975	B-2
Papua New Guinea (Bougainville)	1989	B-2
Philippines (Mindanao)	1970	B-2
Philippines (NPA)	1970	A-2
Sri Lanka	1983	B-1
Latin America		
Guatemala	1980	A-2
Colombia (FARC)	1964	A-2
Colombia (ELN)	1965	A-2
Mexico	1994	B-2
Peru (Sendero)	1980	A-2
Peru (MRTA)	1987	A-2

Key to war types:
A = anti-regime wars, i.e. wars waged at least for the abolition of a regime in power or for the restructuring of the entire social order;
B = other internal wars, such as secessionist wars or wars waged for a higher degree of autonomy;
C = inter-state wars;
D = wars of decolonization.

1 = no foreign intervention;
2 = with foreign intervention (only direct involvement by foreign troops in combat is considered as intervention).[6]
Source: Arbeitsgemeinschaft Kriegsursachenforschung, University of Hamburg.

violent mass conflicts. Anti-regime wars and other internal wars, waged about secession or autonomy of regions, have been the most frequent types of war in recent decades. In 1994, only the wars in Lebanon and Chad showed a strong international component. All other foreign power involvements can be considered as intervention.

CAPITALISTIC TRANSFORMATION AND WAR DEVELOPMENT IN THE 1990S

The ongoing process of imposition of capitalism,[7] which now also includes the former 'socialist' countries, has been accompanied by wars and conflicts from its outset. Neglecting the particular circumstances of each case which allow the explanation of wars as single events, hence the process of decomposition of traditional patterns of *Vergesellschaftung* by the advancement of capitalistic patterns can be discerned as the decisive conflict-engendering feature in contemporary world society. The advancement of the capitalist mode of production, and the faults of its aftermath such as the monetarization of social relations, labour and land increasingly seen as commodities, and the growing importance of market mechanisms, have brought about the dissolution of traditional forms of social integration.

In these periods of tremendous changes, social conflicts easily escalate into violence. The emergence of nation-states is nothing more than a late result of this process of capitalistic transformation, and the simultaneous evolution of market economies and bureaucratic states is the leitmotiv throughout the 500 years of European history of wars. It accompanied the colonial and imperialistic expansion of European powers until the wars of decolonization earlier this century, and it is now also showing its effects in the decaying state-socialist societies. The simultaneous occurrence of contradictory forms of *Vergesellschaftung* is thus the basic fact that characterizes developing countries at war, for whereas the traditional patterns are dissolved by the advancement of a market economy, new 'modern' forms cannot yet be developed sufficiently to resolve emerging social conflicts.

Apart from the conflict potential of these fractures, engendered by the advancement of civic-capitalist patterns, there are two other central lines which can be identified from a historical point of view: conflicts carried over from pre-modern times which are revitalized in the context of current crises; and, on the other hand, conflicts emerging from contradictions within *Vergesellschaftung* itself. The latter have special significance in early capitalistic stages of social development. The essential causes of contemporary wars can thus be reconstructed as a combination of these elements.

On the other hand, transformation to capitalism also has its civilizing side. The democratic constitution of a country, which more or less accompanies increasing industrialization with its division of labour and the functional interdependencies, may not in itself be a sufficient precondition for peaceful policies. However, a number of studies have indicated that societies with democratic constitutions are at least less susceptible to war in their behaviour towards each other. But this is only a late result of the modernization to capitalism which occurs in and between developed civil societies.[8] The balance of powers, the constitutional state, the rule of law, democracy and general welfare obviously constitute a bulwark against the emergence of warlike conflicts within and between developed societies. Consequently, both the violent as well as the civilizing faces of the transformation to capitalism have to be seen in order to reach a consistent and stringent analysis and interpretation of contemporary wars. Fundamental errors result, however, if the violent trail of capitalism in history is understood as a quality of capitalism itself. On the contrary, wars and conflicts have to be seen as conditions of the emergence and advancement of capitalism, this conclusion being fundamental to the fact that developed civil societies no longer wage wars against each other, whereas they behave much less peacefully towards peripheral societies.

Widespread expectations that the collapse of socialism at the end of the 1980s, the dissolution of the global East-West confrontation and that democratic movements in several 'Third World' countries would lead to a rapid and peaceful transition to market economy, democracy and general prosperity have proved to be an illusion. The hasty identification of forthcoming developments with the achievements of bourgeois civilization which have become the world-wide standard of civil order may be understandable against the background of the political developments in the 1980s but it was not realistic. Instead of a general expansion of the civilizing achievements of capitalism, the contradictions in world society are increasing towards the end of the twentieth century, and the conflicting forces of modernization to capitalism are escalating. Even reinforced peace efforts by the United Nations and other regional organizations have failed to contribute to the settlement and pacification of armed conflicts.

In addition to the war-torn 'Third World' regions, the former Eastern bloc states are now emerging as the new crisis centre in world politics. In this region once almost free of war, seven conflicts have already escalated into war since 1989. But the further the decline of social, economic and political structures progresses, the less the blame can be put on the legacy of socialist rule and controlled economy. Rather, it is the process of transformation to capitalism itself that becomes the ever-stronger source of disintegration, violent conflicts and war.

The radical changes in the former Eastern bloc thus confirm a recurring pattern of capitalist modernization in world history: before capitalism becomes a reality in the shape of civil society where the constitutional state, democracy, human rights, prosperity and peace prevail, the radical changes of traditional non-capitalist societies lead to far-reaching deformation of the social order and to violent conflicts and wars. Only in exceptional cases can this phase of disorder and social upheaval be managed without authoritarian or violent means, and this applies to the history of Europe as well as to the transitional societies of the 'Third World' and to the current transformation process in the former Eastern bloc. Moreover, this pattern will also be repeated in the inevitable decay of the Chinese empire.

After the violent European nation-building process during the eighteenth and nineteenth centuries and the independence of the former colonies between 1940 and 1960, the third large process of nation-building is now taking place on the territory of the former Soviet Union, which broke into 15 sovereign states by 1991. After a phase of territorial consolidation, most of these newly formed states will face the same social and economic problems and experience the same forms of violent conflicts that the countries of the 'Third World' experienced after their – in some cases violently secured – formal independence. These are all internal conflicts concerning the subsequent consolidation of a merely formal national status, for example, the struggle for the form of government, state subsidies, autonomy or secession, clashes between rivalling religious, ethnic or locally tied groups, confrontations between the emerging social classes, etc. Under the condition of a merely formal consolidation of the state and unfinished nation-building these conflicts tend to escalate violently.

In contrast to the 'classical' inter-state wars which prevailed from the nineteenth until the early twentieth century, the various internal social conflicts now constitute the predominant form of war. Among the 45 wars registered in 1993, there is not a single inter-state war.

STATEHOOD, DEMOCRATIZATION AND FUNDAMENTALISM

The dominance of internal wars in 1993 reflects the trend of decreasing inter-state wars since the end of the nineteenth century. Conflicts of domination and struggles for autonomy and secession within existing states are the most apparent forms of war in the 'Third World'. These wars reveal a structural characteristic specific to developing societies: the institutions of the developing modern state are usually not capable of mediating social conflicts resulting from society's transformation to capitalism. In most cases, state and society are obviously not congruent, and this cleft between state and society – between political and social integration – is based on the chronic deficit of state authorities' legitimacy. In 'Third World' countries, the state is not the crystallization point of collective identity, but only a formal framework including the social protagonists. It is a framework that was acquired during the colonial past and guaranteed by world state order and international law. The decisive points of reference of personal identity and political loyalty are determined instead by traditional familial, tribal or religious ties and relationships.

The modern state, described by Max Weber as the monopoly of legitimate use of violence, only exists as a territorial and legal cover, as an imposed form to which the social content has yet to consolidate itself. In countless countries the legitimacy of existing political order is disputed by regional, ethnic or religious groups, even with violent means. The subsequent internal consolidation, the state-forming process in the 'Third World', is by far not yet achieved.

At the same time, the international community confronts these fragile political organizations with rising expectations. For example, the distribution of international resources is increasingly linked to an 'obligation for democracy', and development aid from the OECD countries increasingly depends on how far democratic rights and the formal institution of free elections are put into effect. Yet a functioning democracy is not only built on the form but on the content of modern statehood. Democratic political structures depend on a generally acknowledged governmental monopoly of power and a bureaucracy based upon impersonal written rules and, as Weber puts it, the distinction between the office and its incumbent. This distinction requires that neither citizens nor civil servants are liable to familial or religious institutions but to legal regulations which shape social relations based on parties of equal contract. That, however, does not apply to societies in the 'Third World'.

This has led to a paradox: in the 'Third World' the enforcement of governmental monopoly of legitimate use of violence – an immensely conflict-laden process which can only be accomplished against the fierce resistance of social groups which have their own means of physical violence at their disposal – is simultaneously met by the demand for democracy. Thus modern democracy, the late result of long-term modernization to capitalism, becomes the very condition for the shaping of this social process.

The confusing variety of demands and expectations put forward to the states of the 'Third World' clearly shows itself in how to deal with a political phenomenon frequently illustrated by the term 'fundamentalism'. Whether the *Front Islamique du Salut* in Algeria, the Hindu *Bharatiya Janata Party* (BJP) in India or the *Janata Vimukti Peramana* (JVP) in Sri Lanka, fundamentalist parties in Asia and Africa participate in democratic elections with increasing success. A possible government take-over by fundamentalist groups does not necessarily lead to state disintegration and civil war as in Algeria; nevertheless it presents an immense challenge to initiated democratization processes. Malaysia's party in power, for instance, accepts the demands of the Islamist movements and thus endangers the precarious ethnic and political balance. Other countries restrict opposition rights, bringing initiated democratization processes to a standstill.

Beyond the question of whether the term fundamentalism is an adequate expression for the described political phenomena, it nevertheless points to certain common grounds of fundamentalist movements: they claim that government should be rooted in traditional cultural and religious foundations. In doing so, however, they reject basic principles of democratic government defined by formal and rational legitimation, for legal democratic state authority is based on the separation of state and religion, it is grounded on an abstract self-identity as well as on the formal general validity of basic social norms, and it is liable to the ideas of sovereignty of people and human rights.

The claims for the democratization of authoritarian systems in the 'Third World' justified against the background of the modern concept of state authority, however, simultaneously offer fundamentalist groups an access to governmental power. The democratization of political systems, which was meant to have a stabilizing effect, thus threatens to turn into the opposite.

NATIONAL BORDERS AND SOVEREIGNTY

The high share of secession wars in 1993 is not a new phenomenon. Since 1945 almost one-third of all armed conflicts concerned autonomy or secession. Counting the decolonization wars of this period, which were also wars about sovereignty, the share of secession wars has not increased. Present secession wars have no more causes than those of former decades. They are fought between regionally oriented groups about the control over the central state formed during the phase of decolonization. The explosive nature of these conflicts is due to economic motives such as the control over export revenues or the neglect of whole regions in development policies, as well as to the existence of different linguistic or religious communities within the territory of one state.

The tension between the merely territorial state and its fragile social content, which characterizes the states of the 'Third World', is readily illustrated in journalism and science by the term of 'artificial borders'. However, the borders of social organizations are neither artificial nor natural, they are instead the results of historical developments. In Europe, too, national borders have separated linguistic and cultural communities for centuries. Historically the self-determination of communities concerning their political borders was a rare exception; instead internal and external power constellations were the main factors determining borders. The division of cultural communities did not necessarily lead to armed disputes. The term 'artificial borders', however, does not help when analysing armed conflicts. It is a political phrase just like the term 'natural borders', and as an expression for coping with the colonial and imperial past it is part of a moral judgement. Such judgements may be politically necessary, but they hardly contribute to understanding the causes of war.

The borders established during colonial times thus do not point out the 'artificiality' of 'Third World' states but rather show the dependence of nation-building processes in the 'Third World' on international power structures. The form of government is the direct expression of such dependence, because statehood is the precondition for participation in the world market and the global community. The aim of a social group to achieve international recognition as a state therefore characterizes a large part of international war events, because the founding of an independent state allows the appropriation of internal resources as well as access to resources offered by international donors. The formation of an independent state is the key to security guarantees, economic support and social prestige for the community.

ARE THERE 'ETHNIC' CONFLICTS?

Since the end of the Cold War, the slogan 'ethnic conflict' does not only appear more and more often in the media, but also in the discourse of social science. But more profound examination of so-called 'ethnic' conflicts shows that the fundamental causes of conflicts have not changed, even after the collapse of the Soviet Union. It is still the process of nation-building and the fight for the distribution of scarce resources which form the fundamental issues of present wars and armed conflicts. Various languages, different descent and divergent religious confessions are used in such disputes to distinguish friend and foe, and in many cases interest groups consciously politicize such cultural differences in order to mobilize larger groups. In other cases, family ties or religious associations are indeed the only reliable social relations which offer social security. It is consequently not astonishing when warring parties are grouped along those distinctive lines. The phenomenon of 'politicized ethnicity', the polarization of populations according to these imagined communities, is merely another result of the institutional weakness of political systems, caused by the low grade of social differentiation and a simultaneous social fragmentation.

The slogan 'ethnic conflict' is an inexact expression. It seems that neither anthropology nor any other human science has developed a scientific usable definition of 'ethnicity', so all kinds of groups can be covered by this term, linguistic groups as well as groups of common descent or religious communities. All these cultural differences used as delimitations cannot be considered to be decisive war-engendering contradictions. Cases such as the war in the Chittagong Hills (Bangladesh) or the war on the Philippine Island of Mindanao clearly illustrate that conflicts are fought under the guise of cultural differences whereas the causes of these conflicts are much more complex. The economic marginalization of regions – perceived by inhabitants as internal colonialism – political manipulation and the absence of functioning political systems promote the ethnic interpretation of social conflicts. However, wars do not break out merely because there are different ethnic groups.[9]

The internal wars of the 1970s and 1980s were very often classified 'class conflicts' and 'proxy wars'. In the beginning of the 1990s, however, 'ethnic conflict' became the most fashionable term and last resort to explain contemporary social conflicts, although the phrase 'ethnic conflict' does not shed much light on the origins and causes of these wars. Confronted with the failed consolidation of states or with other crises, people seek refuge in the fiction of nations, ethnic identities or religious fundamentalism. They dress themselves up with nationalistic or religious symbols and fight in the name of alleged communities of descent. This might be accepted as an expression of existential uncertainty and longing for a more integrated society that offers unity and security. However, it cannot be accepted that the scientific debate on wars succumbs to these seducing simplicities, contributing to the renewed mythologization of our understanding of society.

To the people involved in war, national or religious issues may appear as a natural impetus of their actions. Examining the causes of ongoing wars, ethnicity turns out to be the result of a preceding process, in the course of which all social mechanisms that previously allowed us to live together are destroyed. The destruction of all these social mechanisms, rules, institutions and the reduction of social differences, groups and classes to the one and only difference of ethnic belonging are the actual causes of these conflicts, and the confusing term of 'ethnic' conflicts is suitable to conceal all these underlying causes. Its popularity proves the recurrence of mythology, which has returned to the Western world with the resurgence of nationalism, even within the scientific community. However, the apologists of the term will be taught a lesson as soon as the supposed homogenous 'ethnic groups' build their own states, in which inner contradictions will be fought out as violently as before. Just like 'class conflicts' and 'proxy wars' the term will then be thrown overboard as an unsuitable collective term for a reality that is much too complex.

CONTINUING CAUSES

The development of war in 1993 was marked by continuing structural causes. The fundamental social transformation, concealed behind the term 'development', with which the 'Third World' is confronted, still engenders the successive decay of traditional political, economic and social structures. This critical process hinders the emergence of a social consensus when even the state's structures are not yet consolidated. These structural weaknesses of political institutions, triggered by the continuing transformation, are the underlying causes of ongoing wars.

There is hardly any reason to hope that these structural causes will disappear in the near future. Even the pressure to democratize will not help to consolidate war-torn or war-prone states. It is not international recognition of state sovereignty that forms a state, nor are formal elections equivalent to a modern democracy. If the pressure to democratize is not accompanied by serious support in the management of economic and social conflicts, it can have a destabilizing effect. Establishing a consolidated state, democracy and a market economy in a short period of time and in a peaceful way – this is the gigantic challenge with which 'Third World' countries are confronted. Under these constraints set by the international system, the ongoing transformation will continue to engender a high number of wars and armed conflicts.

NOTES

1. Classical formulations of the problem can be found in Kenneth N. Waltz, *Man, the State and War: A Theoretical Analysis* (New York: Columbia University Press, 1959); see also Joseph S. Nye, *Understanding International Conflicts: An Introduction to Theory and History* (New York: Harper Collins, 1993), p. 28 ff. The best résumé of research on causes of war is written in German: Martin Mendler and Wolfgang Schwegler-Rohmeis, *Weder Drachentöter noch Sicherheitsingenieur: Bilanz und kritische Analyse der sozialwissenschaftlichen Kriegsursachenforschung* (Frankfurt am Main: Hessian Foundation for Peace and Conflict Research, 1989).

2. The empirical findings presented here are the result of the work of the Arbeitsgemeinschaft Kriegsursachenforschung (AKUF). Since 1980 this study group has registered data on wars since 1945 and has tried to trace trends and tendencies of the world-wide development of armed conflicts. This research is done under the direction of Professor Gantzel, and the first bulk of data was delivered by Professor Istàn Kende, Budapest. The register of wars and a quantitative analysis, covering the period between 1945 and 1992, can be found in Klaus Jürgen Gantzel and Torsten Schwinghammer (eds), *Die Kriege von 1945 bis 1992: Daten und Analysen* (Münster: Lit, 1994).

3. See, for example, the theses in Kalevi J. Holsti, *Peace and War: Armed Conflicts and International Order 1648-1989* (Cambridge: Cambridge University

Press, 1991), pp. 279 ff.; and Ted R. Gurr, *Minorities at Risk: A Global View of Ethno-Political Conflict* (Washington, DC: US Institute of Peace Press, 1993), p. 131 ff.

4. The classical text in this field is still useful to avoid the bulk of confusion. See Carl G. Hempel, *Science, Language, and Human Rights* (Philadelphia, PA: University of Philadelphia Press, 1952), pp. 65-86.

5. This notion, central to the work of classical German sociology, is hard to translate. In this context it signifies the process of insertion of individuals, the determining principles of ties in a given society, formulated in ideal typical notions. See the explication given by Max Weber concerning the term 'associative relationships', in Guenther Roth and Claus Wittich (eds.), *Economy and Society: An Outline of Interpretive Sociology* (New York: Bedminster Press, 1968), pp. 40-43.

6. Note that an armed conflict exists when one or more of the above-mentioned criteria of the war definition is not fulfilled, or the available information is not sufficient to allow a clear classification. A list of other armed conflicts includes: Angola (Cabinda); Burundi; Congo; Egypt; Eritrea; Haiti; India (Nagas); India (Naxalites); India (Assam); Indonesia (West-Irian); Indonesia (Aceh); Iran (Kurds); Kenya; Mozambique; Pakistan (Sind); Russian Federation (Chechnya); Togo; and Zaire.

7. Concerning the theoretical considerations presented here, see Klaus Jürgen Gantzel and Jens Siegelberg, 'War and Development: Theorizing about the Causes of War, with Particular Reference to the Post-1945 Period', in *Law and State* (Tübingen), vol. 44, pp. 1-29; for further reading see also Jens Siegelberg, *Kapitalismus und Krieg: Eine Theorie des Krieges in der Weltgesellschaft* (Münster: Lit, 1994).

8. This does not implicate a view of history as a continuous progress: 'The emergence of modern capitalism does not represent the highpoint of a progressive scheme of social development, but rather the coming of a type of society radically distinct from all other forms of social order'. See Anthony Giddens, *The Nation-State and Violence, Vol. Two of A Contemporary Critique of Historical Materialism* (Cambridge: Polity Press, 1985), p. 32.

9. See Klaus Schlichte, 'Is Ethnicity a Cause of War?', in *Peace Review*, vol. 6, no. 1, pp. 59-65.

Part II

STATE-FORMATION

3

State-Making, State-Breaking and State Failure: Explaining the Roots of 'Third World' Insecurity[1]

Mohammed Ayoob

INTRODUCTION

There are two significant realities of the current international scene which form the backdrop to any discussion of the formation and disintegration of states in the last decade of the twentieth century. The first is the incontrovertible fact that the overwhelming majority of conflicts since the end of the Second World War have been located in the 'Third World'. The second is the equally unassailable fact that most conflicts in the 'Third World' have been, and are, either primarily intra-state in character or possess a substantial intra-state dimension even if they appear to the outside observer to be inter-state conflicts.

The validity of both these assertions is borne out by K.J. Hoslti's tabulation. According to Hoslti's conservative estimate of wars and major armed interventions during the 1945-1989 period, only 2 out of 58 such events occurred outside the 'Third World'. Furthermore, according to his calculation, the large majority of such conflicts, 47 to be exact, were the product in one way or another of one or more of three, often interacting, factors: national liberation from colonial rule, state creation, and regime legitimacy – all firmly rooted in the domestic arena of political activity.[2] Other observers have put the figure for conflicts in the post-1945 period much higher. For example, Evan Luard has estimated that between 1945 and 1986, there were 127 'significant wars'. Out of these, Europe accounted for 2, Latin America for 26, Africa for 31, the Middle East for 24, and Asia for 44. According to Luard's estimate, more than 98 per cent of all international conflicts during that period took place in the 'Third World'.[3]

That these two trends – concentration of conflicts in the 'Third World' and the primacy of domestic sources of conflict – have continued into the 1990s is borne out by the figures presented in the *SIPRI Yearbooks* of 1991 and 1993. According to the former, of the 31 major armed conflicts in 1990, almost all of them in the 'Third World', only one was inter-state in nature. The rest were divided almost equally among those for the control of government (where the legitimacy of regimes was challenged) and state formation conflicts (where the legitimacy of existing states was challenged, in other words, where secession was the goal).[4] The *SIPRI Yearbook 1993* has confirmed this trend by presenting data that demonstrate that of the major armed conflicts that were waged in 30 locations around the world in 1992, all but one were intra-state in character. Almost all of these conflicts were located in the old or new 'Third World'.[5] There is abundant data, therefore, to support the conclusion that the overwhelming majority of conflicts in the international system since 1945 have been 'a ubiquitous corollary of the birth, formation, and fracturing of "Third World" states'.[6]

The end of the Cold War has led not to the irrelevance of the 'Third World' as an explanatory category, but to its expansion, as new states have emerged following the breakup of the Soviet Union and of Yugoslavia and as ethnic antagonisms that had been forced underground by the twin forces of Russian imperialism and Leninist ideology have resurfaced with a vengeance. In terms of their colonial background, the arbitrary construction of their boundaries by external powers, the lack of societal cohesion, their recent emergence into juridical statehood, and their stage of development, the states of the Caucasus and Central Asia, as well as of the Balkans, demonstrate political, economic and social characteristics that are in many ways akin to Asian, African and Latin American states that have been traditionally considered as constituting the 'Third World'.

Amitai Etzioni perceived this similarity clearly when he pointed out that although 'historians tend to treat as distinct the emergence of nation-states from the Ottoman and Hapsburg empires and the liberation of former colonies in Asia and Africa following the Second World War, there are actually great sociological similarities between the two movements'.[7] Above all, the similarities between the Balkan states and the rest of the 'Third World' are symbolized by the multi-ethnic nature of both sets of states and the inadequate integration of the different ethnic groups with each other. Furthermore, as Najdan Pasic had noted more than two decades ago in a prescient article on the Balkans, 'From the Holy Alliance and the Congress of Berlin to the Yalta Conference, where spheres of influence in the Balkans were calculated in percentages, the Balkan peoples had their destinies carved by others. The parcelling out of political and national structures in the Balkans was in a substantial part the product of such external forces. In this respect, the historical circumstances surrounding nation-building in the Balkans bear a close resemblance to those in which nations and independent national states have taken shape in other parts of the economically underdeveloped world'.[8]

Recent events, especially the high incidence of ethnic conflict and the simultaneous operation of secessionist and irredentist forces, have confirmed not merely the affinity of the Balkan states' security problems with those of the 'Third World', but of their status as members of the 'Third World'.

THE WESTERN MODEL OF STATE-MAKING: DANGEROUS COMPARISONS

The events of the last few years, by removing the 'Second World' from the international equation, have helped in presenting the dichotomy between the global core and the global periphery – the 'First World' and the 'Third World' – in very stark terms.[9] By removing the Cold War overlay from 'Third World' conflicts and thus exposing their fundamental local dynamics, the end of bipolarity has also demonstrated the close linkage between these conflicts and the dynamics of state-making (and its obverse, state-breaking and state failure) currently under way in the global periphery. However, the dichotomous representation of the 'First' and the 'Third Worlds' that is currently fashionable hides the essential similarity in their process of state-making, which has been, and is, crucial in determining the political trajectories of states. This point becomes clear if one compares the current situation in the 'Third World', not with that prevailing within and among the industrial democracies today, but with the situation in the seventeenth and eighteenth centuries in Western Europe when the earliest national states were at a stage of state-making that corresponded with the stage where most 'Third World' states find themselves today.[10]

The process of state-making has been most succinctly defined by Cohen, Brown and Organski as 'primitive central state power accumulation'.[11] Thus defined, state-making must include the following: (1) the expansion and consolidation of the territorial and demographic domain under a political authority including the imposition of order on contested territorial and demographic space (war); (2) the maintenance of order in the territory where, and over the population on whom, such order has already been imposed (policing); and (3) the extraction of resources from the territory and the population under the control of the state essential to support not only war-making and policing activities undertaken by the state but also for the maintenance of state appliances necessary to carry on routine administration, deepen the state's penetration of society and serve symbolic purposes (taxation).[12]

All three broad categories of activities outlined above, however, depend on the state's success in monopolizing and concentrating the means of coercion in its own hands in the territory and among the population it controls. That is why the accumulation of power becomes so crucial to the state-making enterprise, and the more primitive the stage of state-building the more primitive and coercive the strategies employed to accumulate and concentrate power in the hands of the agents of the state. As Cohen, Brown and Organski demonstrated in a seminal article, 'The extent to which an expansion of state power will generate collective violence depends on the *level* of state power prior to that expansion ... the lower the initial level of state power, the stronger the relationship between the *rate* of state expansion and collective violence'.[13] One needs to be reminded that violence generated during the process of state-making is the result of actions undertaken both by the state and by recalcitrant elements within the population who forcefully resist the state's attempt to impose order.

The inherent similarity in the logic of the state-building process provides explanations for the current replication by 'Third World' states of several dimensions of the early European experience of state-making. Simultaneously, the difference in the pace at which state-building has to be undertaken and completed in the 'Third World', plus the dramatically changed international environment in which 'Third World' state-making has to proceed, explain the divergence in other dimensions from the earlier European model of state-building. The similarities and the differences are equally important, as is the bearing they have on the security predicament of the 'Third World' state.

It should be pointed out at this stage that state-making in most of Europe usually antedated the emergence of nations and nation-states by a couple of centuries. This is why it is essential not to confuse the building of national states with the emergence of nation-states in the nineteenth and twentieth centuries. The distinction between national states and nation-states has been highlighted by Charles Tilly who has defined the former as 'relatively centralized, differentiated, and autonomous organizations successfully claiming priority in the use of force within large, contiguous, and clearly bounded territories'. Nation-states, on the other hand, are those 'whose peoples share a strong linguistic, religious, and symbolic identity'.[14] Nationalism, the necessary condition for the establishment of nation-states, although not of national states, has been defined by Ernest Gellner as 'primarily a principle which holds that the political and the national unit should be congruent'.[15]

National states that have performed successfully over a long period of time and therefore knit their people together in terms of historical memories, legal codes, language, religion, etc., may evolve into nation-states or at least provide the necessary conditions for the emergence of nation-states, but they are not synonymous with the latter. Historical evidence has convincingly demonstrated that in almost all cases in Europe, with the exception of the Balkans (an exception which may provide the clue to the current violence and strife in that region), the emergence of the modern national state was the precondition for the formation of the nation.[16]

The chronological sequence in the 'Third World' as it relates to the establishment of the national state and the evolution of nationalism bears very close resemblance to that of early modern Europe with the state taking clear historical precedence over the nation. As Anthony Smith has put it very succinctly, '[T]he Western model is essentially a "state system" rather than a "nation system"; and this has been its fateful legacy to Africa and Asia'. Smith goes on to point out that, despite the differences in geopolitical and cultural terms between Europe and the 'Third World':

> The central point ... of the Western experience for contemporary African and Asian social and political change has been the primacy and domi-nance of the specialized, territorially defined and coercively monopolis-tic state, operating within a broader system of similar states bent on fulfilling their dual functions of internal regulation and external defence (or aggression).[17]

In this context, it is instructive to note Tilly's point that '[t]he building of states in Western Europe cost tremendously in death, suffering, loss of rights, and unwilling surrender of land, goods, or labour ... The fundamental reason for the high cost of European state-building was its beginning in the midst of a decentralized, largely peasant social structure. Building differenti-ated, autonomous, centralized organizations with effective control of terri-tories entailed eliminating or subordinating thousands of semi-autonomous authorities ... Most of the European population resisted each phase of the creation of strong states'.[18] Tilly's description of conditions in Europe at the birth of national states has an uncanny resemblance to present conditions in many 'Third World' societies. It helps, therefore, to explain why if one arranges the current state-building strategies employed in the 'Third World' on a continuum ranging from coercion to persuasion with the two ends representing ideal types, even those states like India that fall relatively close to the persuasive end of the continuum are forced to rely on significant amounts of coercion – as witnessed in Punjab, Kashmir and the north-eastern states – to entrench and consolidate the authority of the state in regions where it faces, or has faced, major challenges.

In order to replicate the process by which modern national states are created, 'Third World' state-makers need above all two things – lots of time and a relatively free hand to persuade, cajole and coerce the disparate populations under their nominal rule to accept the legitimacy of state boundaries and institutions, to accept the right of the state to extract resources from them, and to let the state regulate the more important aspects of their lives. Unfortunately for 'Third World' state elites, neither of the two commodities listed above is available to them in adequate measure.

The point regarding the availability of time becomes clear with a closer look at the amount of time it took for the states of Western Europe to emerge as full-fledged national states, enjoying the habitual obedience of their populations, by and large secure in the legitimacy of their borders and institutions, and, therefore, in a position where they could be responsive to societal demands since these demands no longer ran counter to the logic of state-building and the accumulation of power in the hands of the state.

It was not until the beginning of the twentieth century that the states of Western Europe and its offshoots in North America emerged as the responsive and representative national states that we know them to be today – the end products of the state-making process that had unfolded for at least three or four hundred years. Although leading historians of state-building in Europe differ about the exact dating of the origins – in the sense of beginnings – of the modern national state, there is little argument about the fact that 'it took four to five centuries for European states to overcome their weaknesses, to remedy their administrative deficiencies, and to bring lukewarm loyalty up to the white heat of nationalism'.[19]

Unfortunately for 'Third World' state-makers, their states cannot afford the luxury of prolonging the traumatic and costly experience of state-making over hundreds of years *à la* Western Europe. The demands of competition with established modern states and the demonstration effect of the existence of socially cohesive, politically responsive and administratively effective states in the industrialized world make it almost obligatory for 'Third World' states to reach their goal within the shortest time possible or risk international ridicule and permanent peripherality within the system of states. The pioneers of European state-making (although not the latecomers like Germany and Italy) were remarkably free from such systemic pressures and demonstration effects, because all the leading contenders for statehood – England, France, Spain, the Netherlands – were by and large in the same boat trying to navigate the same uncharted sea.

Where European states did not have this chance and had to telescope some of the sequential phases that together constituted the process of state-building into each other, they suffered from a 'cumulation of crises'.[20] This applied particularly to the important states of Germany and Italy that emerged as unified national states only in the closing decades of the nineteenth century and were immediately faced with the pressures of mass politics. In fact, it can be argued that the emergence of Italian Fascism and German Nazism were a result of the Italian and German state elites' inability in the first two decades of the twentieth century to successfully respond, in a context of mass politics, to the accumulated crises threatening their respective states.[21]

If this could be the case – especially with Germany, which had the well-established Prussian state at its core – one can well imagine the enormity of the challenge faced by the post-colonial states of the 'Third World'. The problem for the latter has been compounded by the fact that they are under pressure to demonstrate adequate stateness quickly, as well as to perform the task of state-making in a humane, civilized and consensual fashion, and to do all this in an era of mass politics. The inadequacy of the time element and the consequent fact that several by-and-large sequential phases involved in the state-making process[22] have had to be collapsed or telescoped together into one mammoth state-building enterprise go a long way in explaining the security predicament of the 'Third World' state. Furthermore, the demand for humane treatment of populations during the early stages of state-building has made that task in the 'Third World' enormously difficult and complicated.

Given the short time at the disposal of state-makers in the 'Third World' and the consequent acceleration in state-making efforts necessary to demonstrate that they are moving speedily towards effective statehood, crises erupt simultaneously, become unmanageable as the load they put on the political system outruns the political and military capabilities of the state, and lead to a cumulation of crises which further erode the legitimacy of the already fragile post-colonial state.

INTERNATIONAL NORMS

In addition to these internal factors, the workings of the international system, especially the policies adopted by the superpowers during the Cold War era, have also complicated the process of state-making in the 'Third World'. By exporting superpower rivalry to the 'Third World' in the form of proxy wars, both inter-state and intra-state, as well as through the medium of weapons' transfers to governments and insurgents in fragile polities existing in volatile regional environments, the bipolar global balance during the Cold War era greatly accentuated the insecurities and instabilities in the 'Third World'.[23] At the same time, it must be acknowledged that superpower apprehensions of being directly sucked into regional conflicts placed certain restraints on the conflictual behaviour of 'Third World' protagonists. To this extent, the superpowers cooperated in insulating their rivalry from unwelcome 'Third World' intrusion.[24]

Even more important, certain international norms, which have crystallized relatively recently, have also had mixed effects on the security and stability of 'Third World' states. Some of these new norms were, in fact, adopted as a result of the entry of the post-colonial states into the international system, and because of the pressure generated by the 'Third World' majority both within international forums like the UN General Assembly and outside.

The first of these norms relates to the inalienability of juridical sovereignty or statehood, once conferred by international law and symbolized by membership of the United Nations. The sanctity of borders of post-colonial states forms the logical corollary of this norm. While this international norm has done much to preserve the existence of several 'Third World' states which may not have otherwise been viable, it has also, paradoxically, added to the security predicament of the 'Third World' state. This point can best be understood by recalling that the elimination of states not considered viable, either because of their internal contradictions or because their existence did not suit Great Power aspirations, was perfectly acceptable to the European international community, virtually until the end of the First World War.

The international consensus on the alienability of juridical statehood began to change during the inter-war period and crystallized after the Second World War in the context of the decolonization of Asia and Africa. Colonies, once granted independence, acquired the right to exist as sovereign entities even if many of them, especially in Africa, did not possess 'much in the way of empirical statehood, disclosed by a capacity for effective and civil government'.[25] This change has meant that while this newly crystallized international norm has protected the legal existence of post-colonial states without regard to their internal cohesiveness, it has been unable to solve or even to mitigate the security problems that such states face as a result of the contradictions present within their boundaries and inherent in their state-making process. In fact, this international norm has possibly made the security problems of some post-colonial states more acute by preventing the legal demise of even the least viable of these entities, like Lebanon, Somalia, Angola, Afghanistan, and Liberia. In other words, the crystallization of this norm has transformed what in an earlier age would have been the existential dilemma of such states – 'To be or not to be'! – into their perpetual security predicament. Gabriel Ben-Dor, writing about Lebanon, pointed out this reality very sharply in the following words: '[C]ountries still may – and do – fail in state-building. The cost of failure, however, is not disappearance, but incoherent, uncontrollable conflict ... But even this process is not irreversible; the price of failure is no longer absolute.'[26]

It is worth noting here that this guarantee encompassing juridical statehood and territorial integrity seems to have begun to weaken in the post-Cold War era. However, this change in international norms, if consolidated, is unlikely to alleviate the 'Third World's' security predicament. In fact, it may considerably worsen the situation and add to the prevalent instability and disorder. It appears, therefore, that the 'Third World' is caught in a no-win situation as far as this set of international norms is concerned, and this point will be discussed further later in this chapter.

A second set of international norms that has affected the security problems of the 'Third World' is related to the issue of human rights, with the primary emphasis on civil and political rights. While the modern conception of human rights can be traced to the natural law approach as developed in eighteenth-century Europe,[27] the recent normative force that human rights have acquired in the international arena is a result of the acceptance by the vast majority of states of the existence and validity of such rights for all human beings irrespective of their status as citizens of particular states. This was demonstrated by the inclusion of references in the Preamble and Article 1 of the UN Charter to human rights. The latter listed, as one of the fundamental purposes of the UN, 'To achieve international cooperation in ... promoting and encouraging respect for human rights and for fundamental freedoms for all without distinction as to race, sex, language, or religion'. The changing attitude towards human rights, as a legitimate concern of the international community that needed to be brought within the ambit of international law and rescued from its status as the exclusive preserve of sovereign states in relation to their own citizens, led to their codification in the Universal Declaration of Human Rights adopted in 1948 and the two International Covenants on Human Rights which were opened for signature and ratification in 1966 and became operative in 1976. This change in the international consensus regarding human rights was a major development in the evolution of norms that govern the international system, for it acknowledged more clearly than ever before that individuals, in addition to states, could now be considered subjects of international law. It also signified the international acceptance of the principle that there were rights of individuals and groups that were independent of their membership of individual states and that did not derive from such membership but from their status as members of the human species.

The major problem with the implementation of human rights in the 'Third World' is the fact that the concept of human rights owes its empirical validity to the existence and successful functioning of the industrialized, representative, and responsive states of Western Europe and North America. These states set the standards for effective statehood as well as for the humane and civilized treatment of their citizens. They do so by their demonstrated success in simultaneously meeting the basic needs of the large majority of their populations, protecting their human rights, and promoting and guaranteeing political participation. But these are states that have, by and large, successfully completed their state-building process, are politically satiated, economically affluent, and possess unconditional legitimacy in the eyes of the overwhelming majority of their populations. They can, therefore, afford to adopt liberal standards of state behaviour in relation to their populations, because they are reasonably secure in the knowledge that societal demands will not run counter to state interests and will not put state structures and institutions in any grave jeopardy.

What are currently considered in the West to be norms of civilized state behaviour, including those pertaining to human rights of individuals and groups, are in the 'Third World' often in contradiction with the imperatives of state-making which, as has been pointed out more than once, not only sanction but frequently require the use of violent means against recalcitrant domestic groups and individual citizens. Furthermore, the international norm upholding human rights runs directly counter to the norm which prescribes the inalienability of juridical statehood for 'Third World' states.[28] While the latter uncompromisingly upholds the legality of the existence of 'Third World' states within their colonially constructed boundaries, the former undermines the political legitimacy of these same states by prescribing standards and yardsticks in terms of the output functions of political systems that most 'Third World' states, struggling to perform the minimum tasks of maintaining political order, will be incapable of meeting for many decades to come.

Moreover, the simultaneous but contradictory operation of the two norms contributes to the creation and augmentation of internal discontent within 'Third World' states. It does so by, on the one hand, forcing all the diverse and dissatisfied elements within 'Third World' states to remain within their post-colonial boundaries, and, on the other, encouraging these very elements to make political, administrative and economic demands on these states to which they cannot respond even minimally, either because they lack the capabilities to do so or because doing so could seriously jeopardize their territorial integrity.

One can make the argument on behalf of 'Third World' states, still struggling to translate their juridical statehood into empirical statehood, that the case for human rights, whether of individuals or groups, and against the state's use of violent means to impose order is not as morally unassailable as it may appear at first sight. This point can be made most effectively in the context of the 'failed states' phenomenon, where state structures have completely collapsed.[29] In these cases it can be demonstrated that in the absence of even rudimentarily effective states as providers of a minimum degree of political order, as in Lebanon for the fifteen years of civil war, or as currently in Somalia, Afghanistan, Angola, Burundi and Liberia, to mention just a few examples, the concept of human rights remains nothing more than a pure abstraction. In such contexts the human rights' ideal is incapable of even minimal implementation, because in the absence of the sovereign a truly Hobbesian state of nature prevails and the very physical survival of large segments of populations cannot be assured. Hence, irrespective of the nature of their regimes and the predatory or developmental character of the states themselves,[30] 'Third World' states at this juncture in their historical development will almost inevitably take recourse to violent means, some more frequently and more brutally than others, in order to pursue their objectives of state-making, state consolidation, and regime survival. In the process, human rights are likely to be violated, both of groups and individuals. However, most of these instances of human rights' violation by states, while deplorable, often turn out to be less serious when compared to the violence that usually accompanies the failure of the state itself, as in Lebanon, Afghanistan or Somalia. These comments should not be taken as an apologia for authoritarian regimes in the 'Third World' that ostensibly emphasize order at the expense of both justice and political participation. Authoritarian regimes and predatory states (and the two must be analytically distinguished, for authoritarian regimes can exist in developmental and intermediate, in addition to predatory, states), the former frequently and the latter invariably, contribute a great deal to the creation and augmentation of disorder in 'Third World' states, despite paying lip-service to the objective of maintaining and promoting order. Iran under the Shah, the Philippines under Marcos, Zaire under Mobutu, Nicaragua under Somoza, to quote but a few instances, all provide good examples of this tendency.

It is also true that most regimes in the 'Third World', but especially authoritarian ones, attempt to portray threats to their regimes as threats to the state. Discerning analysts must, therefore, carefully make the distinction between issues of regime security and those of state security. However, in many cases, given the lack of unconditional legitimacy both of the regime and of the state structure in the 'Third World' and the close perceptual connection between regime and state as far as the majority of the state's population is concerned, the line between regime security and state security becomes so thin, and the interplay between the two so dense, that it is virtually impossible to disentangle one from the other. As one perceptive scholar pointed out in connection with the Middle East, 'those who rule must attempt to encourage loyalty to the state, of which they hope themselves to be the chief beneficiaries, while at the same time seeking to disguise the fact that their system of power, and thus the identity of the political structure itself, frequently owes more to the old ties of sectarian and tribal loyalty'.[31] Currently, Iraq, Jordan, Saudi Arabia and Kuwait in the Middle East, and Sudan, Angola and Mozambique in Africa, to name but a few cases, provide classic examples of the fusion between state and regime security. In many of these countries the fall of the regime is also likely to signal the failure of the state. Any student of Tudor England or Bourbon France will find this to be a very familiar phenomenon.

ETHNO-NATIONAL SELF-DETERMINATION

One further point needs to be touched upon here in connection with the human rights issue. This relates to the highly positive emotive response that the advocacy of human rights can draw from diverse constituencies when used as the normative basis to justify group rights. As a result, human rights' rhetoric and justifications for political action when applied to groups, especially ethnic groups, can facilitate the transformation of attempts by such groups for the recognition of their ethnic identities within existing states into their quest for national self-determination.

Given the multi-ethnic nature of most 'Third World' states, if human rights are interpreted to include the right to ethno-national self-determination, they are likely to pose grave threats to the territorial integrity and juridical statehood of post-colonial states, thus once again pitting one set of international norms against another. The renewed legitimation of the notion of ethno-national self-determination, above all in Europe, symbolized by the prompt recognition accorded to the successor states to the Soviet Union and Yugoslavia and the separation of Slovakia from the Czech Republic, is likely to give a fillip to demands for ethnic separatism in the 'Third World'. The acceptance in principle by the major European powers and by UN representatives of the division of Bosnia – despite the opposition of the Bosnian government – into three ethno-national states is bound to further confirm the legitimacy accorded to the right of ethnic groups to self-determination. The ethnic strife that has accompanied and followed the demise of the Soviet Union in Azerbaijan, Georgia and elsewhere has provided greater evidence of the increasing popularity and the escalating destructiveness of the ethno-nationalist ideal.

Given the latent tensions between ethnicity and state-defined nationalism even in functioning federal polities like India, and the clear contradiction between ethno-nationalism and state-defined nationalism in much of the 'Third World',[32] any development anywhere in the international arena that may encourage ethnic separatist demands in the context of state and regime fragilities prevalent in the 'Third World' is bound to add to the great strains already existing within these polities. The veracity of this assertion is borne out by the fact that 'under the banner of self-determination, there are active movements in more than sixty countries – one-third of the total roster of nations – to achieve full sovereignty – or some lesser degree of "minority" rights. A number of these movements have developed into ongoing civil wars.'[33]

In this context, the international community's, and especially the major powers', endorsement of the doctrine of ethno-national self-determination, even if limited to exceptional cases as in the Balkans, the former Soviet Union, and former Czechoslovakia, is bound to augment the challenge to the legitimacy of the principle that post-colonial states in their present form are territorially inviolable. The effects of such a contagion spreading have been summed up in a recent Council on Foreign Relations study, which has concluded that 'while the creation of some new states may be necessary or inevitable, the fragmentation of international society into hundreds of independent territorial entities is a recipe for an even more dangerous and anarchic world'.[34]

A major problem with ethno-national self-determination relates to the definition of the ethnic self that is seeking to determine its future. The self-perception and self-definition of ethnicity is usually subject to change depending on the context in which it operates at any point in time. As a leading scholar of South Asian ethnicities has pointed out, ethnicity is a fluid and flexible concept: 'its boundaries expand or contract. Its multiple attributes assume a different order of pre-eminence in diverse situations.'[35] This is what Crawford Young has referred to as 'the dynamic and changing character of contemporary ethnicity: far from representing a fixed and immutable set of static social facts, cultural pluralism is itself evolving in crucial ways, and is in major respects contextual, situational, and circumstantial'.[36] Therefore, to link such a potent ideology as self-determination to a malleable idea like that of ethnicity, and then to legitimize this combination by reference to the principle of group human rights, is bound to introduce even greater disorder in the 'Third World' than is already present, because it would endow the demands of every disgruntled ethnic group with the legitimacy of the ideal of national self-determination. The danger is that this is exactly what the renewed popularity of the idea of ethno-national self-determination may end up achieving, to the great detriment both of order and justice in the 'Third World'.

It may be possible to argue that the current international toleration of state-breaking and the re-formation of states on ethnic lines is limited and a product of the specific circumstances that accompanied the end of the Cold War, especially the demise of the Soviet Union, and cannot be equated with a long-term trend in the international system. However, the damage may already have been done in terms of the demonstration effect of the disintegration of established states on the more fragile 'Third World' states, and especially on groups agitating for their fragmentation. At a minimum, as a Carnegie Endowment study has stated, 'the old assumption that the boundaries set after the Second World War were permanent has been shaken by events in the Soviet Union and Yugoslavia'.[37] Even the temporary and limited diversion from the norm, that the political boundaries of states once established and recognized were guaranteed by the international community, is likely to exacerbate the security problems of insecure 'Third World' states that are faced with secessionist challenges.

STATE FAILURE

Related to the issue of ethno-national self-determination is the failed states phenomenon. Jack Snyder has succinctly described the link between the two by describing ethnic nationalism as 'the default option'. According to Snyder, ethnic nationalism 'predominates when institutions collapse, when existing institutions are not fulfilling people's basic needs and when satisfactory alternative structures are not readily available'.[38] While this may not provide the total explanation for the revival of ethno-nationalism, it does capture a very major ingredient – namely, the lack of effective statehood – that has contributed to the recent popularity of the ethno-nationalist ideology. This is true not only in the case of the components of the former Soviet Union and of former Yugoslavia but of many parts of the 'Third World' as well. It was the lack of effective statehood that was responsible for the emergence of what Robert Jackson has termed 'quasi-states' in the 'Third World'.[39] These quasi-states can now clearly be seen as precursors of failed states in the global South.

The end of the Cold War has had an important impact on the transformation of some of these quasi-states into failed states. This is especially true in the case of those states that had witnessed high levels of superpower involvement especially in the military sphere, including the arena of arms' transfers, during the Cold War era. At the height of the Cold War the superpowers attempted to shore up client governments in internally fragmented states, often with a view to maintaining a semblance of stability within countries that were allied with one superpower or the other. One major instrument of such support was the transfer of large quantities of relatively sophisticated arms to friendly regimes. In several instances such arms transfers led to countervailing transfers of weaponry by the rival superpower to forces opposed to the central authorities. Afghanistan during the 1980s came to epitomize this action-reaction phenomenon.[40]

Past superpower policies of pouring arms into fragmented polities have, however, become a major source of instability and disorder in the post-Cold War period. As one observer has pointed out in relation to Somalia, 'today the prevalence of modern weapons, Somalia's most significant legacy of superpower involvement during the Cold War, has undermined the very foundation for order in Somalia's society – the authority of clan elders'.[41] The presence of large quantities of relatively sophisticated weaponry, ranging from AK-47s to Stinger missiles, combined with the withdrawal of superpower support to weak and vulnerable regimes – support that was essential to prevent the central authorities from being overwhelmed by domestic rivals who, in turn, were divided among themselves – have created near-total anarchy in countries like Afghanistan and Somalia where central authority has completely collapsed, thereby turning these quasi-states into failed states.

The recent Lebanese and the current Somali, Afghan, Liberian and Zairean experiences demonstrate very clearly that the failure of the state in the 'Third World' constitutes a much greater source of human tragedy than the repression of people by even the most autocratic, but functioning, states like Iraq and Syria. This is why the combination of a juridically sovereign but empirically non-functioning central authority, which is what the failed state phenomenon has come to mean, could well be the major source of both suffering and disorder in the 'Third World', and possibly in the international system as a whole, not only in the 1990s but well into the next century.

THE OUTCOME OF STATE FAILURE

There is another major factor that makes the prospect of any acceleration in the process of state failure in the 'Third World' appear very dangerous for international and regional stability. This is the likelihood that in the last decade of the twentieth century the outcome of state failure will be dramatically different from what it had been in the seventeenth and eighteenth centuries when European states were at a stage of state-building that roughly corresponds to where most 'Third World' states are today. During that earlier period, when conquest and annexation were permissible under the norms then governing the international system, many non-viable states were annexed by, or partitioned among, their stronger and more viable neighbours. This led to a dramatic reduction in the number of political entities that comprised the European international system from about 500 in 1500 AD to 25 in 1900 AD.[42]

Annexation and conquest are no longer feasible in the current climate prevailing in the international system for two reasons. First, conquest and annexation will in all probability continue to remain impermissible under international law (although this does not mean that there will be no exceptions to this rule), even if the norm relating to the territorial integrity of post-colonial states is relaxed. Second, now that the era of direct and formal colonialism is over, conquest and annexation can only be undertaken by neighbouring states. They can, therefore, be ruled out in most cases because 'Third World' neighbours of failed or failing 'Third World' states usually have neither the capability nor the will to annex and integrate failed states, or even parts of them.

It is true that several 'Third World' states may not be averse to dismembering hostile neighbours if the international environment becomes more permissible in this regard. However, as the Indian involvement in the East Pakistan crisis in 1971 demonstrated, dismemberment is one thing and annexation quite another. While some 'Third World' states may profess irredentist designs against neighbouring states, the overwhelming majority of them will certainly not be interested in annexing large chunks of their neighbours' territories and populations because this would immensely complicate the already acute problems of ethnicity and ethno-nationalism faced by most such states themselves.

Failed states will, therefore, be left with only two options: either to continue to revel in anarchy and the consequent suffering this causes their populations (Somalia); or to splinter into a number of mini-states carved out mainly around temporarily self-defined dominant ethnic groups in particular regions of the failed states (Yugoslavia). Ethnic self-definitions in such cases are likely to be used as surrogates for failed political institutions, thus providing further evidence that ethnicity 'has now become the ultimate resort of the politically desperate'.[43]

If this comes to pass on a large scale, it is likely to lead to a situation against which Hurst Hannum has forcefully warned: 'full exercise of ethnic self-determination, grounded on linguistic, religious, or other self-defining criteria, might better protect current incarnations of "nationalities", "minorities", and "indigenous peoples". Nevertheless, the prospect of 5,000 homogeneous, independent statelets which define themselves primarily in ethnic, religious, or linguistic terms is one that should inspire at least as much trepidation as admiration. As frontiers are shifted and minorities displaced to make way for greater purity, a new age of intolerance is more likely to follow than is an era of mutual respect and tolerance for all.'[44] Even if the number of states increases to 500 instead of the 5,000 envisaged by Hannum, it would make for a much more anarchic situation than the one prevalent today, with full membership of the system of states bestowed on over 180 states. This would especially be the case since most of the newcomers will be even more insecure and vulnerable than the most insecure and vulnerable states that emerged in the wake of decolonization.

THE DEMOCRATIC EXPERIMENT

Many state's elites in the 'Third World' seem to have realized that the only way to prevent state-making from being transformed into state failure is to allow for greater political participation to those sectors of society – whether ethnic or socio-economic – that were heretofore excluded from the exercise of political power. The recent wave of democratization in the 'Third World' is in substantial part the result of the realization among ruling elites in the developing countries that the survival of their states and regimes is crucially dependent upon defusing the severe crisis of legitimacy that they face in the last decade of the twentieth century. It would be too naive to suggest, however, that democratization by itself, and in all contexts, will succeed in neutralizing ethnic separatism. As the example of Congo currently demonstrates, merely holding elections without adequate sensitivity to ethnic fissures can turn out to be counterproductive, especially if the fairness of the elections itself is in doubt and if the post-election regime has a distinctive ethnic hue. Such an outcome may end up widening ethnic rifts and heightening internal tensions as has happened in Congo since the overthrow of the one-party Marxist-Leninist regime in Brazzaville in 1991 and the holding of elections in late 1992.[45]

The success of the democratic experiment in defusing ethnic tensions will, therefore, depend on a number of factors which have been identified by de Nevers to include 'the speed with which ethnic issues are recognized; the level of ethnic tension when the democratization process begins; the size and power of different ethnic groups within the state; the ethnic composition of the previous regime and its opposition; the political positions of the leaders of the main ethnic groups; the presence or absence of external ethnic allies; and the ethnic composition of the military'.[46]

There is, however, another side to the democratization coin. The demands of state-building and democratization can only be reconciled if the democratizing state in the 'Third World' is able to monopolize credibly the instruments of violence within its territories so as to preclude dissident groups from attempting to change the state's boundaries when political controls are relaxed. This is essential because 'often the first act of forces liberated by the introduction of democracy is to seek some permanent escape from the state they see as having oppressed them'.[47]

This is where the most severe problems are likely to arise even if democratic political systems become the norm rather than the exception in the 'Third World'. For democratic regimes cannot afford to be seen as weak when confronted by separatist challenges, and cannot, in the final analysis, give up their right to lay down and enforce the rules (even if some rules have been negotiated with the opponents of the state) by which the game of politics is to be played within the boundaries of states over which they preside. Otherwise, 'a democratic centre may be questioned for its inefficiency in creating or its weakness in handling the secessionist crisis, opening the way for military intervention'.[48]

This is a point inadequately understood by most proponents of democratization in the 'Third World' who tend to equate democratic states with weak states on the assumption that strong states are bound to be autocratic by nature.[49] By making this assumption they fail to learn from the European experience that democracy emerged as the final stage of the state-building process and not at the latter's expense. Even if in today's context, when democratization cannot wait until state-building is completed, it cannot thrive in the absence of the political order that only a strongly embedded state can provide.

Democratization, therefore, must complement rather than contradict the process of state-making, for without the political order that can only be provided by effective states the gains of democratization cannot be sustained. Anarchies, as the examples of Lebanon, Somalia, Liberia and Afghanistan clearly demonstrate, are no respecters of democratic values. This truth prompted a perceptive scholar of the Middle East to declaim more than a decade ago in the context of the failure of the Lebanese state that '"Seek ye the political kingdom first" – not because it matters more, but because, in the lack of political order, no normal social development is possible. The state cannot replace society, but it must protect society. In the lack of political order, social and individual values are meaningless; they cannot be realized, nor can they be protected from assault, violence and chaos.'[50]

CONCLUSIONS

The reconciliation of the two imperatives of consolidation of state power and democratization is not, and will not be, an easy task even if tremendous goodwill is present on all sides. Major tensions are bound to arise between state elites and their ethnic and political opponents who would like to put significant curbs on the power of the central state. In addition, where separatist insurgencies are already under way, major problems between separatists and democratizing central governments are likely to centre around two basic questions: What is the guarantee that groups espousing separatism will indeed surrender all arms and reconcile themselves to autonomous or semi-autonomous status that will continue to be essentially dependent upon the good faith and the continuing political sagacity of the central government? And what is the guarantee that central authorities, after persuading separatist ethnic groups to lay down their arms and thus having overcome immediate internal security crises, will continue to abide by their commitment to popular political participation, the constitutional protection of minority rights, and regional autonomy?

The answers provided by the 'Third World's' historical record to both these questions do not leave much room for optimism. Furthermore, if one goes by the earlier European experience, one is likely to conclude that the historical juncture at which most 'Third World' states find themselves today is unlikely to permit a great deal of ethnic accommodation and political participation, because these two processes usually run counter to the overriding imperative of the consolidation of state power and the fashioning of a national state. However, one can make an effective argument that the context of the late twentieth century is so dramatically different from those of the late eighteenth or even the late nineteenth centuries that radically new solutions must be found for this dilemma.

In other words, the problem of reconciling the demands of state-making with those of democratization and human rights will have to be addressed much more creatively, and mutually acceptable solutions found, if the twin spectres of failed states and destructive ethno-nationalism are to be kept at bay. However, after all is said and done, one has to be realistic enough to recognize that even in cases (and there will not be many) where there is no dearth of goodwill and of creative thinking, the imperatives of state-building and the demands for group rights and democracy may turn out to be irreconcilable. Given the stage of state-making at which most post-colonial states currently find themselves, this should not come as a surprise to seasoned observers of the 'Third World'. All it means is that one should then be prepared for a future where internal conflicts, based on ethnic, social and ideological divisions, will be further accentuated in many 'Third World' regions, leading either to state repression or state failure and, often, to a combination of the two.

This is a combination that is sure to spill over political boundaries and increasingly fuel inter-state conflict. Together, intra-state and inter-state conflicts will then continue to perpetuate the vulnerabilities and insecurities from which the 'Third World' has traditionally suffered. The only difference will be that these vulnerabilities and insecurities are likely to become more acute in the post-Cold War era. This would be so because of the transformations that have occurred, and are likely to occur, both in the nature of Great Power relations, where many of the Cold War restraints on 'Third World' conflicts have been removed, and in some of those norms governing the international system that have been, and are, crucial to the security and integrity of 'Third World' states.

With the overwhelming majority of the members of the international system still undergoing the traumas that invariably accompany the early stages of state-making, and that in an international environment that immensely complicates the essential task of imposing political order on fragmented societies, conflict and insecurity are likely to be the rule rather than the exception in the 'Third World' as we enter the twenty-first century. Conflict, instability and insecurity in the 'Third World' can be expected to lead not only to refugee flows into neighbouring states but to migrations to the developed countries as well, thus creating racial tensions within the industrialized democracies.[51] In this era of nuclear weapons and jet travel, the core of industrialized democracies, despite its best efforts, cannot insulate itself from the conflicts and instabilities in the global periphery. There may be an element of poetic justice in this outcome after all.

NOTES

1.   This paper draws heavily upon the analysis in my book *The Third World Security Predicament: State-Making, Regional Conflict and the International System* (Boulder, CO: Lynne Rienner, 1994). Written under the auspices of the Watson Institute for International Studies, Brown University, the book forms a part of the Institute's series 'Emerging Global Issues'.

2.   Kalevi J. Holsti, *Peace and War: Armed Conflicts and International Order 1648-1989* (Cambridge: Cambridge University Press, 1991), Table 11.1, pp. 274-8. The only two cases in Holsti's tabulation that fell outside the 'Third World' were the Soviet interventions in Hungary (1956) and Czechoslovakia (1968). Holsti's estimate is termed conservative because he has used rather

stringent criteria to determine whether outbreaks of armed violence fall under his definition of wars and major armed interventions.

3. Evan Luard, *War in International Society: A Study in International Sociology* (London: Tauris, 1986), appendix 5, p. [Check page].

4. Karin Lindgren, Birger Heldt, Kjell-Ake Nordquist and Peter Wallensteen, 'Major Armed Conflicts in 1990', *SIPRI Yearbook 1991: World Armaments and Disarmament* (Oxford: Oxford University Press, 1991), p. 345.

5. Ramses Amer, Birger Heldt, Signe Landgren, Kjell Magnusson, Erik Melander, Kjell-Ake Nordquist, Thomas Ohlson and Peter Wallensteen, 'Major Armed Conflicts', *SIPRI Yearbook 1993: World Armaments and Disarmament* (Oxford: Oxford University Press, 1993), p. 81.

6. K.J. Holsti, 'International Theory and War in the Third World', in Brian L. Job (ed.), *The Insecurity Dilemma: National Security of Third World States* (Boulder, CO: Lynne Rienner, 1992), p. 38.

7. Amitai Etzioni, 'The Evils of Self-Determination', *Foreign Policy*, no. 89, winter 1992-93, pp. 21-2.

8. Najdan Pasic, 'Varieties of Nation-Building in the Balkans and Among the Southern Slavs', in S.N. Eisenstadt and Stein Rokkan (eds), *Building States and Nations*, vol. 2, (Beverley Hills, CA: Sage, 1973), p. 130.

9. Shahram Chubin has made a similar agument forcefully in his 'The South and the New World Order', *Washington Quarterly*, vol. 16, no. 4, autumn 1993, pp. 87-107.

10. I have made this argument in greater detail in Mohammed Ayoob, 'The Security Predicament of the Third World State: Reflections on State-Making in a Comparative Perspective', in Job, *The Insecurity Dilemma*, pp. 63-80.

11. Youssef Cohen, Brian R. Brown, and A.F.K. Organski, 'The Paradoxical Nature of State-Making: The Violent Creation of Order', *American Political Science Review*, vol. 75, no. 4, 1981, p. 902.

12. For expanded discussions of the process of state-making and its relationship with organized violence, see Keith Jaggers, 'War and The Three Faces of Power: War-Making and State-Making in Europe and the Americas', *Comparative Political Studies*, vol. 25, no. 1, April 1992, pp. 26-62; and Charles Tilly, 'War-Making and State-Making as Organized Crime', in Peter B. Evans, Dietrich Rueschemeyer, and Theda Skocpol (eds), *Bringing the State Back In*, (New York: Cambridge University Press, 1985), pp. 169-91.

13. Youssef Cohen, 'The Paradoxical Nature of State-Making', *American Political Science Review*, p. 905.

14. Charles Tilly, *Coercion, Capital and European States, AD 990-1990* (Cambridge, MA: Basil Blackwell, 1990), pp. 3, 43.

15. Ernest Gellner, *Nations and Nationalism* (Ithaca, NY: Cornell University Press, 1983), p. 1.

16. For details of this argument and the data on which it is based, see Charles Tilly (ed.), *The Formation of National States in Western Europe* (Princeton, NJ: Princeton University Press, 1975). Also, see Cornelia Navari, 'The Origins of

the Nation-State', in Leonard Tivey (ed.), *The Nation-State: The Formation of Modern Politics* (Oxford: Martin Robertson, 1981), pp. 13-38.

17. Anthony D. Smith, *State and Nation in the Third World* (New York: St Martin's Press, 1983), pp. 11, 17.

18. Charles Tilly, 'Reflections on the History of European State-Making', in Charles Tilly (ed.), *The Formation of National States in Western Europe* (Princeton, NJ: Princeton University Press, 1975), p. 71.

19. Joseph R. Strayer, *On the Medieval Origins of the Modern State* (Princeton, NJ: Princeton University Press, 1970), p. 57.

20. Stein Rokkan, 'Dimensions of State Formation and Nation-Building: A Possible Paradigm for Research on Variations within Europe', in Charles Tilly (ed.), *The Formation of National States in Western Europe*, p. 586.

21. For theoretically informed accounts of the 'cumulation of crises' in Italy and Germany, see the chapters on Italy and Germany by Raymond Grew and John R. Gillis respectively in Raymond Grew (ed.), *Crises of Political Development in Europe and the United States* (Princeton, NJ: Princeton Unviersity Press, 1978).

22. The earliest modern states of Western Europe were able to complete their state-making process in three near-distinct phases: (1) the establishment of the centralized, 'absolutist' state at the expense of a feudal order that had begun to lose much of its economic and political utility; (2) the welding together of the subjects of the centralized monarchy into a people with a common history, legal system, language, and, quite often, religion (in the sense of Christian schisms), thus leading to the evolution of a national identity and the transformation of the centralized monarchical state into a nation-state; and (3) the gradual extension of representative institutions (dictated by the necessity to co-opt into the power structure new and powerful social forces that emerged as a result of the industrial revolution) over the decades if not centuries. Above all, as Stein Rokkan has pointed out, 'What is important is that the Western nation-states were given a chance to solve some of the worst problems of state-building before they had to face the ordeals of mass politics'. Stein Rokkan, 'Dimensions of State Formation and Nation-Building: A Possible Paradigm for Research on Variations Within Europe', in Charles Tilly, *The Formation of National States in Western Europe*, p. 598.

23. For details of this argument, see Mohammed Ayoob, *The Third World Security Predicament: State-Making, Regional Conflict and the International System*, forthcoming.

24. For the argument that the Cold War had a cooperative as well as competitive element built into it, especially as far as conflict in the 'Third World' was concerned, see Benjamin Miller, 'Explaining Great Power Cooperation in Conflict Management', *World Politics*, vol. 45, no. 1, October 1992, pp. 1-46.

25. Robert H. Jackson, 'Quasi-States, Dual Regimes, and Neo-classical Theory: International Jurisprudence and the Third World', *International Organization*, vol. 41, no. 4, autumn 1987, p. 529.

26. Gabriel Ben-Dor, *State and Conflict in the Middle East: Emergence of the Post-Colonial State* (New York: Praeger, 1983), p. 233.
27. R.J. Vincent, *Human Rights and International Relations* (Cambridge: Cambridge University Press, 1986), pp. 19-36.
28. As Seyom Brown has pointed out, the intellectual position that 'servicing ... basic human rights is the principal task of human polities, and that the worth of any polity is a function of how well it performs this task, has put the legitimacy of all extant polities up for grabs, so to speak. Whether particular nation-states, and the prevailing territorial demarcations, do indeed merit the badge of political legitimacy is, according to this view, subject to continuing assessment; accordingly, neither today's governments nor today's borders are sacrosanct.' Seyom Brown, *International Relations in a Changing Global System: Toward a Theory of the World Polity* (Boulder, CO: Westview Press, 1992), p. 126.
29. For a discussion of failed states, see Gerlad B. Helman and Steven R. Ratner, 'Saving Failed States', *Foreign Policy*, no. 89, winter 1992-93, pp. 3-20.
30. For a valuable analysis of different types of states - predatory, developmental and intermediate - in the 'Third World', see Peter B. Evans, 'Predatory, Developmental, and Other Apparatuses: A Comparative Political Economy Perspective on the Third World State', *Sociological Forum*, vol. 4, no. 4, 1989, pp. 561-87.
31. Charles Tripp, 'Near East', in Robert S. Litwak and Samuel F. Wells Jr (eds), *Superpower Competition and Security in the Third World* (Cambridge, MA: Ballinger, 1988), p. 113.
32. For an incisive discussion of the difference between ethnicity and ethno-nationalism, see Ashutosh Varshney, 'Contested Meanings: India's National Identity, Hindu Nationalism, and the Politics of Anxiety', *Daedalus*, vol. 122, no. 3, summer 1993, p. 230.
33. Lloyd N. Cutler, 'Foreword', in Morton H. Halperin and David J. Scheffer with Patricia L. Small, *Self-Determination in the New World Order* (Washington, DC: Carnegie Endowment for International Peace, 1992), p. xi.
34. Gidon Gottlieb, *Nation Against State: A New Approach to Ethnic Conflicts and the Decline of Sovereignty* (New York: Council on Foreign Relations Press, 1993), p. 2.
35. Urmila Phadnis, *Ethnicity and Nation-Building in South Asia* (New Delhi: Sage, 1990), p. 241.
36. Crawford Young, 'The Temple of Ethnicity', *World Politics*, vol. 35, no. 4, July 1983, p. 659.
37. Morton H. Halperin, *Self-Determination in the New World Order*, p. 119.
38. Jack Snyder, 'Nationalism and the Crisis of the Post-Soviet State', *Survival*, vol. 35, no. 1, spring 1993, p. 12.
39. Robert H. Jackson, *Quasi-States: Sovereignty, International Relations and the Third World* (Cambridge: Cambridge University Press, 1990).

40. For details of the situation in Afghanistan in the 1980s during the height of superpower involvement in that country's civil war, see Olivier Roy, *Islam and Resistance in Afghanistan* (Cambridge: Cambridge University Press, 1990).

41. Jeffrey Clark, 'Debacle in Somalia: Failure of the Collective Response', in Lori Fisler Damrosch (ed.), *Enforcing Restraint: Collective Intervention in Internal Conflicts* (New York: Council on Foreign Relations Press, 1993), pp. 207-8.

42. Charles Tilly, 'Reflections on the History of European State-Making', in Charles Tilly, *The Formation of National States in Western Europe*, p. 15.

43. John Chipman, 'Managing the Politics of Parochialism', *Survival*, vol. 35, no. 1, spring 1993, p. 143.

44. Hurst Hannum, *Autonomy, Sovereignty, and Self-Determination: The Accomodation of Conflicting Rights* (Philadelphia, PA: University of Pennsylvania Press, 1990), pp. 454-5.

45. For details of the Congo case, see Kenneth B. Noble, 'Democracy Brings Turmoil in Congo', *New York Times*, 31 January 1994, p. A3.

46. Renee de Nevers, 'Democratization and Ethnic Conflict', *Survival*, vol. 35, no. 2, summer 1993, pp. 31-2.

47. John Chipman, 'Managing the Politics of Parochialism', p. 168.

48. Larry Diamond, Juan J. Linz, and Seymour Martin Lipset, 'Introduction: Comparing Experiences with Democracy', *Politics in Developing Countries: Comparing Experiences with Democracy* (Boulder, CO: Lynne Rienner, 1990), p. 29.

49. For example, Rajni Kothari, *State Against Democracy: In Search of Humane Governance* (Delhi: Ajanta Publications, 1988).

50. Gabriel Ben Dor, *State and Conflict in the Middle East: Emergence of the Post-Colonial State*, p. 244.

51. For an insightful analysis of the nexus between international migration on the one hand and security and stability on the other, see Myron Weiner, 'Security, Stability, and International Migration', *International Security*, vol. 17, no. 3, winter 1992-93, pp. 91-126. Also, see Gerald Dirks, 'The Intensification of International Migratory Pressures: Causes, Consequences, and Responses', in Gerald Dirks, *et al.*, *The State of the United Nations, 1993: North-South Perspectives*, ACUNS Reports and Papers 1993, no. 5, (Providence, RI: Academic Council on the United Nations System, 1993), pp. 65-81.

4

Integration and Disintegration: An Approach to Society-Formation

Joel S. Migdal

INTRODUCTION

Internal wars and other forms of instability have taken millions of lives in 'Third World' countries since the Second World War. The Cold War fuelled many of these conflicts, but the end of that prolonged stand-off did not bring a respite from continuing tension, even outright slaughter, in numerous internal disputes in Africa and Asia. And new political and communal violence has since flared in hot spots throughout the former communist countries. How can we understand domestic conflict in a broad comparative framework? While every set of tensions holds its own distinctive grudges and sparks, a state-society approach helps us discern some of the key obstacles in establishing an accepted set of rules for peaceful resolution of disputes within a country.

In this article, I will argue that serious attention must be given to the process of *society formation* if we are to understand the bases of today's internal social and political struggles. Speaking of society formation – and the role of states in that process – demands a clear understanding of what we mean by society. But surprisingly little self-consciousness thinking by those working in the state-society framework has gone into the question of what we mean by both state and society beyond rather perfunctory definitions. Much of the literature has tended to regard states in fairly undifferentiated terms, usually, following Max Weber, as a complex organization that holds a monopoly over the means of violence in a territory. In presenting them as holistic, some scholars have given the misleading impression that at key junctures in their histories all or most states have pulled in single directions. Some researchers have taken this tendency so far in order to reify and anthropomorphize the state, treating it as a unitary actor that assesses its situation strategically and then acts accordingly to maximize its interests. Unfortunately, in regarding the state as an organic entity and giving it an ontological status, they have obscured the fragility of many states, as well as the dynamics of the struggle for domination in societies in which powerful forces vie against the state or co-opt significant parts of it.[1] Many scholars and policy-makers have simply overstated the capabilities of states.

To appreciate the limitations of states (as well as their sometimes formidable powers), we can best understand them as one organization – among many other social organizations – in a society. While such political organizations have existed since ancient times, modern states – those that began emerging in Europe in the seventeenth century and that have since proliferated in all parts of the globe – have made extensive claims in regulating the minutiae of their subjects' daily lives. This now universal modern dimension of states, the assumed right to make the rules of behaviour in many realms of people's personal affairs in the society, has had two important effects. First, state rules – its laws and regulations – have often pitted its officials against others in society promoting different norms for daily behaviour, especially when state leaders have staked out new regions or dimensions of life that they have sought to regulate. And, second, the insinuation of the state into people's daily lives through these countless laws and regulations has frequently blurred the boundaries between it and other social forces, such as markets and families. The state is a large and complex organization and, like other big institutions, its different parts may work at cross purposes with each other; indeed, parts of the state may become so remote from central control that they become indistinguishable from other local social organizations.

It is impossible to understand states – whether we want to look at international or domestic relations – without placing them in the contexts of the societies within which they interact with other social organizations, for it is from these interactions that states draw their strength and find their limitations. The myth of sovereignty assumes the freedom of states to pursue their own interests in the international arena, and the myth of state autonomy takes the coherence of states for granted, as it does the distance from other societal forces. In fact, whether states are sovereign or autonomous is a historical question that cannot be decided a priori. A more fruitful approach is to examine the state in the context of those forces impinging upon its ability to act unfettered.

This chapter seeks to look at state-society relations within this framework. Two different ways of thinking about society will be discussed, although each perspective is a distillation, rather than a historical representation. The historiography of particular societies demonstrates two independent sets of principles for assessing state-society relations. Some thoughts on how these conceptions may be joined in order to approach questions of societal instability and violence, as well as possible integration, in the 'Third World' and elsewhere, will then conclude the chapter.

Two Views of Society

The first view understands society as fragmented, often conflictual, organizations exercising social control; the emphasis here is on the components of society – its innards – and how the parts of this melange interact. Social, economic, and cultural relations within and among social organizations – states, churches, clans, businesses, informal bonds marked by patron-client ties, and more – are marked by conflict and accommodation. Organizations clash over who has the right, authority, and power to set the rules for people's behaviour in particular areas of their lives; their aim may be extraction of surplus, imposition of a particular religious order, or simply power for power's sake.

Some of these forces enter into coalitions, gaining leverage over other organizations in order to establish firm social control. By one measure, then, society is delineated by these partially overlapping arenas of social relations and social control: organizations, including the state, band together (often giving up on some of their goals in order to entice others into a coalition) in order to thwart the designs of opposing social forces and to set their own rules for behaviour and belief. This is a conception of society that stresses fragmentation and particularly questions of domination (conflict, coalitions, social control, power, struggle between social classes, etc.).

A second view posits society as 'the outermost social structure for a certain group of individuals who, whatever might be their attitude toward it, view themselves as its members and experience their identity as being determined by it'.[2] Here, the stress is on society as a whole, rather than on its parts. What keeps society together? What makes it a social unit? This is a definition that points to the unity of society and, in particular, questions of integration (identity, legitimacy, consensus, shared values, civil society, etc.). This second view holds that it is the cumulation of peoples' shared experiences, particularly through their common interaction with the state, which is the key in creating boundedness, or that outermost social structure.

While the two perspectives seem to be at odds with one another, a closer look will reveal an important complementarity between them. To understand recurring social and political violence and the obstacles to the institutionalization of accepted rules for behaviour, we must scrutinize these two perspectives on society, because each, unfortunately, has been fraught with myths. Our question is whether there is a way to unite these two approaches and to comprehend when a melange of social organizations, often in conflict over social control, manages to create a recognized outermost structure.

STATES AS A MELANGE

It is simply wishful thinking to assume that all societies manage to create strong outermost structures. Cases such as Rwanda and the former Yugoslavia demonstrate that any shared sense of history and identity may be overwhelmed by conflict and struggle. Marxist, liberal, and state-centric theories have all been too quick to assume that some kind of hegemony or outermost structure necessarily results from (or comes prior to) social struggle. The outcomes of struggles for social control in society have not automatically aggregated to create broad classes with cohesive projects that could shape society (as Marxists would have it). Nor have such conflicts necessarily been channelled within a widely agreed upon normative framework (as liberals suppose). An autonomous and capable state organization (the prerequisite for state-centric theorists) might have been entirely absent. In short, no outermost structure may emerge at all. And, even if we find such classes or frameworks of states, must we assume that they will hold together beyond the short or medium term?[3]

Viewing society as a melange of organizations does not necessitate seeing social forces as cohering into an integrated whole with an outermost structure. It may be more useful to accept the possibility that varying elements may each pull in different directions, leading to unanticipated patterns of domination and transformation. Patterns of domination are determined by key struggles that are spread through society's multiple 'arenas of domination and opposition'. Such arenas are the key for analysing state-society relations. Officials from different levels of the state are crucial figures in these struggles, interacting, and at times conflicting, with an entire constellation of social forces in the arenas in which they are engaged. Any individual part of the state may respond as much (or more) to the distinctive pressures it faces in particular arenas as it does to the rest of the state organization.

In many societies, attention to local and regional events – to the cumulation of struggles and accommodations in society's multiple arenas – may explain far more than easy assumptions about unified bodies like states (represented in the capital city) or social classes. Events at the 'centre' may not be decipherable without a clear understanding of the so-called periphery. And patterns of social control broadly dispersed through society may prevent a 'centre' from making a broadly accepted outermost structure.

Social forces in society, even ones far from the formal trappings of power (such as squatters' movements in Peru or patron-client ties in Senegal), have represented powerful mechanisms for associative behaviour. The efficiency of their hierarchies, their ability to use resources at hand, their adroitness in exploiting or generating symbols to which people develop strong attachments, all have affected their ability to influence or control behaviour and beliefs. The social control they have exercised could rob those holding formal offices of the ability to affect people's behaviour in particular realms. In Lebanon from 1975-1990, it was obvious that the state controlled little more than the presidential compound, while a variety of militias, clans, and sectarian political organizations governed many dimensions of daily life. Other countries may do far better in masking the weakness of putatively powerful organizations with their headquarters in the capital city – the state, church, political parties – but much social control may nonetheless be invested in fragmented social forces dispersed in urban slums and poor villages. Even highly centralized states, such as China and Mexico, while able to place firm limits on what people can and cannot do in certain realms of behaviour, have found themselves stymied on a host of issues because of the insidious social control exercised by social forces, even those in the outermost reaches of society.

These diverse social forces have not operated in a social vacuum. Their leaders have attempted to mobilize followers and exercise power in environments in which other social forces have been doing the same. And there has rarely been a neat division of the population or of issues keeping various social forces from conflicting or overlapping. The notion of arenas focuses on those environments where various social forces engage one another over material and symbolic issues, vying for supremacy through struggles and accommodations, clashes and coalitions. Approaches that start with a presumption of large-scale integrated organizations that dominate society – whether the state, social classes, or others – have missed this key dynamic of domination. They have also overlooked the dispersed, ongoing struggles for social control – the shifting coalitions, the effects of exogenous forces on existing coalitions – which are the bases of transformation. Indeed, one might argue that the failure of social scientists to see the fragility of the Soviet Union and its East European allies stemmed from a gaze too strongly fixed on what one took to be the integrated organizations at the centre, the state and the Communist Party, while missing the dispersed struggles for actual social control dispersed throughout these countries.

The arenas in which such struggles have occurred are not simply 'policy arenas' in which various groups attempt to shape public policy.[4] In addition to contests over governmental policy, struggles and accommodations have taken place over the basic moral order and the very structure within which the rights and wrongs of everyday social behaviour should be determined: Who has the right to interpret the scriptures? Who is to be respected over others? What system of property rights will prevail? How will water and land be distributed within the context of the prevailing system of property rights? *Conflict has been as much over rules for engagement and who will control the procedures as over substantive issues.* Social scientists must not assume that the battles over state policy are necessarily the determining ones in society. Other much less obvious struggles may be much more determining in the overall divisions within society and in the patterns of social behaviour.

Attempts at domination by any social organization have invariably been met with opposition by others also seeking to dominate or by those trying to avoid domination. Rarely could a social force achieve its goals without finding allies, creating coalitions, and accepting accommodations: landlord and priest, entrepreneur and sheikh, have forged such social coalitions with power enough to dictate wide-ranging patterns of belief and practice. Arenas point us not only to hierarchical relations of social control, but to these key horizontal ties as well, involving coalitions of figures with important material and symbolic resources (such as land or the means to spiritual salvation).

The struggles and accommodations of social forces in any local or regional arena of domination and opposition have not been hermetically sealed affairs. Resources have been reallocated from one arena to another in order to influence the outcome of struggles. Social forces have enhanced their position by sporting resources garnered from outside, by reassigning trusted personnel, or by riding on the backs of pervasive and powerful symbols, such as religious beliefs or ethnicity. Factors such as the overall structure of production in society, existing institutional arrangements, and the saliency of certain symbols have all influenced who would be in a position to reallocate resources and symbols from arena to arena.

To return to our notion of the state as one organization among many in society, representatives of the state have been among the actors struggling within arenas for social control. Indeed, the first cut at understanding the state should not be as a single actor in society but as a participant in scattered arenas throughout the territory that state leaders seek to rule. What has distinguished most modern states from political organizations of the past and from many other contemporary social organizations has been its leaders' aspirations to be present and achieve dominance in all of society's arenas. But aspirations have not necessarily been transformed into reality. In some societies, especially in sub-Saharan Africa, representatives of the state have not even been present in many arenas where struggles for social control have occurred. In many societies, the state office designated to put forth the state's agenda in a given arena has been co-opted by leaders of other social organizations with different agendas. The result may be that state resources have flowed into the arena, but they have been used in the service of another social organization, such as a clan or a landlord's gang. This sort of co-optation is one way that the lines between the state and other social organizations have been blurred.

Even in instances where state offices have not simply been resources for other organizations, state officials have frequently faced tremendous pressures within the arenas they have entered. While they have carried with them formidable resources from the state organization as a whole, they have also been subject to the pushes and pulls of the struggles within their arenas. The result may be a state with little overall coherence, as the state's parts reflect the distinctive pressures of the individual arenas within which state officials have been engaged, rather than some larger overall agenda generated by the state's leaders in the far-off capital city.

Like states, international and transnational organizations have been among the players in societies' arenas. They, too, have brought impressive resources to the struggles within arenas. But they have also had liabilities in their arena interactions: irrelevant sets of symbols, little staying power in the struggles, the inefficient use of surrogates to distribute resources, difficulties of control and command. Just as it makes little sense to make a special level of analysis for the state, rather than to see it as one of many organizations seeking control and entering into coalitions, setting international donors and other organizations apart from the struggle within arenas does little to advance our understanding of who holds power and how change is effected in particular societies.

In short, the image of society as a melange of organizations cautions us not to jump to conclusions concerning the integration of society. It warns us, too, not to assume that conflict in society is marked by large-scale, integrated social forces, such as social classes, or widely accepted frameworks for the rules of competition. The dynamics of society, rather, can be seen in the struggles and accommodations that mark the arenas of domination and opposition. In the dispersed conflicts and coalitions within those arenas lie insights into the distribution of power and key cleavages in society. The state, as one of the organizations of society, is an actor in most arenas, but that does not mean that it will be dominant. Indeed, arenas may have a greater effect on the state (undermining its leaders' hopes for state coherence, robbing it of key resources) than states have on the outcome of struggles for social control within arenas.

SOCIETY AS THE OUTERMOST STRUCTURE

Besides the conception of a melange, where different groups vie for social control, the other notion of society emphasizes common identity created by an outermost structure. It stresses the commonality among society's members, what binds them together rather than what divides them. This notion of a common outermost structure is critical, but it is not unproblematic. It comes to us by way of some long-standing myths that make it difficult to assess its usefulness in judging the ability of societies to deal with their differences peacefully.

Again, some fundamental misunderstandings about the character and capabilities of states have led to difficulties in employing the conception of society as an outermost structure in useful ways. It came to be assumed in the eighteenth century and after, when political legitimacy was increasingly associated with the will of the people, that states' authority was over a population with shared experiences and some common identity. Indeed, the claim was that states' authority derived from the common will of those people, thereby assuming their basic unity (or an 'outermost structure').

States, the thinking went, did not come on the scene of world history to unite disparate peoples (as empires had) but were an expression of, and drew their authority from, *pre-existing* societies. Society predated the state, in this view, and, ultimately, gave birth to the state. Indeed, the tendency to analyse the rise of the state in contractual terms was an early manifestation of the belief that a society already present contained people with enough in common so that they (or an elect group that could claim to represent all of society) could make a binding political contract (either with each other or the ruler). The state, in such a view, was a tool invented by societies in order to defend them and to give expression to their wills. Its right of existence, its legitimacy in forcing people to do what they would otherwise not do, derived from the fact that it was merely a creation of society and was articulating the will of society as a whole (against the wills of wayward individuals).

Because of limitations of space, the notion of the 'nation' will not be dealt with at any length in this chapter – but problems with understanding society are similar to those of sorting out the myth of the nation. As a number of scholars have pointed out, the nation has been mistakenly presented by historians and social scientists in mythic terms, as a natural, ontological phenomenon, rather than as a humanly constructed entity. Societies, too, took on such ontological meanings. Even when the state was exported outside Europe, colonial officials spoke as if they were somehow hunting for the *natural* societies or nations in this place or that, which could sanction the establishment of particular state boundaries and, ultimately, legitimate the colonial state itself. Even colonial rulers sought some form of societal sanction in the establishment of their rule. The key here is that state rulers, whatever their ilk, have never claimed that what the state's political boundaries are, or should be, is arbitrary. They have justified political boundaries in terms of some larger calling, whether a manifest destiny (as in the case of the United States) or a correspondence to societal boundaries that mark off their society from others. The attempt to establish the relationship of the state's political boundaries to societal boundaries lies at the heart of the central ideological project of many states.

Some British rulers' disappointment in Palestine during the Mandate period, for example, stemmed from the dawning reality of the absence of such a natural society there, shattering their earlier naivety. Note the self-revelatory and didactic tone of the Palestine Royal Commission (or Peel Commission) Report in 1937: 'It is time, surely, that Palestinian "citizenship"... should be recognized as what it is, as nothing but a legal formula devoid of moral meaning'. This sense of resignation, coming almost 20 years after the British assumed rule in Palestine, indicated not only their ingenuousness, to be sure, but also their disappointment that they could not find indigenous legitimacy for their rule in a mythical all-Palestinian society. Indeed, the Peel Commission Report was written in the years of an all-out Arab revolt, impelling the British to re-examine their justification for ruling the country. While arenas marked by social control and other forms of social relations occasionally (but not always) encompassed both Jews and Arabs in Palestine, the dimension of society where people see themselves as part of the same outermost structure marking common identity was entirely absent, and it was this reality with which the British were coming to terms.

In Europe and then elsewhere, state leaders have sought affirmation for themselves and their states in the 'moral meaning' of society, referred to in the Peel Commission Report, or in the 'naturalness' of society itself. If the state is an outgrowth of the will of a natural society, then the privileged position of political rulers could be more easily explained in their roles as the executors of society's will. There is barely a state in Asia or Africa today, no matter how new its vintage and how diverse its population, which has not had its founders and subsequent heads ground it and define it in terms of a pre-existing society in its territorial and social space. Through the putative naturalness of society, state officials have sought a moral justification and consensual basis for their use of coercion in everything from collecting taxes to fighting wars. As Weber and others have pointed out, domination is nearly impossible without a belief by the dominated that those dominating them are right in seeking their obedience. Propagating the idea of a natural society helped meld the minds of dominator and dominated about the appropriateness of the political arrangement.

Part of the project of state leaders in justifying themselves and the state, then, was to make the notion of the pre-existence of their nations and, if their space was clearly multi-national, their societies a truism. It is consequently not surprising that state leaders have nurtured myths of pre-existing societies in order to legitimate the state and their own rule. Such myths are problematical when they become incorporated into social scientists' and historians' understanding of why states and societies are structured as they are.

These understandings entail a kind of essentialism, which has seeped into the study of state-society relations. It has been written elsewhere about the state side of the equation, charging that current theories have tended to reify the state.[5] The result has been that questions of state formation have too often been blurred and the state has appeared to be much more unified and purposive in its actions than seems warranted by the evidence.

A similar claim may be made about our understanding of society. The essentialism has come in taking the totality of the society and its particular structure as a known fact – as pre-existing entities rather than as artifacts of specific conditions. What state leaders used as means to gain legitimacy for their own positions and actions became accepted canons of social science. It is the assumption of society's naturalness rather than it stemming from particular contingencies that is the underpinning for many of today's discussions about state-society relations.

How, then, do we approach this element of an outermost structure if not through the naturalness or pre-existence of society? We must get away from an ontological approach and turn, instead, to what we might call *society formation*. Here the focus is on how the outermost social structure determining identity is itself constructed. Such construction is a conjunctural process, dependent on a large number of contingencies. Indeed, all sorts of forces may be involved in forming and re-forming societies – war, powerful states, topographical factors, natural disasters, and more. Societies are not immutable: internal and external forces exert pressures, making the outermost societal boundaries and the internal structure of society subject to change. The important point is that societies are an outgrowth of human action, combined with the physical opportunities and limitations people find in their environment. Understanding society as an outermost structure, then, means accepting that such a structure is a human construction. The structure may change its character internally and it may change its boundaries in relation to other societies. Of course, such a view undermines states' claims that their political boundaries must come from the society's *natural boundaries*.

COMBINING THE NOTIONS OF MELANGE AND OUTERMOST STRUCTURE

We are still left with the question of how these contingent forces – from typhoons to tyrannies – interact with society so as to change its pattern of relations and, ultimately, its outermost structure. The answer lies in combining the two understandings of society discussed in this chapter: society as a melange of contending organizations, and society as an outermost structure. It is the numerous past and ongoing struggles in arenas of domination and opposition that have shaped the distinct structure of every society. The process of society formation involves the construction of forms of control and societal boundaries that emerge out of the struggles and accommodations in arenas of domination and opposition. It is within these arenas that the contingent forces have been absorbed, changing the balance of power within them as the scarcity or abundance of labour has changed, as some groups have benefited from new infusions of resources, and so on. The collapse of the Soviet Union and its effect on neighbouring societies, a Bengali tidal wave, the delinking of the French Franc from currencies in Africa, the absorption of fundamentalist Islam in southern Lebanon, changing birth rates in Mexico, the penetration of the world economy throughout the 'Third World', are all contingent conditions that have created winners and losers and thus changed the balance of forces in arenas. And changes in the balance within individual arenas have had ripple effects, changing societal boundaries and the outermost structure of society, even ultimately the identity of those in society (who is included in society and who is excluded).

Through its distinctive ideology and organization, the modern state has been at the core of destabilization of existing arenas during the nineteenth and twentieth centuries. Indeed, modern society has been marked by a common ideology among state leaders: to create a hegemonic presence - a single authoritative rule - in multiple arenas, even in the far corners of society. While such an image is an ideal, we can identify the emergence of transformative states in cases where political leaders have succeeded in widespread penetration of society, where most other social organizations have been subordinated to the authority of the central political organization. While such states, through constitutional arrangements, have often given way to other organizations, such as the family or the market, which may establish rules in certain spheres, the ultimate limits of the authority of these other organizations has frequently rested with the state. States have thus dissolved families that abuse children because those families have overstepped the authority that the state had delegated to them. Similarly, individual rights establish checks on the state, but states have maintained the prerogative to abrogate those rights, as in times of national emergency. The goal of leaders in transformative states has been to penetrate society deeply enough to shape how individuals throughout society identify themselves, and the purpose of the complex organization of the state has been to effect such far-reaching domination. Where states have been powerful, they have overridden people's multiple other identities – religious, ethnic, regional, tribal, etc. – creating a framework for domination under the umbrella of a broad societal (often, national) identity.

Even states falling far short of the ideal have made extraordinary demands upon those they have claimed as their subjects: to sequester their children in state institutions for 30 hours a week, to dispose of their bodily wastes in only prescribed ways, to treat their sick exclusively with state-licensed healers, to prove a proprietary relationship to land solely through state-issued deeds. Whatever their specific programmes, states have shaken up existing social relationships, renewing active struggles for domination in arena after arena. Eugen Weber's fine account of nineteenth century France, for example, depicts how the state moulded, indeed created, French society; the state was not the simple outgrowth of an already formed French society, but through its activist role entered arenas of domination and opposition from which it had previously been largely absent.[6]

What is as interesting as the role of the French state in changing society is the changes forced upon the state as it penetrated numerous arenas with particular distributions of social control. Indeed, both the French state and society came to be formed and reformed in an ongoing series of interactions, alliances, struggles, and accommodations. Just as much as the state is an actor in affecting the struggles in arenas and influencing the formation of society's outermost structure, it is also a prize (to be secured and itself moulded) for groups competing to define society. It is in this relationship of moulding and being moulded that we find the crux of state-society relations. As state officials and resources have entered into arenas, they have been the subjects of intense pressure and competition. Local actors have offered strong incentives to co-opt these state officials and resources, thereby changing the very nature of the state. In short, the state has often fallen far short of being a transformative state; true, it has been a force that shapes society, but it also has been a force shaped by society.

State and society boundaries have often been coincidental, but this does not necessarily have to be the case. Especially in cases where the state's capabilities have fallen quickly, where its ability to defend society's members has plummeted, people have constructed different societal boundaries – a new outermost structure – reflecting new or renewed identities. Where people have suspected the state's power, its ability to dominate has often dropped dramatically, as the bond between dominator and dominated has broken apart. In such cases, the societal (or national) identity imposed by the state has given way to other identities – religious, ethnic, tribal, etc. – which have appeared to offer more protection.

This relationship between falling state capabilities and new identities has been a particularly important notion in the era following the Cold War. A number of the props that fortified states – alignment with a superpower, foreign aid, military support – have been pulled out from under them, and we have witnessed a period of state retreat rather than continuing state penetration of society. Like penetration, retreat signals a change in the balance of forces in dispersed arenas in society, setting off intense struggles and conflicts. As much as any factor, the state's weakening ability to maintain its own territorial integrity, as in Yugoslavia, the Soviet Union, and Ethiopia, has shattered the outermost structure of society. State retreat has rippled inwards to numerous arenas of domination and opposition, sparking often violent confrontations as newly empowered social organizations have offered alternative primary social identities with different bases of inclusion and exclusion.

These arena struggles have not been totally self-contained. As mentioned earlier, key social forces have brought resources from one arena to another, allowing the outcomes of struggles in one area to affect those in other areas. It is these multiple, connected struggles and accommodations that have spawned the conditions for creating the overall pattern of domination in society and for maintaining that dominance - what social scientists call the reproduction of power within society. In some cases, where the contingent conditions have been right, the numerous struggles have moved a society towards *integrated domination*, in which the state as a whole (or possibly even another social force) has established broad power. In other instances, the conflicts and complicities in the multiple arenas have sometimes led to *dispersed domination*, where neither the state (nor any other social force) has managed to achieve broad domination and where parts of the state have been pulled in very different directions. By changing the contingent conditions in a number of areas, including the Balkans and Africa, the end of the Cold War has led to increasingly dispersed domination along with violent ethnic and tribal warfare. In these cases, the state may have remained as a shell (for example, in Angola during its prolonged civil war), or the state and society may have fragmented, as in Yugoslavia and the Soviet Union.

Where there has been a sense of permanence, even sacredness, about the state's boundaries, integrated domination has become more likely and society can become encased in seemingly stable outer limits. Such sacredness has derived from the sense on the part of citizens – the dominated – that it is proper for the state to make laws and rules demanding obedience. Under these circumstances citizens have created reinforcing societal institutions and myths – what we may call a civil society – to develop within those boundaries. Social and political struggles have then been over the control and content of those institutions and beliefs, not over their ultimate legitimacy and scope. But when the state has been in retreat, when territorial integrity has been in question, political and social struggles have shifted from struggles over control of legitimate institutions whose scope is widely accepted to those marked by broad disagreement on the limits of society and over which boundaries are truly sacred. In short, with the state's own borders in flux, the question of society's boundaries and character has had something of a life of its own. In the end, the outcome of arena struggles has determined the outermost structure of society.

CONCLUSIONS

Establishing a civic basis of association in society is a delicate enterprise. It entails some risk-taking by groups and individuals who must depend for their security on the forging of a public space and fair rules to govern interactions in that space, all with people that they mostly do not know personally. Uncertainty over who will be in the society and who not and over the scope of state boundaries undermines the stability necessary to undertake that fragile exercise. A civic basis for association depends, in the end, on firm outermost limits for society, ones coincidental with the political boundaries of the state, which is the ultimate guarantor of that critical public space.[7] It is the coincidence of societal and political boundaries that allows for the development of market relations, both the informal trust needed for basic interaction and the ultimate knowledge that a legal framework exists to uphold contracts. Similarly, it is under these circumstances that the foundation is laid for both civil and political rights. In the disintegration of the Ottoman, Austro-Hungarian, and Soviet empires, it was precisely this sort of uncertainty about the political boundaries that promoted national or ethnic conceptions of society, with their exclusive premises. Diverse contingent forces led to the downfall of these empires. In each case, however, these forces had powerful effects on local societies, as the balance of forces in arenas of domination and opposition changed quickly and dramatically. The struggles that ensued destroyed both the existing integrated domination of those societies and, ultimately, the outermost structure of the societies themselves.

From Poland to Cambodia, from Angola to Peru, questions are in the air about the conception of society, about what ties people in particular territories together. The changing dimensions of state territory, or at least questions about the permanence of territorial boundaries, highlights the struggles in arenas of domination and opposition. Immediate political contingencies, not least of which is the perceived permanence of political boundaries, help determine whether society formation will tend towards association based on 'the gross actualities of blood, race, language, locality, religion, or tradition...' or will be grounded in 'practical necessity, common interest, or incurred obligation...'[8] It is to the arenas of domination and opposition that we must turn our attention in order to understand (and possibly intervene against) the changing outermost structure of society and the potential for mass violence that it carries.

NOTES

1. By domination, I refer to the ability to gain obedience through the power of command. Weber used such a designation for domination in *Wirtschaft und Gesellschaft*. See Max Rheinstein, (ed.), *Weber on Law in Economy and Society* (Cambridge, MA: Harvard University Press, 1954), pp. 322-37. The motivation to obedience can be coercion or voluntary compliance that comes when one sees the rulemaker as the legitimate authority. (Weber speaks of the sources of domination in slightly different terms, seeing domination as a virtue of one's interests, the monopoly position of the dominator, or by virtue of authority, the power to command and the duty to obey; p. 324.) Domination, as used here, is thus more inclusive a term than just coercion or just legitimate authority.

2. Liah Greenfeld and Michel Martin, (eds), *Centre: Ideas and Institutions* (Chicago, IL: University of Chicago Press, 1988), p. viii.

3. See E.P. Thompson, 'Eighteenth-Century English Society: Class Struggle without Class?' *Social History*, 3, (May 1978), p. 150. Stedman Jones ends up taking a different position from Thompson but is even more adamant about the tenuous relationship between heuristic devices and what was found in history. 'One should not proceed upon the assumption that "class" as an elementary counter of official social description, "class" as an effect of theoretical discourse about distribution or production relations, "class" as the summary of a cluster of culturally signifying practices or "class" as a species of political or ideological self-definition, all share a single reference point in an anterior social reality.' Gareth Stedman Jones, *Languages of Class: Studies in English Working Class History, 1832-1982* (New York: Cambridge University Press, 1983), pp. 7-8. See also Thompson's *The Poverty of Theory and Other Essays* (New York: Monthly Review Press, 1978), p. 255.

4. Arenas of domination and opposition thus differ in some fundamental respects from Lowi's arenas of power. Such arenas of power, he writes, include 'events, issues, and leadership [which should] be studied within defined areas of govern-

mental activity. These areas are, in effect, the functions of government defined more broadly than a single agency, more narrowly than government with a single political process.' Theodore J. Lowi, *At the Pleasure of the Mayor: Patronage and Power in New York City, 1898-1958* (New York: Free Press, 1964), p. 139. In contrast, arenas of domination and opposition are not functions of government (although they may include government actors), nor are they limited to governmental activity.

5. Joel S. Migdal, 'The State in Society: An Approach to Struggles for Domination' in Migdal, Atul Kohli, and Vivienne Shue, *State Power and Social Forces: Domination and Transformation in the Third World* (New York: Cambridge University Press, 1994).

6. Eugen Weber, *Peasants into Frenchmen: The Modernization of Rural France 1870-1914* (Stanford, CA: Stanford University Press, 1976).

7. For a related but more restricted view, see David L. Blaney and Mustapha Kamal Pasha, 'Civil Society and Democracy in the Third World: Ambiguities and Historical Possibilities', *Studies in Comparative International Development*, 28 (spring 1993), pp. 3-24.

8. C. Geertz (ed.), 'The Integrative Revolution', in *Old Societies and New States: Modernity in Africa and Asia* (New York: Free Press, 1963), pp. 108-9.

Part III

ETHNICITY AND NATIONALISM

5

Ethnicity and Nationalism

Kingsley M. de Silva

INTRODUCTION

The deep concern in Europe today about the nature and consequences of the link between ethnicity[1] and nationalism[2] stems from the revolutionary events of the late 1980s, the present turbulent state of affairs in parts of Central and Eastern Europe and the Balkans, and the contemporary ethnic resurgence within Europe, sustained by the ideology of nationalism, which seeks the creation, by any means necessary, of political entities which emphasize ethnic interest. North-western Europe, grown a trifle too self-confident and complacent as a result of the unprecedented prosperity and political stability of the last four decades, is seeking to come to terms with the outbreak of ethnic violence in the Balkans and the states of the former Soviet Union. In doing so, two interconnected questions are asked. What makes the combination of nationalism and ethnicity so dangerous to the stability of the state system that has emerged from the collapse of Soviet domination imposed on Central and Eastern Europe and the Balkans by the victors of the Second World War through the Yalta settlement? Could this combination of ethnicity and nationalism help resolve conflicts rather than make them more complex, help maintain stability rather than subvert the political structures that the successor states of collapsed empires have inherited?

The term nationalism, of course, has been around much longer than ethnicity, but both – and in particular ethnicity – have eluded the efforts of generations of scholars to give them any great precision in definition. The present upsurge of political violence in some of the states of the former Soviet bloc, and in the successor states of the former Soviet Union, has given greater currency to the two terms, especially to ethnicity, in the descriptions and analyses pouring forth from journalists in the print and electronic media, and of course from politicians. The common assumption in many of these cases is that the two terms, ethnicity and nationalism, are closely intertwined, indeed that they are interchangeable.

109

ETHNICITY

Over 60 years ago, Pareto pointed out that the term ethnicity 'is one of the vaguest known to sociology'.[3] The efforts of scholars since then to capture its meaning in a short and precise definition have not yielded any great success, and we are no nearer a standard definition of ethnicity today than in Pareto's time. This is not to deny the merits of the substantial contribution by anthropologists, beginning with Edmund Leach[4] in the early 1950s and Frederik Barth[5] a little over ten years later, and of others, in clearing away some of the confusion in the use of the term. In defining the term ethnicity, Leach and Barth adopted two distinctive approaches, with Leach emphasizing what anthropologists have called structural relationships and along with it identity formation, a more subjective process. Barth's important contribution lay in his emphasis on 'boundary-maintenance' as a critically important factor in ethnicity, something dependent on structural differences of groups. In Barth's view structural relationships are more important in defining ethnicity than cultural factors, as well as in the processes of state formation and the emergence of ethnic identity. Counter to this were the views associated with Edward Shils,[6] and Clifford Geertz,[7] which became especially influential in the late 1950s and early 1960s: the primordialist approach, as it was called. This emphasized the importance of culturally distinctive characteristics such as myths of origin, ritual, religion or genealogical descent in distinguishing groups and peoples from one another. The primordialists stopped short of placing these characteristics within a historical context although that seemed the logical outcome of their arguments.

The contraposition, real and apparent, between these two viewpoints was a central theme in the debate among anthropologists and others on the term of ethnicity in the 1970s, a debate which continues to the present day. In the early 1980s another anthropologist, Charles Keyes, in an effort to reconcile these two viewpoints, began to emphasize the significance of culture as the 'primary defining characteristic' of an ethnic group, and went on to argue that 'ethnicity' is only salient to the extent that it helps people to determine their own distinctiveness from others who are seen to have ethnic identities of their own.[8]

The circular reasoning one sees in Keyes's efforts at straddling the contrasting views of men like Barth on the one hand and the primordialists on the other, also characterizes the efforts of others. One case in point is the US political scientist Cynthia Enloe who, in an effort to provide a coherent definition of ethnicity, began with the contention that its 'basic function is to bind the individual to a group'.[9] She then proceeded to argue that an ethnic group becomes one 'because [it] successfully present[s] [itself] as one', and that such a group 'must have reality in the minds of the members and not just in the eye of the beholder'. Eventually her definition of ethnicity comes close to the primordialist position in emphasizing 'an awareness of a common identity' as its principal feature.

An 'awareness of a common identity' brings us to three other elements essential to an understanding of ethnicity. The first of these is the vital importance of the past – an awareness of the history of a country or a people – in understanding the complexities of the present, whether in the Balkans and Central and Eastern Europe, or the Baltic states, or in South and South-East Asia, in all of which discussion or analyses of ethnic tensions are often framed in terms of historical legacies in which language, culture and religion are the essential points of distinctive identity. Ethnic identities often carry with them memories of historical enmities with very deep roots. Tensions and hostilities arise from attempts at a redress of historical griev-ances, sometimes going back several centuries into the past. Secondly, there is the 'politicization of ethnicity', a process 'that preserves ethnic groups by emphasizing their singularity [and yet] also [facilitates] their modernization by transforming them into political conflict groups for the modern political arena'.[10] And thirdly, there is the elasticity of the term ethnicity and the wide variety of potential ethnic groups: Barth, for instance, would include 'com-munity', 'culture', language group, corporation, association or population group. One could sum up by arguing that for most such groups the core of their identity would be the cultural traits that set them apart from others.[11]

Paul Brass, another US political scientist, uses the term 'community' to refer 'to ethnic groups whose members have developed an awareness of a common identity and have attempted to define the boundaries of the group'. The critically important issue is with regard to the transformation or transi-tion of a community into a nationality or a nation. This happens, Brass argues, when a community 'mobilizes for political action and becomes politically significant ... makes political demands and achieves a significant measure of success by it own efforts'.[12]

There are two distinct processes at work: national liberation in a colonial setting, and separatism in post-imperial and post-colonial situations, the transition from consciousness of a separate ethnic identity within a nation to the creation or emergence of another in which a nationality insists on the congruence between the political and national unit.[13] This transition to national independence is generally resisted by the empire in which the ethnic group is located, just as when separatism is sought, the state resorts to violence to prevent the separation from taking place. That violence stems from the fact – as Lord Acton pointed out earlier in this century – that while 'a state in course of time produces a nationality ... that a nationality should constitute a state is contrary to the nature of modern civilization'.[14] While a great many political commentators of the present day would be inclined to disagree with this contention, Acton's epigram contains an element of truth. Acton would have heartily endorsed the views expressed by Walker Connor in the well-known article 'Nation-Building or Nation-Destroying?',[15] not so much the contention that 'ethnic identity constitutes the only "true nationalism"' but the conclusion that Connor reached, namely that since the process of building state loyalties often involves overcoming ethnic identities, the proper term for the development of state loyalties is nation-destroying rather than nation-building.

Part of the problem of capturing the essence of ethnicity lies in its complexity. There is no pure form of ethnicity. Some identities have amazingly withstood the passage of time and form part of the consciousness of people, whether they are rooted in language and culture, or linked to religion. However, despite the durability of ethnic identity, it is not immutable but as liable to change as most other social phenomena. Indeed one is all too aware that identities are changeable and have changed through the centuries. Change could come from the operation of a number of factors: emigration or changes in political boundaries; subjugation by conquest; or assimilation, either voluntary or involuntary. Nevertheless, one is struck by the adaptability of ethnic identity to changing circumstances and its remarkable powers of survival.

In a world racked by ethnic conflict as it is today, many conflicts are presumed to have an ethnic component even when ethnicity is not the root cause, as, for example, in the violent onslaught on the Peruvian political system by the *Sendero Lumuniso* (Shining Path). Historically, conflicts in the Balkans, no less than in South and South-East Asia, have often been ethnically based, but they are also struggles for power, territory, security, scarce resources, prestige, and other issues – the age old causes of conflict – not necessarily rooted in ethnic differences. Quite often, as the case of Bosnia-Herzegovina shows, the sources of conflict are too intertwined to separate. Here we come up against two important issues: how national governments perceive and respond to conflicts between groups within their borders; and how ethnicity may be created, reinforced, and exploited by both sides as a political mechanism.

The current situation in the Horn of Africa also serves to illustrate the point that ethnicity is not the only factor in deep-rooted conflict. The separation of Eritrea from Ethiopia, at least for the moment, came after several years of violent conflict in which ethnic identity was a significant but never a dominant factor. It is estimated that Ethiopia has no less than eighty 'ethnic groups' and Eritrea has at least nine, yet the present line of political demarcation between the two countries is not congruent with any ethnic divide. On the other hand, Somalia, which is ethnically homogeneous, is in the throes of self-destructive violence which has reduced it to a failed state. Indeed the Somalian situation raises questions about the salience given by scholars to the ethnic factor as a cause of contemporary conflict. Nevertheless, it is entirely possible that distinct ethnic identities could emerge among Somalia's rival clans as a result of this conflict some time in the future. The Somali situation apart, ethnicity is often manipulated to serve purely political ends in separatist agitation. The danger is that every ethnic group determined to secede and convert itself into a majority, has within its new territory another minority that seeks to escape from the new majority. In a political sense, self-determination on the basis of ethnic identities securing majority status by changing sovereign boundaries, is a more limited right. Generally, self-determination that is limited to regional or local autonomy based on cultural distinctions, freedom of religion, language and association gains greater acceptance, although that acceptance is also often rather reluctant and conceded only after much agitation and resort to violence by both sides in the encounter. State-building or state-maintenance in a post-colonial context becomes a self-defeating exercise unless ethnic identity ceases to be the only true nationalism.

NATIONALISM

Apart from its political impact on the state system of Europe, the current recrudescence of ethnic tensions and the outbreaks of violence associated with them have revived interest in the search for an understanding of nationalism as a political phenomenon. The fact that the term nationalism has been around so much longer than ethnicity only makes the problems of definition more complex.[16] Scholars seek to distinguish nationalism from ethno-centralism; and to deny that mere evidence of the experiences of national consciousness is proof of the existence of nationalism in the form in which Western scholars understand the term. The recent outpouring of books, monographs, scholarly articles and journals on ethnicity and ethnic or group tensions is symptomatic of the world-wide concern over the destabilizing effects of the current upsurge of nationalism linked with politicized ethnicity. Until now, most of the writing has been done by Western scholars using Western – that is, European – models and Western experience to explain it.

Three trends are discernible in these recent writings. First of all, these is a tendency to wish that this will all go away, and to believe and argue that it will. Thus we have Eric Hobsbawm claiming in his recent study of *Nations and Nationalism since 1780* that

> anyone likely to write the world history of the late twentieth and early twenty-first centuries will see 'nation-states' and 'nations' or eth-nic/linguistic groups primarily as retreating before, resisting, adapting to, being absorbed or dislocated by, the new supranational restructuring of the globe ...
> It is not impossible that nationalism will decline with the decline of the nation-state ... It would be absurd to claim that his day is already near. However, I hope it can at least be envisaged. After all, the very fact that historians are at least beginning to make some progress in the study and analysis of nations and nationalism suggests that, as so often, the phenomenon is past its peak. The owl of Minerva which brings wisdom, said Hegel, flies out at dusk. It is a good sign that it is now circling round nations and nationalism.[17]

The second tendency is confined to responses to the violence in the Balkans and Eastern Europe, and here one sees a disdainful effort to suggest that it was all happening in a part of the world that is only geographically part of Europe, not historically so. A good example is a book entitled *The Wrath of Nations* by William Pfaff[18], a staff writer on the *New Yorker*, and an ardent Europhile. He begins the fourth chapter of his book thus:

> The past lies in strata of human experience, never totally forgotten even when deeply buried in a society's consciousness, but too often, in East Europe, still raw at the surface. 'We have been waiting for this moment for eight centuries', the defence minister of newly independent Croatia said in August 1991, as his country's struggle began. These strata are layers of sophistication, accumulated experience – even of thought. There is an important division between those societies which have been through the modern experience – which means Reformation, Renais-sance, Enlightenment, and Revolution – and those which have not. The division largely coincides with a religious split – between the Europe of Catholicism and Protestantism, progenitors of the modern West, and the Europe of Orthodox Christianity and Islam.

Pfaff cites in his support Krzysztof Pomian, an analyst at the French Na-tional Scientific Research Centre, who views this line of religious division as more like a zone. Pomian, quoted by Pfaff, goes on to say:

This line thus goes from the White Sea to the Adriatic and corresponds with the line between Latin and Greek Christianity. It is also a line of historical division. Between the twelfth and fourteenth centuries the territory north of the Dniester was controlled by the Mongols and the Golden Horde. Later, little by little, it fell into Russia's holding at the time of Russia's furthest advance in the west, after the Polish partitions. In the south, the Balkans were dominated by the Ottomans from the fourteenth century to the end of the nineteenth. During these long centuries these two regions which made up Eastern Europe were literally cut out of European history.

The third trend is exemplified by Paul Brass's recent publication entitled *Ethnicity and Nationalism* – a collection of essays on Indian politics but with the addition of some material seeking to compare the Indian situation with recent developments in Central and Eastern Europe – which revives the old debate between the so-called situationalists and the scholars of the primordialist persuasion. Brass places himself, quite emphatically, against those

> who consider ethnicity and nationalism to be reflections of primordial identities and who have searched the past to find evidence of the existence of ethnic identities and nationalism throughout recorded history. My position, on the contrary, is that ethnic identity and modern nationalism arise out of specific types of interactions between the leaderships of centralizing states and elites from non-dominant ethnic groups, especially but not exclusively from the peripheries of those states.[19]

In so doing, Brass challenges the views of scholars like Anthony D. Smith and John A. Armstrong[20] who emphasize the importance of the historical background, the local memories and ways of thinking as no less important than religious and cultural traditions and political inheritance as factors in the emergence of nationalism. This brings us to the fourth distinguishing feature in contemporary studies of nationalism, the fresh emphasis being given to an examination of the historical roots of the national question in a country or region. This is seen in the increasing scholarly output on the historical origins of nationalism in Western and Central Europe, no less than in the Baltic region and the Balkans, in the attempt to understand its complexities and strength.[21]

Finally, the fifth point, despite the new awareness of the historical factor in nationalism and the development of ethnic identities, there is still the tendency to treat, and indeed to assume that nationalism is an essentially modern phenomenon, that Europe itself is the single source of modern nationalism, that no other form exists, and that if it does, it is not quite genuine, not quite legitimate. Opposition to colonial intrusion, even fierce and prolonged opposition in the nineteenth century or earlier, is relegated to the category of 'resistance movements' even where that resistance stimulates political sentiments that are distinctly nationalist. Terence Ranger, who popularized this concept in the late 1960s and early 1970s, evolved a hierarchy of such movements, with primary resistance movements yielding place to secondary resistance movements and finally, in the twentieth century, to modern nationalist agitation.[22] He was basing his not very complicated and rather beguiling concept on the African experience, and it was influential enough to have others seeking to extend the same concept to India[23] and Sri Lanka.[24]

Anyone studying the long and complex history of South Asia is often confronted with the reality of events and movements which have a remarkable similarity to twentieth-century assertions of regional or even national identity: an emphasis on religion and language as essential points of distinction in societies, and assertions of separation from others drawn in terms of language, religion and region, if not 'nation' – in short, the roots of nationalism going back to pre-colonial times, several centuries into the past. Western theoreticians of nationalism, however, have generally ignored these. Efforts to deny their relevance to the understanding of the current crises in our societies have not entirely ceased, but they are now less than wholehearted, because the ideological certainties of Marxism and Liberalism are giving way in the face of the revival of ethnic identities in Europe, itself looking back to more violent periods of Europe's past. In the Baltic states and Central and Eastern Europe, current events have served to demonstrate that a people's past deeply influences the way they adapt to current issues, for that past is never totally forgotten.

It is consequently no longer possible to dismiss the current hostilities of Sinhalese and Tamils in Sri Lanka, of Hindus and Muslims in India as essentially modern developments to which elite groups give a historical colouring, for the fact is that historic differences are somehow being transmitted through the generations. This happens today, but more significantly it also happened in the past, long before the emergence of print capitalism and mass education. Political scientists, anthropologists and sociologists alike have no clear idea as to how this transmission was and is made, and sustained. But the fact that it happens in most South Asian societies, and no doubt in other areas as well, especially in Central and Eastern Europe, is left to historians to record, if not to explain.

This brings us to the issue of history and imagination and the influence of Anderson's book *Imagined Communities*[25] on the world-wide debate about the links between ethnicity and nationalism. This book has now gone into an enlarged version (in 1991), a response, no doubt, to contemporary events in the European continent. There is a kernel of truth in Anderson's contentions. Nowhere is this seen more clearly than in the efforts of nationalists, politicians and publicists alike to look at a country's past and choose from it those elements which support their case, especially in the search for evidence for claims to territory, or the long record of the machination of the traditional enemies. Anderson has his critics both within and without his own ideological tradition. The latter would argue that in treating nationalist claims as essentially spurious, merely a matter of clever invention and something deliberately concocted, his book becomes no more than a companion volume to Ranger's and Hobsbawm's *The Invention of Tradition*.[26]

One critic from within that tradition is the Indian scholar Partha Chatterjee,[27] whose riposte to Anderson used the provocative title 'Whose Imagined Community?'[28] Chatterjee's principal criticism of Anderson is that he compels 'nationalists in the rest of the world ... to choose their imagined community from certain "modular" forms already made available to them by Europe and the Americas'. If that is the case, Chatterjee protests, 'what do they have left to imagine?':

> I object to this argument, not for any sentimental reason. I object because I cannot reconcile it with the evidence on anti-colonial nationalism. The most powerful as well as the most creative results of the nationalist imagination in Asia and Africa are posited not on an identity, but rather on a *difference*, with the 'modular' forms of the national society propagated by the modern West.

This is a powerful argument with which I sympathize, especially in its emphasis on the *differences* between the processes of historical evolution in Asia and Europe. Nevertheless, like most South Asian scholars of the Marxist tradition, Chatterjee has not given sufficient attention to identifying these differences or engaging in a quest for evidence from the past of the roots of nationalism, free of the ideological framework to which they themselves adhere.

In their search for such differences, historians, like political scientists and anthropologists, face an uncomfortable fact. For many nationalists, politicians and scholars, history is no more than a distorting mirror, yet perhaps the metaphor of a distorting mirror is intrinsically unsatisfactory in this regard. The failure is at a different level. The historical imagination of the nationalist is often focused on the *distant* past so that flaws, distortions and inventions have all been more realistically creative than in the examination of the more recent past. In South and South-East Asia this would be especially true of the failure to understand the nature of the state structure that successors of the *raj* and the British colonial governments inherited. The legatees of the *raj* have generally assumed that their inheritance, obtained at the partition through struggle and unparalleled bloodshed, is no more than a contemporary version of a similar structure or structures in India's ancient past. Here we see the failure of historical imagination, the easy assumption that something akin to the British *raj*, in scale and extent of territory controlled, had existed in the past. For firm evidence of this distortion of the historical imagination, one needs only to turn to Nehru's own well-known study, written while in jail in the early 1940s, *The Discovery of India*.

Similar processes of adjusting memories of the past to fit the needs of the present are at work in Central and Eastern Europe and the Balkans today, where we see the same identification of nation with linguistic and cultural or religious affiliations. In many instances historical tradition overrides present demographic realities, for example in Serbian insistence that Kosovo is essential to the maintenance of a Serbian identity in the Balkans, despite being almost entirely Muslim Albanian in population. There is also the case of Transylvania in Romania, where the population is largely Hungarian, but the region is regarded as essential to the Romanian national identity. These are only two of many such cases in Central and Eastern Europe's post-colonial situation. There are, for instance, the problems of the Transcaucasus, especially the situation in the disputed region of Nagorno Karabakh, a predominantly Armenian enclave within the former Soviet republic of Azerbaijan. The roots of the conflict there go back several centuries to the hostilities between Christian Armenia and the Muslim communities in the surrounding region, and these animosities were aggravated by Stalin's deliberately divisive nationalities policy. With the collapse of the Soviet Union this has become once more an area of violent conflict.

THE CRUMBLING OF EMPIRES

The current reality in South and South-East Asia, as in Central and Eastern Europe, is that language, culture, religion and ethnicity stemming from pre-colonial times and acting separately or in combination, have assumed the proportions of explosive forces threatening the stability of the post-independence political settlement. The separatist threat in South and South-East Asia, dangerous though it may be in some parts of the regions, is not as ominously menacing to peace as that in the Balkans and Central and Eastern Europe. While there are substantial differences between the two regions as they emerge from the dissolution of imperial rule in the case of South and South-East Asia,[29] and the collapse of empire in Central and Eastern Europe and the Balkans,[30] the tensions in both stem generally from four factors, either acting on their own or in combination with each other to stimulate separatist agitation. These are: religion; language; the redress of historic grievances; and the question of territorial boundaries, both external and internal. The tensions are seen in their most acute form in the separatist agitation that is now endemic in the Caucasus and in some of the successor states of the former Soviet Union with large Russian minorities, whose insecurity is aggravated by feelings of relative deprivation.

One key to understanding the strength of separatist forces is to identity the stages by which empires were constructed, and to examine the nature of the administrative and other mechanisms of control devised to absorb the new territories thus acquired within the wider colonial political structure. Many of those stages are identifiable as political fault-lines whether in Russia, some of the successor states of the former Soviet Union, or for that matter in India. Here we come up against the fact that much more attention has been focused on the overseas expansion of European powers – primarily but not entirely British – than on the creation of the Tsarist empire and its expansion and consolidation under Stalin. The latter is in many ways an academic *terra incognita*, although it was a larger empire in terms of territory than Britain's and had a longer history. The British empire in India was unique in controlling the whole Indian subcontinent. But in welding it together and consolidating it, the empire builders of the *raj* incorporated within it peoples and territories which Indian rulers of the past had seldom been able to control. The north-east and north-west frontier territories of the *raj*, acquired through the conquest of Burma and the subjugation of the Sikhs, are examples of these, and from them spring some of India's most troublesome separatist movements.

In Central and Eastern Europe the problem is much the same. History has triumphed over ideology, and ethnic identities with long and turbulent pasts have reasserted themselves with a vigour that has baffled the ideologues. It is the recrudescence of unresolved European ethnic rivalries of the past – and here we speak of centuries not decades – which have reasserted themselves with a passion reminiscent of the conflicts that dominated their past. We are confronted here with the collapse of the last of the European colonial systems – the Russian/Soviet empire – the final stage in a process of dissolution of empires which began in general in the aftermath of the First World War; and along with it – and giving it greater significance – the collapse of an ideological framework which minimized the role and function of ethnicity. Somehow Liberal, Marxist and social democratic thinking absorbed the dissolution of the British empire in South and South-East Asia, the US empire in the Philippines, and the collapse of the French and Dutch empires as though it was merely a logical sequence of events inherent in the triumph of anti-colonial nationalism. They failed to see, or refused to see, the salience and durability of ethnicity emphasized through language and culture or religion in this triumph of nationalism. Liberals, social democrats and Marxists alike believed until very recently that ethnicity was a residual inheritance from a country's past that would surely disappear as society modernized, whether through peaceful social or economic change or through the processes of revolutionary upheaval and purposeful ideological reconstruction. The persistence of ethnicity in the face of all efforts to undermine, obliterate or simply ignore it – as in Central and Eastern Europe – has shaken earlier certainties regarding its inevitable obsolescence. Post-revolutionary societies, especially in Central and Eastern Europe, in whose dominant Marxist ideology ethnicity was contemptuously dismissed as an evanescent irrelevance, proved to be as vulnerable to the pressures of ethnic solidarities as other societies.

The legitimacy of the political system imposed by the victors of the Second World War on the states of Central and Eastern Europe as part of the post-war political settlement, which recognized and consolidated the dominance of the Soviet Union as regional superpower, was eventually undermined by the failure of the introduced social and economic changes to yield the benefits they were designed to do. As it was, acute economic stagnation and industrial obsolescence made the patently unequal political relations between the metropolitan power and the states over which it established domination, and the structure of relationships between the state and the people in each of these 'nations', more unpalatable than they may have been if there was at least the compensation of economic buoyancy or prosperity.

The common factor in both post-colonial South and South-East Asia and the post-colonial states of the former Soviet bloc and component states of the former Yugoslavia is that with the end of colonialism ethnicity has become a major, if not the principal, source of internal tensions and conflicts through the rivalries of different ethnic groups living within the boundaries. In both cases these tensions have been carried over from the movement of peoples, either willingly or by force of arms, through the centuries: they have been left behind, in one case, as the empires of the Hapsburgs, the Hohenzollerns, the Ottomans, and the Romanovs (which Stalin and his successors expanded) collapsed; and in the other as the Islamic and British empires expanded and contracted.

The present reality is that all these post-colonial states, European no less than the Asian, face agitation by minority groups, the more vocal and powerful of whom are seeking the creation of new states in which the minority could convert itself into a majority. None of these states face as strong a challenge from ethnic minorities as the former Soviet Union.

The principal features of the historical evolution of South Asia since independence illustrate some of the consequences that flowed from the end of empire there and have relevance to the situation in Central and Eastern Europe. The first, of course, was that the critical event, the British decision to dismantle the *raj*, was a confession that it was no longer possible to resist the nationalist upsurge directed by the Indian National Congress. There is an amazing parallel here in the recent collapse of Russian domination in Central and Eastern Europe and in the former Soviet Union itself. But soon – and this is the second of the consequences – the partition of the *raj* demonstrated the subversive effects of ethnicity, linked to religion, in becoming a major source of internal tensions and conflicts in societies striving to free themselves from the bonds of colonial rule. Third, the partition of the *raj* was expected to have settled at least some of these problems, since the largest segment of the Muslim minorities was brought within the boundaries of a new state through one of the most terrible cataclysms of modern times. But within twenty-five years another set of South Asian events demonstrated the destructiveness of another form of ethnic identification, a link between ethnicity and language. When the state of Pakistan was divided once more and Bangladesh emerged, it marked the superior strength of language and culture as points of identity in a state – the original Pakistan – that was constructed on the basis that religion was the principal bond of its people's identity.

When conflicts based on language issues appear in the states emerging from the collapse of the old Soviet bloc, such as in the Baltic states and Kazakhstan for example, it is possible to turn to South Asia for recent examples of the destructiveness of nationalism and ethnic identities based on language. But nineteenth and twentieth century Europe, and Central and Eastern Europe in particular, was the original home of linguistic nationalism. More than forty years ago, Sir Lewis Namier spoke of the explosive impact of linguistic nationalism on mid-nineteenth century Central and Eastern Europe:

> The demand that the state should be co-extensive with linguistic nationality was an internationally revolutionary postulate which, seeing that nations are seldom linguistically segregated, proved destructive both of constitutional growth and of international peace.[31]

A century later the same phenomenon had a near-revolutionary impact on the politics of post-colonial South Asia. It compelled a sceptical Nehru to yield to pressures which redrew the internal boundaries of India on the basis of linguistic states; it led to the separation of Bangladesh from Pakistan; and in Sri Lanka it helped destroy civil peace for a decade or more. Sinhalese politicians who sought power through championing linguistic nationalism soon confronted the rival linguistic nationalism of the Tamils, with all its attendant risks.

The political establishments of the British empire's successor states are often embroiled in protracted conflicts with ethnic and religious minorities which seek to resist the expanding powers and demands of the state. South Asia provides a large number of examples of such conflicts: the Punjab; Jammu Kashmir and Assam in India; the problems of the Sind and of Baluchistan in Pakistan; and, not least among them in their destructive impact on a post-colonial polity, the current problems of Sri Lanka. In almost all of these post-colonial societies of South and South-East Asia, newly emerging from colonialism, ethnicity is a major, if not the principal, source of internal tensions and conflicts through the rivalries of different ethnic groups living within the boundaries of the new states. The minority ethnic resistance more often than not takes the form of separatist movements seeking the creation of new states in which the minority could convert itself into a majority.[32]

CONCLUSIONS

The combination of ethnicity and nationalism reviewed here has two facets. In its more constructive form as the instrument of national integration it gives greater depth to human civilization and culture. As the two anti-colonial revolutions of the post-Second World War period have shown – one in South and South-East Asia and the other in the former Soviet Union and former Yugoslavia – it assumes the proportions of an irresistible force in liberating captive nations. On the other hand, it is the principal cause of internal disharmony and discord in the post-colonial worlds of South and South-East Asia and in the successor states of the former Soviet Union and Yugoslavia alike. It is also the most powerful source of irrational behaviour in politics and rigidly uncompromising attitudes, whenever the issue of redress of historic grievances comes up.

In most of these societies the past is a powerful presence and often carries with it painful memories of losses suffered and of territories lost. Ethnic consciousness in combination with nationalism raises expectations of attempts to preserve or restore the past, to preserve the past and to transform it into something new, to create a new society upon ancient foundations. Attempts to restore the past often involve efforts at securing a redress of ancient grievances to the point where the past is an incubus which dominates the present, and carries with it the danger of destroying the future. In the Balkans and Central and Eastern Europe, as in parts of South Asia, what happened several centuries ago has an immediate significance that distorts political thinking and makes governance all that much more difficult. Indeed, some of the grievances that activist groups seek to redress go back 400 to 500 years, as in the case of the demolition of the Babri Masjid in India, or in that potential flashpoint in the incipient conflict between Serbia and Albania, the historical memories associated with the state of Kosovo.

The politicization of ethnicity has a historical dimension and looking for the roots of a problem is not a mere academic exercise, nor does it only strengthen the hands of recalcitrant activist groups and unscrupulous politicians anxious to exploit an issue for their own political ends. In that search lies the beginning of a process of understanding about why the encounter between ethnicity and nationalism is as likely to erupt in violence as it is to stabilize a political situation disturbed by people's efforts, nationalities and nations – to seek a congruence between ethnicity and national identity.

NOTES

1. W.W. Isajiw, 'Definitions of Ethnicity', *Ethnicity*, I (July 1974), pp. 111-24.
2. See Isiah Berlin's reflections on the neglect of nationalism by scholars in the essay 'The Bent Twig: On the Rise of Nationalism', *The Crooked Timber of Humanity* (New York: Vintage Books, 1992).
3. V. Pareto, *The Mind and Society: A Treatise on General Sociology* (New York: Harcourt Brace, New Edition 1963), p. 1837.
4. Edmund Leach, *Political Systems of Highland Burma*, (Cambridge: Cambridge University Press, 1954), p. 15.
5. Frederik Barth, 'Introduction', *Ethnic Groups and Boundaries* (Boston, MA: Little Brown, 1969), pp. 9-38.
6. Edward Shils, 'Primordial, Personal, Social and Civil Ties', *British Journal of Sociology*, 7, 1957, pp. 113-45.
7. C. Geertz, 'The Integrative Revolution: Primordial Sentiments and Civil Policies in the New States', *Old Societies and New States* (New York: Free Press, 1963), pp. 105-57.
8. Charles Keyes, 'Towards a New Formulation of the Concept of Ethnic Group', *Ethnicity*, 3, 1976, pp. 202-13; and 'The Dialectic of Ethnic Change', in C.

Keyes (ed.), *Ethnic Change*, (Seattle, WA: University of Washington Press, 1981), pp. 3-30.

9. Cynthia Enloe, *Ethnic Conflict and Political Development*, (Boston, MA: Little Brown, 1973), p. 187.

10. Joseph Rothschild, *Ethnopolitics: A Conceptual Framework*, (New York: Columbia University Press, 1981), p. 3.

11. T.R. Gurr, *Minorities at Risk: A Global View of Ethnopolitical Conflict* (Washington, DC: US Institute of Peace, 1993).

12. Paul Brass, *Language, Religion and Politics in North India*, (Cambridge: Cambridge University Press, 1974), p. 8.

13. Ernest Gellner, *Nations and Nationalism*, (Oxford: Basil Blackwell, 1983), is an example of books that make this point.

14. Lord Acton, *Essays on Freedom and Power* (New York: Meridien Books, 1957), p. 162.

15. Walker Connor, 'Nation-Building or Nation-Destroying?', *World Politics*, XXIV(3), 1972, pp. 319-55.

16. See particularly, Anthony D. Smith, *Theories of Nationalism* (London: Duckworth, 1983); John Breuilly, *Nationalism and the State* (Manchester: University of Manchester Press, 1982); and older works such as Elie Kedourie, *Nationalism* (London: Hutchinson, 1960); Hans Kohn, *The Idea of Nationalism* (New York: MacMillan, 1945); and Carlton Hayes (1931), *The Historical Evolution of Modern Nationalism* (New York: R.R. Smith, 1931).

17. E.J. Hobsbawm, *Nations and Nationalism Since 1780* (Cambridge: Cambridge University Press, 1990), pp. 182-3.

18. W. Pfaff, *The Wrath of Nations: Civilization and the Furies of Nationalism* (New York: Simon & Schuster, 1993).

19. Paul R. Brass, *Ethnicity and Nationalism: Theory and Comparison* (New Delhi: Sage, 1991), pp. 8-9.

20. Paul Brass's reference was to Anthony D. Smith, *The Ethnic Origins of Nations* (Oxford: Basil Blackwell, 1986); and John A. Armstrong, *Nations before Nationalism* (Chapel Hill, NC: University of North Carolina Press, 1982).

21. For a recent study see Mikulas Teich and Roy Porter (eds), *The National Question in Europe in Historical Context* (Cambridge: Cambridge University Press, 1993).

22. T.O. Ranger, 'Connections Between "Primary Resistance" Movements and Modern Mass Nationalism in East and Central Africa', Part I, *The Journal of African History*, IX, 3, 1968, pp. 437-53; Part II, IX, 4, 1968, pp. 631-41.

23. See Eric Stokes, 'Traditional Resistance Movements and Afro-Asian Nationalism: The Context of the 1857 Mutiny Rebellion', *The Peasant and the Raj* (Cambridge: Cambridge University Press, 1978), pp. 120-39.

24. K.M. de Silva, 'Nineteenth-Century Origins of Nationalism in Ceylon', in K.M. de Silva (ed.), *History of Ceylon*, Vol III (Colombo/Kandy: University of Ceylon Press, 1973), pp. 249-61.

25. B. Anderson, *Imagined Communities* (London: Verso, 1983).

26. T. Ranger and E. Hobsbawm, *The Invention of Tradition* (Cambridge: Cambridge University Press, 1983).

27. Partha Chatterjee, *Nationalist Thought and the Colonial World* (Minneapolis, MN: University of Minnesota Press, 1993).

28. Partha Chatterjee, 'Whose Imagined Community?', *Millennium: Journal of International Studies*, vol. 20, (2), 1991, pp. 521-5.

29. On South-East Asia see Lim Joo-Jock and Vani S, *Armed Separatism in South-East Asia* (Singapore: Institute of South East Asian Studies, 1984); and Chandran Jeshuran, *Governments and Rebellions in South-East Asia* (Singapore: Institute of South East Asian Studies, 1985).

30. I. Banac, *The National Question in Yugoslavia: Origin, History and Politics* (Ithaca, NY: Cornell University Press, 1984); J. Bugajski, *Nations in Turmoil: Conflict and Cooperation in Eastern Europe* (Boulder, CO: Westview, 1982).

31. L. Namier, 'Nationality and Liberty', *Vanished Supremacies* (London: Peregrine, 1962), pp. 46-7.

32. See, for instance, Ruth McVey, 'Separatism and Paradoxes of the Nation-State in Perspective', in Lim Joo-Jock and Vani S, *Armed Separatism in South-East Asia*, pp. 3-29. See also, R. Premdas *et al.* (eds), *Secessionist Movements in Comparative Perspective* (London: Pinter, 1990).

6

Ethnic Conflicts Versus Development in Africa: Causes and Remedies

Omari H. Kokole

INTRODUCTION

Most countries across the globe are ethnically pluralistic societies. While ethnic diversity by itself need not generate ethnic conflict, it is evident that ethnicity can be exploited and manipulated enough to generate social conflict, especially in the developing world. Indeed, ethnic conflict is definitely a major hindrance to national stability and cohesion, and to the quest for socio-economic development, in many Asian and African countries. However, ethnic conflicts are not a monopoly of the South, as events in Eastern Europe, the former Soviet Union, and former Yugoslavia in the 1990s clearly demonstrate.

Ethnicity is basically ascribable collective identity and is related to cultural affinity, a shared myth of origin or belief in a unique past, and a belief in being distinctive as a collectivity. To quote Donald Horowitz, ethnicity, like nationalism to some extent, can be based on 'colour, appearance, language, religion, some other indicator of common origin, or some combination thereof'.[1]

In many developing countries, ethnic consciousness and loyalties tend to be particularly strong and lend themselves to easy manipulation, partly because other identities and loyalties are either weak or altogether absent. Peace and stability may not be sufficient conditions for socio-economic development, but both are indisputably necessary elements for any society to grow, develop, and prosper. For our purposes development is essentially defined as a process of modernizing society minus the demon of dependency. African societies that have experienced serious and armed ethnic conflicts internally in the post-colonial era – like Rwanda, Uganda, Burundi and Liberia – have been devastated as a result and are further behind developmentally than they were at the time of independence some 30 years ago.

This chapter addresses social conflict generated by ethnic competition, especially ethnicity reinforced by religion and language and how this impacts

126

on socio-economic development, with special reference to Africa. In particular, the republic of Uganda will loom large in the illustrations provided.

As affirmed by recent horrors in Rwanda, Burundi, Somalia and elsewhere, Africa is ethnically a conflict-ridden continent. This analysis attempts to identify the multiple sources of these conflicts. At the minimum, the conflicts can be categorized in two ways: a) political; and b) non-political. The implications and consequences of these conflicts for socio-economic development in Africa are also examined, and the article concludes by advancing some tentative recommendations pertinent to conflict-prevention, conflict-management and conflict-resolution in Africa.

Needless to say, many of Africa's conflicts are of domestic or internal origin, but Africa is not an island entire unto itself. Some of its conflicts are, at least partly, imported into Africa rather than generated internally, so the interplay of domestic and external sources of conflict shall also be addressed.[2]

Apart from a handful of exceptions, the rest of the African countries are multi-ethnic in composition.[3] Africa also has countries that are ethnically or racially dual – the so-called 'dual societies' (for example, Rwanda, Burundi, Zimbabwe, and, in a sense, the Sudan and Algeria). What is more, the boundaries in which Africa's more than 50 post-colonial countries are individually enclosed were arbitrarily drawn by Europeans towards the end of the nineteenth century.

Most African countries comprise a plurality of ethnic groups and have little historically common or shared experiences and cultural values to cement them internally. True, the colonial experience was widely shared across ethnic lines, but then that historical experience, averaging less than a century, was neither long enough, nor deep enough, to forge a solid sense of shared identity.[4] Indeed, some European imperial policies, especially that of British indirect rule practised in Uganda and Nigeria, tended to divide rather than unite Africans.

Additionally, the anti-colonial struggle, though unifying to some extent, was even briefer, averaging a decade or two at the most. Once the colonial master departed, the nascent nationalism that was mobilized during the decolonization struggle atrophied, so that, for example, even the liberation and anti-apartheid struggles in the Republic of South Africa and Namibia have basically failed to unite all Africans in the two countries.

National integration remains woefully lacking in most of Africa. Ethnic conflict is a disease afflicting many African countries; instability and violence are the symptoms, while the cure is national integration.

Most African countries experienced a kind of nationalism directed against colonial rule, without necessarily developing nationhood internally first. The post-colonial era has revealed that many, if not all, African countries are culturally and politically highly differentiated and perhaps not even to be maintained as states as such. Some of the serious conflicts and instability on the continent have been triggered by causes such as: the ethnic heterogeneity of various countries and the resultant 'wrong chemistry'; the newness, and in a sense the 'artificiality', of those countries; and the competition for political power and scarce socio-economic resources within them.[5] But even culturally or ethnically coherent countries like Somalia and Lesotho have undergone serious internal conflicts. When armed and militarized, these conflicts can exact a massive toll on society. What the experience of these few ethnically homogenous countries suggests, is that the fundamental causes of internal conflicts in Africa transcend ethnicity and ethnic competition.

While it is not easy to tell empirically where on one side the non-political ends and on the other the political begins, for analytical purposes this chapter has placed Africa's ethnic conflicts into two categories – non-political and political. It is to these categories that we next turn.

NON-POLITICAL CONFLICTS

Religious Sources of Conflict

While pre-colonial Africa did not have religious wars *per se*, the intrusion of Christianity and Islam into Africa have introduced conflicts animated or inspired, at least in part, by sectarian differences, and sometimes sectarian conflicts have occurred within the same religion, as, for example, the Protestant/Catholic divide in Uganda.[6]

Uganda's many serious conflicts and civil wars since attaining independence over 30 years ago have, at least in part, been organized around religious groupings. As a Ugandan political scientist has put it:

> The fact is that religion and the modern political Uganda were like Siamese twins that saw the light of day at the same time. And, to continue with the metaphor, the two had not been really separated even when independence came some eighty years after.[7]

Several years later Yoweri Museveni's National Resistance Movement (NRM) reiterated this basic fact about the intrusion of religion into Ugandan politics. In the words of the founding document of the NRM:

The politics of Uganda at independence was unabashedly sectarian: DP [Democratic Party] mainly for Catholics, UPC [Uganda People's Congress] mainly for Protestants outside Buganda, and KY [Kabaka Yekka] for Protestants in Buganda.[8]

While it would be erroneous to label the internal conflicts and even civil wars that have raged in the Sudan, Algeria, Ethiopia, Uganda and elsewhere as 'religious' wars, it is indisputable that the religious factor was in some way relevant in all of them, albeit in combination with other variables. More recently some 'religious violence' has manifested itself in Egypt and Algeria, and elsewhere on the continent ethnic wars have sometimes interacted with religious factors, as universalist religions have paradoxically and inadvertently created new ethnicities in Africa.

It is definitely clear that where the religious divide coincides with ethnic identity and regionalism as in Nigeria (roughly Muslim Hausa in the north versus Christian Igbo in the south-east), this convergence has tended to sharpen social conflict. The bulk of the Hausa people in Nigeria are to be found in the northern segment of the country and are mainly Muslim by faith. In contrast the Igbo people are located in the south-east and are mostly Christian. (The Yoruba have occupied an intermediate position partaking in Islam, Christianity and indigenous Yoruba authenticity.) No doubt the north-south divide in Nigeria has been reinforced and made much more dangerous by this coincidence of ethnicity and religious affiliation. One remedy that has been attempted is the redivision of Nigeria into more culturally mixed states, so the northern and southern identities have been gradually diluted in Nigeria.

Additional Cultural Sources Of Conflict

Linguistic nationalism has been weak on the African continent, and as a result language-based conflicts have been rare. Indeed, ironically, the anti-northern sentiment in southern Sudan did not include hostility to the Arabic language; many southern Sudanese speak, and have spoken for decades their own version of Arabic despite their anti-Muslim and anti-Arab stance.

The multitude of indigenous African languages has, rather paradoxically, forced Africans to choose not their own languages, but instead alien idioms, either as official languages or lingua francas. Per capita, Africa's languages outnumber those of any other continent. Yet this 'mother of languages' has mainly tended to borrow European languages for official business, primarily because it was politically prudent to do so. Most African executives and legislatures, judicial and educational systems conduct their business in some

European language. Arab Africa is a little different in this regard, although there are many North Africans in the Maghreb who feel more at home in the French language than they do in Arabic. The Maghreb has also witnessed some language-based conflicts in the form of competition between Arabization and the more indigenous Berber language.

It is telling that many educated Ugandans derided, even despised, President Idi Amin's (or Tito Okello Lutwa's) 'broken English', almost as if any Ugandan who did not know the English language well enough was not entitled to be President of the country. And yet Idi Amin was fluent in several indigenous African languages – none of them politically salient of course. In the words of a British officer under whom Idi Amin once served as soldier in the colonial era: 'severely limited in so many intellectual spheres and often ridiculed for his slender knowledge of English, Idi was in fact fluent in at least a dozen African languages'.[9] And yet had Amin mastered three or four times more indigenous African languages than he in fact did, that would still have been unsatisfactory for many of his educated and culturally Westernized detractors. By contrast, had Amin mastered the English language alone (and not spoken any other indigenous Ugandan language) he would have been deemed qualified to be President by many of his compatriots. Competence in the language of the departed colonial master as a credential for political office has been a widely shared attribute across Africa, particularly south of the Sahara.

There is little doubt that the carnage and massive destruction that have occurred in such African countries as Idi Amin's Uganda, Bokassa's Central African Republic, and Macias Nguema's Equatorial Guinea were the result of the mutual hostility between educated and articulate politicians on one side and basically semi-illiterate soldiers drawn from peasant origins on the other. Many African soldiers were suspicious of their articulate and often internationally well-connected politicians. The politicians were often perceived as players of 'dirty games', and as a manipulative, loquacious, and arrogant lot. Similarly, the politicians looked down upon the soldiers as 'illiterate', 'primitive' even basically 'uncultured'. And yet politically these two groups – the soldiers and members of the intelligentsia – would play major roles in their respective societies, although these mutual stereotypes about each other did set the stage for serious domestic conflicts. Civil-military relations in many African countries need to be redesigned and restructured if peace, stability, and development are to occur.

Civil-military tensions and stresses in Africa often degenerate into conflict situations partly because the current political institutions and the armed forces are alien arrangements unilaterally imported into Africa by the Europeans. The Africans who best understood these alien institutions, and who in fact have run them, were the educated and culturally Westernized Africans – a small minority compared to the rest of their national populations. Such African politicians as Nnamdi Azikiwe, Kwame Nkrumah, Milton Obote, Agostincho Neto and Patrice Lumumba belonged to this category of Africa's political elite. They talked, behaved, and even dressed like the departed colonial master.[10]

By contrast, those who enlisted in the army, itself an import from Europe, were less formally educated and at most minimally culturally Westernized. Such African soldiers who later became politically influential in their respective countries (like Idi Amin, Francisco Macias Nguema, Jean-Bedel Bokassa, Samuel K. Doe and Joseph-Désiré Mobutu) were culturally more African and closer to the peasants of their societies than they were to the Westernized political elites. These soldiers were also often despised and taken for granted by the suave politicians.

Of course, this is not to suggest that African soldiers like Amin, Bokassa, Doe, and others who captured supreme power in their respective societies, behaved in the barbaric ways that they did while in office *because* they were culturally more 'authentic'. Rather the forces (psychological, cultural, military, etc.) at work were multiple and for these soldiers, just as in the case of the Westernized elites, these variables interacted in non-simple ways.

Confrontations between politicians and soldiers have been commonplace in Africa, to some extent because of the ruthless competition between the two groups for influence, power and other scarce socio-economic resources. Military *coups* arise partly out of the stresses and tensions in civil-military relations. One possible solution to this problem might lie in finding alternative relationships between the military and civil society. These include the idea of *diarchy*, whereby the soldiers are included (but not marginalized) in the polity – what the first President of independent Nigeria, Nnamdi Azikiwe, once described as a 'combined civil and military government'.[11]

It would be false to suggest that African societies consist only of either soldiers or Westernized elites. Indeed, in most African countries, the vast majority of the respective populations do not belong to either of these categories, and leaders like Daniel arap Moi of Kenya, Omer el-Bashir of the Sudan, Bakili Muluzi of Malawi and many others are neither military men nor Westernized personalities. Yet it still remains substantially accurate to submit that African soldiers and Westernized elites have had a massive impact on the post-colonial politics of the continent, out of proportion to their puny numbers.

POLITICAL CONFLICTS

Primary Sources Of Conflict

Ethnic specialization like the erstwhile predominance of Nilotic northerners in the armed forces of Uganda, and the concomitant demilitarization of the Bantu peoples of southern Uganda, could have conflictual and anti-developmental consequences later on. It is hence reassuring that since 1986, under President Yoweri Museveni, the Ugandan army has become more nationally integrated and ethnically representative of the entire country. There is little doubt that the ethnic integration of the military is an imperative that could also reduce the inter-ethnic conflicts that bedevil many African countries.[12] It is reasonable to assume that African armies that are dominated by one or two ethnic groups in an otherwise ethnically plural society are more likely to carry out military *coups d'état* than armies that are ethnically more mixed.

Comparable remedies to ethnic conflict and polarization in Africa probably include A. Milton Obote's proposals for 'electoral polygamy' in Uganda as well as the separate institution of 'National Service' programmes that obligate the youth of a given country to serve in areas other than their own ethnic base or home-towns.

Perhaps the most fundamental issue springs from the question of whether one belongs, or does not belong, to the body politic (or political community) in any given African country. We might term this kind of issue one of *primary political conflict*. Idi Amin's tenure as President of Uganda (1971-79) demonstrated the nature of the political conflicts related to the question of ethnic origins.

In Idi Amin's case the issue arose primarily because he belonged to the small ethnic group of the Kakwa which is only partially lodged in Uganda. The colonial experience had scattered the Kakwa people three ways, making them politically accountable to three divergent capital cities – Kampala, Khartoum and Kinshasa. Some of the Kakwa people were made Ugandans, others became Sudanese, and yet others were made nationals of what later became Zaire. The decision to disperse the Kakwa people so arbitrarily is of colonial origin, yet to many who disliked Amin's regime or were critical of his policies, it was fair game to label the man an 'alien' or a 'stranger' in Uganda. After all, his group was also Sudanese as well as Zairean. Many preferred not to remember that the Kakwa people of what is now Uganda, Sudan and Zaire had arranged their lives in other ways for centuries before the European boundaries were drawn.

It is arguable that the single most serious *coup d'état* attempt mounted against Idi Amin during his entire reign was partly motivated by this anti-foreign sentiment. In the words of a Ugandan who served in Amin's cabinet:

> One reason for the revolt was that Arube [Brigadier-General Charles Arube, then Chief-of-Staff of the Uganda Armed Forces and officially on leave at the time] and a number of senior officers resented the rule of the southern Sudanese [in Uganda] and the way in which they were bringing the army into disrepute. The revolt was an attempt to drive them out.[13]

At least two Presidents of Uganda since Amin have also been accused of being foreigners: Tito Okello Lutwa (1985-6) and Yoweri Kaguta Museveni (since 1986), branded as Sudanese and Rwandan respectively. Again, this was partly because they belonged to ethnic groups that are transnational in twentieth-century Africa. And, in neighbouring Zaire, President Mobutu has sometimes been accused of being from the Central African Republic masquerading as a Zairean, allegedly because his ethnic group, the Ngbandi, traverse the Zaire/Central African Republic border. Zambia's first President, Kenneth David Kaunda, was often dismissed as the 'Malawian' by some of his hostile compatriots. Why? Because his father had migrated to Zambia from Malawi. Where Kaunda was born, or what his legal status was in Zambia, seemed singularly irrelevant to these kinds of super ethnically conscious critics. Similarly, some Ghanaians accused their first President, Kwame Nkrumah, of being a Côte d'Ivoirian because his ethnic group, the Nzima people, happen to traverse the Ghana/Côte d'Ivoire border. All these contested citizenships and nationalities belong to what we will term primary political conflicts in Africa. Africa's secessionist wars also belong to this category. The Nigerian civil war (1967-1970), the Sudanese civil war (1956-1972), and the Eritrean civil war (1960-1993) were all attempts at reconstituting political communities.

Although basically internal in their origins, these conflicts did in fact involve varying degrees of foreign intervention. Indeed, both superpowers were often participants, as were other foreign actors. With the successful independence of Eritrea, and the *de facto* declaration of independence by the Somaliland (former British Somaliland or Northern Somalia), however, it is conceivable that future attempts to redraw colonial boundaries in Africa might succeed. Indeed John Agami's Lado Republic movement in the area where the borders of Zaire, Uganda, and Sudan meet and intersect, the Rwenzururu movement in western Uganda, the current Shaba rebellion in Zaire, the Casamance problem in Senegal, and possibly even others, belong to this category of primary conflict, basically internal but not entirely without external intervention even after the Cold War has ended.

When armed and militarized, these conflicts have cost several millions of African lives and destroyed not only property but the very ecology of Africa itself. As a process of destruction, wars – civil or otherwise – are wasteful and they divert attention from constructive efforts. It is quite obvious that in the 1960s the massive Republic of Nigeria did not assume its natural role as leader and spokesperson of the African continent basically because it was embroiled in its own civil war. Approximately two million Nigerian lives were lost, much property destroyed, and the natural environment of the former eastern region of Nigeria devastated as federal troops fought the self-styled Biafran secessionists.[14] Not all Biafrans were ethnically Igbo, though the majority of them were. However, the war essentially erupted because the former easterners no longer wanted to be part of an entity called Nigeria, left behind by the British, which they felt short changed them as citizens. Their secessionist ambition failed at a very high cost, yet the resolution of the conflict could be argued to have enhanced the prospects of national integration in Nigeria.

Given the 'artificiality' of Africa's nation-states, and considering the fact that there are millions of partitioned Africans across the continent, there have been surprisingly few international wars arising from border disputes among these countries.[15] Indeed, the OAU Charter which entered into force in May 1963 declared Africa's frontiers virtually sacred. And for many African political elites the prospect of redrawing the colonial boundaries has been too nightmarish to contemplate. Many believed that to tamper with the European-drawn boundaries would be like opening up a 'Pandora's box', since the process of 'correcting' them would be indefinite and infinite. Rather, many Africans decided to accept the foisted territorial divisions and to begin their post-colonial lives within them.

In the same vein, instances of political union of the Tanganyika/Zanzibar type which resulted in the formation of the United Republic of Tanzania, or similar attempts at political federation in Arab Africa have been few and far between. Even with regard to Tanzania, there is now an emerging sentiment among many Zanzibaris and even Tanganyikans to pull out from the 1964 union.

Secondary Sources of Political Conflict

However, there have been other kinds of sources of conflict that have traumatized Africa that fall short of attempts at redefining the political community as defined by the colonial boundaries. These might be placed under two categories: *secondary*, and *ecological* (or *tertiary*) conflicts. Secondary political conflicts relate to conflicts centring on aims, directions, objectives, priorities and purposes of the extant political community. Many of the political assassinations in Africa are of this variety, and the military *coup* has sometimes served as the functional equivalent of a competitive election whereby a regime change occurs, often violently.

Often the *coup*-makers do not aim at reconstituting the political community, but rather seek to redirect the same political community. From the Free Officers of Egypt, who included colonels Muhammad Naguib and Gamal Abdel Nasser in Egypt in 1952, to the first military *coup d'état* in black Africa in Togo from 1963 onwards, post-colonial Africa has experienced over 100 successful military *coups d'état*. The unsuccessful *coups* are even more numerous than that, but essentially they all represent political conflicts of the secondary kind. The basically Tutsi invasion of Rwanda from Uganda in 1990 and the continuing struggle of the Rwandese Patriotic Front (RPF) to re-enter their ancestral land and even change its politics, and the Tutsi *coup* attempt in Burundi which cost Hutu President Melchior Ndadaye his life in late 1993 also belong to this secondary category.[16]

The ongoing trend of political democratization has also created secondary political conflicts. Indeed the number of political parties formed across the continent in the 1990s is staggering.[17] These contending political groups are attempting to capture the political centre and mould the extant society in their own image. Traditionalist versus modernists, monarchists versus republicans, socialists versus capitalists, centrists versus rightists, leftists versus rightists, and secularists versus religious fundamentalists are competing against each other politically, and occasionally militarily, in many parts of Africa, both north as well as south of the great Sahara desert.[18]

What all this means is that ideological differences sometimes degenerate into serious political conflicts in Africa. When values, perspectives, orientations and public policy preferences diverge, they could generate serious conflicts, especially when external actors intervene (such as the antagonists of the Cold War ideological conflict drama). Political pluralism, ideological tolerance and coexistence are possible remedies for such ideologically inspired conflicts, yet too much political liberalization, and too rapid an introduction of pluralism, could present the danger of ethnic polarization in many African countries. Past experiences of this have often led to violence and chaos.

Events in the 1990s in such diverse African countries as Kenya, Angola, the Gambia, Mozambique and elsewhere suggest that too hurried an introduction of political pluralism may do more harm than good, at least in the short run. Clearly, there is therefore a case to be made for *planning* the democratization and liberalization of the politics of a hitherto authoritarian society. The precise details of this planning will vary from country to country as well as from year to year, but it remains clear that none of the African societies can simply 'muddle through' to successful politics and democracy.

Moi's Kenya, in particular, illustrates that an incumbent president can easily divide and render farcical the opposition. By 1994, the opposition in Kenya was haemorrhaging profusely as an embarrassing number of members of parliament rejoined Moi's Kenya African Nation Union (KANU) party in power. Had the Kenya of the 1990s had too many political parties for its own good? In an ethnically plural society, is too much multi-party democracy bad? Is Museveni's 'no party democracy' in Uganda worthwhile? Should there be a limit to the number of political parties permitted in any given African society. The right mix of possibilities will inevitably vary from one African society to another.

Tertiary Sources of Conflict

In addition to the primary and secondary political conflicts already discussed, some of Africa's conflicts have grown from the political environment of the various countries located in the wider global context in which they operate. Indeed the tragic case of the nomadic Somalis is a good illustration of how contending clans have competed for scarce land and pasture.

Similarly, the tensions between the Hutu and the Tutsi in both Rwanda and Burundi have been stimulated by the high population density and the 'land hunger' in both countries. This has been compounded by the lack of geographic separation between the Hutu and Tutsi. Both are spatially so intermingled that armed conflict inevitably results in massive destruction of lives and property.

Additionally, the drought that swept the Sahelian region of Africa resulted in new forms of political instability in that part of the continent. For example, the Ethiopian revolution of 1974 was partly a consequence of the drought and related famine.

Meanwhile, Africa's fast-expanding populations at a time of decreasing infant mortality rates and relatively improving health care facilities has meant that more Africans are living in either shrinking or stagnating economies. Some of the serious political conflicts in Africa are the result of either underemployment or unemployment and form the real consequences of the demographic reality within the context of ethnic competition.

The wider global environment in which Africa seems to be inescapably entrapped also generates problems. For example, many African countries are currently implementing World Bank/IMF policy prescriptions (so-called structural adjustment programmes, SAPs) which are directly related to Africa's mounting debt. Such policies, which often require cutbacks on social services, health care and education, are most likely to hurt the weakest members of African society – children, women, the aged, and the physically challenged.

The highly unstable financial situation of African farmers, sellers of primary products, exists in a wider global economy which is biased in favour of industrial or manufactured goods. The African has to pay more each year for the same industrial good, while the African primary producer earns less and less. The results of these growing internal inequalities are widespread misery, desolation, and hardships of the lower classes, which sometimes erupt into violent conflicts.

During the nuclear age, the populations of the developing world – including those of Africa – have been used as pawns in the game of global expansionism, as the nuclear powers transferred their rivalries to the southern hemisphere where they confronted each other indirectly. Consequently, some conflicts in Africa are related to either the existence of the Cold War (for example, Angola) or its termination (for example, Somalia).

PREVENTION AND RESOLUTION OF CONFLICTS

Africa's Under-Utilized Resources

Africa's extended family tradition and its spirituality have been under-utilized by African policy-makers as possible remedies for ethnic conflict across the continent in the post-colonial era. These cultural resources need to be rediscovered and applied to new national purposes.

Equally neglected have been the following resources:

a. The Palaver Tradition – the culture of talking things out, of discussing issues, of 'sitting down under the tree and talking until they agree', as Julius K. Nyerere once put it. In his first administration as Prime Minister of Uganda (1962-71), Apolo Milton Obote used to boast about 'government by discussion', as a preference and his *modus operandi*. While in practice he often fell short of that ideal, he was essentially making a valid point that talking things out was better than shooting them out. Africa has an indigenous tradition of discussion which has not been fully mobilized in the post-colonial era.

b. The Elder Tradition – consultation of elders in efforts to build national communities and in resolving societal conflicts and tensions. In the former northern Somaliland, which has now declared itself independent as the Republic of Somaliland, a remarkable degree of peace and security exists in contradistinction with other parts of Somalia. This may well be due to the traditional councils of elders as structures of authority and governance. Similarly, the tiny kingdom of Swaziland in Southern Africa – one of the more stable and peaceful African societies – institutionalized the Liqoqo as a body of elders, virtually as a council of advisers to government; and former Ugandan President Idi Amin's initial rule involved periodic consultation with elders, and this period turned out to be the least bloody and destructive of his eight years in power. This 'elder' tradition is also an additional resource that has yet to be fully mobilized in post-colonial societies.

c. What Ali A. Mazrui calls 'Africa's Short Memory of Hate' could be encouraged and strengthened. An impressive range of Africans have manifested the capacity for forgiveness and magnanimity: Kwame Nkrumah, Joshua Nkomo, Robert Mugabe, Nelson Mandela, and Jomo Kenyatta are among African leaders (dubbed 'prison graduates') who were victimized and mistreated by colonial masters and white settlers before black majority rule and yet managed to 'suffer without bitterness'. The first President of independent Kenya, the late Jomo Kenyatta, once published a book with precisely the title *Suffering without Bitterness*.[19] And like many other African ex-political prisoners turned heads-of-state, Kenyatta proved to be forgiving and even generous to his former white tormentors. This propensity could be further cultivated and utilized in resolving conflicts in post-colonial societies.

d. Indigenous Tradition of Reparations and Compensation as mechanisms of resolving conflicts between individuals and ethnic groups (to be distinguished from the imported criminal justice system). In many pre-colonial societies, conflicts were partly resolved peacefully by compensation and reparations paid to the victim or the victim's family (as opposed to the state or government). This tradition has been largely forgotten in the post-colonial era and yet could be usefully resurrected.

e. Spiritual Values – Africans are a very religious (non-secular) people. Religion could be used as a mechanism of social control and of promoting non-violence and tolerance. Religious leaders in Africa need to be utilized more consistently in resolving conflicts in society, such as Archbishop Laurent Monsengwo Pasiniya's role in Zaire's ongoing transition to democratic politics;[20] and during the heat of the anti-apartheid struggle in the

Republic of South Africa, Nobel Peace Laureate Archbishop Desmond Tutu often served as a restraining and moderating influence on many enraged and potentially violent black South Africans. Religious leaders elsewhere on the continent have been less active in conflict-management and conflict-resolution, but could be usefully employed in these domains. Those who respected and listened to Archbishops Pasiniya and Tutu did so out of their deep African spirituality and fear of God. This resource can be extended to the political field.

NOTES

1. See Donald Horowitz, *Ethnic Groups in Conflict* (Berkeley, CA: University of California Press, 1985), pp. 17-18; and Larry Diamond, 'Ethnicity and Ethnic Conflict', *The Journal of Modern African Studies*, 25:1, 1987, pp. 117-28.
2. Many of the ideas in this paper have been inspired and informed by my close intellectual association and colleagueship over the last 25 years with Professor Ali A. Mazrui, to whom I am deeply indebted.
3. Somalia, Lesotho, Swaziland, Botswana, and the bulk of Arab Africa are arguably ethnically singular, but this is subject to qualification and even debate.
4. See Roland Oliver, *The African Experience: Major Themes in African History from Earliest Times to the Present* (New York: HarperCollins, 1991), p. 226.
5. By 'artificiality' we mean these nation-states were not the product of local or internal forces and processes, but rather of external (European) intervention. See Basil Davidson, *The Black Man's Burden: Africa and the Curse of the Nation-State* (New York: Random House, 1992). Of course, in the final analysis, all countries possess not natural, but rather artificial or humanly contrived borders.
6. See, for example, Jan Jelmert Jorgensen, *Uganda: A Modern History* (London: Croom Helm, 1981).
7. A.G.G. Gingyera-Pincywa, *Apolo Milton Obote and his Times* (New York: NOK Publishers, 1978), p. 23.
8. Founding document of the National Resistance Movement, the current government of Uganda. This quote is from Article 3, 10-point programme of the NRM, reprinted in Y. Museveni, *Selected Articles on the Uganda Resistance War* (Kampala: NRM, 1986), p. 52.
9. Iain Grahame, *Amin and Uganda: A Personal Memoir* (London: Granada, 1980), pp. 38-9.
10. Consult, for example, Ali A. Mazrui, *Political Values and the Educated Class in Africa* (London and Berkeley, CA: Heinemann and University of California Press, 1978).
11. See Richard L. Sklar, 'Nnamdi Azikiwe', in Harvey Glickman (ed.), *Political Leaders of Contemporary Africa South of the Sahara: A Biographical Dictionary* (Westport, CT: Greenwood Press, 1992), p. 21. Also see Michael S.O. Olisa

and Odinchezo M. Ikejiani-Clark (eds), *Azikiwe and the African Revolution* (Onitsha, Nigeria: Africana-FEP Publishers, 1989).

12. See Omari H. Kokole and Ali A. Mazrui, 'Uganda: The Dual Polity and the Plural Society', in Larry Diamond, *et al.*, *Democracy in Developing Countries*, vol. 2, *Africa* (Boulder, CO and London: Lynne Rienner and Adamantine, 1988), pp. 259-98.

13. See Henry Kyemba, *A State of Blood: The Inside Story of Idi Amin* (New York: Paddington Press, 1977) p. 135.

14. See, for example, T.C. McCaskie, 'Nigeria: Recent History', in *Africa South of the Sahara 1990*, 19th edition (London: Europa Publications, 1989), pp. 764-5. See also John J. Stremlau, *The International Politics of the Nigerian Civil War, 1967-1970* (Princeton, NJ: Princeton University Press, 1977).

15. A.I. Asiwaju (ed.), *Partitioned Africans: Ethnic Relations across Africa's International Boundaries, 1884-1984* (London and Lagos: Hurst and University of Lagos Press, 1985).

16. For one report on the *coup* and assassination on 21 October 1993, see *The New York Times*, 25 October 1993, p. 11.

17. The number has ranged from country to country. For example, Mali in West Africa has had over 40, while Ghana has 9.

18. See, for example, Dunstan M. Wai, *The African-Arab Conflict in the Sudan* (New York: Africana, 1981).

19. See Jomo Kenyatta, *Suffering without Bitterness: The Founding of the Kenya Nation* (Nairobi: East African Publishing, 1968).

20. 'Zaire: A Three-Headed Monster', *The Economist*, 17 April 1993, p. 42.

Part IV

ECONOMIC FACTORS

7

Destabilizing Consequences of Sequential Development

Henk W. Houweling

INTRODUCTION

This chapter focuses on the destabilizing consequences of development in late-industrializing countries, in both domestic politics and in international relations. Section One addresses the notion of development as viewed from the Western experience, and argues that (economic and political) development is closely related to the process of state formation, which is a violent process for the North as well as for developing countries in the South. In Section Two, late development is introduced, in relation to the income distribution in developing countries, and in Section Three, recent work on linkages between income concentration and conflict in 'Third World' countries will be reviewed. In Section Four, issues of environmental scarcity and of violence in developing countries will be touched upon, and Section Five deals with the problem of the weak state. Some conclusions will be drawn in Section Six.

THE NOTION OF DEVELOPMENT: THE WESTERN EXPERIENCE

Building on the Western experience, development of a human group may be defined as the combined process of long-term rise in its aggregate and per capita income and of its members becoming subjected to, identifying with and participating in the apparatus of a non-confiscatory, impersonal and bureaucratic-legal state apparatus through the exercise of rights of citizenship. In terms of social organization, 'development' ultimately means the transition from a social order in which power accrues to the fighter and his organization, to one in which productive and consumption organizations, and values derived from them, predominate in societal institutions and in individual behaviour. Note that by defining 'development' in this way, it is not implied that world population as a whole can, or cannot, become as developed as rich countries are at present times. Nor is it implied that the development of first-comers can go on forever, or that it some day will come to a halt.[1]

When development is linked to the long-term rise of aggregate and per capita income, we talk about *intensive* growth, which should be distinguished from *extensive* economic growth, in which population and income grow at about the same rates.[2] During the last six centuries, China, with its population increasing from about 65/80 million people in 1400 to about 430 million in 1900, and with its inhabitants living at about the same per capita income level as their ancestors, is an example of social change due to extensive growth. Meanwhile, the Netherlands, which had about 2,047,000 inhabitants in 1816, living at a per capita income of about $1,307 (at 1985 US prices) in 1820, increased its population to 14,804,000 inhabitants in 1989, living at a per capita income of $12,737 (at 1985 US prices),[3] and thus demonstrates change due to intensive growth. Institutions generating extensive, respectively intensive, growth are radically different. And the transition from one type to the other is often violent. The Chinese empire embedded politics, economics and family life.[4] Intensive growth, on the other hand, is due to international markets embedded in a competitive system of internally pacified nation-states.[5]

Uninterrupted intensive economic growth is a feature of market society, embedded in the framework of an impersonal, rational-legal and bureaucratic state organization which is also a member of an inter-state system. In a market society, all types of factors of production have been brought under at least partial control of managers in investor-owned business, from the point of view of their most profitable allocation for the firm. In such society, everyday material needs are met by private enterprise.[6] A precondition for the emergence of such a society is that ethics of doing business within groups have given way to nation-wide, impersonal, and rationally calculable standards of success and of failure from the firm's point of view,[7] thus irrespective of traditional status, ties of blood, religion or location, or in any other criterion which may be used to distinguish its human owners and workers from each other. At a normative level, in a fully developed market society, extra-economic characteristics of people are normatively irrelevant for economic transactions within society. Deviations from this norm are called 'discrimination' or 'racism' or 'corruption'. Because of international competition, such deviations are self-punishing. This lesson, however, is not hammered in by studying ideas, but by learning from experience. Between states, extra-economic marker criteria return in the form of protectionist nationalism, especially in times when economic opportunities for all states become less abundant. The self-punishing nature of these practices was revealed during the depression of the 1930s, the subsequent outbreak of the Second World War and the defeat of those powers resorting to conquest of territory in order to regain economic autarky, although as the saying now goes: the losers of that war are the winners of the economic game. After the Second World War, therefore, the legitimacy of discrimination in economic transactions on the basis of nationality has been undermined as far as transborder transactions of goods and capital, although not of labour, are concerned.

'Development is a Violence-Generating Process, But Peace Comes in its Tail End'

The conclusion may be drawn from the history of the rise of the Western world during the past five centuries that the process of switching from imperial institutions, or their feudal legacy, to the growth-generating institutions of competitive markets operating in a multi-state system, is extremely violent, both within and between states. The development record of early Europe is in this respect dismal. Three types of violence may be distinguished.

The first type of violence generated by development is the collision between the emerging state and responding society. The achievement of state supremacy in society and the spread of markets into the domain of the provision of daily needs has many losers. State power and market transactions each break down barriers which previously separated different cultural groups. Unpleasant as it may be to recall, the levelling powers of the state – in the form of what we would now label as 'ethnic cleansing' through expulsion and/or genocide – are part of the developmental history of the now developed states. In the early modern period of European history (1445-1650), nation-states in Western Europe were put together under the domination of one ethnic culture. In this region of world society, state-builders emerged from the traditional elite (nobility and clergy) of society, both sharing the same uninterrupted literary and religious tradition. Those who were considered to fall outside this culture were expelled or eliminated. The long series of atrocities that accompanied this phase in the history of Europe's developing states is now rather neutrally characterized as the 'process' of nation-building. Or, to summarize in different words, in the development history of the now rich and rather pacified countries of the North, the victory of economic values over the values of the fighter runs through violent nationalism, as a response to the uprooting consequences of 'development' as defined above.

After this violent process of achieving state supremacy in society, came the more peaceful[8] involvement of state bureaucracies in matters of language, script, education, and conscription. The result is the assimilation of regional cultures into one nation-wide culture. The subsequent democratization of these states, and the development of welfare states in the twentieth century, has finally taken away the state as an uncontested privileged province of one particular estate or family or class.[9]

Democratization also removed the use of the state's compulsive power as a direct source of exploitation, both at home and overseas. The state as an institution could then slip away from the direct control of society's elite that up until then had controlled the military capability of society,[10] and as no particular actor in society is in control of the state, all have to compete for positions to influence state policy. The result of this centuries-long process of political development is correlated with an initially very slow but persistent rise in per capita income in what is still the core area of world society. In integrating Western Europe, this process of societal homogenization is now peacefully working across national borders, leading to a transnational civil society which will translate itself into the political fusion of state administrations.

The second type of violence generated by development is state collapse and its consequences. Since early modern times, European states have been repeatedly struck by revolutions and episodes of total state collapse. Between 1550 and 1650, a wave of political crises struck virtually all the major polities of the northern hemisphere. That century of unrest was followed by a prolonged period of increasing domestic peace in most of them until the mid-eighteenth century. State collapse was sharply on the increase again in the period 1750-1850, but state supremacy, leading a sharp decline in the number of years characterized by revolution,[11] has been achieved in the Netherlands since 1648, in England and France since 1691, and in Russia since 1791. The end result of this political development is the destruction of both traditional political authority from the pre-capitalist era, as well as of its charismatic would-be successor from the instable period of transition during which the growth-generating institutions, embodied in capitalism and political pluralism, were incorporated into society. Revolutions and state collapse ultimately increased the penetrative capability of the state apparatus in society.

To understand better the violent nature of state development it is important to realize that the population's identification with the state occurred after all the alternative sources of identification, such as Church and empire, feudal lords, guilds, village community, family clan, and

region, had been deprived of their independent power to offer viable strategies of survival to followers. Their role was taken over by the ever more
intrusive power of the impersonal legal and bureaucratic state to penetrate
and regulate social life, and the development of markets interacted with and
reinforced this homogenizing effect of state supremacy in society and vice
versa.

The third type of violence generated by development is the escalation of
primitive warfare from the pre-development era, of low-level intensity but
with high frequency, to interrupted warfare at ever higher levels of intensity,
separated by periods of time without war of increasing length, to possibly
stable peace.[12] Since the Second World War, the major power sub-system
has moved into what appears to be a phase of indefinite prolongation of
peace in relations among its members. The great capitalist and democratic
states of the Western world have developed into a rich and stable zone of
peace in the international system through their mutual relations, and these
mutual relations are no longer dominated by the reality or threat of war,
while their internal systems are dominated by electoral politics and peaceful
transitions of power among governments within stable state institutions.
Within the developed core, we are now experiencing the longest period of
international peace and domestic tranquillity since the beginning of the inter-
state system in the early modern period of European history.

Development, Violence and the Role of the Economy

During the process of development defined above, the economy becomes
more visible and more autonomous as a sub-system of society, relative to
family relations, to traditional elite groups and to political-military force.
The economy becoming a sub-system in this way – regulated by markets but
supported by an administrative-bureaucratic, impersonal, non-tributary
state – implies an unprecedented upheaval in the organization of the state, as
well as in society and state-society relations, sometimes leading to revolution
and even total state collapse. Why this linkage to violence?

Market penetration, interacting with the establishment of state supremacy
in society, implies the disentanglement of economic decisions from family
relations, religion, traditional status, race or sex. Economic development
increases the number of households losing control over the means of subsistence and thus becoming dependent on labour power as a commodity.
Losing control over means of subsistence, in conjunction with the emergence
of new centres of wealth, mobilizes previously separated groups, leading to
them competing in the same market for economic opportunities. This market

penetration and the build-up of state power change the relations between contenders within the elite group between established and aspiring sub-elites. Competition between rivals within the elite group may be followed by the breakdown of institutionalized restraints on competition for power over the apparatus of the state due to the building of rival coalitions.[13] The challenge to governments in developing states is to reunite an internally divided elite by peacefully including aspiring elites into the political system without alienating more conservative elite factions. From the European experience it may be concluded that a ruling elite coalition consisting of an agrarian-aristocratic group, bureaucrats from a labour-repressive state organization, and a modernizing entrepreneurial class is prone to fail to include the emerging civil society into the apparatus of government, leading to the breakdown of weakly institutionalized democratic governance that Europe saw in the 1920s and 1930s.[14] In Britain, the Netherlands and France, leaders of civil society became dominant in the apparatus of the state because of a mixture of domestic revolution and peaceful inclusion through electoral reform. Meanwhile, in Austria, Germany and Japan, civil society leaders became hegemonic in the apparatus of the state because of the destruction in both world wars of a pre-industrial, feudal-agrarian and conquest-oriented elite embodied in the military and aristocracy. In the former Soviet Union, civil society and nation-states are just beginning to develop and still threaten to get overwhelmed by the behavioural legacies of empire.

The causes of revolution, the causal trends in demographic, economic, financial and political variables, caused by industrialization and which have led to state collapse, have been extensively studied, empirically documented, and quantitatively studied by Goldstone.[15] His impressive model of state collapse is based on four measured independent variables, the conjunction of which leads to state collapse: [i] elite factionalization, which is related, though not invariably, to [ii] a shortfall in government finance relative to expenditure commitments, to [iii] mobility into and out of the elite group, and [iv] to the increased potential for mobilization of the population. Market penetration in a subsistence society of self-employment is such a process leading to mobilization. These processes of change are now under way in the 'Third World'. There is little evidence so far about the ability of governments in developing states to respond in timely fashion to changes in the value of variables that correlated with revolution and state collapse in Europe's developmental history. It thus seems unlikely that these governments are able to skip the tragedies of mass murders that litter the European road to the welfare state and democracy, but we cannot know this for sure.[16]

The Clustering of Patterns at the Regional Level

Contemporary world society, created by the rise of Western Europe to global dominance, is characterized by unprecedented inequality in living standards and in state capacity of human groups that live in state-organized societies. International inequality is of rather recent origin. However, though in itself predating industrialization, the dramatic increase in inequality is because of the industrialization of the first states of the Western world to develop.

Despite the fact that industrialization has spread beyond the Euro-Atlantic core, the group of 'middle-income countries' at the international level is losing ground relative to the numbers of people in the bottom and top layers of income in world society. In its *World Development Report 1993*, the World Bank estimated that the ratio of the number of people in its 'low-income' category (in 1991 up to or below the threshold of $635 per capita) to world population increased from 54 per cent in 1965 to 58 per cent in 1990; the expectation is that in 2030, 63 per cent of world population will live in 'low-income countries'. In the terms of the World Bank's classification in the same *Development Report*, the ratio of the number of people living in 'high-income countries' to world population is estimated to have decreased from 20 per cent in 1965 to 15 per cent in 1990; and it is expected to decline further to 11 per cent in 2030.[17] Between 1965 and 2030, the proportion of people in the 'middle-level' income group, earning incomes between $635 and $7,911 per year in 1991, is estimated to have remained constant at about one-quarter of world population. In terms of the ratio of the number of people in the low-income group, however, it is becoming less significant, for in relation to the low-income group, the middle group is estimated to have decreased from 46 per cent in 1965 to 43 per cent in the year 2000, and is expected to have decreased further by 2030.

In international society, a virtually constant proportion of world population in the middle layer of the world's income distribution, faces an increasing proportion of people at the bottom and a decreasing proportion of the world's inhabitants in the top rank. The ratio of high-income earners to those in the middle layer is estimated to have decreased in recent years. In 1965, each middle-level income earner faced 0.81 persons in the top-income bracket; in 1973 that ratio had become 0.72, in 1980 the ratio of rich people to those earning middle incomes had become 0.66, in 1990 the ratio decreased to 0.59; in the year 2000, the World Bank expects that the ratio will be 0.53, while in 2030, the ratio of high-income earners to the number of people earning middle incomes is expected to be 0.40.

This trend of a shrinking group at the middle-income level is likely to undermine political stability in world society. Twentieth-century democracies are characterized by a majority of the population in the middle-income group, with minorities in top and bottom groups. This is, after all, why stable democracies are considered to be 'middle-class' societies, having middle-class values. In world society as a whole, on the other hand, a constant proportion is in the middle. This middle group faces, in terms of its own numbers, a shrinking proportion of world society at the top and an expansion of those at the bottom.

In national societies of Western Europe and North America, the wealthy few at the top of the income hierarchy are protected, precisely because the sizeable proportion of society[18] is in the middle-income group, from which most members of the political elite originate, and by the redistributing state which is dominated by the middle-income group. In the now stabilized rich part of the world, the historic task of the middle group has been to discipline the poor by showing them the way to go, while its members themselves learned what is desirable and what has to be avoided from both the top and from those below, thus preventing social polarization. In world society, however, the opposite process of bifurcation of the distribution of world income is under way. Because of the spread of industrialization into the 'Third World', the increasing numbers of poor people find new centres of wealth at their doorstep.

The remarkable thing about the area differentiation of human society in terms of per capita wealth and state capacity, is that it is observed at the regional level. There is no Switzerland-like state in Africa; likewise, there is no Mozambique-like entity in Western Europe or in North America. Apparently, a government in a poor country is unable to elevate its own national society far above its regional average. Decisions taken by governments in developing countries no doubt do matter, although within the limits of the effects of common regional factors. In other words, a region has powerful factors common to the nations within it. States and their populations thus do not differ at random in respect of wealth and in state capacity to create conditions favourable to the creation of wealth.

The next section focuses on late development in relation to income distribution in developing countries and its effect on political violence and conflict.

DOMESTIC INCOME INEQUALITY AND LATE DEVELOPMENT

The pioneering work of Kuznets suggests an inverted U-shape form for the relationship between income concentration and per capita income growth.[19] What was launched as a hypothesis about national economic development in

1955, inspired by the observation that incomes in developed countries had become more equal during the course of the twentieth century and by Kuznets' guess that there may have been a widening gap in incomes during the initial stage of intensive economic growth, has now become a widely accepted fact about national economic development.[20]

High-quality time series data on income distribution for 'Third World' countries are not, however, available. We thus do not know whether or not 'Third World' countries replicate the Western experience of increasing income concentration in the initial stage of intensive economic growth. However, cross-national evidence available on income concentration is compatible with Kuznets' findings. Using World Bank data on domestic income distribution, as reported in *World Development Report 1994*, Table 30, as a measure of income inequality, the ratio may be used of the income share of the poorest quintile to the share of the richest quintile, getting a score between 0 and 1. Nineteen 'Low-Income Economies' for which data are given, have an average score of 0.15, comparable with the average score of 0.14 for 17 'High-Income Economies' for which data was also available.[21] However, the range differs greatly between both groups of countries. The scores for the World Bank's Low-Income Economies vary between 0.03 for Tanzania to 0.25 for Bangladesh. Countries belonging to the World Bank's High-Income Economies, on the other hand, have score values from 0.10 for the United Kingdom and Australia to 0.22 for the Netherlands, Belgium and Spain. Compatible with Kuznets' inverted U-shape relationship between income concentration and income growth is that the average share of the top quintile income earners in Low-Income Economies is 47.2 per cent compared with an average share of 40.8 per cent in High-Income Economies. The average share of the top quintile income earners in Lower-/Middle-Income Economies is 51.9 per cent; in Upper-/Middle-Income Economies, the average income share of the bottom quintile is 54.6 per cent. With regard to the income shares of the bottom quintile, the rank order is reversed. In High-Income Economies it is 6.3 per cent, in Lower-/Middle-Income and Upper-/Middle-Income Economies the average shares are respectively 5.4 per cent and 4.4 per cent. Consequently, the poorest segments in both poor and rich countries get more than the poor segments in Middle-Income Countries; the poor in the Upper-/Middle-Income Economies get the smallest share of national income.

These findings suggest that developing countries moving from Low-Income Economies into Middle-Income Economies get new centres of wealth simultaneous with a falling share of income for the bottom quintile of society. During the onset of intensive economic growth, these countries thus seem to replicate at the domestic level the bifurcated income distribution of world society as a whole.[22]

It should be noted, however, that in addition to the level of per capita income, other variables affect the distribution of income. In bi-variate and multi-variate analyses, in addition to the level of per capita income, the stock of foreign direct investment contributes rather strongly to income concentration in developing countries.[23] It may overtake the positive effect of the level of per capita income on concentration levels. Stock and inflow levels of foreign investment capital improve the income share of the top quintile and worsen the position of the poorest 40 per cent. It is thus not likely that rapid per capita growth in poor countries, among other things due to the inflow of foreign direct investment, will make it more easy to solve the problem of relative poverty, because of its effect on widening the gap in income between top and bottom layers.

For a sample of approximately 50 developed and developing countries for which data are available, Muller[24] found that stable democracies, as measured by the number of years of unbroken democratic rule, have lower levels of income concentration, irrespective of the level of per capita income. Democracies initiated in polities with high levels of income concentration which fail to produce a more equal income distribution, have a very high probability of breaking down within two decades after the transition to democracy. Generally, the association between levels of inequality in income distribution and the probability of the breakdown of democracy is rather strong, irrespective of the level of per capita income. These findings suggest that the process producing the gap in living conditions during the initial stage of 'development', at the same time mobilizes the poorest segment and impoverishes it in relation to the 'top guys'. In a subsequent stage, however, the number of years of democracy has a delayed but rather strong effect on equalizing income, which stabilizes democracy.

Psychological Mobilization in Late-Comers in Development

However, latecomers do not simply repeat the experience of the early industrializing European countries. With regard to the timing of increasing life expectancy and decreasing levels of income concentration, the development history of the West differs from developing countries. The average life expectancy of populations in West European states greatly increased during the first half of the twentieth century, and in the same time period, the concentration of income in these populations sharply decreased. For the birth cohort born at the beginning of the twentieth century, Kuznets' inverted U-shaped curve started to run down as the distribution of income became much more equal. Consequently, 'historical graphs of life-time income inequality, reflecting both the distribution of annual incomes and the distribution of length of life, would show Kuznets' inverted U-pattern switching from no clear equalization trend before the late nineteenth century to dramatic equalization within this century'.[25]

Comparing the development of rich and poor countries with respect to the timing of the onset of a sharp increase in life expectancy, relative to the timing of the bending down of Kuznets' inverted U-curve for birth cohorts, is obviously a matter for further study. However, it is known that during the last 30 years, the life expectancy gap between 'First' and 'Third World' populations has been slowly reducing. With regard to average life expectancy, several countries with rather low levels of per capita income even approximate the life expectancy of populations of developed countries. In 1950-55, the average mortality rate of children under five years old in 'Third World' countries was 281, compared with 73 in industrialized countries. In 1990-95 rich countries had reduced their child mortality rate to 14, and developing countries to 106 per thousand. The absolute difference thus reduced from 108 to 92.[26] However, the further reduction in mortality rates in rich countries coincides with these countries shifting to less than replacement rates of fertility during the same period, which will in the next two decades or so reduce the absolute number of people living in these countries. In developing countries birth rates are still very high relative to declining child mortality rates. Consequently, even as birth rates are going down, the population growth will continue because of further decreases in child mortality rates. As already reported, an average of 95 million people are added to the world's population each year in the 1990s,[27] approximately 95 per cent in poor countries.

Sustained improvements are also reported for health and education in most 'Third World' countries. The suggestion is that, because of Kuznets' inverted U-form of the relationship between income growth and income concentration, these more healthy, better educated, longer living and growing populations probably experience increasing income concentration because of the onset of intensive growth, which is slowed down by the disjointed phases at the beginning of intensive economic growth and very high population growth. In early European developers, the sharp reduction of death rates during the first half of the twentieth century coincided with falling birth rates and decreasing income concentration. In sub-Saharan Africa, most countries have lost per capita income in the last decade, in some cases by up to one-third. Even so, life expectancy and educational achievement levels in these countries improved, but were accompanied by the highest regional population growth-rate in the world. Regions of world society with growing per capita incomes, better educated and longer living 'Third World' cohorts with growing per capita incomes may also experience growing domestic income concentration. Their members are exposed to mass media which demonstrates wealth, both inside and outside their country, and in rapidly growing developing countries high-status models are observed, which demonstrate 'First World' wealth at home.

Lerner, in his study of 'modernization',[28] called attention to the far-reaching impact of the process of 'development' on the mental habitus of those who participated in it. He argues that in 'traditional societies' people have great difficulty in imagining themselves living a different way of life than they actually do, or to imagine a complete reordering of traditional status hierarchy. Eighteenth-century Russian peasants, for example, could not imagine not being ruled by a Tsar. During the Pugachev rebellion of 1773, crowds of serfs and workers were in search of a new and hopefully better Emperor.[29] However, more than one century later, under the impact of intellectual side effects from Western Europe's industrialization, Lenin and his associates had little difficulty in imagining a completely restructured Russia.

In Lerner's view, the ability to imagine one's social conditions as radically different from what they actually are, is the realm in which members of 'modernizing societies' excel.[30] If true, this should create a vast multiplication of the sources of initiative and change. As estimates by UNESCO vividly demonstrate, access to mass media, especially to television, is rapidly increasing in all parts of the poor world. However, broadcasting from abroad presumably informs more about the end product and enjoyments of consumption and the power it brings, than about the institutions required to produce the things on display. Waste contains evidence of wealth accumulated and consumed elsewhere and thus gives scavengers, who make a living from it, the message of opportunities missed. End-product reports probably raise aspirations more easily than conveying new knowledge about means to raise living conditions. This may be indexed to the spread of patents outside the rich world, relative to the levels of technological sophistication of goods consumed in poor societies. Subjective awareness of poverty may increase faster than opportunities to satisfy needs created in this way. In this derailed sense, Lerner's 'modernity' has become a world-wide phenomenon,[31] implying that in 'Third World' countries, not only population growth and urbanization, but also media access, educational achievement and the increase in life expectancy, may be out of step with the rate of growth of the per capita income and its level of concentration. The precise nature of these leaps and lags in several regions is a matter for further study. Nevertheless, available evidence strongly suggests that in this restricted sense, the psychological mobilization required for development runs ahead of the multiplication of new opportunities to satisfy the energies and needs created.[32]

FROM INCOME CONCENTRATION TO CONFLICT BEHAVIOUR

Theory: Methodological Individualism and Collective Violence

On the global level, a process of accumulating inequality, that is, a bifurcated income distribution, can be witnessed, and processes of this sort are often known to end in violent efforts of redistribution. Will the process of accumulating inequality in world society also end in violence? Below, some theoretical notions derived from rational choice theory are discussed, introduced by Gupta in his study of collective violence.[33]

Gupta's application of rational choice to collective violence has given empirical results that are superior to the application of deprivation theory applied to collective violence. The explanatory strength of Goldstone's theory of revolution, introduced above, together with Weede's observation that elite rebellions are much more frequent than rebellions by the most deprived sectors of society, are compatible with the assumptions of rational choice and are incompatible with the notion of aggregated societal deprivation as a cause of collective violence.

In terms of motivating factors of individuals, Gupta distinguishes between the preferences of individuals for respectively individual or collective goods, for values, and environmental constraints as well as opportunities. Collective goods are subdivided into excludable and non-excludable collective goods, both resulting from collective action. The non-excludable part of the collective good refers to benefits accruing to all group members, irrespective of whether or not they participated in collective action. This is the political, ideological, or group-serving part of human activity. The guess is that this group-serving part is particularly strong in ethnically fragmented societies in which individuals may link their fate to group membership.

The attainment of collective goods by group action does, however, also entail individual goods such as positions of power and privilege within the group, and loot [all personal income factors resulting from participating in collective action] obtained by it. Income concentration, and its changes over time, refer to group phenomena. However, it also contains a strong component of individual well-being. A more equal income distribution – although a public good for rich and poor members alike – may be expected by those at the bottom of the hierarchy to bring benefits particularly to them.

The absolute level of earnings of an individual, and its changing value over time, are individual-level properties. By assuming that participants in collective violence are motivated by the prospects of achieving excludable individual benefits – the latter to be obtained by individual participation in group action – the free-rider problem is circumvented.

The distinction between individual income and group income to be shared by all and only by members, brings the matter of allocating time between the pursuit of individual and group interests within the realm of individual decision-making on the basis of opportunity costs. Being poor or unemployed may decrease the opportunity cost of time spent on initiating or participating in collective violence. The presence of a wealthy sub-group creates opportunities for individual rewards through group action. Adding the notion of opportunity cost in time allocation between participation and non-participation, a decision-making framework is created for studying the initiation and participation by individuals in acts of collective violence. Circumstantial factors relevant to participating in collective violence are, among others, the degree of repressiveness of the political regime, the severity of punishment of acts of rebellion,[34] the degree of ethnic ranking in fragmented societies, and the stability of the balance of power between ethnically ranked groups.

According to Gupta, the role of income concentration in outbreaks of violence relates to individuals' preferences for both a higher level of individual income and a desire to improving the relative income position of the group to which the individual feels himself attached. Group action may reinforce pre-existing group boundaries, or even create new ones, and thus connect moral indignation to individual grief as a cause for behaviour. Marker criteria derived from culture or race probably have a more potent mobilizing effect, compared with the abstract categories of class invented by Ricardo and Marx. From the moment an individual ascribes his or her position at the bottom of the income hierarchy to his group membership, a psychological basis is created for group formation and mobilization for conflict. Whether or not such conflicts escalate or are channelled towards institutions for settlement will depend on the level of development achieved by the state. Strong state organizations possess conflict management capabilities short of (frequent) use of violence. In cases where ethnic groups are traditionally ranked, the top group – finding itself in control of a weak state and being under the threat of development from the bottom group (as in, for example, Rwanda and Burundi) – may use the apparatus of the state to liquidate the bottom group in the economic struggle for survival.

Income concentration and poverty hence will not cause turmoil unless combined with some form of group identity being mobilized for collective action in which excludable values are also to be gained. In homogenized societies governed by a strong state organization – contrary to such ethnically or nationalist divided countries – identity expresses itself at the country-wide national level in nationalist fervour against (foreign) enemies of the state, not in acts of rebellion by intra-state groups against the state. For example, during the great depression in the 1930s, developed countries did not experience a sharp increase in domestic turmoil because of frustration, compared with the feverish nationalism and warfare in international relations.

Empirical Findings on the Relationship between Income Concentration and Violence in Developing Countries

A comprehensive, tested, and thus widely accepted model of latecomer development does not exist. Most researchers, therefore, work with weakly connected sets of *ad hoc* hypotheses, so not all the relationships suggested earlier have been tested. Several of them, however, have been scrutinized and some replication studies have been made. Below, several empirical findings on the relationship between inequality and/or its determinants, conflict behaviour at different levels of intensity and government responses to it are discussed.[35] Perhaps because of the prominence of international and domestic income inequality in developing countries, more replication studies have probably been performed on this set of relations than on any other.

Using a cross-national design of 84 developing countries in the time intervals 1976, 1980 and 1983, Rothgeb[36] regressed political conflict, as mentioned by frequency counts of public demonstrations against the government, political strikes, calls for resignation of government officials, and so on,[37] on stocks of foreign direct investment in mining and manufacturing which were normalized for the size of the national income of the host country. Government responses are measured by the frequency of events such as the imposition of travel restrictions, the imposition of censorship and the closing of universities. Separate analyses were performed for the poorest and more wealthy developing countries, and a pacifying effect was found from foreign direct investment stocks in the poorest countries. However, in richer developing countries, higher levels of concentration from foreign direct investment, especially in manufacturing, significantly increase the frequency of political conflict after a time delay of six years. However, the level of government repression is negatively related to the stock of direct foreign investment in these more wealthy developing countries. Thus, a high level of foreign direct investment in more wealthy developing countries provokes domestic conflict, but counteracts the escalation of conflict because of moderate levels of government repression.

Unfortunately, the level of unemployment is not controlled in this study. It is also unknown who was involved in the unrest. It is therefore impossible to make any statement in the empirical domain of opportunity cost in the time spent by protesters, as suggested by Gupta's theory and mentioned above. One may guess, however, that at very low levels of income, the opportunity costs of organizing for collective action are more severe, because no income can be missed at this level. At higher levels of income, when the proportion of time spent earning food decreases, it may be more promising to invest in capturing a portion of wealth accumulated by others through collective action. In Rothgeb's study, no information is given about the level of income, the age, the level of education and exposure to television, if any, of the protesters versus non-protesters. Data on group formation among non-governmental group actors are among the most difficult to acquire, as they require documentary evidence or reports from on-the-spot observers.

The negative relationship observed between the size of the direct investment stock and government repression may be mediated by the uncontrolled variable 'legal development of the state'. Foreign investors desire a legal base for their operations, implying company law, labour law and legal conflict-settlement procedures. The time-lag in the cross-section findings reported above makes it unlikely that the positive relationship between investment stock and political conflict can be ascribed to self-selection, because foreign investors in manufacturing prefer host countries with stronger consumer publics, despite unrest.

Findings for the poorest and for the more wealthy group of developing nations contradict each other, but are compatible with a positive relationship between a country moving through Kuznets' inverted U-shaped relationship between income concentration and level of per capita income and political conflict. As already remarked, higher levels of direct foreign investment rather strongly predict income concentration in host countries. Consequently, the findings by Rothgeb indirectly demonstrate a link between income concentration and political conflict in developing polities with middle-level per capita incomes.[38]

The intensity of political conflict in the research reported by Rothgeb is rather low. As part of a debate between deprivation theorists and rational choice theorists of collective violence, Muller, Dixon and Seligson,[39] and Weede,[40] have investigated possible links between levels of income concentration, severity of lethal political conflict, level of a political regime's repressiveness and severity of government sanctions. As a part of this work, the relationship between the income share of the top quintile in a polity and the number of deaths due to political violence in these polities have been extended to include the degree of regime repressiveness and severity of government sanctions. In a sample of over 60 polities, the level of income inequality, as measured by the percentage share of the top quintile in national income, strongly predicts the cumulative number of deaths per million people because of political violence in polities with a semi-repressive regime and a strong separatist movement. In polities without both conditions the curvilinear function that relates income inequality to political violence accelerates more slowly.

Another important finding is that the relevance of inequality in land ownership for explaining differences in the observed level of political violence is only to the extent that it is associated with nation-wide income inequality. Land reform thus contributes to peace only as far as it affects a less unequal income distribution. These findings are neither dependent on the particular estimation method used nor on the sample under study, a charge that had been brought against these findings by Weede. However, a comprehensive model for latecomer development does not exist, so further replication studies in different social settings are required to figure out the precise conditions under which high income concentration provokes violence. Perhaps fragmented societies in which ethnic groups are ordered in an inherited-status hierarchy that coincides with the income hierarchy are more vulnerable to disruption due to increasing income concentration than fragmented societies with parallel, or internally ranked, groups, even if these groups are hostile to each other. In the studies mentioned above, the social position of persons involved in violence, nor their time budget, is known. It is implausible that those from top incomes became involved in lethal conflict, although their children may well have been. Participation by members from the bottom rank is not plausible either, unless certain prior conditions are met. The suggestion is that the lower/middle-level echelons of society are most likely to be involved. Therefore, in addition to replication, extending research to variables peculiar to latecomers in industrialization is urgently needed.

Another observed regularity is the strong inverse influence of income inequality on the stability of democracy, as measured by years of unbroken democratic rule in a country. According to Muller and Seligson 'the most important determinant of changes in level of democracy is income inequality'. While controlling for the level of per capita income, they find that an increase of 10 per cent in the size of the upper quintile income groups' share in national income is associated with a substantial decrease in the level of democracy, although the level of economic development has by itself, irrespective of its distribution, no direct effect on democratic stability. As the breakdown of democracy is seldom peaceful, this finding may give further indirect evidence between income inequality and violence.

ENVIRONMENTAL FACTORS AS CAUSES OF INSTABILITY IN LATE-INDUSTRIALIZERS

First-comers in industrialization had the privilege of having access to untapped stocks of environmental goods. They still enjoy that benefit. One example is military capability. The estimate is that during Cold War years the US military establishment used more nickel, copper, aluminium and platinum than all the developing countries together.[41] During the rise of the West, first-developing states had the opportunity to withdraw – world-wide – units of non-renewable resources such as oil and gas, to downgrade or exhaust, for their exclusive benefit, reproducing stocks of renewable resources such as woods and ocean fisheries, and to dump waste in a yet unspoiled natural environment. A contemporary example of such a first-comer advantage is the decision by rich states not to ratify the initial text of the *Convention On The Law Of The Sea*, which prescribed that benefits from exploitation of mineral resources on the seabed beyond the limits of national jurisdiction should be shared with poor states unable to exploit these resources.

By experiencing a complete demographic transition induced by the domestic transition from agriculture to industry, and by profiting from land expansion in the Western Hemisphere, driving native inhabitants into extinction, first-industrializers could prevent the degradation of agricultural land by population growth. It seems plausible to assume that latecomers, who still have to climb up the technological hierarchy, will be particularly affected by environmental scarcity and by conflicts over environmental goods, especially arable land, pasture, forest and water. Homer-Dixon has collected case studies of violent conflict between human groups in which responses to environmental scarcity involving overpopulation played an unambiguous role,[42] that is, he finds cases of lethal conflict because of migration caused by land scarcity. His findings are of importance, since the poorest developing countries are particularly affected by environmental and land scarcity, sharply increasing food dependence, especially in Africa and Latin America. More generally, population growth in 'Third World' agricultural countries is virtually always a factor in the marginalization of peasants because of shrinking landholdings. Between 1977 and 1983/4, average holdings in Bangladesh shrank from 1.4 to 0.92 hectares. The story is the same for the Ethiopian highlands, where the bulk of its farmers live. But let us assume that these peoples all industrialize. Presently known stocks of mineral resources would be rapidly depleted if world population consumed per capita at the same rate as inhabitants of rich countries do. So the charge initially levelled against the work of the Club of Rome that the more we consume the greater the untapped stock becomes, because of the discovery of new inventories if prices rise and technologies improve, is true as long as the consuming population is considered to be less than 20 per cent of world population.

Nevertheless, because of technological advances, known reserves of mineral deposits are constantly changing. For example, in 1950 copper reserves were estimated to be about 100 million tonnes. During the next 30 years consumption was as high as 156 million tonnes, while reserves were re-estimated at 494 million tonnes. However, these estimates refer to a consuming population of industrialized countries. If the consuming population is taken to be world population of 2100, estimated in the UN's medium-level forecast to be 11.5 billion people, the 1988 world stock of copper will be gone in 4 years.[43]

Whether it is realistic from an environmental and (non-)renewable resources point of view to expect that 'development' will some day elevate the per capita consumption and waste production of people living in the 'Third World' to the per capita level of the inhabitants of rich countries, is often contested. If it is not realistic, efforts by late-industrializing countries to close the gap in living conditions will be in vain. Unless a new policy of coping with ecological scarcity is invented, resource and waste conflicts between and within nations may be expected to rise and increase. A policy to close the gap, however, may collide with domestic opinion in rich countries. Rich countries' desire to make trade 'greener', and thus limit the import of 'Third World' products believed to be produced in ecologically harmful ways, will collide with the observation by developing countries that the industrialized world consumes most of the world energy production. The United States alone, with about 6 per cent of world population, consumes about 30 per cent of world energy production. 'Third World' countries will thus not be greatly impressed by rich countries' calls for the 'greening of trade'.

THE WEAK STATE AS A SOURCE OF VIOLENCE

In most regions of the 'Third World', especially in Africa, the state itself is an underdeveloped institution;[44] instead of being part of the solution to the poverty problem, it is often a crucial part of the problem. A 'developed' state is able to penetrate society and to regulate the behaviour of its members by administrative means, backed by the credible threat of force in cases of overt non-compliance. Most 'Third World' states are able to penetrate society to a certain extent by means of violence, but find it difficult to regulate behaviour by administrative means. The absence of state supremacy in society is precisely reflected in the rootedness of its members' behaviour, especially of its traditionally leading members, in survival strategies offered by pre-state institutions.[45] The imposition of a state apparatus and efforts by the state to establish supremacy in society and to implement modernizing policies may even reinforce pre-state institutions. The intermingling between the two occurs when traditional power wielders become incorporated into the apparatus of the state without completely losing their traditional power base, and this problem becomes imperative when governments have to take into account the positions and local influence of traditional power wielders. In these cases the reform capacity of the central government is neutralized at lower levels within the government itself. Moreover, since it is almost impossible to displace entirely and/or on short notice the more archaic systems of social order that persist in most developing countries, the competition between state power and more traditional forms of influence within state boundaries will remain unresolved. In some cases this can lead to factionalism, 'tribalism', corruption and regionalism within the government or the country.

This problem emphasizes once more the role of state formation and democratization as a precondition for economic development, especially in Africa and Latin America. Most of Asia, however, has a long-standing state tradition, and Europeans entering the region had to reckon with state organizations before they could get access to local communities. In Asia, unlike in Africa and in Latin America, there was not much room for the application of titles of discovery for occupation of *terra nullius* or the imposition of artificial boundaries as on the African partition model.[46]

CONCLUSIONS

Because of the shrinking of distance in travel time and transport cost for persons, goods, ideas, images, and diseases, influences radiating from the South into industrialized Western Europe will multiply and become stronger. Yet external influences radiating into Europe are rather new. During the twentieth century, the impact from the extra-European world feeding back to the West European region has emanated primarily from the United States and from the Russian empire.[47] However, in the twenty-first century, extra-

European influences upon rich countries will come from even the remotest corners of the globe.

This reveals serious policy dilemmas for governments of developed states as well as for the publics who have to support the government policies dealing with these influences. For reasons of domestic legitimacy, these governments cannot maintain friendly relations with governments that openly and grossly violate human rights. However, it is also in their interest to keep former colonial states together. Governments of rich states also preside over economies with important weapon-manufacturing capabilities. They thus have to balance public respect for the observance of human rights against interests in successful 'Third World' nation-state building and interests in weapons' exports. Some of the trade-offs involved in these choices are revealed by empirical regularities between weapon deliveries, military *coups* and length of military rule in 'Third World' states.[48] Domestic foes are the most likely target of these weapons, thus implying the violation of human rights. Rich countries teach poor countries to industrialize, to open up their economies and then complain about unfair low-wage competition and 'job snatchers' in successful 'Third World' countries. Rich countries want to 'green trade', but also want to dump their waste in poor countries. Rich countries also want to liberalize markets, yet dump meat and grain produced in their highly protected markets in 'Third World' countries; they want to preserve rain forests but they harvest with large nets in the major fishing regions of the world.[49]

To secure their own safety, the response by the enlightened part of Western elites to the discovery of their poverty by the poor has been the creation of the welfare state. Its development, since the late nineteenth century, nicely coincided with the need of Western Europe's political elites for mass armies composed of healthy men. The Dutch international lawyer Röling, taking the values associated with the rise of the welfare state at face value, in the late 1950s discerned a trend of change in international law away from 'the international law of liberty' of states towards a new 'international law of welfare': 'The world community is bound to become a welfare community, just as the nation-state became a welfare state'.[50] Röling was certainly right with regard to the trend of change in diplomats' language about their former colonies. Indeed, the late-nineteenth-century dichotomy of 'civilization' versus the 'barbarism' of the natives, had given way to the rhetoric of development aid. The late 1960s until the mid-1970s were the heyday of development aid policies in terms of this rhetoric,[51] yet the gap in living conditions strongly increased during this period of development aid. Accordingly, the famous principle from the Gospel of Matthew ruled unabated that 'to him that hath shall be given'. As already discussed, that principle still rules world-wide in relations between large aggregates of people. If the suggestion that first-comer advantages have taken the best development opportunities makes sense, one may expect a further increase in the ratio of poor people to world population in the future. In 1956 Dag Hammerskjöld noted that 'What we have done so far has been on the margin of the real difficulties ... Our ultimate aim must be to level off the dangerous and unacceptable differences between the standard of living and of economic development in various countries'.[52] This message seems to be more urgent than ever.

Emphasizing first-comer advantages versus latecomer disadvantages suggests a cumulative, irreversible, gap in development. Emphasizing social preconditions for growth and the geographic spread of growth-generating institutions implies a speedy reversal of the gap in development. The rising gap in development discussed in this chapter suggests that first-comer advantages/latecomer disadvantages still outweigh the benefits from the partial spread of capitalism and democracy outside the industrialized core.

What can developed countries do to speed up economic and political development in the 'Third World'? Development planning should first take more notice of the history of state- and nation-building and its relationship with economic growth in the West European region (including its detrimental consequences for latecomers). To incorporate that knowledge could prevent a lot of disappointment. Second, governments of rich, industrialized countries should give much more attention to the trade-offs between nation-state building, trade expansion, weapon exports and human rights' observance. The levelling powers of market expansion on conflicts between ethnic groups are much more thorough and less costly in the long run than anything state power can achieve, short of complete extermination of unwanted groups. Capitalist democracy is not dependent on extra-economic differentials, such as tariffs and non-tariff-based measures of protectionism of national economies. Yet both capitalism and democracy originate historically in rather homogeneous societies whose internal differences were further levelled by their combined impact. Third, developed countries should help to build regional trade coalitions that connect countryside and cities in the least developed 'Third World' countries and also help host governments to acquire an impeccable tax-collecting apparatus to levy taxes on production and trade. This would bring the state on a legal footing. Fourth, rich countries, by upgrading their own economies, should create room at the bottom of the product cycle for those at the beginning of it, thus allow competing imports into currently heavily protected sectors, such as textiles, processed agricultural products including leather products, and steel. In this scheme, there is no place for subsidized food production and the dumping of food surpluses on the markets of underdeveloped agricultural economies, and these programmes could be negotiated with 'Third World' governments on the basis of trade-offs in the fields of migration, drugs control and debt reduction.

NOTES

1. Whether or not first-comers are viable over time falls far beyond my capacity to answer. Two threats to viability come to mind. First, developed societies are now below, and in Catholic Southern Europe far below, replacement-level fertility. Unless replenished by immigration, societies below replacement-level fertility ultimately face extinction. Second, individualism in political life means, among other things, the organization of political life on the basis of individually calculated reciprocity. Elections in which candidates running for office are closely tied to their financiers who buy and thus capture them, compel those lacking political investment funds to stay at home.
2. See Lloyd G. Reynolds, *Economic Growth in the Third World: An Introduction* (New Haven, CT: Yale University Press, 1986), p. 7ff.
3. Income figures taken from Angus Maddison, *Dynamic Forces of Capitalist Development* (New York: Oxford University Press, 1991), Table 1.1.; population figures taken from B.R. Mitchell, *European Historical Statistics 1750-1975* (London: Macmillan, 1980), Table B1.
4. Imperial institutions are analysed in John H. Kautsky, *The Politics of Agraristocratic Empires* (Chapel Hill, NC: University of North Carolina Press, 1972), esp. Parts II and III.
5. The notion of growth-generating institutions builds upon the work of, among others, Max Weber. See Randall Collins, *Weberian Sociological Theory* (New York: Cambridge University Press, 1986), esp. Part I.
6. This definition is borrowed from Randall Collins, *Weberian Sociological Theory*, p. 21ff.
7. Wage costs, not survival cost, of the labour force are the basis of recruitment and dismissal decisions by firms. Firms may thus rationalize by deferring the survival cost of dismissed members to society. This implies the posibility of Bauer's *Fehlrationalisierung*.
8. Not necessarily peaceful. The initial draft of the Convention on the Crime of Genocide prepared by the legal section of the UN Secretariat, UN doc. E/447 (1947), subsumed under genocide not just massacres but also such acts as the desecration of shrines, the prohibition of language and the destruction of books. By finding this unacceptable, governments evidenced their continuing interest in having available the option to destroy within their borders a culture they do not like. Unfortunately, there seems to be no way to prevent cultural diversity from being destroyed by governments.

9.   See Anthony Giddens, *The Nation-State and Violence* (Cambridge: Polity, 1985), pp. 148-72.
10. State institutions and market exchange 'bind' the excercise of raw power by individuals and groups to rules. The development of the state as an institution brings the human potential for violence under social control by binding it either to the army, to police forces or by prosecuting and punishing it as 'crime', allowing exchange and production to disassociate institutionally from the excercise of raw power.
11. Charles Tilly, *European Revolutions, 1492-1992* (London: Blackwell, 1993), Table 7.1, p. 243.
12. See H.W. Houweling and J.G. Siccama, 'The Neo-Functionalist Explanation of World Wars: A Critique and an Alternative', *International Interactions*, vol. 18, no. 4, 1993, Table 1, for a breakdown of the number of military deaths during the phase of permanent warfare and interrupted warfare since 1494.
13. For an educated guess of the increase in proportion of dependent persons in Europe's total population between 1500 and 1990, see Tilly, *European Revolutions*, Table 2.1. Absolute rulers not only eliminated domestic rivals and expelled unwanted population groups by abolishing guilds and liberating peasants, they also imposed nation-wide markets. In his inaugural address in 1895 at the University of Freiburg, Max Weber applied a domestic capability transition model to relations between Junkers and contenders from industrializing Germany, to explain why Germany as a state was in deadly danger, despite a booming economy.
14. See John D. Stephens, 'Democratic Transitions and Breakdown in Western Europe, 1870-1939: A Test of the Moore Thesis', *American Journal of Sociology*, vol. 94, no. 5, March 1989, pp. 1019-77.
15. Jack A. Goldstone, *Revolution and Rebellion in the Early Modern World* (Berkeley, CA: University of California Press, 1991). For the application of insight derived from his model of state breakdown derived from European revolutions to revolutions in late twentieth-century conditions, see Jack A. Goldstone, *et al.*, *Revolutions of the Late Twentieth Century* (Boulder, CO: Westview, 1991).
16. European and Asian settings are too different for results of research obained for Europe's developmental history to be generalized to latecomers elsewhere. I agree with Paul Kennedy's rather optimistic view, according to which all of the major shifts in the world's military power balances have followed from alterations in the productive balances, but economic prosperity does not always translate into military capibilities.
17. World Bank, *World Development Report 1993* (New York: Oxford University Press, 1993), Table A. 1, p. 199.
18. At present time, top quintiles in OECD countries take between 37% and 45% of national income, the bottom quintile gets between 5% and 8%, resulting in a share of about 60% of the population getting about 50% of national income.

19. For empirical work on the Kuznets' curve for European countries, see Y.S. Brenner, *et al.*, *Income Distribution in Historical Perspective* (New York: Cambridge University Press, 1991).

20. It should be observed, however, that the side of the inverted U-shaped curve reflecting movement towards greater equality, fits better than the trend towards concentration during the early phase of economic growth. The facts about income concentration at lower levels of development are not well documented and populations entering intensive growth vary greatly in the level of pre-growth income concentration. Tribal communities enter intensive growth from fairly low levels of income and of wealth concentration compared with landlord states. For an informative review of literature and further analyses of determinants of income concentration in developing countries, see S. Chan, 'Income Inequality among LDCs: A Comparative Analysis of Alternative Perspectives', *International Studies Quarterly*, vol. 33, 1989, pp. 45-65.

21. However, the top 5 or 10 per cent in poor countries are getting much bigger shares than in rich countries.

22. For further evidence on the stimulating effect of the levels of per capita income on income concentration, see S. Chan, 'Income Inequality among LDCs'.

23. Like earlier studies by Weede and Tiefenbach, Chan also finds that weapon deliveries from abroad have a negative impact on income concentration. However, this variable reduces the income share of the rich more than it increases the share of the poor.

24. E.N. Muller, 'Democracy, Economic Development, and Income Inequality', *American Sociological Review*, vol. 53, no. 2, 1989, pp. 50-68.

25. Y.S. Brenner, *et al.*, *Income Distribution in Historical Perspective*, p. 214.

26. United Nations Department of International Economic and Social Affairs, *Mortality of Children under Age 5: World Estimates and Projections, 1950-2025*, in Lester Brown, *et al.*, *Vital Signs 1993: The Trends that are Shaping our Future* (New York: Norton, 1993), p. 97.

27. Demographers estimate that in the 1990s the number of individuals added to human stock equals the world population size around the year 1810. It is known that the reproductive power of humans is not under environmental control: humans have no rutting season. Due to development, as defined above, social controls of reproductive behaviour change during a relatively short period of time known as the 'complete demographic fertility transition'.

28. Daniel Lerner, *The Passing of Traditional Society: Modernizing the Middle East* (New York: Free Press, 1968).

29. Nicholas V. Riasanovsky, *A History of Russia* (New York: Oxford University Press, 1984), p. 260ff.

30. 'High empathic capacity is the predominantly personal style only in modern sociey, which is distinctively industrial, urban, literate and participant.' In 'traditional society ... without an urban-rural division of labour people's horizons are limited by locale and their decisions involve only other known people in know situations'. Lerner, *The Passing of Traditional Society*, p. 50.

168 *Destabilizing Consequences of Sequential Development*

31. For varieties of Lerner's modernization scheme, see the stimulating exercise of Erich Weede, *Enwicklungsländer in der Weltgesellschaft* (Opladen: Westdeutscher Verlagsanstalt, 1985), ch. 2.

32. For a more optimistic view, see Ithiel de Sola Pool, *Technologies without Boundaries: On Telecomunications in a Global Age* (Cambridge, MA: Harvard University Press, 1990), ch. 9.

33. Dipak K. Gupta, *The Economics of Political Violence: The Effect of Political Instability on Economic Growth* (New York: Praeger, 1990).

34. For effects of regime repressiveness and intensity of sanctions on collective violence, see Erich Weede and Edward Muller, 'Rationalität, Repression und Gewalt', *Kölner Zeitschrift für Soziologie und Sozialpsychologie*, vol. 42, no. 2, 1990, pp. 232-47.

35. For a critical, although not fully convincing, review of several empirical studies on the relationship between inequality and violence, see Mark Irving Lichbach, 'An Evaluation of "Does Economic Inequality Breed Political Conflict?" Studies', *World Politics*, vol.41, no. 4, July 1989, pp. 431-70.

36. John Rothgeb, 'Investment Dependencies and Political Conflict in Third World Countries', *Journal of Peace Research*, vol. 27, no. 3, 1990, pp. 255-72.

37. This sort of event represents 10 on the intensity scale in the Conflict and Peace Data-Bank. COPDAB gives data on, *inter alia*, domestic conflict events. The data are described by Edward Azar, 'The Conflict and Peace Data Bank (COPDAB) Project', *Journal of Conflict Resolution*, vol. 24, 1980, pp. 143-52. See also Edward Azar, *The Codebook of the Conflict and Peace Data Bank* (College Park, Maryland: Center for International Development, 1982).

38. This finding calls into question the explanatory power of deprivation theory versus rational choice theory. Collective rebellion by the poorest segment of society is much less frequent, and rebellion by the better off more frequent than one would expect on the basis of deprivation theory. See Erich Weede, 'Ungleichheit, Deprivation und Gewalt', *Kölner Zeitschrift für Soziologie und Sozial Psychologie*, vol. 45, no. 1, 1993, pp. 41-55.

39. Edward Muller and Mitchell A. Seligson, 'Inequality and Insurgency', *American Political Science Review*, vol. 81, no. 2, June 1987, pp. 425-51; T.Y. Wang, 'Inequality and Political Violence Revisited', *American Political Science Review*, vol. 87, no. 4, December 1993, pp. 979-83; and William Dixon, Edward N. Muller and Mitchell A. Seligson, 'Response', *American Political Science Review*, pp. 983-93.

40. Probably the best short review of studies of collective violence at hand is in Erich Weede, *Mensch und Gesellschaft: Soziologie aus der Perspektive des methodologischen Individualismus* (Tübingen: Mohr, 1992), pp. 262-84.

41. William Ophuls, *Ecology and the Politics of Scarcity Revisited: The Unravelling of the American Dream* (New York: Freeman, 1992), p. 272.

42. Thomas F. Homer-Dixon, 'Environmental Scarcities and Violent Conflict', *International Security*, vol. 19, no. 1, summer 1994, pp. 5-40.

43. Taken from Paul Harrison, *The Third Revolution: Population, Environment and a Sustainable World* (London: Penguin, 1993), pp. 40-41.

44. For penetrating analysis of variables involved in various state-society relations in the 'Third World', see Joel S. Migdal, *Strong Societies and Weak States: State-Society Relations in the Third World* (Princeton, NJ:Princeton University Press, 1988).

45. 'The lord prevented deviance and fostered a social structure of atomized households in order to maintain complete peasant dependency'. Joel S. Migdal, *Peasants, Politics and Revolution* (Princeton, NJ: Princeton University Press, 1974), pp. 44-5; escapes may be risky for peasants, because in times of distress the lord may offer help where the state fails, leading to debt peonage.

46. See C.H. Alexandrowicz, *An Introduction to the History of the Law of Nations in the East Indies (16th, 17th and 18th Centuries)* (Oxford: Clarendon Press, 1967), p. 41ff.

47. Russia's vast expansion westwards during the eighteenth century, leading to contiguity with the Prussians and the Austrians, was primarily caused by France's inability to help its traditional allies, the Poles, the Swedes and the Ottomans, to block the expansion.

48. Data-based research by Maniruzzaman suggests that if arms transfers to 'Third World' governments go up as a percentage of GNP per capita of the recipients' economies, the probability of a military *coup* shoots up, as well as increasing the length of military rule. He also finds that civilian deaths from political violence are related to military takeovers as a result of military rule, not as its cause. His findings imply an external political link between internal violence and political underdevelopment of 'Third World' countries. Talukder Maniruzzaman, 'Arms Transfers, Military Coups, and Military Rule in Developing Countries', *Journal of Conflict Resolution*, vol. 36, no. 4, December 1992, pp. 733-56.

49. According to the FAO, all 17 major fishing regions of the world are currently harvested beyond capacity. See Lester Brown and Hal Kane, *Full House: Reassessing the Earth's Population-Carrying Capacity* (New York: Norton, 1994), p. 76.

50. B.V.A. Röling, *International Law in an Expanded World* (Amsterdam: North-Holland Publishing, 1960), p. 83.

51. See, for example, the documents on 'development law' and on the 'right to develop' of poor countries, in F. Snyder and P. Slinn (eds), *International Law of Development* (Abingdon: Professional Books, 1987).

52. David Halloran Lumsdaine, *Moral Vision in International Politics: The Foreign Aid Regime, 1949-1989* (Princeton, NJ: Princeton University Press, 1993), p. 253.

Part V

ARMAMENTS

8

Armaments and Conflict: The Causes and Consequences of 'Military Development'

Keith Krause

INTRODUCTION

Between 1987 and 1991, more than 176 billion US dollars worth of weapons flowed into the developing world, and since 1963, more than three-quarters of a trillion (constant 1991) dollars have been spent on armaments.[1] Every year, military expenditures in the developing world exceed 200 billion dollars, spending which keeps more than 17 million men under arms.[2] It also sustains an arsenal that today includes more than 50,000 main battle tanks, 17,000 combat aircraft, 8,000 military helicopters and 80,000 armoured fighting vehicles.[3] At the same time, most of the world's wars and violent conflicts since 1945 have occurred in the developing world. The actual number varies widely according to one's counting rules (anywhere from 58 to 135), but since 1945 these wars and conflicts have resulted in between 20 and 40 million war-related casualties and deaths.[4]

Many of these conflicts have been protracted and extremely resistant to resolution. Most of them also fit uncomfortably into a conventional 'inter-state' paradigm, and involve issues of ethnicity, race, religion, or other forms of identity. An exclusive concentration on inter-state conflict and war thus excludes many of the important forces and factors that must be understood if we are to untangle the complex insecurity-armaments-conflict-war nexus.

Understanding the linkage between armaments, insecurity and conflict is thus a pressing issue, for both intellectual and human reasons. This chapter addresses this linkage not only by concentrating on the 'military aspects of security', but through a broader focus on the *role of institutions and instruments of organized violence in conflicts and insecurity in the developing world*. The reasons for formulating the problem in this fashion, and for dealing with the issues raised, will be addressed along the following outline:
— what is the scope and nature of the problem?

— what motive forces explain patterns of arms acquisition, military development and militarization?
— what (if any) is the linkage between armaments and conflict?
— what are the policy implications of different formulations?

To foreshadow the conclusions somewhat, the motive forces that drive states in the developing world to acquire arms are located at the systemic, regional and internal level, and hence the linkage between armaments and conflict is more complex than simplistic analyses would suggest. Arms acquisitions and the creation of modern military establishments are not necessarily directly (causally) linked to the outbreak of wars and conflicts, but they exacerbate certain sorts of insecurities that can lead to conflicts (inter-state or domestic), and they have a negative impact on the 'quest for security', for peoples and states in the developing world. Although this chapter concentrates on armaments and armed forces, it is inextricably entangled with the host of other issues – ethnicity, state-formation, economic change – that are dealt with in this volume. The goal is to clarify the issues surrounding this more narrow topic, and to build towards a more nuanced account of the connections between armaments and conflict.

One caveat must be registered: an examination of the linkage between conflict and development could lead to the conclusion that this is an exclusively Southern phenomenon. Likewise, a focus on the arms traded between states conceals the fact that the majority of arms (about three-quarters) are produced and 'consumed' within the advanced industrial states.[5] This is misleading, in so far as both Northern and Southern states participate in the 'global military order', and respond to various pressures and forces that are imposed upon them. With these caveats, an examination of the relationship between conflict and development is still valuable, if only because of the critical role played by the post-colonial processes of state-formation, nation-building and economic transformation.

THE STOCKS AND FLOWS OF ARMAMENTS IN THE DEVELOPING WORLD

The four following tables present an overview of the arms build-up in the developing world, and highlight significant regional differences. Table 8.1 details the flow of arms to the developing world since 1963, and illustrates the shifts in regional concentration that have tracked different patterns of conflict: from a focus on East Asia and the confrontation between NATO and the Warsaw Pact in the early 1960s, to the predominance of the Middle East and Africa in the 1970s and early 1980s. The late 1980s marked the ascendence of South Asia, and a slight upsurge in East Asia, with a decline in the Middle Eastern and African share. But despite the increased activity in Asia, the Middle East has accounted for fully one-third of weapons' acquisitions during the past two decades, and has become the most heavily armed region of the developing world.[6] Already there appears to be a loose relationship between arms' flows and violent conflicts, associated with the Indo-China wars in the 1960s and early 1970s, the Middle Eastern wars of 1967 and 1973, the Iran-Iraq war, and the Afghan conflict. That arms flow towards war zones is not surprising; the deeper question is whether or not this actually causes or exacerbates conflicts.

Tables 8.2 and 8.3 show how these flows of weapons have contributed to the arsenals of different regions in the developing world.[7] The Middle East and North Africa account for about half the tanks and armoured fighting vehicles in the developing world (excluding China); and Egypt alone has more tanks than all of Latin America or sub-Saharan Africa! East Asia and China possess the next largest arsenals, while sub-Saharan Africa and Latin America remain relatively less well armed. Although the most rapid growth of arsenals has occurred in sub-Saharan Africa, this is a result of the small size of the military establishments that existed in the early post-independence period. Table 8.3 tracks the increase in the number of states possessing advanced weapons' systems, and although it does not document the increase in sophistication of the armaments possessed by states in the developing world, this too has climbed with advances in military technology. Despite many simplifications, what these data demonstrate is that the flow of arms into the developing world has created powerful, modern military establishments in several states in a short span of time. These armed forces do not approach the industrialized states' arsenals in size or technology, but the absolute increase in destructive potential in the developing world has been enormous.

Potentially the most significant data are contained in Table 8.4, which presents cross-regional comparative military indicators. It illustrates that regions vary widely in their levels of military expenditure, size of arsenals, and relative economic burden and societal 'weight' of the armed forces. Although these data obscure differences within regions, and the near-dominant role of particular states (such as South Africa, Egypt and India), it does illustrate the great differences that exist, and the possible linkages between armaments and other indices of 'military development' that must be explored. Most importantly, the developing world does not present an undifferentiated picture of wholesale 'militarization', and only the Middle East approaches the level of militarization that existed between the two opposing blocs during the Cold War.[8] These figures also suggest that whatever frame-

TABLE 8.1 *Regional Distribution of Arms Imports, 1963-1991*

Years	1963-67	1968-72	1973-77	1978-82	1983-87	1987-91	(%popul. 1982)
Africa	4.2	3.6	11.3	18.7	12.3	7.8	(9.8)
East Asia	28.7	34.6	15.6	10.7	11.5	12.7	(35.1)
Latin America	3.1	3.6	4.8	6.8	7.4	5.9	(8.1)
Middle East	9.2	16.6	33.6	37.5	37.8	34.7	(3.1)
South Asia	6.8	4.3	4.0	3.9	7.3	12.7	(20.4)
North America	3.0	3.5	2.0	1.7	1.5	4.9	(5.6)
Oceania	2.0	1.4	0.9	1.0	1.5	1.5	(0.5)
NATO (Eur.)	20.3	18.3	10.2	8.7	7.4	12.0	(7.1)
Warsaw Pact	19.1	11.2	14.7	8.3	10.4	6.0	(8.2)
Other Europe	3.6	2.7	2.8	2.7	2.4	1.6	(2.0)
Developed	41.7	28.9	25.7	19.5	20.9	22.4	(23.1)
Developing	58.3	71.1	74.3	80.5	79.1	77.5	(76.3)

Source: WMEAT, various years.

Note: Regions are classified as follows: *Oceania:* Australia, New Zealand, Fiji, Papua-New Guinea; *Africa:* does not include Egypt; *Middle East:* Egypt to the Persian Gulf, Iran and Cyprus; *Latin America:* Mexico south, all Caribbean states; *North America:* Canada and the US; *South Asia:* Afghanistan, India, Pakistan, Nepal, Bangladesh, Sri Lanka; *East Asia:* Mongolia, both Koreas, both Chinas, Japan and from Burma to Indonesia; *Other Europe:* Albania, Austria, Finland, Ireland, Malta, Spain, Sweden, Switzerland, Yugoslavia; *Developed:* all of NATO, except Greece and Turkey; all of the Warsaw Pact except Bulgaria; Japan, Australia, New Zealand, Finland, Austria, Ireland, Sweden and Switzerland; *Developing:* all others.

TABLE 8.2 *Number of Weapons by Region and Weapons System, 1993-94*

	Middle East/ North Africa	Sub-Saharan Africa	South Asia	East Asia	China	Latin America/ Caribbean
Main Battle Tanks	22,549	1,817	6,641	9,705	8,000	2,517
Other AFVs	39,544	9,209	4,732	19,561	4,800	9,016
Combat Aircraft	4,143	917	1,557	3,605	6,064	1,640
Helicopters	2,110	709	864	3,088	630	1,476
Naval Vessels	598	232	365	2,594	1,344	654

Source: International Institute of Strategic Studies, *The Military Balance* (London: IISS, various years), compiled by Ken Boutin.
Notes: IISS data is subject to great variation from year to year; these figures are meant as trend indicators only. Central Asian republics of the former Soviet Union have been excluded.
Main battle tanks includes heavy and medium tanks; *Other AFVs* includes light tanks, reconnaissance vehicles, armoured personnel carriers and infantry fighting vehicles; *Combat aircraft* includes fighter, strike, reconnaissance, counter-insurgency and ASW aircraft; *Naval vessels* include all surface and submarine vessels of greater than 100 tons displacement (excluding hovercraft).

work one constructs to reveal the relationships between armaments and conflict, other military, economic and social factors must be included, if only because the armaments by themselves cannot be said to do or cause anything!

Evidence from the early 1990s suggests that although some of the major trends governing defence and security policies in the developing world have changed, the fundamental picture painted by these statistics has not altered. Although arms' imports have dropped to between one-third and two-fifths of the levels of the late 1980s, military expenditures have only declined by about ten per cent since 1985.[9] Likewise, although the flow of arms to the developing world has declined, arsenals have not shrunk, and their potential for use in violent conflicts has not been diminished by arms control or confidence-building processes analogous to those which have unfolded in Europe. The evidence also suggests that the decline in the number of conflicts since the end of the Cold War has been, if anything, very gradual.[10]

TABLE 8.3 *Numbers of States in the Developing World with Selected Weapons Systems, 1950-1992*

	1950	1960	1970	1980	1985	1990	1992
Supersonic aircraft	-	1	28	55	55	61	66
Missiles	-	6	25	68	71	75	81
Armoured Vehicles	1	38	72	99	102	102	105
Main Battle Tanks	-	32	39	-	62	57	64
Modern Warships	4	26	56	79	81	80	79

Sources: Figures for 1950-1985 (except for main battle tanks) from Edward Kolodziej, *Making and Marketing Arms: The French Experience and its Implications for the International System* (Princeton, NJ: Princeton University Press, 1987), p. 183. Figures for main battle tanks (1950-1985) estimated from Michael Brzoska and Thomas Ohlson, *Arms Transfers to the Third World* (Oxford: Oxford University Press, 1987), p. 12. Figures for 1990 and 1992 are from the *Military Balance*, and have been checked against Kolodziej's figures to ensure comparability.

LINKAGES BETWEEN ARMAMENTS, INSECURITY AND CONFLICT

What explains these patterns of arms acquisitions, and how might they be related to patterns of conflict in the developing world? To begin, it is worth sketching, in almost caricatured form, three simple models of the relation-

TABLE 8.4 *Selected Military Indicators, by Region, 1991*

	Military Expenditure (1990 $US)	Milex/GPN (per cent)	Milex/capita ($US)	Armed forces (thousands)	Population (millions)	Soldiers/ thousand
Africa	16,000	4.1	26	1,629	620.4	2.6
East Asia	119,700	2.1	66	8,058	1,820.5	4.4
Latin America	15,800	1.5	35	1,561	452.1	3.5
Middle East	88,300	20.1	466	2,560	189.6	13.5
South Asia	11,000	3.2	10	2,283	1,157.2	2.0
North America	291,800	4.7	1,044	2,201	279.5	7.9
Oceania	8,100	2.4	320	88	25.3	3.5
NATO Europe	188,100	2.9	464	3,391	405.3	8.4
Warsaw Pact	276,600	9.3	710	3,854	389.4	9.9
Other Europe	22,600	2.5	382	393	59.2	6.6
Developed	796,500	4.1	678	8,667	1,174.8	7.4
Developing	241,700	4.5	57	17,350	4,223.8	4.1
World	1,038,100	4.2	192	26,020	5,398.6	4.8

Source: WMEAT 1991-1992 (Washington: ACDA, 1994), pp. 47-50.

ship between armaments and conflict. First, one could posit that there is a direct, causal link between armaments and conflicts, such that increased levels of armaments (or a more rapid rate of acquisition) can exacerbate the security dilemma and/or increase the potential for misperception to lead to war. This relationship, the 'spiral model of conflict', captures the underlying argument behind the vast (and inconclusive) literature on the relationship between arms races and conflict or war. As Robert Jervis analyses it, 'the spiral model of conflict sees the [resulting] action-reaction dynamic as accelerated by each side's inability to understand the other or to see how the other is interpreting its own behaviour. These processes generate and magnify conflict, leading to unnecessary wars.'[11]

Second, one could posit that armaments are a purely dependent variable that is not causally connected to the occurrence of war. This view argues that conflicts have roots in social and political struggles between states over the distribution of economic and political power. Increased levels of armaments could be a manifestation of these tensions, but it is the underlying conflict that causes arms' acquisitions (and wars).

Finally, one can argue that the direction of causality is irrelevant; that 'whether the conflict begets the arms or the arms beget the conflict, they go together; the increase in military capability will most certainly be accompanied by an increase in conflict'.[12] This view assumes that levels of armaments and levels of conflict are linked on a deeper level: the same structures, forces and processes that cause the acquisition of arms also lead to increased conflict. The exact relationship between armaments and conflict remains unclear: the acquisition of arms may be symptomatic and not causal, or there could be a linkage that exacerbates further conflicts that have already been catalysed.

There are analytic problems with each of these stripped-down formulations. The first enjoys little empirical support unless a host of ancillary causes are introduced; the second reifies the causes of conflict by rooting them in historical or socio-cultural conditions that are seldom considered amenable to change; and the third, while admitting somewhat more complexity, is analytically not very useful. Although each can be tested empirically, their state-centricity and lack of historicity excludes precisely the systemic, domestic and historical forces that must be included in order to understand particular conflict dynamics.

The relationship proposed in this chapter differs from the first two stark alternatives, and elaborates on the third in order to make it analytically and prescriptively useful. It argues that the relative 'strength' of the instruments and institutions of organized violence within a state can change the costs or benefits associated with the various options that state rulers possess to achieve peace and security, and can tilt the balance in favour of particular 'solutions' to insecurities and conflicts (that is, peaceful negotiation and resolution versus confrontation and violent conflict). Thus arms and armed forces can accelerate the momentum towards conflicts that have been created by a constellation of other factors. In and of themselves, armaments do not cause anything, but under certain circumstances their presence or 'influence' can fuel conflict tremendously and exacerbate insecurities. The goal is to specify more precisely in what ways and under what circumstances increased levels of armaments contribute to exacerbating conflicts, and how this effect can be dampened or reduced.

MOTIVE FORCES DRIVING ARMS' ACQUISITIONS, MILITARY DEVELOPMENT AND 'MILITARIZATION'

The first step is to embed the discussion of armaments within the broader context of the creation and expansion of the institutions of organized violence within the developing world. As Nicole Ball has noted, 'in the public mind, security expenditure in the Third World is firmly linked with the arms trade', but the bulk of military spending in the developing world goes to operating and personnel costs.[13] Hence armaments' acquisitions can only be a small part of the problem of 'military development', and the transfer of weapons is only one aspect of this complex process by which institutions, ideas and instruments for defining and achieving 'security' are transmitted to the developing world.[14] Yet we have few case studies of security policy-making in the developing world that would shed light on these processes.[15] The best one can do at this point is to present suggestive illustrations that could form the foundation for future research, and the first task is to unpack the various motive forces that propel the accumulation of large arsenals in various parts of the developing world.

The forces that fuel the patterns of arms' acquisition and military developments suggested by the above tables operate (often simultaneously) at systemic, regional, internal and 'state-formation' levels.[16] Systemic forces include the pursuit of status and hegemony; the influence of patron-client relationships that can 'socialize' clients into accepting particular understandings of security (the source of threats and the appropriate means to respond to them); and the 'halo of prestige' that surrounds modern weapons and military establishments and makes them desirable as symbols and trappings of a modern state. The pursuit of power or status appears to have played a significant role in the arms' acquisition decisions of states such as Iran, Egypt, or India, all of which have aspired to a prominent regional role.

Likewise, tight patron-client relationships (the US with Iran, Pakistan or the Philippines, the former Soviet Union with Iraq, Cuba and Vietnam) have doubtless shaped the resulting military establishments.[17] What is important to highlight, however, is that these factors are *systemic*, in the sense that they rely on the diffusion and acceptance of ideas about the proper role of armed forces and modern weapons in the quest for security that shape the way in which rulers and elites define their interests, and the alternative courses of action that they face.

Regional motive forces are those directly associated with the need to fight wars or guarantee security against specified external threats. This level captures the traditional idea of 'national security', and accords well with the argument that armaments are acquired to deter or defend against attacks from other states. Regional actors' perceptions of security threats are in part determined by the military capabilities of other actors in the same 'security complex', and military expenditures and the acquisition of weapons represent concrete responses.[18] Although this inter-state security dilemma also rests on subjective perceptions of intentions, its acuteness is tied to the military potential of possible opponents. Prominent prima-facie examples of regional security complexes that would be dominated by this set of forces would be the Arab-Israeli conflict, the Persian Gulf (since the early 1970s), and the China-India-Pakistan conflict.

As Mohammed Ayoob and others have pointed out, however, security and armament policies in the developing world are not solely determined by systemic or regional imperatives.[19] Rather, the third and fourth sources of insecurity stem from the weakness of regimes that have a narrow base of political support, or from the low legitimacy of the state itself. Regime insecurities do not necessarily translate into the desire to acquire armaments, but the most immediate method by which to secure a regime against internal threats is to increase its control over the means of organized violence. In many cases in the developing world, the military has emerged as a significant prop for the state, existing in a symbiotic relationship with the ruling elite (sometimes ruling itself, sometimes acting as the 'power behind the throne'), and it frequently exercises a claim on a significant share of national resources. Similarly, in many states in the developing world, military development and arms' acquisitions are fuelled by the tensions inherent in the process of 'state-formation'. In states in which the institutions (or existence) of the state are in question, the result is often a hypertrophied military establishment, with tentacles of influence reaching into all levels of society. This is most clear in Africa and the Middle East, where the percentage of GNP absorbed by military expenditures is the greatest in the developing world. Classic examples would include Iraq, Zimbabwe or Algeria.

Not all of these motivations would operate in every case, and this list of factors should be seen as a set of prima-facie hypotheses that need further research and testing. Anecdotal evidence can, however, be offered for each of them. What is most important is to underline that most analyses of the relationship between armaments and conflict have concentrated on the regional level, in which the primary focus of attention is the threat of inter-state war. Consequently, providing a more nuanced or comprehensive answer to the question of why states acquire armaments, facilitates a more sophisticated account of the relationship between armaments' acquisitions and conflict.

ARMAMENTS, INSECURITY AND CONFLICT

The debate on the concept of security has in recent years highlighted the weaknesses of any formulation that ties security tightly to the idea of 'securing the nation-state from externally generated threats to its survival'. [20] Scholars such as Barry Buzan have suggested that the concept needs to be deepened to draw attention to the different levels (individual, state, regional and systemic) on which security is achieved. Others have suggested that the concept needs to be broadened to include issues other than those associated with traditional 'military-security', such as environmental, economic, or human rights' dimensions. [21] This same logic applies to discussions of conflict: if we define the scope of our concern solely as the incidence or possibility of inter-state war, we exclude from scrutiny many possible negative consequences of armaments' acquisitions and military development. But if increased conflict results from increased insecurity, as a corollary, the object of study should be the *consequences* of this process of military development (including the acquisition of armaments) on the quest to achieve security at the regional, state and individual level. [22] This extends our understanding of conflict to include not just inter-state wars, but also conflicts between organized groups within the state, or between the state (regime) and its citizens.

At each level of analysis, different sets of possible consequences can be outlined, and since only anecdotal evidence for each of these can be offered here, these sets of consequences should be regarded almost as hypotheses for further research. The broad claim is that the ideas, institutions and instruments of organized violence within a state facilitate the development of particular understandings of what security is, how security is to be achieved, and what the source of threats are; and that these exert a critical influence on the strategies chosen to achieve regional, state and individual security. This claim establishes the parameters of a more complex and sophisticated account of the linkages between 'armaments and the causes of conflict', or of the 'military aspects of security', and its propositions are summarized in Figure 8.1.

The regional consequences encompass traditional conceptions of the threats that states pose to each other. Three elements of the armaments-insecurity-conflict nexus can be highlighted that could be important. First, acquisitions of increasingly sophisticated armaments have intensified the destructiveness of regional wars, even if they have not caused them. Second, external patronage (arms transfers and/or security alliances) has lowered the opportunity cost of participating in arms races or wars, and made co-operative solutions to regional conflicts less likely. As Mullins has demonstrated, even relatively poor states such as Somalia, Ethiopia, Nicaragua or Syria have been able to make convincing bids for regional status and have fought wars, based on military capabilities far in excess of their economic resources and obtained almost solely as a function of superpower patronage.[23] Third, large or hypertrophied military establishments in such states weaken or marginalize those groups that would benefit the most from the transformation of a regional conflict environment, and hence groups which would advocate most strongly non-conflictive ideas about how to achieve regional security. The slow process by which Egypt decided to seek peace with Israel, for example, was influenced by (and was simultaneous with) President Sadat's economic opening to the West and the world economy. After the 1973 debacle, Egyptian technocratic and state capitalist elites articulated an interest in lowering the cost of security in order to maximize their domestic and international economic opportunities.[24] By contrast, similar groups in Syria have been relatively weak and subordinate to the military, and Syria is only now opening its economy to private capital and enterprise.[25] This balance of social forces almost certainly contributed to the reluctance of President Assad's regime to countenance even a cold peace with Israel.

The second set of consequences manifests itself at the level of the state, and it concerns the threat that those who control the institutions and instruments of organized violence can pose to state institutions. The development of European states involved rulers amassing greater and greater resources to finance expanding military machines, and war preparation facilitated the innovation of public debt, led to the creation and expansion of taxes, and exercised a 'ratchet effect' on government expenditures. Emerging political and socio-economic institutions (the modern bureaucracy) were essential to mobilize resources to build modern armies, and they could bargain on relatively equal footing with them.[26] This created a symbiotic relationship between 'war-makers' and 'state-makers' which, over time, resulted in the

FIGURE 8.1   *Military Development, Insecurity and Conflict – Research Hypotheses*

REGIONAL SECURITY AND INTER-STATE CONFLICT

- spiralling acquisitions of increasingly sophisticated armaments intensify regional wars even if they do not cause them
- external patronage (weapons or security alliances) lowers the opportunity cost of participating in arms races or wars, making cooperative solutions to regional conflicts less likely
- large military establishments weaken or marginalize groups that would benefit most from the transformation of a regional conflict environment, and that would advocate most strongly non-conflictive ideas about how to achieve regional security

STATE OR REGIME SECURITY AND SOCIETAL CONFLICT

- increased armaments and rapid military development tilt the balance of social and political power between the military and other social forces, and skew the distribution of resources between military and other ends
- rapid military development results in state institutions and elite groups being bent to the purposes of the institutions of organized violence

INDIVIDUAL SECURITY AND CONFLICT BETWEEN THE STATE AND CITIZENS

- states with strong external patronage do not draw upon citizens' resources (taxes) to construct modern military establishments, thus reducing the claims citizens have upon the state to constrain military power or influence
- when modern institutions of organized violence develop more rapidly than other social institutions or structures, rulers rely upon them to a greater degree for surveillance and social control
- the armed forces, as a reservoir of political power, can be captured by groups within fractured states that have no interest in creating a broader consensus for representative rule

---

subordination of the military and security policy to civilian control and institutions. In much of the developing world, however, the armed forces appear as the first, and most highly developed, 'modern' institution, and there is little evidence of a symbiotic and evolving relationship with other groups and forces in society. The practical consequences of this are two-fold. First, this unequal balance of social and political power skews the distribution of resources between military and other ends. Even if there is no evidence that military spending exerts a negative impact on economic growth, there are opportunity costs of these choices, and armed forces consume resources which could in principle be used for other purposes.[27] Although it is notoriously difficult to define 'excessive' military spending, there is little evidence to justify the claim that the threat faced by the over-whelming majority of states in the developing world is as dangerous as levels of military spending and arms acquisitions would prima facie suggest. As one study of 46 'new' states shows, there is no evidence that [these] 'states are arming themselves in response to external considerations [ie: regional threats]; on the contrary, the size of their economies and their relationships with the Soviet Union more than any other factors explain the level in any given year of their military capability'.[28] This suggests that armed forces behave like any powerful social or bureaucratic actor, advancing claims on national income that are based on maintaining or expanding their share of resources, rather than being based on national security imperatives. What-ever the *causal* factors that determine levels of military expenditure, the *consequences*, in a domestic political environment in which other social groups are weak, can be extremely negative.

The second result is that state institutions and elite groups in the develop-ing world are fused with, and bent to the purposes of, the institutions of organized violence. Again, to offer an example from the Middle East, the Syrian military has institutionalized economic corruption to satisfy the demands of the armed forces for resources, and has hindered the emergence of an independent economic or technocratic elite. As Raymond Hinnebusch notes

> from the moment Ba'thi officers brought the party to power ... it was likely that the military would be an equal or senior partner in the new military-party state, and that institution building would have to go on in concert with military leadership, not apart from it.[29]

Although the military has retreated from direct political control in many states, it is a mistake to assume that the 'return to the barracks' necessarily subordinates the armed forces to civilian control. Instead, as Nicole Ball has noted

> most Third World armed forces have not supported the growth of partici-
> patory forms of government ... rather they have become important both
> as mediators between different elite groups ... and as guarantors of elite-
> dominated political and economic systems.[30]

This argument may be able to demonstrate a direct (quasi-causal) link between social conflict, military rule, and military expenditures or arma-ments.[31] Even if it cannot, it suggests that the process of military develop-ment, when aided and abetted by external powers, has as a consequence the creation of conditions under which the development of strong and indepen-dent social and political institutions in civil society is thwarted. Without such institutions, social conflict (whether rooted in economic conditions or other circumstances) is endemic, and the potential for reducing insecurity through political dialogue and compromise is limited.

The final set of consequences concerns individual security: the threat posed by the institutions and instruments of organized violence to citizens. This draws our attention to conflicts manifest exclusively within the state, between a state/regime and its citizens, and to the role of instruments and institutions of violence in creating or perpetuating authoritarian rule. By the middle of the nineteenth century, many Western states had relieved the army of its internal security functions, and another reciprocal relationship emerged. As state-makers extracted resources from nascent citizens for war-making, they promised security in return. This 'gave civilian groups enforce-able claims on the state', which were politically enfranchising, and contrib-uted to the evolution towards representative government.[32] But the creation of modern military institutions, sustained by patron-client or alliance rela-tionships with powerful states, has made this process of 'democratization' more difficult in the developing world, for three reasons.

First, states that enjoyed strong external patronage did not have to turn to their citizens to construct large, modern military establishments. This reduced the need for bargains to be struck between state-makers and other social groups that would eventually give citizens claims on the state.[33] Anecdotal evidence for this can be found in the experience of many African and Middle Eastern states.

Second, modern institutions of organized violence appeared in an envi-ronment in which other social structures were struggling to emerge, or were actively suppressed. This has given rulers unprecedented means of control: in the absence of other social institutions capable of commanding loyalty from the citizens, the armed forces, and their concomitant modern techniques of surveillance and social control, became the most prominent tools of statecraft.[34]

Third, the armed forces have been a tremendous reservoir of political power that can be captured by particular groups within a state that have no interest in creating a broader social consensus for rule. In states with weak 'national' identities, religious, ethnic, racial or cultural minorities can, by dominating or controlling the institutions of violence, entrench their positions and thwart the emergence of more pluralist or representative politics. This directly contradicts the argument advanced by early modernization theorists that the armed forces would act as an integrative force in a fractured polity, and authoritarian rule in these states has probably been deepened rather than weakened as a consequence of military modernization.[35] Obviously, other economic and social forces are at work in the creation and perpetuation of authoritarian rule, but, as Jill Crystal notes in the Middle East context

> political violence ... is central to the longevity of these regimes, ... once established these [coercive] institutions may assume an independent internal dynamic.[36]

CONCLUSION: THE POLICY-RELEVANT IMPLICATIONS

Figure 8.1 summarized the central hypotheses for the relationship between armaments, military development, insecurity and conflict, hypotheses that could form the core of a programme to investigate the military aspects of security. But what (if any) would be the policy implications of this research? Different accounts of the relationship between armaments and conflict have, of course, very different policy implications. Those who believe that armaments are in themselves a causal contributor to regional and inter-state conflicts would put their faith in controls for the continued proliferation of conventional weapons, either through supply-side efforts (such as the Missile Technology Control Regime, or a renewed CoCom), or via supplier-recipient initiatives (such as the Chemical Weapons Convention). Those who argue that armaments are not an independent factor in such conflicts, but a symptom of deeper problems, would either argue that the real causes could not be addressed by arms control, or that regional and inter-state conflicts could only be resolved through peace-building and conflict resolution processes. Those who believe that armaments can exacerbate insecurities, even if they do not directly cause conflicts, would grant a small meliorative role to efforts to increase transparency (as in the UN Register of Conventional Arms) or to implement regional military-oriented confidence- and security-building measures, but would not expect major shifts in regional conflict dynamics as a consequence.

This chapter suggests a somewhat different approach. First, it implies that policies that concentrate exclusively on the role of armaments in inter-state conflict dynamics are misguided: such a focus leads inevitably towards the goal of 'stabilizing' potentially explosive conflict regions, but does not promote stability at lower levels of armaments. It is also open to self-interested manipulation by arms suppliers, who can defend virtually any decision to export arms as a stabilizing measure![37] Perhaps most importantly, a focus on inter-state or regional stability neglects the other potential negative consequences that manifest themselves at the state and individual level.

Second, by placing the problem of armaments in the broader framework of the creation and expansion of modern military establishments in post-colonial states, the analysis draws attention to issues beyond arms' imports, such as levels of military spending. Levels of arms' imports closely track the pattern of global military spending, suggesting that an exclusive focus on controlling armaments is misguided, as the forces that give rise to arms' acquisitions are rooted more deeply in the processes of military development.

Finally, this chapter argues that many of the tensions that generate high levels of military expenditures and an intrusive role for the military in politics are the result of the historical process of state-formation in the developing world.

Taken together, these arguments suggest that the proper focus of policy attention should be on ways to constrain military expenditures and the growth of military establishments, and on the nature of civil-military relations in the developing world. Three particular practical measures merit closer study: increasing the transparency of arms' acquisitions and security policies; linking security expenditures and international financial assistance; and promoting – under the rubric of 'good governance' – different patterns of civil-military relations.

Efforts to increase transparency have focused on the recently established UN Register of Conventional Arms.[38] At the inter-state level, those who believe in the 'spiral model' of conflict would argue that the Register could diminish uncertainty and misperception, reduce crisis instability, and potentially lower levels of military and armaments' spending.[39] The argument presented here, however, suggests that this understanding of the motive forces behind arms' acquisitions and military expenditures is too narrow. If attention is paid to the inter-locking regional, state and individual levels of

security, the goal of increased transparency would be to reduce the armed
force's privileged status as the custodian of national security policy by
making possible a greater debate over the allocation of resources within
society, and over security policy in general. A closely related goal would be
the provision of 'early-warning' indicators (such as rapid increases in arms
imports) that could be used by governments and international or non-governmental organizations to raise awareness of the rising potential for violent
conflict. Although it may be impossible to link (in any formal way) levels of
armaments (or of particular types of armaments), to levels or types of violent
conflict, an approach that considers the regional context of policies concerning military spending and arms' imports is more likely to highlight outstanding and worrisome cases.[40]

On this account, the Register of Conventional Arms would have to be
improved to include national procurement and weapons' holdings, and inter-
governmental consultative processes would have to be established. Data
from the Register would also have to be widely disseminated and used by
non-governmental groups (such as Human Rights Watch or Amnesty International) to promote policy changes. This is a more complex task than simply
improving inter-governmental discussions on security and armaments, but
it is a logical corollary of this argument, and it highlights the necessary role
of non-governmental organizations in promoting a dialogue within society
on the best means to achieve security.

Efforts to link restraint in arms' acquisitions or military spending to
access to the international financial system have received increasing attention
since 1989, when IMF and World Bank officials began speaking out on the
excessive resources devoted to military and security policy in many parts of
the South.[41] Concrete measures would tie restraint on the part of Southern
states to development assistance, World Bank lending, credits from the
International Monetary Fund, or other multilateral financial instruments for
development. Individual states (in particular Japan, Germany, the Nordic
countries and Canada) have also stated that their overseas development
assistance programmes will consider military spending and security policies
in their decisions, albeit on a case-by-case basis. The most straightforward
initiatives threaten to reduce bilateral or multilateral development assistance
or credits in cases of 'excessive' arms' acquisitions or military spending, and
the comparative indicators that have been used to assess this include the level
of armament spending relative to military (or government) spending, the
percentage of GNP (or government spending) devoted to the armed forces,
the relationship between arms imports or military spending and fiscal defi-
cits, and the level of personnel in the armed forces (soldiers per thousand of
the population).

There is, however, no easy mechanism for assessing comparatively the impact of armaments and military spending on economic development and conflict and insecurity, and measures to link economic development programmes to reductions in military spending must be approached with caution. As noted in Table 8.4, indicators of 'militarization' vary widely from region to region and offer no easy benchmarks, but within particular regional contexts there are always one or several outlying states that appear to devote disproportionate resources to the military. These are not always, however, the states most susceptible to multilateral pressure. Levels of military spending in one state remain closely linked to changes in the level of military spending in neighbouring countries, suggesting that the classic security dilemma still plays a role in setting levels of military expenditures (and hence, arms' build-ups), even if the consequences of these choices are felt most acutely at the state and individual level. Initiatives that target individual states outside the context of regional initiatives could thus exacerbate rather than ameliorate conflicts. Such measures are also discriminatory if they exclude states that do not rely on the international community for financial resources (such as resource-rich states), if they affect only states that must import weapons (allowing producers to arm themselves with impunity), or if they affect only states that borrow from multilateral financial institutions, rather than those which obtain credit in the private market (as is increasingly the case, for example, in East Asia).

Instead, perhaps the most important initiatives concentrate on offering inducements and assistance to those states that actively promote 'good governance', defined by the World Bank as 'the manner in which power is exercised in the management of a country's economic and social resources for development'.[42] This concept can easily be oriented towards security policy, and three specific areas have been highlighted to date: the demobilization and reintegration of military personnel in the aftermath of conflicts or a transition to democratic rule (in Argentina, Uganda, Central America, Russia); the conversion of defence industries (as in Slovakia, Poland and the former Soviet Union); and the rebalancing of military expenditure with other government spending (for example, much of sub-Saharan Africa and India). Each of these issues goes beyond simple declaratory policy linkages, and requires concerted assistance from the international community in such matters as restructuring civil-military relations, retraining military personnel, or providing investment and export assistance. At the official level, states could be encouraged as part of 'good governance' to participate in regional confidence- and security-building processes, multilateral non-proliferation regimes, and domestic demilitarization programmes. At the domestic level, strategies of 'capacity-building' could concentrate on enhanc-

ing the power of groups in civil society (such as community groups, entrepreneurial elites, social service networks) that have a vested interest in non-
conflictual solutions to regional conflicts, and in reducing or constraining the
resources that go to maintaining the institutions of organized violence in
developing states. Strategies for good governance must, however, be conscious of the role that the institutions of organized violence play in many
states, and the disruptive potential they contain.

None of these strategies will provide a short-term fix for a deep and
seemingly intractable problem that has been many years in the making. But
the end of the Cold War at least provides the opportunity to move beyond the
outworn ideological formulations that fuelled so many regional conflicts and
to address the quest for security in all its dimensions, and these opportunities
should at least be seized by policy-makers.

NOTES

1. The $176 billion figure is from the United States Arms Control and Disarma-
   ment Agency, *World Military Expenditures and Arms Transfers, 1991-1992*
   (Washington, DC: Arms Control and Disarmament Agency, 1994); hereafter
   cited as *WMEAT*. The $750 billion figure for total armament spending has been
   compiled from successive ACDA publications and recalculated in 1988 dollars.
   The definition of 'developing world' or 'Third World' is contestable, especially
   since the emergence of new states in the territory of the former Soviet Union,
   but since the purpose is to concentrate on broader patterns, the conventional
   definition (states in Africa, the Middle East, Latin America and all of Asia
   except the former Soviet Union) has been adopted.
2. Military expenditure in the developing world for 1991 was 241 billion dollars,
   WMEAT, 1991-1992, p. 47. The total number of soldiers is from the same
   source.
3. International Institute of Strategic Studies, *The Military Balance, 1992-93*
   (London: IISS, 1993).
4. The low figure for the number of wars is from Kalevi J. Holsti, *Peace and War:
   Armed Conflicts and International Order 1648-1989* (Cambridge: Cambridge
   University Press, 1991), p. 278; the higher figure from Ken Booth (ed.), *New
   Thinking about Strategy and International Security* (London: HarperCollins,
   1991), p. 355. The low figure for war-related deaths is from Booth, p. 355; the
   higher figure is from David Morrison, 'Sounding a Call to Arms for the 1990s',
   National Journal, 13 November 1993, p. 2728.
5. See Keith Krause, *Arms and the State: Patterns of Military Production and
   Trade* (Cambridge: Cambridge University Press, 1992), p. 93.
6. On Asian weapons' acquisitions see Desmond Ball, 'Arms and Affluence:
   Military Acquisitions in the Asia-Pacific Region', *International Security*, 18:3

(winter 1993/94), pp. 78-112; Michael Klare, 'The Next Great Arms Race', *Foreign Affairs*, 72:3 (summer 1993), pp. 136-52. On the Middle East see Keith Krause, 'Middle Eastern Arms Recipients in the Post-Cold War World', *The Annals of the American Academy of Political and Social Science*, 535 (September 1994), pp. 73-90.

7. Material in this section is drawn from Krause, *Arms and the State*, pp. 187-92, and has been updated by Ken Boutin.

8. For a discussion of the definitional difficulties with the term 'militarization', see Andrew Ross, 'Dimensions of Militarization in the Third World', *Armed Forces and Society*, 13:4 (summer 1987), pp. 561-78.

9. SIPRI figures for arms exports to the developing world for 1988 and 1992 are $23,688 million and $9,320 million (constant 1990 dollars) respectively; Richard Grimmett's figures for the same period are $46,743 and $12,720 (constant 1992 dollars). See Stockholm International Peace Research Institute, *SIPRI Yearbook 1993* (Oxford: Oxford University Press, 1993), pp. 392, 444; and Richard Grimmett, *Conventional Arms Transfers to the Third World, 1985-1992*, Congressional Research Service, report 93-656F, July 1993, p. 60.

10. The *SIPRI Yearbook 1993* suggests that the number of conflicts declined from 32 in 1989 to 30 in 1992, pp. 86-8. For a discussion of the various arguments concerning the 'decompression' effect of the end of the Cold War, which suggests that the number of conflicts might actually increase in the short term, see Amitav Acharya, 'Third World Conflicts and International Order after the Cold War', *Working Paper 134* (Canberra, ACT: Australian National University Peace Research Centre, 1993).

11. Robert Jervis, 'Arms Control, Stability and Causes of War', *Political Science Quarterly*, 108:2 (summer 1993), p. 244. Another strand in the literature calls this the 'tinderbox hypothesis', which states that 'arms races do not necessarily cause wars, but they do create an inflammable situation between the racing nations where even the slightest spark can push a blaze to war ... [it] implicitly assumes that arms races do not cause disputes'; James Morrow, 'A Twist of Truth: A Re-examination of the Effects of Arms Races on the Occurrence of War', *Journal of Conflict Resolution*, 33 (September 1989), p. 502. For a recent review of the literature, see Randall Siverson and Paul Diehl, 'Arms Races, the Conflict Spiral, and the Onset of War', in Magnus Midlarsky, (ed.), *The Handbook of War Studies* (Boston, MA: Allen & Unwin, 1990).

12. A.F. Mullins, *Born Arming: Development and Military Power in New States* (Stanford, CA: Stanford University Press, 1987), p. 114.

13. Nicole Ball, *Security and Economy in the Third World* (Princeton, NJ: Princeton University Press, 1988), p. 107. Her appendix I offers data on this for several states.

14. Military development refers not only to the growth and modernization of armed forces, but to the broader process of diffusing modern military technologies and techniques of organization to the developing world. It encompasses choices about military doctrines (mass versus elite armies, defensive versus offensive

194   *Armaments and Conflict*

force postures), the development of ancillary social and political institutions (civil-military relations, a military educational system), and choices among different overarching concepts of who or what represent the threat, and how best to counter them.

15. For comparative case studies, see Stephanie Neuman (ed.), *Defense Planning in Less-Industrialized States: The Middle East and South Asia* (Lexington, MA: Lexington Books, 1984); Robert Harkavy and Edward Kolodziej (eds), *Security Policies of Developing Countries* (Lexington, MA: Lexington Books, 1982). For macro-statistical studies, see Robert Looney, *Third-World Military Expenditure and Arms Production* (London: Macmillan, 1988); and Robert McKinlay, *Third World Military Expenditure: Determinants and Implications* (London: Pinter, 1989).

16. See Krause, *Arms and the State*, pp. 193-8. These motivations have been dealt with differently by many authors concerned with explaining not only arms acquisitions but also military expenditures. For a general account see Andrew Pierre, *The Global Politics of Arms Sales* (Princeton, NJ: Princeton University Press, 1982), pp. 131-5, 136-271; Stockholm International Peace Research Institute, *The Arms Trade with the Third World* (Stockholm: Almqvist and Wiksell, 1971), pp. 41-85. For a detailed statistical correlative analysis see Robert McKinlay, *Third World Military Expenditure*.

17. On patron-client relationships and security doctrines, see Keith Krause, 'Military Statecraft: Power and Influence in Soviet and American Arms Transfer Relationships', *International Studies Quarterly*, 35:3, (September 1991), pp. 313-36; and Mullins, *Born Arming*.

18. Barry Buzan, *People, States and Fear* (London: Harvester Wheatsheaf, 1991), pp. 187-95.

19. See Mohammed Ayoob, 'Security in the Third World: The Worm About to Turn', *International Affairs*, 60:1, pp. 41-51; Ed Azar and Chung-In Moon, 'Third World National Security: Towards a New Conceptual Framework', *International Interactions*, 11, 1984, pp. 103-35. See also Edward Azar and Chung-In Moon (eds), *National Security in the Third World* (Aldershot: Edward Elgar, 1988); and Mohammed Ayoob (ed.), *Regional Security in the Third World* (Boulder, CO: Westview, 1986), pp. 3-23.

20. For an extensive listing and discussion of orthodox formulations of the concept of security, see Buzan, *People, States and Fear*, pp. 16-18.

21. See Caroline Thomas, *In Search of Security* (Hemel Hempstead: Harvester Wheatsheaf, 1987); Yezid Sayigh, 'Confronting the 1990s: Security in the Developing Countries', *Adelphi Paper 251* (London: IISS, 1990). On specific issues see, Jessica Tuchman Mathews, 'Redefining Security', *Foreign Affairs*, 68:2 (spring 1989), pp. 162-77; Brad Roberts, 'Human Rights and International Security', *Washington Quarterly*, (spring 1990), pp. 65-75; Patricia Mische, 'Ecological Security and the Need to Reconceptualize Sovereignty', *Alternatives*, 14:4, 1989, pp. 389-427.

22. Since it is not possible to deal with both the 'deepening' and 'broadening' aspects of the reconceptualization of security, the first set of issues will be concentrated upon. An analysis of the 'broadened' agenda of security would examine how choices around military security affect the ability of states and peoples to achieve, for example, economic security (as in the classic 'guns-butter' trade-off).

23. Mullins, *Born Arming*, pp. 107-8.

24. As Yahya Sadowski has described it, the Egyptian business elite wants a state weak enough to loot, but strong enough to be worth looting. Cited in Jill Crystal, 'Authoritarianism and its Adversaries in the Arab World', *World Politics*, 46:2, January 1994, p. 272. See also Robert Satloff, *Army and Politics in Mubarak's Egypt* (Washington, DC: Washington Institute for Near East Policy, 1988).

25. Yahya Sadowski, 'Patronage and the Ba'th: Corruption and Control in Contemporary Syria', *Arab Studies Quarterly*, 9:4, pp. 442-61; 'Liberated Syrian Economy Takes Off', *Manchester Guardian Weekly*, 6 March 1994.

26. See Charles Tilly, 'War-Making and State-Making as Organized Crime', in Peter Evans, Dietrich Rueschemeyer and Theda Skocpol, *Bringing the State Back In* (Cambridge: Cambridge University Press, 1985), pp. 169-91; Charles Tilly, *Coercion, Capital, and European States, A.D. 990-1990* (Oxford: Blackwell, 1990); and William Thompson and Karen Rasler, *War and State-Making* (Boston, MA: Unwin Hyman, 1989).

27. Ball, *Security and Economy*, pp. 123-57, 405-8, discusses at length the findings, strengths and shortcomings of the many studies that have attempted to link military expenditure to development. She concludes that 'the considerable variations in the ways in which Third World economies actually function and in their potential for development, as well as differences in the size and nature of the security outlays of individual countries, greatly reduce the likelihood that one pattern could be discovered to describe the situation in all developing countries at all times'; p. 390.

28. Mullins, *Born Arming*, p. 77. He concludes that the overall growth of weapons capabilities in the developing world is closely correlated with rising GNP, although this relationship does not hold for individual states; pp. 68-9.

29. Raymond Hinnebusch, *Authoritarian Power and State Formation in Ba'thist Syria* (Boulder, CO: Westview, 1990), p. 157. Details on military corruption and its role in the economy from Sadowski, 'Patronage and the Ba'th'.

30. Ball, *Security and Economy in the Third World*, p. 391.

31. See Talukder Maniruzzaman, 'Arms Transfers, Military Coups and Military Rule in Developing States', *Journal of Conflict Resolution*, 36:4, December 1992, pp. 733-55. His study 'suggests that arms transfers facilitate the occurrence of *coups d'état* ... lengthen the period of military rule ... [and] indicate that large-scale deaths from political violence might be the result rather than the cause of military rule'.

32. Tilly, *Coercion, Capital and European States*, p. 206.

33. This is also the case for *rentier* states (such as Saudi Arabia) which increase their extractive ability by drawing upon resources, rather than taxation.
34. As Samir al-Khalil puts it in his portrait of early twentieth-century Iraq, 'before civil society had any chance to constitute or define itself ... modernity suddenly appeared in the form of a parliament and an army'. Samir al-Khalil, *Republic of Fear* (New York: Pantheon, 1989), p. 162.
35. See John Johnson (ed.), *The Role of the Military in Underdeveloped Countries* (Princeton, NJ: Princeton University Press, 1962).
36. Crystal, 'Authoritarianism and its Adversaries in the Arab World', pp. 267, 282.
37. American policy since the 1990-91 Gulf War seems to have rested on this justification.
38. See Edward Laurance, Siemon Wezeman and Herbert Wulf, *Arms Watch: SIPRI Report on the First Year of the UN Register of Conventional Arms* (Oxford: Oxford University Press, 1993); Malcolm Chalmers *et al.*, *Developing the UN Register of Conventional Arms* (Bradford: University of Bradford, 1994).
39. As Jervis puts it, 'because the security dilemma and crisis instability can exacerbate if not create conflicts, potential enemies [in the Third World] will have an interest in developing arms control arrangements'; Jervis, 'Arms Control, Stability and Causes of War', p. 251.
40. See Frederic Pearson and Michael Brzoska, 'The Register as an Early Warning System: Case Studies and Empirical Evidence of the Role of Conventional Arms in Conflict', in Chalmers, *Developing the UN Register of Conventional Arms*, pp. 225-50. As Aaron Karp has also argued, the most important weapons for so-called ethnic conflicts are 'light weapons', which are not covered by the Register, or indeed by any other publicly available sources; Aaron Karp, 'Arms Control for a New Era', *The Washington Quarterly*, 17:4 (autumn 1994), pp. 65-77. Accelerated imports of small arms to Rwanda in 1993 and early 1994 would seem to provide a poignant illustration of this issue.
41. See *SIPRI Yearbook 1993*, pp. 394-6; Nicole Ball, 'Development Assistance and Military Reform', *International Security Digest*, 1:2, 1993, p. 3; Nicole Ball, *Pressing for Peace: Can Aid Induce Reform?*, policy essay no. 6 (Washington, DC: Overseas Development Council, 1992); and Robert Miller (ed.), *Aid as Peacemaker: Canadian Development Assistance and Third World Conflict* (Ottawa: Carleton University Press, 1992).
42. See World Bank, *Governance and Development* (Washington, DC: IBRD, 1992), p. 58. The OECD Development Assistance Committee uses the term to cover a range of issues associated with participatory development, respect for human rights, transparency in decision-making and democratization.

9

Arms and Conflicts in the Post-Cold War Developing World

S.D. Muni

INTRODUCTION

The end of the Cold War seems to have simultaneously generated two mutually competing and incompatible tendencies with regard to the situation for peace and security in the 'Third World'.

One comprises the moves towards resolving and moderating conflicts, and pursuing arms control and confidence-building measures, and the resolution of conflict in Cambodia, the peace agreement between Israel and the Palestine Liberation Organization, the initiation of an arms control process in West Asia, talks between India and Pakistan to find mutual confidence-building measures, and now at least a glimmer of hope towards dousing the fires, if not immediately resolving the conflict, in the former Yugoslavia through UN and NATO intervention, may be mentioned in this regard. There is also a growing awareness among the developed as well as developing countries to see whether their respective defence budgets can be reduced. And the establishment of the UN Arms Trade Register, even with its limitations, may prove to be a major step towards ensuring greater transparency in acquisition, supply and storage of conventional weapons by states[1]. In the field of nuclear and missile proliferation, supplier controls are being tightened and streamlined, and efforts are also under way through the use of various 'carrots and sticks' by multilateral agencies as well as major powers, particularly the United States, to limit and 'roll-back' demands and aspirations for these weapons of mass destruction. Many such attempts at conflict prevention, moderation and/or resolution, including arms control and confidence-building, are not yet fully effective and successful, but their powerful positive impact on the global security situation deserves notice.

The other tendency, at odds with this positive development, is characterized by the rise in the spread of conflicts and turbulence. The data calculated at Uppsala University and relied upon by SIPRI show a broad consistency since the end of the Cold War. There are regional variations, but the total number of 30 to 32 conflicts throughout the world is not a comforting figure (SIPRI, *Arms Watch 1993*, pp. 86-7). Additionally, we have to keep in mind the fact that this figure does not include conflicts where casualty figures are less than 1,000, and the data also exclude those conflicts that were raging in previous years but have witnessed a decline in intensity, or are passing through a phase of temporary lull. Since such conflicts are neither resolved, nor moderated or regulated, the possibility of them again becoming intense always exists. The sudden re-eruption of intense conflicts in countries like Yemen and Rwanda in early 1994 brought this point home. In these conflicts, the casualty figures crossed the 1,000-mark in a matter of only a few days, and the killing fields continue to be active. If this numerical threshold of 1,000 casualties is lowered for compiling conflict lists, the number of raging conflicts may well be over 100[2]. One wonders what the dimensions of such conflict data would be if we were to include in our criteria of conflict categorization the number of persons not only killed, but disabled and displaced, as well as potential flashpoints where hostilities have not yet broken out.[3] The spread of conflicts and turbulence has been so extensive that analysts are rejecting the prevailing categories of global differentiation in terms of 'First', 'Second' or 'Third Worlds', or the North-South division, and instead see the world being gradually divided into 'Zones of Peace and Zones of Turmoil'.[4]

The spread of conflicts and turbulence does not match the continuous downward trend in the trade of major conventional weapons which has been evident since 1987, that is, before the Gulf War and the disintegration of the Soviet Union. In 1992, the decline from previous years in the recorded value of such trade was significant, to the tune of 25 per cent, and both imports and exports of major conventional weapons have registered a gradual decline of more than 50 per cent since 1988[5]. There is a possibility that this declining trend in arms' transfers will stabilize and may even reverse, but it may not attain the dimensions of the Cold War years. This mismatch between conflicts and armaments deserves a closer look.

CONFLICT SPREAD AND SMALL ARMS

In order to understand the mismatch between the spread of conflict and the declining trade in major and conventional weapons, it is important to bear in mind the nature of the spreading conflict as well as the type of arms used therein. The interesting fact from the conflict data is that of the 30 conflict locations listed for the year 1992 in SIPRI data, only one, between India and Pakistan, is identified as an inter-state conflict. The rest occur within states, waged between the state and one or more rebellious groups, adequately armed and fighting for ethnic, religious, regional or ideological assertions and rights. In some of these conflicts, the objective of control of the existing state or the creation of a new one through secession is also inherent. In analysing the dynamics of these intra-state conflicts in the developing world, various social and historical distortions, mismanagement, the failure of state-building processes and discriminating distribution of developmental gains, or the absence of such gains, are highlighted as critical factors[6]. Recently, the debate has centred on the prospects of these emerging conflicts as the clash of civilizations[7]. There is considerable merit in all these explanations. History provides strong evidence of the fact that state-building in Europe, Asia and elsewhere, throughout the evolution of history, has been a very painful, violent and tortuous process. It has involved the extraction of resources from the producers and the ordering of social evolution to facilitate that extraction, while strengthening the legitimacy and hegemony of the state over society. These explanations, however, do not adequately take into account the fact that state-building in present times is different from the past and it is carried out under a complex internal and external environment. The developing countries no longer have the freedom and autonomy in their respective state-building exercises that were enjoyed by European states. And many of them have had their economies ravaged and societies distorted by more than a century of colonial domination and exploitation. Their people are exposed to value systems and developmental aspirations emanating from, and reinforced at, the global level which would not permit easy and orderly state-building. Above all, the turbulence resulting from state-building processes in the developing countries has an unmistakable external dimension, not only in terms of consequences across the borders, but also in terms of input from across the borders to generate, perpetuate and intensify these conflicts. There is also the role of ideological projections such as human rights, self-determination, democracy and material affluence, which fire the imagination and arouse the aspirations of the warring groups against the state which is in the process of organization and consolidation. There is consequently much more to the 'state-' and 'ethnicity-'based explanations of internal conflicts in the developing world which have been discussed earlier in this book.

Many 'Third World' conflicts, and the supply of arms that feed them, have a Cold War lineage. It was during the mid-1960s and early 1970s, while the Soviets and Chinese planned their own wars and 'spread revolutions' to secure strategic advantages and influence in the Cold War rivalry, that the United States and the Western alliance almost outpaced them by creating, pampering and promoting the forces of 'counter revolution'.[8] In the evolution of these conflicts, it may not be too far fetched to see a link between, on the one hand, the development of nuclear and conventional deterrence between the superpower-led military alliances, and on the other, the emergence of proxy wars. With the strategic deterrence in place, war between the power blocs became unrealistic and the only way left to secure a favourable balance of power was through small, manageable proxy wars in the strategically important regions of the world. Consequently, not only surrogate and supportive states, but also militant and rebellious groups, were encouraged by the respective superpowers to fight it out among themselves, as in Nicaragua, the Horn of Africa, Cambodia, Angola and Mozambique.[9] The war in Afghanistan was also an example of a proxy war, with the difference that there, the former Soviet Union committed the folly of directly intervening and becoming a party itself.

Once precipitated or encouraged, these East-West proxy wars gained their own dynamics and momentum, so much so that the retreat of these wars' mentors, as a result of the end of the Cold War, has made no material difference to some of the conflict situations, as in Afghanistan, Cambodia, Mozambique and Angola. The stockpiles of sophisticated weaponry amassed by the Cold War warriors and their proxies have now easily been transformed into the instruments of carrying out diverse struggles for power along ethnic, regional, religious or ideological lines. Arms' supply-lines established during the Cold War period have continued to be operational, although they are less widespread. Meanwhile, some of these conflicts continue with the same or even greater intensity, although the forms and character of warring parties have registered significant changes.

In Afghanistan, for instance, the folly of indiscriminately supplying arms to anti-Soviet Mujahidin groups has had a wide range. Such supplies created enemies among the allies for the then identified cause because of the discriminate preferences for one group or another; and the capabilities provided to fight a common enemy are now being used by the erstwhile allies for political dominance and control of the state. That the arms supplied and fighters trained for the anti-Soviet war in Afghanistan are also active in Kashmir through the Pakistani conduit, demonstrates that internal wars in developing countries are more complex than they are generally thought to be.[10] A similar situation was evident in Cambodia, where the arming of the Khmer Rouge and other anti-Vietnamese groups by diverse suppliers from Western, Asian and Chinese sources led to the development of local and regional vested interests who do not see any advantage in a lasting solution of the problem. Examples of such vested interests are the Thai army and the drug barons and gem traders in Thailand and Burma, who continue to keep the Khmer Rouge's aspirations of political dominance in Cambodia alive by keeping the arms' supply-lines active. Consequently, a simmering conflict and the potential for its further eruption persist in Cambodia, even after the Vietnamese withdrawal and the establishment of a UN-supervised political order. A similar situation is evident in Somalia where the Somali war-lords have kept the conflict alive on the basis of stockpiles and supply-lines established during the Cold War's proxy war in the Horn.

As the conflicts are internal, have also been of low intensity, and are thus fought with small arms, the available data on 'major conventional arms' do not reflect the consequences of spreading conflict in the developing world. The prevailing definition of 'small arms' is wide enough, as it includes 'all crew-importable direct fire weapons of a calibre less than 50mm and will include a secondary capability to defeat light armour and helicopters'.[11] This covers shoulder-fired anti-tank and anti-aircraft missiles which are not even counted in the UN Convention on Arms Transfer Register. In addition to this broad range of weapons are the RDX and other explosives, even petrol bombs and land-mines. Additionally, there are no authentic data about the flow of these arms. In fact, there can be none, because these weapons mostly travel through clandestine channels, including drug routes, they are captured from rival forces or looted from state armouries, their supply channels are established and operated by powerful covert agencies, and in many cases are even produced indigenously by the involved states as well as the rebellious groups, so as to defy any attempt to measure the volume of the trade.[12]

But the trade or transfers of such arms is significant in view of its impact on the emerging regional and global security situation. Even in terms of value, although it is not as high as the trade in major conventional weapons, it is not insignificant. Even the known accounts of the value of arms supplied to internal war situations are staggering. For instance, the Afghan anti-Soviet war was supplied at the rate of $670 million annually by the United States alone. Similar supplies to Nicaraguan contras and Angolan UNITA militia were in the range of $70 million and $30 million per year respectively. Meanwhile, the supplies by the former Soviet Union to its client states and preferred insurgent groups, and by China to insurgent groups such as the Khmer Rouge in Cambodia, will remain unknown for a long time to come.

Recently, *The Economist* estimated that the value of trade in small arms could be as much as $10 billion per year,[13] and an executive of South Africa's state-owned arms corporation, the Armscore, said that in view of raging conflicts in Africa, the export of arms by the company is expected by 1996 to be 'at least double, and possibly quadruple'.[14]

An important role in supplying weapons to the combatants in internal conflicts has been played by external sponsors of the state, including, as mentioned above, the role of the superpowers during the Cold War-sponsored proxy wars. However, during these proxy wars, the role of regional powers and usually a neighbouring state – playing sponsor as well as a conduit for supplying weapons to the insurgent groups – has also been central. The role of Syria, Yemen, Libya and East European countries in building the PLO's arsenals; of China, Thailand, and Burma in equipping the Khmer Rouge; of Pakistan in arming anti-Soviet Afghan Mujahidins and anti-Indian Sikh and Kashmiri militants; of India in supporting the Tamil insurgency until 1987; of African states, including South Africa, in the conflicts in Mozambique, Angola, Yemen and Rwanda; and of Bulgaria, Hungary and Romania in fuelling the conflict in the former Yugoslavia, may all be mentioned here as examples and should be a subject of continuing and much needed research. The role of the neighbouring state is influenced more by strategic and religious or ethnic considerations, although commercial interests may not be absent.

One way to deal with this situation of spreading conflicts is to intervene through multilateral forces under the UN umbrella.[15] The sobering effect of NATO brinkmanship on the Serbian forces has raised some hopes in this regard, but the earlier neglect of conflict in Bosnia-Herzegovina, and the frustrating experience of American and other UN forces in Somalia, call for a balanced and careful approach to the issue of internal conflicts. The issues involved are extremely complex, as they expose the lack of political will in accepting human lives and costs in material terms by the major powers, the problems of coordinating policy directions and operational guidelines in any multilateral UN operations, and the absence of a proper legal framework within which the UN can undertake peace-keeping and peace-enforcing operations in the increasing number of diverse internal conflicts.[16] Imposing solutions from above may create a temporary lull at best, but it will leave the conflict simmering as a potential flashpoint for the future. And yet such a temporary peace is also vital if it can be used as a window of opportunity to build on a process of maintaining peace and resolving the inherent conflict through determined socio-economic developmental measures.

As another small step in meeting the challenge, the UN may be encouraged to widen the scope of the UN Convention on Arms Transfer Register and cover the small arms as well, particularly those such as anti-aircraft and anti-tank missiles, to monitor their production, movement and even use. This is easier said than done, but a beginning has to be made somewhere. International institutions like SIPRI and the IISS may also consider compiling data on small arms and their pipelines to countries and areas of conflicts. SIPRI has done excellent work by mapping out major-arms producers,[17] so how about venturing to do a similar job for small-arms producers? Even important national institutes such as the Arms Control and Disarmament Agency in the United States, the Institute for Defence Studies and Analyses in New Delhi, the Centre for International and Strategic Studies in Jakarta may also join in the effort. Put together, all such efforts will generate data in a field where authentic accounts are badly needed, and will also arouse consciousness, so as to make concern on small arms a policy input into arms control, disarmament and regional security measures. Means and methods to restrain the flow of small arms cannot be evolved without broad assessments about their quantities and flows.

No less important may be to rethink the ideological parameters of the so-called values of the 'New World Order', such as self-determination, which have proved to be counterproductive in cases like the former Yugoslavia and will be so in many other situations of internal conflict.[18] Greater caution and circumspection is also called for in the use of 'human rights' as an instrument to pressurize states for strategic objectives. One may even build a strong case for consolidating and strengthening the state in the 'Third World', with adequate safeguards for the state to be as accountable and accommodating as possible under the given social and political context within which it has to operate and seek legitimacy. Countries of the world are at different levels of socio-economic development and they cannot be expected to follow standards and criteria applicable in the few developed countries.

REGIONAL UNCERTAINTIES, IMBALANCES AND ARMS ACQUISITION

The declining trend in defence expenditures and acquisition of major conventional weapons in the developing countries has wide variations. While this trend is reasonably stable in Latin America and Africa, Asia presents a mixed picture. Over the last five years or so, East and South-East sub-regions of Asia are showing growing tendencies of rising defence expenditures and increasing imports of major-weapon systems.[19] In East and South-East Asia, Japan, South Korea and Thailand are among the top ten arms' importers for the period from 1988-92. All the countries of these sub-regions have shown significant growth in their defence expenditures, with China topping the list with an increase of more than 60 per cent since 1985. India and Pakistan also figure prominently among the top ten importers of major conventional weapons for the period 1988-92.

In West Asia, gross figures of arms expenditures and arms imports have come down but these figures need to be taken with caution and qualification. There are a number of countries, particularly the Gulf Council members and Iran, which defy this trend.[20] Even so, experts question the complete reliability of the arms trade and expenditure statistics in West Asia, as they do not reveal military aid and the official accounts fudge defence expenditure figures.[21] No wonder then that Saudi Arabia and the United Arab Emirates have refused to comply with the UN Arms Trade Register obligations. Even the major powers, who have committed themselves to ensuring the effectiveness of, and compliance to, arms control measures in the region, have often hesitated about behaving otherwise in reality.[22]

There are a number of factors behind the continuing endeavour for arms and military build up in the Asian regions in a period of reduced inter-state conflicts (with South Asia as an exception). Strategic uncertainty is one of the most important factors. This is the result of changing strategic and security relationships between regional actors and the major powers since the end of the Cold War. The prospects of reduction in the US military presence in Asia, particularly in East and South-East Asia, is giving rise to the fears that a power vacuum may be in the offing. And such a power vacuum may be filled by regional influences such as China and Japan in East and South-East Asia, and Egypt, Syria, Saudi Arabia and Iran (even Iraq in the mid- to long-term prospects) in West Asia. Alarming trends in the military acquisitions of some of these regional influences, particularly by China which has also indicated its capacity and willingness to use force for its strategic objectives in the South China Sea region, give credence to such fears of uncertainty and assertion by the regional powers.[23] The fact that China has unresolved territorial disputes with most of its Asian neighbours makes the situation worse. It is interesting to note in this respect that both the ASEAN and Gulf Cooperation Council (GCC) members have decided to augment their respective regional organizations with security dimensions. It will take time to evolve such security arrangements within the existing regional cooperation organizations because of divergent threat perceptions and security needs of the member countries on the one hand and preferences of the major powers actively involved in the respective regional affairs.[24] However, whenever that happens, a new regional balance among the regional influences, the regional actors and the extra-regional major powers may emerge. In the process, the regional actors are likely to become better armed, without concrete threats, and the external arms' supplier may coordinate and streamline the regional arms' markets better. However, the tendency on the part of the external suppliers to induct newer weapons and technologies to create regional imbalances and generate local demands for arms' acquisitions should also not be overlooked here. The US supply of F-16s to Taiwan and Saudi Arabia, Patriot Missiles to South Korea and pressure on Japan for collaboration in the Theatre Missile Defence Systems may be mentioned here to illustrate the point. Meanwhile, China has done the same by supplying M-11 missiles to Pakistan and Gulf countries.[25]

An important role in accelerating or decelerating the drive for arms' acquisition is played by the economic factor, and there are many dimensions of this factor. In West Asia, for instance, since the mid-1970s, the decline in arms' imports and military expenditure has been matched by a decline in oil revenues. In view of falling oil revenues, West Asian countries have not only had to engage in arms control measures but have also started to divert funds from military to developmental projects, and so may find proposals to swap arms for debt attractive.[26] Meanwhile, in East and South-East Asia, growing economies are facilitating drives for arms' acquisition. There is a direct positive relationship between the GNP growth and increasing defence expenditures in this region, although the latter may not match the level of growth in the former.[27] The faster growing economies in this region are not only making surplus cash available for the purchase of weapons, but are also laying increasing emphasis on the development of domestic arms' industries and new technologies, particularly in the field of electronics, to upgrade weapon systems already acquired.[28] The emphasis on modernization, through the introduction of precision technologies and greater kill-capacities, is clearly evident in this region and elsewhere. This urge for modernization received a boost as a consequence of the Gulf War, which in some ways elevated military technologies and transformed battle strategies. And since the economies of this region are expected to grow continuously into the next century, the region should continue to be in focus for its arms' build-up activities. South Asia may also join this line-up if the Indian and Pakistani economies also pick up growth momentum under their current reform programmes. This should not be surprising, because development and arms' build-up have traditionally had a positive relationship in the case of most of the major powers and developed regions when there are potential conflicts and active rivalries.

Adding to the drives for arms' acquisitions by the developing countries are the commercial pressures of the arms industries in the industrialized as well as other countries to seek and encourage customers, and more so than earlier, since orders from national consumers (like the Pentagon in the United States) are dwindling. The US Secretary of Defense, William Perry, admitted in a television interview that the United States was fast emerging as the largest weapons' supplier in the world, filling the vacuum created by the collapse of the former Soviet Union. The pressure from the manufacturers of the F-16 fighter aircraft line, McDonnel, has been evident in the US decision for sales of these planes and other weapons to countries like Saudi Arabia($9.2 billion), Israel ($26 billion), and Taiwan.[29] The State Department's proposal to supply 38 F-16s to Pakistan as a one-time exception to the imposition of the Pressler Law on Pakistan for its proliferation drive, also falls into the same category. Attacking the US arms' sales policy, *The New York Times* wrote:

> In effect, the Pentagon is acting like a salesman for private industry. American taxpayers foot a sizeable bill to subsidize US arms' exports. According to William Hartung of the World Policy Institute, the Government spends $500 million a year directly on arms export promotion. It finances foreign arms' purchases with an additional $3.2 billion in grants and $800 million in subsidized loans, and millions more in foreign aid to arms' buyers – which really amounts to indirect subsidies.[30]

It is this pressure which has also been forcing industry to indulge in illegal trade in arms. Under the provisions of the 1994 Defense Department Authorization Act, the US Senate approved subsidizing arms exports to 'NATO Members, Australia, Japan, South Korea and Israel'.[31] With assured political backing, it is not a surprise that American firms collected orders to sell weapons worth $32 billion in 1993. This was much above the 1992 level of $28 billion and 1991 of $12 billion.[32] But the United States is not alone in this. The arms industry has become a powerful factor in many countries – Russia, Western Europe, Poland, former Czechoslovakia, Turkey, South Africa, China, Japan and Australia – to exert pressures for export.[33] The British attempts to induce arms' sales through overseas development aid disbursements in the case of Malaysia have recently been exposed in the international media. This, however, would not be the only case of its type and the United Kingdom is not the only country which indulges in offering incentives for arms' purchases. And all this happens when the end of the Cold War is supposed to generate peace dividends and the G7 group of industrialized countries have evolved guidelines to deny overseas development aid to such countries that do not control their defence budget arms' imports.

The end of the Cold War has put the former Soviet Union and the East European countries under unprecedented economic hardships, forcing them to activate the global arms bazaar by selling their products at highly competitive prices, to the delight of many in the 'Third World'. There is no way to account for the value of such transactions, and the nature and number of weapons sold.[34] The Czech President, Vaclav Havel, soon after assuming office in 1989, promised to do away with his country's arms' exports, but after the split of Czechoslovakia into the Czech Republic and Slovakia, both new countries have aggressively resumed arms' sales.

Meanwhile, China's push for arms' exports is also well known. During the 1980s, China's income from such exports was estimated at $1 billion annually. By the latter half of the 1980s, the Chinese People's Liberation Army was allowed to keep 75 per cent of its arms' export earnings for its own modernization as an incentive for exports. Increasingly, besides the strategic and political considerations, commercial and profit motives are playing an important role in Chinese arms' exports.[35]

Consequently, we find that arms' build-up in the 'Third World' regions is a process, related not only to the possible causes of conflicts, tensions and insecurity, but also to the strategic and economic interests of the extra-regional arms' suppliers and technological advances in the weapon systems themselves. Added to this is the stimulant of regional and national wealth that finds expression in the acquisition of more and better arms. This being so, regional arms control and confidence-building measures, necessary components as they are for the peace and security-building processes, may not be enough by themselves to contain or eliminate regional arms races.

SPREAD OF NUCLEAR AND MISSILE CAPABILITIES

As in the case of regional conventional arms' build-up, Asia has also become a focus of attention in the field of spreading nuclear and missile capabilities, outside the five nuclear powers. Of the eleven 'Third World' countries identified for their nuclear capabilities and active programmes, excluding those created after the collapse of the Soviet Union, eight are in Asia.[36] Similarly, an overwhelming number of countries engaged in missile technology development are also in Asia.[37] Among these countries, while some – like the new states born out of the Soviet disintegration, such as Kazakhstan, Belarus and Ukraine – got their nuclear weapons as an 'inheritance', others like Israel, India, Pakistan, and South Africa, built their capabilities through determined efforts. Of those countries that are still at the nuclear threshold, newspaper and intelligence reports claim that North Korea has already acquired the capability to fabricate a nuclear explosive device. Iraq, on the other hand, has been pushed back years on the road to nuclear status through UN sanctions and international pressure after its defeat in the Gulf War of 1991.

Since the five official nuclear powers attained their nuclear status, nuclear aspirations by other states have remained active. In fact, by the beginning of the 1970s, Israel and South Africa had made significant advances and India had successfully conducted an underground explosion in 1974. Why, then, is there such a renewed and heightened concern about nuclear proliferation in the developing world since the end of the Cold War? Three issues deserve attention in this respect, besides the frequently expressed fears that if proliferation is not contained, its spread would be faster and wider than envisaged during the Cold War period.

First is the end of the Cold War itself. During the Cold War, strategic considerations had prevailed over the major powers to ignore their proliferating 'Third World' allies. The case of Pakistan, where the United States looked towards the other side of Pakistan's fast and determined efforts to acquire nuclear capabilities because its cooperation in the anti-Soviet war in Afghanistan was necessary, is a case in point.[38] Not only that, but senior US military officers like General Christ, the Commander-in-Chief of the Central Command in 1987, even considered a Pakistani nuclear weapon as a welcome deterrent against a possible Soviet push southwards from Afghanistan. With the Cold War having come to an end, however, there is no need to show such indulgence, and hence the United States imposed restrictions under the Pressler Law on Pakistan for its nuclear advances in 1990, this in turn leading Pakistan to indulge in loud claims and assertive rhetoric about its nuclear status, to attract some of the lost strategic attention from the United States.

Second, as a result of the multinational Gulf War against Iraq, the spectre of a developing country using missiles, possibly loaded with nuclear or chemical weapons against the interests of the major powers, has become much more realistic and probable than ever before.[39] Accordingly, there have been reports of nuclear retargetting by the Pentagon to aim at new sources of threats in the 'Third World'.

And finally, the threat of proliferation has increased because of the disintegration of the former Soviet Union, as there are now significant quantities of nuclear material and know-how on the loose, looking for customers who have cash and willingness to pay.[40] There are reports of increasing attempts in Russia, of underpaid and unpaid workers at the nuclear plants stealing enriched uranium. The smuggling of weapon-grade uranium from other parts of the former Soviet Union has also increased.[41]

The heightened concern regarding proliferation has led great powers, particularly the United States, to clamp as many, and as fast, non-proliferation restraints on as many 'Third World' nuclear aspirants as possible. This is being done from the supply as well as demand sides of the proliferation chain, and several measures have been included in this effort. A strong consensus among the developed Western powers at the G7 level is being built for halting proliferation through the tightening of technology exports and leakages suspected to benefit potential proliferators. There was also a strong G7 move to get the Non-Proliferation Treaty extended indefinitely at the Review Conference in 1995. In some cases, the non-proliferation consensus is being widened through UN resolutions and guidelines, even sanctions, as shown by present moves in the United Nations to deal with the North Korean defiance.

In May 1993, the UN Disarmament Committee adopted guidelines for regional approaches to disarmament, including non-proliferation. Similarly, later in the year (November 1993), the General Assembly considered and subsequently approved the resolution on fissile material 'cut-off'. At the level of individual countries, incentives are offered and pressures increased on the nuclear aspirants and capable 'Third World' countries to accept non-proliferation restraints, of either multilateral or regional and bilateral nature. Ukraine's acceptance of such restraints, after considerable resistance, marked a success in this direction, but the dilemma of getting North Korea back into the NPT regime and under IAEA safeguards persists. So, also, in the case of South Asia, the pressures and incentives for nuclear 'cut-off', 'freeze' and 'roll-back' have so far failed to produce tangible results.

The difficulties in halting the spread of nuclear capabilities in the 'Third World' arise from two major sources. One is that the restraint regimes have many shortcomings that have been exploited for commercial and strategic considerations in the past. The commercial nuclear suppliers in the developed countries have continued to violate export controls under pressures of commercial competition and profit earning, with or without the connivance of their respective governments.[42] Within the NPT regime, provisions of inspections and verifications are neither perfect, nor have they been properly carried out. They cannot be, if nearly 70 per cent of the IAEA resources are spent on selected countries like Japan, Germany and Canada. The NPT provisions on issues like the accounting of nuclear material, in its stockpiling and movements are also highly inadequate.[43] The US Congress has expressed concern about the limited area of export control being exercised in actual practice,[44] but the supply-side restraints have been made more difficult and imperfect by the rise in the number of countries that have developed capabilities to export nuclear material and know-how.[45] This is particularly the case when a supplier country is either passing through political and economic crisis, as in Russia and the newly independent states from the Soviet Union's collapse, or is not well enough integrated with the Western-dominated restraint regimes and maintains a defiant stance like China.

Closely related to the weaknesses of the supply-side restraints is the lack of credibility, at least in the perceptions of the nuclear aspirants, of the restraint regime as it is based on discrimination. There are no credible restraints on the nuclear haves and the NPT has been widely criticized for discriminatory non-proliferation obligations on the part of the nuclear haves and have-nots. The indefinite extension of the Non-Proliferation Treaty will consolidate this discriminatory regime in perpetuity. Not only that, but three of the five nuclear-weapon powers have not joined the nuclear arms reduction process, and all five of them continue to keep the nuclear weapons' option intact in one form or another, and to improve and streamline their nuclear arsenals.[46] The fact that the nuclear powers have carried out 107 tests between 1988 and 1992 speaks for itself. Of these, the United States conducted the largest number, with 46 tests, followed by France at 28, and the former Soviet Union, United Kingdom and China conducted 25, 3 and 6 tests respectively.[47] Additionally, there are no credible non-proliferation pressures on chosen allies of the West like Israel. South Africa accepted the NPT restraints only in July 1991, to avoid nuclear weapons falling into the hands of the Blacks, and Japan, on its part, continues to stockpile plutonium ignoring all advice contrary to this.

The other source of difficulty is the under-lying assumption of nuclear restraint efforts in the 'Third World' that as their nuclear aspirations are related to bilateral and regional security concerns, the non-proliferation moves also need to be confined to regional and bilateral parameters. This assumption is, at best, only partially valid. The nuclear question in the 'Third World', while no doubt linked to regional security concerns, goes far beyond the bilateral and regional contexts, and in most of the cases is part of the global nuclear dynamics. It is thus not irrelevant to the question of global disarmament and security. Approaches like the 'carrots and sticks' for working out regional non-proliferation arrangements cannot therefore fully answer the question. Countries like India would like to take up the question of nuclear disarmament (and not selective, regional arrangements) in a comprehensive, universal and non-discriminatory framework. India's late Prime Minister Rajiv Gandhi's plan for a gradual and comprehensive approach to the global disarmament issue was presented at the United Nations in 1988. The problem is that this comprehensive approach is not acceptable to the major and nuclear weapon powers who prefer a differentiated approach so as to keep their nuclear capabilities at effective, operational levels. The 'Third World' countries' demands for comprehensive disarmament measures that include nuclear non-proliferation are viewed in the West as diversionary and unrealistic.

However, there is a way to deal with the question of nuclear proliferation. Two possible approaches may be considered. One is to acknowledge the fact that 'nuclear weapons cannot be disinvented' and accordingly pursue policies that seek 'balance and deterrence' as legitimate objectives to ensure global and regional security.[48] A systematic case along realist lines for proliferation as a means to deterrence and security was made by Kenneth

Waltz, who argued that the spread of nuclear weapons in Europe and developing countries may not really endanger world security as is being apprehended, and, instead, may ensure peace through deterrence as witnessed during the Cold War years between the superpowers.[49] Building on the same theme, Mearsheimer has pleaded for allowing countries like Germany and even Ukraine to develop credible nuclear deterrence to ensure stability of the post-Cold War world.[50]

In the case of South Asia, arguments for a nuclear 'safe zone' as against a 'nuclear-weapon-free zone' have also been advanced, emphasizing the need for nuclear confidence-building between India and Pakistan, while recognizing that each has the capability to assemble nuclear weapons. There has also been a proposal for 'non-weaponized deterrence', based on acknowledgement of nuclear capabilities, and yet commitment on the part of India and Pakistan that they will not make and deploy nuclear weapons against each other.[51] And in the case of North Korea, reacting strongly to the pressures being exercised, Philip Bowering concluded his argument in the *International Herald Tribune*:

> In short, Korea is a good place to start reminding ourselves that nuclear weapons' technology cannot be stopped, only slowed. The doctrine of deterrence, of balance of terror, along the borders between the Koreas as well as in Punjab, has at least as big a role to play in a multipolar world as in a bipolar one. The job of big powers should not be to decide who can and cannot have a weapon, through selective and bullying attempts. It is to help keep balances.[52]

The danger in the 'deterrence' approach is that it may unleash a process of considerable nuclear uncertainty and chaos, which may even generate insecurity, at least in the immediate context. This is particularly so because the evolution of proper national safekeeping of fissile material and nuclear devices, command and control systems and capabilities to deal with accidents will take both considerable time and resources of the nuclear aspirants to reach levels of credible deterrence. The other alternative approach may, therefore, be to evolve a judicious synthesis of existing control systems and link them up with a serious and honest process of achieving a 'universal, comprehensive and non-discriminatory' regime of nuclear disarmament. Accordingly, while the export controls may be streamlined and strengthened, the NPT may be *revised* to accommodate nuclear-capable powers in a non-discriminatory manner. Simultaneously, there is a need to pursue vigorously the goals of fissile material cut-off, comprehensive test ban, no-first use, with a credible and broad-based international verification system. Gradually even nuclear R&D may be brought under international control within the UN umbrella. This is a tall order and may appear to be very ambitious, even unrealistic, at initial stages, but if a sincere beginning is made in the right direction, nuclear concerns may be eased at the global level and eventually nuclear weapons may be completely eliminated and outlawed. A comprehensive and universal approach worked in the case of chemical and biological weapons, so there is no reason to doubt that it cannot be attempted in the nuclear field. The only requirement is for the nuclear-weapon powers to demonstrate sufficient political will in favour of such an approach, which is unfortunately not forthcoming at the moment.

CONCLUSION

The security challenge unfolding in the post-Cold War world seems to be concentrated on two divergent areas: of intra-state conflicts and small arms on the one hand, and proliferation of weapons of mass destruction on the other. Both these dimensions of the security challenge will have to be met simultaneously. While urgent need exists in the field of monitoring the dimensions and directions of transfers of small arms, the real challenge of mitigating internal conflicts will have to be met through processes of socio-economic development and political accommodation in the affected countries. In stimulating and sustaining such processes, concerted efforts and support from the international community are required.

In the nuclear field, the nuclear-weapon states may have to demonstrate the sincerity of purpose by committing themselves to a universal and non-discriminatory approach to non-proliferation. In the absence of such an approach, the proliferation threats may be slowed down but the world will settle to the reality of balance and deterrence in the nuclear field.

NOTES

1. Edward J. Laurance, Siemon T. Wezeman and Herbert Wulf, *Arms Watch: SIPRI Report On the First Year of the UN Register of Conventional Arms* (Oxford: Oxford University Press, 1993).
2. Jan Egeland, 'New and Emerging Conflicts in the New World Order', A Keynote Speech, International Alert, London, November 1992, p. 2.
3. *The Independent* (Sunday, 1993) prepared a map entitled 'The World At War', which showed many flashpoints not counted in the SIPRI data. There are also ethnic conflicts, such as in Bhutan, where it is extremely difficult to have

authentic figures of the dead and wounded persons, but informal accounts suggest more than 1,000 casualties. Conflict in Bhutan also does not figure in the SIPRI data, and the Uppsala University team admits the difficulty in computing authentic data on conflict situations.

4. Max Singer, 'Zones of Peace, Zones of Turmoil: A New Order of Hope', *International Herald Tribune*, 2 September 1993.

5. *SIPRI Year Book 1993: World Armaments And Disarmament* (Stockholm: Stockholm International Peace Research Institute, 1993), pp. 443-5.

6. Mohammed Ayoob, 'Security Problematic of the Third World', *World Politics*, vol. 43, January 1991, pp. 257-83. See also his 'Security in the Third World: The Worm About to Turn?', *International Affairs*, vol. 60, no. 1, winter 1983-84. John Chipman, 'Third World Politics and Security in the 1990s: The World Forgetting; By the World Forgot', *Washington Quarterly*, vol. 14, no. 1, winter 1991.

7. Samuel P. Huntington, 'The Clash of Civilizations', *Foreign Affairs*, summer 1993. For responses to his argument, see *Foreign Affairs*, September/October 1993 and November/December 1993.

8. Clair Sterling, *The Terror Network* (London: Weidenfeld & Nicolson, 1981). Also Edward J. Laurance, 'Political Implications of Illegal Arms Exports from the United States', *Political Science Quarterly*, vol. 107, no. 3, pp. 501-34.

9. William E. Odom, *On Internal War: American and Soviet Approaches to Third World Clients and Insurgents* (Durham, NC: Duke University Press, 1992).

10. Chris Smith, *The Diffusion of Small Arms and Light Weapons in Pakistan and Northern India*, London Defence Studies, no. 20 (London: Brasseys, 1993). Also Jasjit Singh, 'Confidence- and Security-Building Measures in South Asia', A Conference Paper (New Delhi: Institute for Defence Studies and Analyses, 1993).

11. *Jane's Infantry Weapons, 1992-93*, as cited in Prashant Dixit, 'Proliferation of Small Arms and Minor Weapons', in *Asian Strategic Review* (New Delhi: Institute For Defence Studies and Analyses, 1993), pp. 205-31.

12. Laurance, *Arms Watch*. Also Michael T. Klare, 'The Thriving Black Market for Weapons', *Bulletin of Atomic Scientists*, vol. 44, no.3, April 1988; and Aaron Karp, 'Arming Ethnic Conflict', *Arms Control Today*, vol. 23, no. 7, September 1993.

13. *The Economist*, 12 February 1994, pp. 19-21.

14. Frank Smyth, 'Arms and Mandela', *Washington Post*, 22 May 1994.

15. Boutros Boutros-Ghali, 'UN Multilateralism: A Cure for Ugly New Nationalisms', *International Herald Tribune*, 21-23 August 1993.

16. For a discussion of some of these issues, see the contributions by Surge Sur, Sverre Lodgaard, David Ruzie and Leiutenant-General Satish Nambiar in *UNIDIR News Letter*, no. 24, December 1993, pp. 3-22. Also US General Accounting Office, *US Participation In Peace-keeping Operations*, Report to The Chairman, Committee on Foreign Affairs, House of Representatives, Washington DC, GAO/NSIAD-92-247, September 1992. Michael Doyle and

Nishkala Suntherlingam, 'The UN in Cambodia: Lessons for Complex Peace-keeping', *International Peacekeeping*, vol. 1, no. 2, summer 1994.

17. Herbert Wulf (ed.), *Arms Industry Limited* (Oxford: Oxford University Press for the Stockholm International Peace Research Institute, 1993).
18. Emile Atzioni, 'Limits of Self-Determination', *Foreign Policy*, winter 1992-93.
19. *SIPRI Year Book, 1993*, pp. 453-6. See also Paul Dibb, 'Asians Are Arming: A Prospect of Trouble Ahead', *International Herald Tribune*, 26 November 1993; and Michael T. Klare, 'The Next Great Arms Race', *Foreign Affairs*, vol. 72, no. 3, summer 1993, pp. 136-52.
20. *Military Balance 1992-93*, (London: International Institute of Strategic Studies, 1993), p. 219.
21. Anthony H. Cordesman, *After the Storm: The Changing Military Balance In the Middle East* (Boulder, CO: Westview, 1993), p. 30.
22. William D. Hartung, *And Weapons for All* (New York: HarperCollins for World Policy Institute, 1994).
23. David E. Long, 'Prospects of Armed Conflict in the Gulf in the 1990s: The Impact of the Gulf War', *Middle East Policy*, 1993; Chin Kin Wah, 'ASEAN: External Security Concerns in a Post-Cold War Era', *The Round Table*, no. 326, 1993, pp. 169-85.
24. See S.D. Muni, *Post-Cold War Regionalism In Asia: With Special Reference to the SAARC Sub-region* (Tokyo: Institute of Developing Economies, 1994).
25. R. Bates Gill, *Chinese Arms Transfers: Purposes, Patterns and Prospects in the New World Order* (Westport, CT: Praeger, 1992).
26. Yahya Sadowski, 'Scuds Versus Butter: The Political Economy of Arms Control in the Arab World', *Middle East Report*, July-August 1992, pp. 2-13.
27. Desmond Ball, 'Arms and Affluence: Military Acquisitions in the Asia-Pacific Region', *International Security*, vol. 18, no. 3, winter 1993/94, pp. 78-112; also in the same issue, Richard K. Betts, 'Wealth, Power and Instability: East Asia and the United States After the Cold War', pp. 34-77. Jonathan Sikes, 'Asia Puts its Wealth in Military', *Washington Times*, 12 February 1990, p. 17.
28. See Klare, 'The Next Great Arms Race'; Dibb, 'Asians are Coming'; Gerald Segal and David Mussington, 'Economics Power Asia's Arms Acquisition', *Japan Times*, 29 November 1993.
29. *Washington Post*, 1 February 1993; *Wall Street Journal*, 28 January 1994.
30. *New York Times*, 3 April 1993, editorial.
31. Jeff Bingaman, 'Let's Stop Subsidizing the Arms Trade', *International Herald Tribune*, 23 September 1993.
32. Ralph Vertabedian and Marshall Tyler, 'US Defense Industry Heeds Calls to Arms - By Foreigners', *Los Angeles Times (World Report)*, as reproduced in the *Daily Yomiuri*, 4 December 1993.
33. Herbert Wulf, *Arms Industry Limited*.
34. *SIPRI Year Book, 1993*, pp. 448-51; Ralph Boulton, 'Guns For Sale', *Financial Times*, 5 February 1994; Steven Erlanger, 'Turning Swords into Plowshares:

No Fun for Russians', *New York Times*, as reproduced in *Asahi Evening News*, 14 December 1993.

35. Eric Hyer, 'China's Arms Merchants: Profits In Command', *The China Quarterly*, no. 132, 1992, pp. 101-18.

36. Leonard S. Spector, *Nuclear Ambitions: The Spread of Nuclear Weapons, 1989-90* (Boulder, CO: Westview, 1990).

37. Lora Lumpe, *Zero Ballistic Missiles and the Third World*, PRAC Paper no. 3, University Of College Park, March 1993; Aaron Karp, 'Ballistic Missiles Proliferation', in *SIPRI Year Book, 1991* (Stockholm: SIPRI, 1991); Steve Felter, 'Ballistic Missiles and Weapons of Mass Destruction: What is the Threat? What Should be Done?', *International Security*, vol. 16, no. 1, summer 1991, pp. 5-42.

38. Seymour M. Hersh, 'On the Nuclear Edge', *The New Yorker*, 29 March 1993. Also, William E. Burrows and Robert Windern, *Critical Mass: The Dangerous Race for Super Weapons in a Fragmented World* (New York: Simon and Schuster, 1994).

39. Aspen Strategy Group Report, *New Threats: Responding to the Proliferation of Nuclear, Chemical and Delivery Capabilities in the Third World* (Aspen Institute, University of America, 1990); Lawrence K. Greshwin, 'Threats to US Interests from Weapons of Mass Destruction', *Comparative Strategy*, vol. 12, pp. 7-13.

40. Joachim Krause, 'Risks of Nuclear Proliferation following the Dissolution of the Soviet Union', *Aussen Politik*, vol. 43, 4th quarter, 1992, pp. 352-61; William C. Potter, 'Nuclear Exports from the Former Soviet Union: What's New, What's True', *Arms Control Today*, vol. 23, no. 1, January/February 1993, pp. 3-10.

41. Such attempts by Russian workers to steal enriched Uranium were admitted by the official spokesman of Russia's Nuclear Power Ministry, *Daily Yomiuri*, 11 February 1994. Similarly, the reports about nuclear material being smuggled by the terrorist groups were published by the German magazine *Der Spiegel*, on the basis of information from German intelligence sources, as cited in the *Daily Yomiuri*, 7 February 1994.

42. Paul L. Leventhal, 'Nuclear Export Controls: Can we Plug the Leaks?' in Jean François Rioux (ed.), *Limiting the Proliferation of Weapons: The Role of Supply-Side Strategies* (Ottawa: Carleton University Press, 1992), pp. 39-53; Jennifer Scarlott, 'Nuclear Proliferation after the Cold War: A Merry-Go-Round of Mayhem', *World Policy Journal*, vol. VIII, no. 4, pp. 687-710; Peter Rudolf, 'Non-Proliferation and International Export Control', *Aussen Politik*, vol. 42, 4th quarter, 1991, pp. 390-401.

43. Leonard S. Spector, 'Repentant Nuclear Proliferants', *Foreign Policy*, fall 1992, no. 88, pp. 21-37; Lewis A. Dunn, 'NPT 1995: Time to Shift Gears', *Arms Control Today*, vol. 23, no. 9, November 1993, pp. 14-19.

44. United States General Accounting Office, *Nuclear Non-Proliferation: Export Licensing Procedures for Dual-Use Items need to be Strengthened*, Report to the

Chairman, Committee on Governmental Affairs, US Senate, Washington DC, GAO/NSIAD-94-119, April 1994.

45. William C. Potter, 'The New Nuclear Producers: The Main Threat to Supply-Side Restraints?', in Jean François Rioux (ed.), *Limiting the Proliferation of Weapons*, pp. 22-37.

46. William M. Arkins, 'Nuclear Junkies: Those Lovable Little Bombs', *The Bulletin of Atomic Scientists*, July/August 1993, pp. 22-7; Jim Mann, 'China Upgrading Nuclear Arms, Experts Say', *Los Angeles Times, World Report*, November 1993.

47. 'World Nuclear Testing, 1945-93', *Arms Control Today*, vol. 23, no. 9, November 1993, p. 29.

48. Robert J. O'Neill, 'Nuclear Weapons in the Nineties: A Question of Purpose', in Beatrice Heuser (ed.), *Nuclear Weapons and the Future of European Security* (London: Centre for Defence Studies, 1991), pp. 5-14.

49. Kenneth N. Waltz, 'The Spread of Nuclear Weapons: More May be Better', *Adelphi Papers*, no. 171 (London: International Institute of Strategic Studies, 1981).

50. John J. Mearsheimer, 'Back to the Future: Instability in Europe after the Cold War', *International Security*, vol. 15, no. 1, summer 1990; also his 'The Case for a Ukraine Nuclear Deterrent', *Foreign Affairs*, vol. 72, no. 3, summer 1993.

51. The concept of 'nuclear-weapon-safe zone' was discussed between Indian and Pakistani strategic analysts in the *Neemrana* series of informal dialogue sponsored by the Ford Foundation and the IISS. For the 'non-weaponized deterrent' concept, see George Perkovich, 'A Nuclear Third Way in South Asia', *Foreign Policy*, no. 91, summer 1993, pp. 85-104. While the 'safe zone' concept is based upon deployed deterrence at the minimum and somewhat crude level, the 'non-weaponized' concept is based on capabilities just short of a fabricated and deployed nuclear device.

52. *International Herald Tribune*, 11 September 1993.

Part VI

REGIONAL ANALYSIS

10

Anatomy of Conflicts in Africa

Francis M. Deng

INTRODUCTION

Over the last few years, the intensification of internal conflicts around the world has resulted in unprecedented humanitarian tragedies and in some cases led to partial and even total collapse of states. For sources and consequences of conflict, UN Secretary-General, Boutros Boutros-Ghali, has said: 'Poverty, disease, famine, oppression and despair abound, joining to produce 17 million refugees, 20 million displaced persons and massive migrations of peoples within and beyond national borders'.[1]

Although the global dimension of the crisis needs to be stressed, Africa is perhaps the continent most devastated by internal conflicts and their catastrophic consequences. About 15 million of the internally displaced persons, now estimated at 25 million world-wide, and 6 million of the world's 17 million refugees are African. These groups represent only samples or microcosms of a much more embracing catastrophe affecting larger numbers of people.

Perhaps the most conspicuous aspect of the crisis is that by uprooting such large numbers of people, they, and ultimately the nation, are deprived of their resource-base and capacity for self-reliance. They must therefore depend on international humanitarian assistance for basic survival. Such assistance, while pivotal in saving lives, may also have the effect of encouraging dependency and undermining development as a self-generating and self-sustaining process from within, which reinforces the vicious circle of poverty, underdevelopment, competition for scarce resources, and, ultimately, conflict over state power and control over resources and the distributive system.

DEFINING CONFLICT AND CONFLICT RESOLUTION

To understand conflicts and the prospects for their resolution, it is necessary to have a working definition of the concepts involved. Descriptively, conflict can be defined as a situation of interaction involving two or more parties in which actions in pursuit of incompatible objectives or interests result in varying degrees of discord. The principal dichotomy is between normally harmonious and cooperative relations and a disruptive adversarial confrontation, culminating at its worst in high-intensity violence. Conflict resolution can be defined as a normative concept aimed at reconciling, harmonizing, or managing incompatible interests by fostering a process of institutionalized peaceful interaction. Conflict resolution envisages strategies aimed at restoring or establishing the normal state of affairs and raising the level of peaceful, harmonious, cooperative, constructive, and productive interaction, even with competition.

It is sometimes argued that conflict is the normal state of human interaction.[2] This can only be valid if it is understood to mean that grounds for conflict exist in normal human relations or that the occurrence of conflict is normal in the sense that it happens. If it is intended to mean that conflict is the normal pattern of life, then such a position is empirically questionable and normatively ambiguous. Since people are more apt to cooperate and harmonize their incompatible or potentially conflictual positions, conflict is in fact a crisis which signifies a breakdown in the normal pattern of behaviour. It involves a collision of incompatible positions resulting from a failure to regulate, reconcile, or harmonize the differences.

In the normal course of events, society is structured around fundamental values and norms which guide behaviour and regulate relations so as to avoid such a destructive collision of interests or positions. If people observe the principles of the normative code, which they generally do, the normal pattern would be one of relative cooperation and mutual accommodation, even in a competitive framework. To call that state one of conflict would be to put a negative value judgement on positive motivations, endeavours, and a relatively high degree of success in peaceful interaction.

Even more important than strict empirical interpretation would be the normative implications of holding conflict as the normal state of existence, which would tend to foster a disposition that is fundamentally adversarial, suspicious, and conflictual. The extent to which members in a community or group reflect this disposition may depend in large measure on the culture and its normative code. Culture in this context can be defined as 'a set of shared and enduring meanings, values, and beliefs that characterize national, ethnic, or other groups and orient their behaviour'.[3] As Morton Deutsch has noted:

'Social interaction takes place in a social environment – in a family, a group, a community, a nation, a civilization – that has developed techniques, symbols, categories, rules and values that are relevant to human interactions. Hence, to understand the events that occur in social interactions one must comprehend the interplay of these events with the broader socio-cultural context in which they occur.'[4]

In the African cultural context, because of the family and kinship orientation of society, where people in conflict are expected to settle their differences and resume cooperative, interpersonal relations, methods of conflict resolution aim at consensus and reconciliation. Despite the frequency of violent conflicts, this underscores mediation and conciliation as conflict resolution techniques. 'Talking it out', even after a bitterly violent dispute, is a prevalent aspect of African settlement of disputes.

Generally, as Deutsch has observed, 'the characteristic processes and effects elicited by a given type of social relationship (for example, co-operative or competitive) also tend to elicit that type of social relationship'.[5] This means that 'cooperation induces and is induced by a perceived similarity in beliefs and attitudes; a readiness to be helpful; openness in communication; trusting and friendly attitudes; sensitivity to common interests and deemphasis on opposed interests; an orientation towards enhancing mutual power rather than power differences; and so on'. Likewise, 'competition induces and is induced by the use of tactics or coercion, threat to deception, attempts to enhance the power differences between one's self and the other; poor communication; minimalization of the awareness of similarities in values and increased sensitivity to opposed interests; suspicions and hostile attitudes; the importance, rigidity and size of the issues in conflict, and so on'.[6]

It has also been argued that conflict may indeed be a good thing. Considering how destructive conflict can be in its violent form, this can only be valid if it means that conflict draws attention to problems that should be addressed to achieve a sustainable peace. To favour harmony and peaceful interaction is not, or should not, be to support a problematic *status quo*.

SOURCES AND CONSEQUENCES OF CONFLICT

Conflicts as they now pertain in the new states of Africa have their roots in the formation of the colonial state. This is not to say that there were no conflicts in Africa before colonial intervention; quite the contrary, conflicts were rampant and in some cases catastrophic. Indeed, although colonialism was inherently oppressive, and during the pacification phase brutally violent, colonial intervention ironically established conditions of law and order which in many instances contrasted with the Hobbesian state of affairs that had prevailed. The ravages of the slave trade constituted an example of the havoc that had devastated the continent.

Nevertheless, a different political and social order existed in pre-colonial Africa which involved largely horizontal relations among groups of varying levels of organization. African political systems ranged from highly central-ized kingdoms to stateless societies with a segmentary lineage system.[7] Ethnic groups interacted, cooperated, conflicted, and reconciled in accor-dance with the established rules of kinship and the normative code of the wider community. Over time, communities developed rules of coexistence and interrelationships embodied in local agreements or customary norms, predicated on autonomy and reciprocity. While groups jealously guarded their lands, borders remained porous and neighbours interacted as economic activities dictated and in accordance with established rules of conduct.

However, the colonial state, with its rigid borders and centralized struc-tures and procedures, was an artificial creation that tore apart regional ethnic groups and affiliated them with other groups. But while these groups were supposedly united by incorporation into the modern state, they were kept apart. Indeed, their relations were manipulated as part of the divide and rule strategy of colonial domination. Hostile historical memories and animosities were kept alive and fanned, but, through law and order, these animosities were not allowed to explode in ethnic violence. When they did, those respon-sible were severely punished. The colonial state was therefore a source of relative peace and stability.

The state also became a source of social services and employment opportunities which, though very limited, introduced a distribution system that was centrally controlled. The autonomous and self-reliant structures and modes of life of the traditional society were gradually replaced by attitudes of dependency on a nascent welfare state system. With resources and capaci-ties that were extremely limited, inequitable sharing of social services, such as education and medical care, and correlative access to employment and development opportunities resulted in grave disparities among regions, ethnic groups, and sectors of society. These inequities in turn affected access to state power. Again, the tensions emanating from these disparities were submerged by the stability of law and order, ruthlessly maintained by the coercive force of the police and military.

Collective opposition to foreign rule, albeit with regional variations, also provided a common purpose in the liberation struggle. Self-determination was seen as a collective right of the people subjected to foreign domination within the borders of the colonial state. Internal diversities and disparities among the various groups comprising the state were overshadowed by the collective quest for national independence.

Although independence initially came as a collective gain for all people of the nation, it soon proved to be the case that an elite and sections of the country succeeded to the power position of the foreign rulers. Power struggles among regions, political factions, and interest groups soon ensued. The demand by regions and ethnic groups, not only to control their own affairs through decentralization but also to participate at the national level on equal footing, was perceived by the power elite as a threat to the unity of the country. The elite's response was to try to repress these demands, which only aggravated the regions and ethnic groups into calls for self-determination or outright secession. The threat that these demands posed for the unity of the newly independent African countries prompted the Organization of African Unity to adopt the principle of preserving the colonial borders against any demands for secession or self-determination. This in turn encouraged the post-colonial governments to suppress any regional or ethnic demands for autonomy or equitable sharing of power. The machinery of the colonial state, now converted to a national apparatus, was fully mobilized to this end without the inhibitions that had constrained the colonial state as an instrument of foreign control.

These domestic measures, sanctioned by regional and international principles of respect for territorial integrity, were further reinforced by the ideological alliance system of the Cold War. In some countries, leaders were wise enough to moderate their policies through a system of regional and ethnic distribution of power positions, public services, employment opportunities, rural development projects, and other pragmatic concessions. In other countries, governments were less compromising in their repressive policies. Supported by the superpowers on the grounds of ideological alignments and geopolitical strategic considerations, these leaders were empowered to suppress their nationals into submission. The ideals of democracy, respect for fundamental human rights, and accountability for the management of the economy and national resources were compromised and subordinated for ideological and strategic interests. This did not entirely inhibit some determined groups from waging civil wars of liberation in the demand for secession, self-determination, or a radical restructuring of the country to allow for equitable participation in the government and economic development.

The end of the Cold War meant the reduction, if not the total withdrawal, of ideological or strategically motivated security and economic assistance from the superpowers and other major foreign sources of support. The resulting dismantling of the bipolar control mechanisms of the Cold War has led to a significant weakening of governments and their instruments of oppression around the world, and has encouraged previously oppressed peoples to assert their demands for democracy, respect for fundamental human rights, and, in some cases, their right to self-determination. The result has been rampant violence, civil wars, massive disorders, and in some instances the collapse of states.

The withdrawal of the Cold War security assistance and economic support based on ideological or strategic considerations has been balanced by massive humanitarian intervention and relief operations which have been stimulated by the suffering of innocent masses affected by these internal conflicts and natural disasters in countries where governments and other controlling authorities lack either the capacity or the political will to protect or assist their nationals. The cleavages of the identity crises behind these ethnic or religious conflicts create vacuums of moral responsibility which the international community is called upon to fill on humanitarian grounds. What makes the tragedy particularly acute is that these conflicts uproot masses of the population, depriving them of their resource base, and their ability to sustain themselves, even at the level of bare subsistence. Large portions of the nation and eventually the country itself become dependent on relief supplies from foreign sources, which in turn distort the economy and retard development.

RECONCEPTUALIZING THE NORMATIVE FRAMEWORK

What seems to be emerging in the aftermath of the Cold War is a universal quest for fundamental human rights, democratic freedoms, and respect for diversity in unity. The artificial borders of the colonial state, although still affirmed, are no longer perceived as sacrosanct, and although self-determination need not entail the dismantling of existing borders, the principle of giving a people the right to determine their future within or outside the framework of the existing state is becoming increasingly recognized.

There is, however, a clear preference for finding remedies to the problems of nation-building within the framework of national unity through good governance. The critical issue is whether the underlying sense of injustice can be remedied in a timely manner that prevents or controls the level of violence. As Boutros Boutros-Ghali has observed: 'One requirement for solutions to these problems lies in commitment to human rights with a special sensitivity to those of minorities, whether ethnic, religious, social or linguistic'.[8] On the need to balance between the unity of larger entities and respect for sovereignty, autonomy, and diversity of various identities, the Secretary-General noted: 'The healthy globalization of contemporary life requires in the first instance solid identities and fundamental freedoms. The sovereignty, territorial integrity and independence of states within the established international system, and the principle of self-determination for peoples, both of great value and importance, must not be permitted to work against each other in the period ahead. Respect for democratic principles at all levels of social existence is crucial: in communities, within states and within the community of states. Our constant duty should be to maintain the integrity of each while finding a balanced design for all.'

Where discrimination or disparity arises from conflicting perspectives on the fundamental issue of national identity, compounded by territorial differentiation, the cleavages involved become extremely difficult to bridge. In some instances, religion, ethnicity, and culture become so intertwined that they are not easy to disentangle. Indeed, these elements are at the core of the challenge of nation-building in countries that are religiously, ethnically, and culturally mixed, especially where these forms of identity correlate and deepen internal divisions.

It is noteworthy that the Kampala Document of the postulated Conference on Security, Stability, Development and Cooperation in Africa (CSSDCA) stipulates under 'The establishment of political bodies: Political organizations should not be created on religious, ethnic, regional or racial basis and considerations and these should not be exploited by leaders'.[9] It also states that 'Religious fundamentalism, no matter from whatever religion, fosters instability. Governments must encourage the principle of separation of state and religion. Religion must remain a personal affair.' Where such cleavages cannot be bridged within a unitary system, varying forms of decentralization, federal or confederate, need to be explored. And where even these arrangements cannot ensure peaceful mutual accommodation, partition may be the residual option.

Although democracy, respect for human rights and responsible economic management are consistently postulated as means of enhancing security, stability and legitimacy, it is recognized that there are no easy short-cuts to the desired goals. Africa must strive to find creative ways of adapting the lofty ideals of democracy to the realities of the African conditions. The dilemma is further heightened by the realization that the Western model for governance and especially its components of democracy, respect for human rights and free market economy, which Africa seems to emulate or is postulated by its international partners and donors as the desired norms, are the outcomes of a long historical process. 'The systems of Africa are being asked to accomplish in the short term – state-making, democracy, and functioning market economies – what it took centuries to accomplish in the United States and Europe.'[10]

What needs to be underscored in the discussion of the normative factors of nation-building is that as long as the root causes of conflicts are not addressed and the framework for consensus within the nation-state is not consolidated, conflict, whether potential or actual, will remain a threat to nationhood. Armed conflicts are followed by gross human rights' violations, disregard for democracy, and the frustration of development, all combining to aggravate the crisis of nation-building. The quest for consensus becomes the key to conflict prevention, management, and resolution. Western-style democracy of the vote, with the 'winner take all' outcome, runs counter to the African indigenous principles of power-sharing and conciliation, and therefore cannot be a basis for conflict resolution in the African cultural context.

THE GLOBAL CHALLENGE OF AFRICAN CRISIS

Africa's crisis of nation-building is the culmination of an evolutionary process in which the colonial encounter played a pivotal role. The postcolonial state, despite independence, was structurally connected to the superpower control mechanisms of the major powers. Even after the withdrawal of these powers from an ideological and strategic national interest perspective at the end of the Cold War, the outside world, particularly the Western democracies, remained engaged in Africa through humanitarian concerns and the activist involvement of non-governmental and voluntary organizations. All this underscores the linkages of the internal and external factors and actors, and the shared responsibility that emanates from that interaction. Although governance as conflict management is a domestic affair, 'it operates in an international context'.[11] This essentially means that the states involved, the OAU, the UN and the international community as a whole are all called upon to make a significant contribution to conflict prevention, management, and resolution. But there is no consensus on the specifics of apportioning responsibility, especially as sensitivities pertaining to national sovereignty constrain international action needed to remedy state failure.

Governance under normal circumstances is a process by which social groups place competing demands before government, assumed to be neutral and objective and held accountable for the way in which it handles them with justice or fairness. But in the African context, conflict is mostly perceived as between groups and the government, which in most cases represents only a faction or factions of the competing and conflicting groups and is therefore inherently partial. Governance in that context implies that the government is managing its own conflicts with others. 'This means that "normal politics" has broken down, the real nature of politics is a war between society [or a faction of the society] and government, which continues even when a new group of society becomes government and takes its turn at the trough.'[12]

In the most severe cases, especially those involving a crisis of national identity, the cleavage between the aggrieved faction of society and the government becomes even more acute and dangerous to the group. Since the ensuing conflict is within state borders and all the groups involved, including those represented by the government (indeed, the government itself becomes party to the conflict), are victims deprived of the protection normally expected from the state. The humanitarian tragedies that often characterize these internal conflicts, such as massive displacement and the use of starvation as a weapon of warfare, directly result from the lack of a moral sense of responsibility on the part of the government. These are in essence a people oppressed by sovereignty and without any sovereignty of their own. It is to the international community that they must turn for assistance and protection from the indignities of a grossly inequitable pluralistic framework of governance.

Protecting and assisting the masses of people affected by internecine internal conflicts entails reconciling the possibility of international intervention with traditional concepts of national sovereignty. One observer has recently summarized the new sense of urgency in the need for international response, the ambivalence of the pressures for the needed change, and the pull of traditional legal doctrines:

> In the post-Cold War world ... a new standard of intolerance for human misery and human atrocities has taken hold ... [S]omething quite significant has occurred to raise the consciousness of nations to the plight of peoples within sovereign borders. There is a new commitment – expressed in both moral and legal terms – to alleviate the suffering of oppressed or devastated people. To argue today that norms of sovereignty, non-use of force, and the sanctity of internal affairs are paramount to the collective human rights of people, whose lives and well-being are at risk, is to avoid the hard questions of international law and to ignore the march of history.[13]

The steady erosion of the concept of absolute sovereignty is making it easier for international organizations, governments, and non-governmental organizations to intervene when governments refuse to meet the needs of their populations and substantial numbers of people are at risk. Sovereignty is becoming understood more in terms of conferring responsibilities on governments to assist and protect persons residing in their territories; if they fail to meet their obligations, they risk undermining their legitimacy.[14] The scrutiny of world public opinion, as represented by the media, makes it difficult for governments to ignore these obligations or defend their failure to act.

But to intervene is not an easy choice. Former UN Secretary-General, Javier Perez de Cuellar, highlighted the dilemmas when he said: 'We are clearly witnessing what is probably an irresistible shift in public attitudes towards the belief that the defence of the oppressed in the name of morality should prevail over frontiers and legal documents'.[15] But he also added, 'does [intervention] not call into question one of the cardinal principles of international law, one diametrically opposed to it, namely, the obligation of non-interference in the internal affairs of states?' In his 1991 annual report, the Secretary-General wrote of the new balance that must be struck between sovereignty and the protection of human rights:

> It is now increasingly felt that the principle of non-interference with the essential domestic jurisdiction of states cannot be regarded as a protective barrier behind which human rights could be massively or systematically violated with impunity ... The case for not impinging on the sovereignty, territorial integrity and political independence of states is by itself indubitably strong. But it would only be weakened if it were to carry the implication that sovereignty, even in this day and age, includes the right of mass slaughter or of launching systematic campaigns of decimation or forced exodus of civilian populations in the name of controlling civil strife or insurrection. With the heightened international interest in universalizing a regime of human rights, there is a marked and most welcome shift in public attitudes. To try to resist it would be politically as unwise as it is morally indefensible.[16]

Meanwhile, the current Secretary-General, Boutros Boutros-Ghali, has written that respect for sovereignty and integrity is 'crucial to any common international progress', but went on to say that 'the time of absolute and exclusive sovereignty ... has passed', that 'its theory was never matched by reality', and that it is necessary for leaders of states 'to find a balance between the needs of good internal governance and the requirements of an ever more interdependent world'.[17] As one observer commented, 'the clear meaning was that governments could best avoid intervention by meeting their obligations not only to other states, but also to their own citizens. If they failed, they might invite intervention.'[18]

Self-interest, therefore, dictates an appropriate and timely action in self-protection. This was indeed the point made by the Secretary-General of the

Organization of African Unity, Salim Ahmed Salim, in his bold proposals for an OAU mechanism for conflict prevention and resolution. 'If the OAU, first through the Secretary-General and then the Bureau of the Summit, is to play the lead role in any African conflict', he said, 'it should be enabled to intervene swiftly, otherwise it cannot be ensured that whoever (apart from African regional organizations) acts will do so in accordance with African interests'.[19] Criticizing the tendency to respond only to worst-case scenarios, Salim emphasized the need for pre-emptive intervention: 'The basis for "intervention" may be clearer when there is a total breakdown of law and order ... and where, with the attendant human suffering, a spillover effect is experienced within the neighbouring countries ... However, pre-emptive involvement should also be permitted even in situations where tensions evolve to such a pitch that it becomes apparent that a conflict is in the making.' Salim went as far as to suggest that the OAU should take the lead in transcending the traditional view of sovereignty, building on the African values of kinship solidarity and the notion that 'every African is his brother's keeper'. Considering that 'our borders are at best artificial', he argued, 'we in Africa need to use our own cultural and social relationships to interpret the principle of non-interference in such a way that we are enabled to apply it to our advantage in conflict prevention and resolution'.

In traditional Africa, third-party intervention for mediation and conciliation is always expected, independent of the will of the parties directly involved in a conflict. Even in domestic disputes, relatives and elders intercede without being invited. 'Saving face', which is critical to conflict resolution in Africa, indeed requires that such intervention be unsolicited. But, of course, African concepts and practices under the modern conditions of the nation-state must still balance consideration for state sovereignty with the compelling humanitarian need to protect and assist the dispossessed.

While the normative frameworks proposed by the OAU Secretary-General and the UN Secretary-General's *An Agenda for Peace* are predicated on respect for the sovereignty and integrity of the state as crucial to the existing international system, the logic of the transcendent importance of human rights as a legitimate area of concern for the international community, especially where order has broken down or the state is incapable or unwilling to act responsibly to protect the masses of citizens, would tend to make international inaction quite indefensible. Even in less extreme cases of acute internal conflicts, the perspectives of the pivotal actors on such issues as the national or public interest are bound to be sharply divided, both internally and in their relationship to the outside world. After all, internal conflicts often entail a contest of the national arena of power and therefore sovereignty. Every political intervention from outside has its internal recipients, hosts, and beneficiaries. Under those circumstances, there can hardly be said to be an indivisible quantum of national sovereignty behind which the nation stands united.

Furthermore, it is not always easy to determine the degree to which a government of a country devastated by civil war can be said to be truly in control, when, as is often the case, sizeable portions of the territory are controlled by rebel or opposing forces. Often, while a government may remain in effective control of the capital and the main garrisons, much of the countryside in the war zone will have practically collapsed. How would such partial, but significant, collapse be factored into determining the degree to which civil order in the country has broken down? No government which will allow hundreds of thousands, and maybe millions, to starve to death when food can be made available to them, be exposed to deadly elements when they could be provided with shelter, be indiscriminately tortured, brutalized, and murdered by opposing forces, contesting the very sovereignty that is supposed to ensure their security, or otherwise allow them to suffer in a vacuum of moral leadership responsibility, can still have a clear face to keep the outside world from stepping in to offer protection and assistance in the name of sovereignty.

The critical question now is under what circumstances the international community is justified to override sovereignty to protect the dispossessed population within state borders. The common assumption in international law is that to justify such action there must be a threat to international peace. The position, now supported by the Security Council, is that massive violations of human rights and displacement within a country's borders may constitute such a threat.[20] Others contend that a direct threat to international peace is too high a threshold because it would preclude action on too many humanitarian crises. Indeed, they argue, the time has come to recognize humanitarian concern as a ground for intervention. To avoid costly emergency relief operations, the international community needs to develop a strategy of preventive response to conflict situations before they deteriorate into humanitarian tragedies. This calls for placing emphasis on peace-making through preventive diplomacy. Such an approach requires understanding the sources and causes of conflicts and addressing them at their roots.

STRATEGIES FOR INTERNATIONAL ACTION

Although addressing the issue of sovereignty and the root causes of conflict are critical prerequisites to intervention, formulating credible operational principles and strategies is the most pivotal factor in the equation. Ideally, from an institutional or organizational perspective, problems should be addressed and solved within the immediate framework, with wider involvement necessitated only by the failure of the internal efforts. This means that conflict prevention, management, or resolution progressively moves from the domestic domain to the regional and ultimately the global levels of concern and action.

Those conflicts in which the state is an effective arbiter do not present particular difficulties since they are manageable within the national framework. The problem arises when the state itself is a party to the conflict, for under those conditions, external involvement becomes necessary. In the African context, it is generally agreed that the next best level of involvement should be the OAU, although there are, however, constraints on the role of the OAU. One has to do with the limitation of resources, financial and logistical. But perhaps even more debilitating is the political will, since in the intimate context of the region, governments feel vulnerable to the generation of conflicts resulting from the problematic conditions of state-formation and nation-building and are therefore prone to resist any form of external scrutiny. And since the judge of today may well be the accused of tomorrow, there is a temptation to avoid confronting the problems. The result is evasiveness and benign neglect.

Beyond the OAU, the United Nations is the next logical organization as it represents the international community in its global context. But the UN also suffers from the constraints that affect the OAU, although to a lesser degree. It has the problem of resources and the reciprocal protectiveness of vulnerable governments.

As recent events have demonstrated, the role of the major Western powers acting unilaterally, multilaterally, or within the framework of the United Nations, though often susceptible to accusations of strategic motivation, has become increasingly pivotal. Indeed, although their motives continue to be questioned, the problem is more one of their unwillingness to become involved or lack of adequate preparation for such involvement. Perhaps the most important aspect of the involvement of Western industrial democracies in foreign conflicts is that they are often moved to act by the gravity of the humanitarian tragedies involved. This makes their involvement both an asset in arresting the tragedy and a limitation from the perspective of prevention at an earlier stage. Even with respect to humanitarian intervention, lack of preparedness for an appropriate timely response is generally acknowledged as a major limitation.[21]

The combination of compelling humanitarian causes and lack of preparation for well-planned response makes Western democracies particularly prone to crisis-induced reactions that are relatively easy to execute and are of more symbolic value than they are effective in addressing the major substantive issues involved, and, in particular, the root causes of these tragedies.

As intervention is a major intrusion from outside, and despite the obvious fact that there will always be elements in the country which will welcome such intervention, especially among the disadvantaged groups to whom tangible benefits are promised, resistance on the grounds of national sovereignty or pride is also a predictable certainty. For that reason, the justification for intervention must be reliably persuasive, if not beyond reproach. 'The difference between an intervention that succeeds and one that is destroyed by immune reaction would depend on the degree of spontaneous acceptance or rejection by the local population.'[22] To avoid or minimize this 'immune reaction', such intervention would have to be broadly international in character. The principles used and the objectives towards which it is targeted must transcend political and cultural boundaries or traditions and concomitant nationalist sentiments. In other words, it must enjoy an effective degree of global legitimacy. 'The rationale that could conceivably carry such a burden presumably involves human rights so fundamental that they are not derived from any particular political or economic ideology.'

The strategy for preventive or corrective involvement in conflict should comprise gathering and analysing information and otherwise monitoring situations with a view to establishing an early-warning system through which the international community could be alerted to act.

The quest for a system of response to conflict and attendant humanitarian tragedies was outlined by the UN Secretary-General when he wrote, referring to the surging demands on the Security Council as a central instrument for the prevention and resolution of conflicts, that the aims of the United Nations must be:

> To seek to identify at the earliest possible stage situations that could produce conflict, and to try through diplomacy to remove the sources of danger before violence results;
>
> Where conflict erupts, to engage in peace-making aimed at resolving the issues that have led to conflict;
>
> Through peace-keeping, to work to preserve peace, however fragile, where fighting has been halted and to assist in implementing agreements achieved by the peace-makers;
>
> To stand ready to assist in peace-building in its differing contexts: rebuilding the institutions and infrastructures of nations torn by civil war and strife; and building bonds of peaceful mutual benefit among nations formerly at war;

And in the largest sense, to address the deepest causes of conflict: economic despair, social injustice and political oppression. It is possible to discern an increasingly common moral perception that spans the world's nations and peoples, and which is finding expression in international laws, many owing their genesis to the work of this organization.[23]

What is envisaged can be conceptualized as a three-phase strategy that would involve monitoring the developments to draw early attention to impending crises, interceding in time to avert the crisis through diplomatic initiatives, and mobilizing international action when necessary.[24] The first step would aim at detecting and identifying the problem through various mechanisms for information collection, evaluation, and reporting. If sufficient basis for concern is established, the appropriate mechanism should be invoked to take preventive diplomatic measures to avert the crisis. Initially, such initiatives might be taken within the framework of regional arrangements, for example, the Conference on Security and Cooperation in Europe, the Organization of American States or the Organization of African Unity. In the context of the UN, such preventive initiatives would naturally fall on the Secretary-General, acting personally or through special representatives. If diplomatic initiatives do not succeed and depending on the level of human suffering involved, the Secretary-General may decide to mobilize international response, ranging from further diplomatic measures to forced humanitarian intervention, not only to provide emergency relief but also to facilitate the search for an enduring solution to the causes of the conflict. A strategy aimed at this broader objective would require a close understanding of the causal link with the conditions and developments leading to the outbreak of the crisis.

CONCLUSIONS

African conflicts are rooted in the problem of nation-building. A central feature of these problems is the diversity and disparity created by the manner in which state formation has separated people with a shared identity, affiliated them with others with different identities, kept them unintegrated and indeed differentiated, and then left them to fend for themselves in the process of building independent, often unitary states. The result is a competition for state power, national resources, and development opportunities. Going beyond these distributional considerations, these conflicts sometimes escalate into identity crises in which the legitimacy of the state and the controlling authorities falls into question. In the polarization that ensues, the government becomes a party to the conflict and large numbers of the innocent civilian population fall into the cracks of the identity crisis between the government and the rebel forces, and are denied the protection and assistance normally associated with state sovereignty and responsibility.

Sovereignty cannot be an amoral function of authority and control; respect for fundamental human rights must be among its most basic values. Enjoyment of human rights must encompass equitable and effective participation in the political, economic, social, and cultural life of the country, at least as a widely accepted national aspiration. This system of sharing must guarantee individuals and groups that they belong to the nation on an equal footing with the rest of the people, however identified, and that they are sufficiently represented and not discriminated against on the basis of the prevailing views of identity.

Although the world is far from a universal government, the foundations, the pillars, and perhaps even the structures of global governance are taking shape with the emergence of a post-Cold War international order in which the internally dispossessed are bound to be the beneficiaries. Unmasking sovereignty to reveal the gross violations of human rights is no longer an aspiration, but a process that has already started. Governments and other human rights' violators are being increasingly scrutinized for such violations. What is now required is to make them fully accountable and to provide international protection and assistance for the victims of human rights' violations and unremedied humanitarian tragedies within their domestic jurisdiction.

NOTES

1. Boutros Boutros-Ghali, *An Agenda for Peace: Preventive Diplomacy, Peace-making and Peace-keeping* (New York: United Nations, 1992), p. 7.
2. I. William Zartman, 'Conflict Resolution: Prevention, Management, and Resolution', in Francis M. Deng and I. William Zartman (eds), *Conflict Resolution in Africa* (Washington, DC: Brookings Institution, 1991), p. 299.
3. Guy Olivier Faure and Jeffrey Rubin (eds), *Culture and Negotiation* (Thousand Oaks, CA: Sage, 1993).
4. Morton Deutsch, 'Subjective Features of Conflict Resolution: Psychological, Social and Cultural Influences', in R. Vayrinen (ed.), *New Directions in Conflict Theory* (London: Sage Publishers, 1991), p. 26.
5. Morton Deutsch, 'Subjective Features of Conflict Resolution', p. 31.
6. Morton Deutsch, 'Subjective Features of Conflict Resolution', pp. 31-2.

7. See E.E. Evans-Pritchard and M. Fortes (eds), *African Political Systems* (Oxford: Clarendon, 1940); and John Middleton and David Tait (eds), *Tribes without Rulers* (London: Routledge & Paul, 1958).

8. Boutros Boutros-Ghali, *An Agenda for Peace*, p. 9.

9. Kampala Document of the Conference on Security, Stability, Development and Cooperation in Africa, p. 14.

10. Thomas Ohlson and Stephen Stedman, *The New is Not Yet Born: Conflict and Conflict Resolution in Southern Africa* (Washington, DC: Brookings Institution, 1994).

11. I. William Zartman, 'Governance as Conflict Management in West Africa', in I. William Zartman (ed.), *Conflict Management in West Africa* (Washington, DC: Brookings Institution, forthcoming).

12. I. William Zartman, 'Governance as Conflict Management in West Africa'.

13. David J. Scheffer, 'Toward a Modern Doctrine of Humanitarian Intervention', *University of Toledo Law Review*, vol. 23, 1992, p. 259.

14. *Human Rights Protection for Internally Displaced Persons: An International Conference* (Washington, DC: Refugee Policy Group, 1991), p. 7.

15. UN press release SG/SM/4560, 24 April 1991. Cited in G.M. Lyons and M. Mastanduno, *Beyond Westphalia?: International Intervention, State-Sovereignty, and the Future of International Society*. Summary pamphlet of a conference held May 18-20, 1992 (Hanover, NH.: Rockefeller Center at Dartmouth College, 1993), p. 2. Portions of the statement are also cited in David Scheffer, 'Toward a Modern Doctrine of Humanitarian Intervention', p. 262.

16. J. Perez de Cuellar, *Report of the Secretary-General on the Work of the Organization* (New York: United Nations, 1991), pp. 12-13.

17. Boutros Boutros-Ghali, *An Agenda for Peace*, p. 5.

18. David Scheffer, 'Toward a Modern Doctrine of Humanitarian Intervention', pp. 262-3.

19. CM/1710 (LVI) Rev. 1, *Report of the Secretary General on Conflicts in Africa: Prospects for an OAU Mechanism for Conflict Prevention and Resolution* (Addis Ababa, June 1992).

20. Note by the President of the UN Security Council, S/25344, 26 February 1993.

21. John Steinbruner, 'Civil Violence as an International Security Problem', a memorandum dated 23 November 1992, addressed to the Brookings Institution Foreign Policy Studies Program staff. See also Chester A. Crocker, 'The Global Law and Order Deficit: Is the West Ready to Police the World's Bad Neighbors?', *The Washington Post*, 20 December 1992, p. C1.

22. J. Steinbruner, 'Civil Violence as an International Security Problem'.

23. Boutros Boutros-Ghali, *An Agenda for Peace*, pp. 7-8.

24. For a more elaborate discussion of these phases as applied to the crisis of the internally displaced, see the UN study in document E/CN.4/1993/35. The study was considered by the Commission on Human Rights at its forty-ninth session, its findings and recommendations endorsed, and the mandate of the Special Representative of the Secretary-General extended for two years to continue to

work on the various aspects of the problem as presented in the study. See the revised version of the study in Francis Deng, *Protecting the Dispossessed: A Challenge for the International Community* (Washington, DC: Brookings Institution, 1993).

11

The Regional Dimension of the Causes of Conflicts: The Middle East

Abdul-Monem Al-Mashat

INTRODUCTION

For the first time since early this century the Middle East seems quiet; regional open conflicts look as if they have been resolved. However, internal conflicts and tensions are growing to an alarming degree, so while the end of the Cold War has had a positive impact on the reduction of inter-state conflicts in the Middle East, it has not increased the level of domestic tranquillity. Moreover, this lack of domestic tranquillity and the increase in societal instability may escalate because of the intrinsic correlation between external factors and regional or international conflicts.

The concept of the Middle East is a vague one. However, for the purpose of this chapter it means Arab states that are members of the League of Arab States, Israel, Turkey and Iran. Countries such as the Islamic republics of the former Soviet Union, Afghanistan or Pakistan are not included.

For the last 80 years, Arabs in the Middle East have lived in the belief that the Arab-Israeli conflict is the trigger of all other conflicts. Since the Balfour Declaration of 2 November 1917, all conflicts against external powers have been regionalized and shifted into a conflict between the Arabs on one hand and the Jews, and then Israelis, on the other. The Declaration, initiated by the British, called for 'the establishment in Palestine of a national home for the Jewish people ... it being clearly understood that nothing shall be done which may prejudice the civil and the religious rights of existing non-Jewish communities in Palestine, or the rights and political status enjoyed by Jews in any other country'.[1]

Between 1917 and 1993 all regional, and even internal, conflicts in the Middle East were blamed on the Arab-Israeli conflict. However, the Camp David Accords of 1978, the Egyptian-Israeli treaty of 1979, the Palestinian-Israeli Declaration of Principles in 1993 – known as the Gaza-Jericho Declaration of Principles – and Cairo Declaration on the Implementation of the

Declaration of Principles are some attempts to resolve the conflict and hence reduce tension and conflict in the area.

It may also be interesting to note that the Iranian revolution of 1979 has diversified Middle Eastern conflicts into a variety of inter-state disputes and fights, and a series of wars, fights and battles which have threatened regional and international peace and security have taken place.

Since the change in the structure of the international system and its transformation into a new world order, there has been an increase in the volume and intensity of internal conflicts, thus raising questions about the causes and types of regional and intra-state conflicts.

A framework of analysis for the Middle Eastern conflicts may be determined as follows:

1. The shift in the international system from bilateral to a system which has not yet been determined raises many questions concerning the patterns of alliance, the volume of interactions and the weight of different forces in relation to each other. The frequency and the intensity of internal and regional conflicts will be determined, in this case, by the perception of the structure of the international order by the parties concerned. If, for example, the United States is perceived as the dominant actor, this leads to a different outcome than in the case of presence of other great powers, so the multipolar system in the making will to a great extent limit the policy of 'benevolent hegemony' initiated by the United States. In this case, types and levels of conflicts in the Middle East will be determined differently.

2. Related to this, the weight given to economic and technological interactions over strategic relations creates real challenges to the regional actors. The establishment of the European Union (EU), the European Economic Association (EEA), the North American Free Trade Association (NAFTA), and other regional economic coordination groupings represent a new challenge to the Middle East actors, who have not yet changed their emphasis from strategic to economic interactions. If they do, lower levels of conflicts and more possibilities for regional *rapprochement* can be expected.

3. The emergence of new values and new areas of emphasis in the new international order – such as human rights, environmental protection, liberalization, democratization and the respect of the rights of minorities – present additional challenges to the Middle East's state system. In most cases, the state apparatus is dominant and powerful and is the main source of any policy, so the new values and initiatives require substantial concessions on the part of the state. Being rigid, as they are, nation-states in the Middle East may risk their stability against any concession concerning their authority and apparatus, thus agitating, alienating and motivating certain sectors in the

society, especially minorities and marginalized groups, to challenge state authority and hence indulge in conflicts and violence.

4. This potential wave of conflicts and violence may expand to influence inter-Arab politics, presenting viable sources of deep inter-state conflicts, even between states that are members in the same sub-regional organization.

PRELIMINARY ANALYSIS OF REGIONAL CONFLICTS

The perceptions of concerned parties in the Arab-Israeli conflict led to the consolidation of Arab political positions against Israel; it also led the Israelis to adopt a unified position against the Arabs.

Between 1948, when Israel was established, and 1978, when the Camp David Accords were signed, the Arab-Israeli conflict played a major role in unifying Arab positions and stands against Israel. Central regional powers such as Egypt played a centripetal role in reaching Arab national consensus against the regional intruder, Israel (Chart 11.1).

CHART 11.1

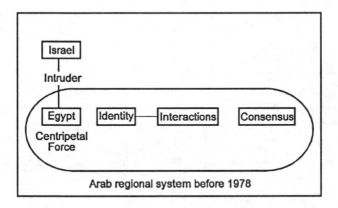

Arab regional system before 1978

Meanwhile, Chart 11.2 shows that between 1978 and 1990 things changed: *rapprochement* took place between Egypt and Israel. The Arab region became divided and consensus was lost. However, Egyptian-Israeli interactions were not developed into a real normalization process. All that happened was the creation of a state of no war, but no more; they were limited to what can be called strategic peace, that is, the state of absence of war. At the same time, Egypt was ousted from the Arab League which was transferred to

Tunisia, and most of the Arab States severed their diplomatic relations with Egypt. Iraq, and perhaps Saudi Arabia, tried to replace Egypt as leader of the Arab sub-system.

CHART 11.2

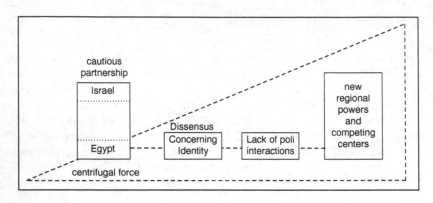

CHART 11.3

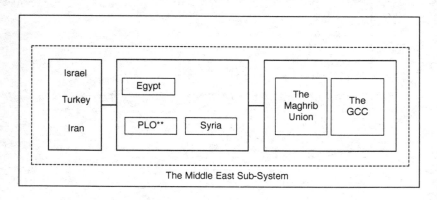

Note:
** *The PLO is not a state actor. Rather, it is a non-state actor. However, since June 1994, it represents the Palestinian National Authority in Gaza and Jericho. It also negotiates with Israel the arrangements for both the interim and final settlement for the peace process.*

After the Palestinian-Israeli Accord of September 1993, known as the Declaration of Principles (DOP), the Arab regional system has witnessed debates digging into its structure, membership and functions. Chart 11.3 discloses some of the changes which reflect rethinking of the identity: for example, a Middle Eastern instead of Arab identity; the inclusion of the three major former intruders, Israel, Iran and Turkey; and the shift from military and strategic interactions to economic, trade and cultural exchanges.

It may be useful, then, to visualize the patterns of interactions among these actors as in Chart 11.4, from which it may be concluded:

1. Cooperation in the region includes Iran and Turkey; Turkey and Israel; Turkey and Egypt; Egypt and the PLO; Maghreb Union, Syria and the Gulf Cooperation Council (GCC); the PLO and Maghreb Union; and Iran and Sudan.
2. Conflict interactions include Iraq and Turkey; Iran, the GCC, Syria and Israel; Israel and Syria; Iran, Sudan and the PLO; and Syria with Israel, Iraq and Turkey.
3. Tense interactions exist between Egypt, Sudan, the GCC, Iran, and Iraq.
4. Ambivalent interactions include those of Sudan, the Maghreb Union, the PLO, and Israel.

Regional conflicts have consequently been reduced, while cooperation is increasing to include former intruders into the Arab sub-system. After the Arab Summit Conference in Amman, Jordan, in 1987, diplomatic relations between the Arab states and Egypt were re-established and the Arab League was transferred back to Cairo. More political cooperative interaction has taken place between most regional actors, and this may legitimize the recent calls for the establishment of a Middle East Common Market which would include members from non-Arab countries such as Iran, Israel and Turkey. In this case, a shift from traditional stereotyped conflicts into new possibilities for regional cooperation is taking place. This was clear at the Casablanca Economic Summit Conference for the Middle East and North Africa held from 31 October to 1 November 1994, when, for the first time in half a century, Arabs, Israelis and others, officials and businessmen met in order to find out ways and means to conduct joint trade and business deals.

The idea of who is an adversary and who is a friend is exposed to thorough scrutiny. For example, Iraq has become the number one enemy to the GCC countries which in turn have disclosed their willingness to interact with the Israelis and support the Palestinian-Israeli Accord. Indeed, some of them have already established political contacts with Israel while they refuse to re-establish diplomatic relations with Iraq.

CHART 11.4

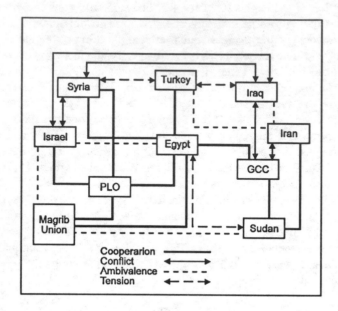

The Iraqi invasion of Kuwait on 2 August 1990, the subsequent Arab Summit in Cairo and the establishment of the international alliance created a new conflictual environment in the Arab region. Inter-Arab tension increased, animosity escalated, and inter-state conflicts were reinforced. A division was created along the lines of both wealth and poverty. Poor states such as Jordan, Yemen, Sudan and the PLO sided with Iraq, which advocated the redistribution of Arab wealth among Arab peoples. The rich states of the Gulf felt vulnerable to their Arab brothers and called for international, especially Western, protection, and Egypt, one of the poor Arab states, took a strong stand with the Gulf states in defence of the principle of non-intervention in others' affairs and non-use of force.

According to Article 5 of the Charter of the League of Arab States, 'any resort to force in order to resolve disputes arising between two or more member states of the League is prohibited'. Consequently, Egypt, as well as other Arab states which defended the liberation of Kuwait, were in favour of resolving the Iraqi-Kuwaiti dispute peacefully and within the Arab regional system.

The war against Iraq and the subsequent embargo against it created more cleavages among Arabs and expanded the level and dimension of inter-Arab conflicts. For example, the tension between Egypt and Sudan, Qatar and Saudi Arabia, Morocco and Algiers, etc., are manifestations of the second Gulf crisis. In addition, intra-state conflicts have also increased; one may mention the civil war in Somalia, as well the fatal conflict in Yemen.

TYPOLOGY OF THE MIDDLE EAST CONFLICTS

The Middle East is not exposed to or confronted with one type of conflict; there are many categories, types and forms of conflicts according to the perspective of each analyst. However, there is consensus that the Arab-Israeli conflict is a protracted social conflict over identity, territory, survival and even the existence of the concerned parties. It is a conflict which is not defined in terms of its parties, its core or the final goals of all parties concerned.

Table 11.1 discloses an attempt to classify the Middle Eastern conflicts in light of their causes:

TABLE 11.1

Type Cause	Domestic			International		
	Civil	Military	C/M	Legal	Military	Cultural
Borders						
Ethnic	**	**			**	**
Religion	**	**				**
Territory				**	**	
Resources			**	**	**	
Social & Political Inequality	**					
Arms Race		**			**	
Demographic Factor	**					**

What we witness is a mixture of causes and types of conflicts which may be labelled open or explicit conflicts. They are conflicts which can be observed, analysed and classified into domestic and/or international, though it is hard to have clear-cut demarcation lines between both. On the other hand, latent conflicts have not been mentioned, that is, conflicts resulting from structural victimization. They have been labelled structural violence, as this is violence resulting from deformed socio-economic structures, on both a domestic and region level (this would also include inadequate and deformed international structures).[2]

Any attempt to initiate a typology of conflicts in the Middle East is confronted by two major facts:

First, there is a strong belief in the Arab world that the Arab-Israeli conflict, and at its core the Palestinian-Israeli conflict, is the nucleus of all other conflicts in the Middle East. Hence, without it being resolved, even if partially settled, it will manifest itself somewhere, somehow, in some form of conflict. In other words, it perpetuates itself, and its devastating consequences will last as long as the unjust, unfair and uneven environment continues. The interruption of the hostile interactions between the Palestinians, and hence the Arabs, on one hand, and the Israelis on the other must become inevitable.

Second, legal and political mechanisms for conflict resolution and crisis management do not exist as binding means to achieve reconciliation, in spite of the fact that the Arab actors are members of the League of Arab States. The League does not have a legal institution such as a Court of Justice or other mechanisms for conflict resolution. Arab and Islamic countries, as well as members of the Organization of Islamic Conference (OIC), have passed a resolution calling for the establishment of an International Islamic Court of Justice, but this resolution, taken by the Islamic Summit in Kuwait in 1987, has not yet seen results. Sub-regional councils such as the Maghreb Union, the Arab Cooperation Council, and the GCC have proved totally ineffective in this regard. Negotiations, mediations, arbitrations, conciliations and the utilization of good officers are rare in the Middle East. Consequently, states resort to force, especially military force, as the first, not the last, resort in order to achieve incompatible national interests. The inability to settle peacefully border, ethnic, religious, territorial, and socio-political conflicts within the regional setting have both prolonged and intensified domestic and regional violence.

These two facts, which may not be unique to the conflicts in the Middle East, add to the complexity of conflict resolution in the area. They generate negative attitudes, as well as rigid stereotypes and false perceptions, among the competing parties in the Middle East.

As Table 11.1 shows, the following causes of conflicts in the Middle East can be distinguished:

Border conflicts

These are widespread among most of the states in the region, both on the Arab side and other Middle Eastern states. Border conflicts spoil the relationships between the Gulf states which are members of the same Council; for example, among GCC states, there has been border conflict between Egypt and Sudan for the Halayeb area, between Yemen and Saudi Arabia, between Iraq and Kuwait, Iraq and Iran, Turkey and Syria, and sometimes between Algiers and Morocco. Some of these disputes have already escalated into wars, really deadly wars such as the Iraq-Iran war from 1980-1988, and others may escalate, once the bilateral and regional balance of power changes or if a radical government comes to power in some states.

The Gulf states, not having the political or legal mechanisms to settle their border disputes, try to ignore the problem, utilize the good offices of elders, or offer some voluntary concessions without even negotiating the issue. This may, however, only work in the short term and will most probably be hard to work out permanently. States may opt for international arbitration, such as Qatar which asked for arbitration from the International Court of Justice. When Bahrain felt embarrassed, Qatar declared its willingness to accept mediation instead. Other Arab states, however, will resort to the use of force, or at least threaten to use it, in their interactions. No final solution to border conflicts can be envisaged for the Arab states, as long as there is no real joint mechanism for conflict resolution.

Ethnic and Religious Conflicts

The Middle East is characterized by a multiplicity of ethnic, religious and sectarian minorities as well as competing tribes. Competition over roles, resources, power and influence among these minorities has turned the Middle East into an intolerable hell. The conflict in Lebanon between 1975 and 1990, the civil war in South Yemen in 1986 and in Yemen in 1994, the internal conflicts in Iraq, the devastating conflict in Sudan and the domestic conflict in Somalia are examples of both explicit and latent conflicts which may escalate at any minute and erupt into open wars. Some of these conflicts have already escalated into wars, as in Sudan, where there is a disastrous war between the south and the north, the southerners fighting for their ethnic, religious and tribal identity. Conflict here is between the need for self-determination on the one hand and the central authority on the other.

The civil war in Yemen which has been taking place since May 1994 is an absurd war. It is a war of cession which is mainly linked to the tribal structure and feud between the two sections of Yemen. The President of

Yemen, a northern citizen, and the Vice-President, who is a southerner, have agitated their constituencies against each other. The factions have fought each other, not as people who belong to the same homeland, but as adversaries and foes who hate each other. In addition, the example of civil conflict in Somalia, which led to the destruction of the state itself, may be added. The Somali tribes, headed by their local leaders, preferred the collapse of their state more than any compromise or reconciliation of differences. Such irrational preferences victimize the masses in these societies.

One may argue that the concept of nation-state has been imposed on tribal, ethnic and religious formations, unlike in Europe where the nation-state is the natural evolution of the societal development and maturity. The imposition of the state on deformed and immature societal structures leads to dissatisfaction among alienated groups, which are always on the alert to challenge state authority in order to satisfy their tribal, religious and ethnic needs and requirements.

Territorial Conflicts and Competition over Resources

Borders disputes may be easy to resolve, as they are linked to the demarcation process implemented by colonial powers. Conflicts over territories, however, are different, since they deal not only with the technical and legal aspects of the problem but also with larger portions of land which may contain natural resources.

The Arab-Israeli conflict is such a case. It is a conflict over territories and resources. The territories allocated to the Jews by the UN General Assembly Resolution 181 of November 1947 were obviously insufficient for the Israelis. They started expanding beyond the UN partition plan for a variety of reasons, such as in 1948, 1967 and 1982 in order to acquire as much territory and water as possible. Their perception of security is based on the assumption that territorial compromises may represent a threat to the survival of the Jewish state.

There is also the territorial dispute between Iran and the United Arab Emirates over the three islands in the Gulf, which are strategically located close to oil resources and the Strait of Hormoz. This has not escalated because of the low-profile diplomacy of the Arab state, although little can guarantee the continuation of this *status quo*. There are other territorial conflicts, such as between Qatar and Bahrain, Iraq and Kuwait, and others.

Competition over resources has also led to wars in the Middle East, although it is sometimes difficult to distinguish between border and territorial conflicts on the one hand and conflicts over resources on the other. The Iraqi invasion of Kuwait and the subsequent Gulf war is an example of this complexity. In addition, there are some who deeply believe that, even if the Palestinian question is resolved, another wave of regional conflicts – especially conflicts over resources such as water or minerals – may erupt. Water has always been an important source of life in the Middle East, and its importance increased in Israel because of Israeli settlement policy in the West Bank and Gaza, when the Israelis diverted 80 per cent of West Bank water to the settlements, resulting in Israeli thinking and Israel's over-emphasis on the settlements being blamed for the shortage of water and potential conflict over it.[3]

Among Arabs, many conflicts and even interstates wars have taken place during the last four decades because of disagreements and disputes over territories, especially areas with potential resources. The conflict between Morocco and Algeria in the early 1960s, the conflict over Western Sahara, the conflict between Egypt and Sudan over Halayeb, the conflict between Iraq and Kuwait, and Saudi Arabia and Kuwait over the neutral zone, and conflicts between most of the Gulf states, are examples of inter-Arab conflicts over territories. In 1990, Iraq accused Kuwait of extracting oil from Iraqi oil fields which lie in Iraqi territory, and blamed both Kuwait and the United Arab Emirates for over-producing oil and hence lowering the price of oil. This, according to Iraq, was considered an act of war against the Iraqi people, who had lost oil revenue while they were at war with Iran. These accusations escalated into the invasion of Kuwait, its annexation and then to war, a war that created deadly consequences which still influence Arab inter-state politics.

Socio-Economic and Political Causes of Conflict

These causes may be the most serious igniters of latent conflicts. Here, we talk not only about substantial economic causes of conflicts, such as economic relative deprivation and lack of fair policies for income distribution, but we also talk about the inability of political systems to mobilize popular participation in politics, lack of institutionalization and the absence of rules for peaceful succession of power. Data about the percentages of income distribution are not available for most Arab and Middle Eastern countries. However, particularly in non-oil-producing countries, it seems that the gap between the rich and the poor is increasing, creating a serious problem of discontent, leading to dissatisfaction and strong tendencies towards violence. Many individuals, as well as groups, feel peripheral to the economic establishment and marginalized in the political process. They hence opt for antagonistic acts against the political system. Combined with the decline in political efficacy and growing social discontent, the economic gap creates dissatisfaction with the existing political systems. This, in the absence of secular ideological alternatives, leads to social frustration and subsequent internal violence. In addition, most of the governments in the Middle East are characterized by a high level of political corruption. There are certain biases built into the political system towards the inner circle of the ruling elite, in both the recruitment and distribution processes. All these factors lead to a polluted social and political environment that is more conducive to conflict than cooperation. Fundamentalists, fanatics and terrorists as well as highly organized and mobilized religious groups are becoming more visible and more active in the politics of the Middle East. The inability of most states to make rational and effective economic and political reform policies, the weak presence of the states in spite of the dominating state apparatus, and the weak civil non-governmental organizations create difficulties in building domestic social equilibrium. What remains are soft states, weak enough to inspire internal resistance.

What adds to this process is that the new trend towards privatization causes more inequalities and lack of government commitment to basic services, which may lead to more dissatisfaction and hence violence. Examples can easily be cited from Algeria, Egypt, Sudan, Yemen, Iraq and others.

In these cases, weak civil society organizations such as NGOs, trade unions, syndicates and professional associations, as well as the absence of national ideological commitments and the inability of governments to mobilize public support for their policies, has led to the emergence of extremists who are well organized and highly disciplined. They appeal to the public, using state inability and inefficiency for their counter attack. They also make use of the absence of democratic traditions in most of the states of the Middle East.

While people had not used to participate in government-sponsored elections, the fundamentalists were able to mobilize them to an alarming degree through their strong and efficient communication lines. They dominate most of the intermediary associations such as syndicates and bar associations. They have also deeply penetrated the psyche of the people through the basic services that they provide. The mosque, church and synagogue are no longer only places for praying. They have been developed as a centre for basic services, for which the government has become incapable of providing, such as education, medical care and financial support.

More important is that the fundamentalists were able to penetrate the education system through both the educators and the curriculum. Their teaching and values were transmitted to the students through these mechanisms and other means such as tape cassettes, and they started to wear a distinguishable uniform so that it was easier to know one another and communicate.

Young people, alienated by economic and political discrimination as well as unemployment, were easily coopted by these groups. Both cooptation as well as recruitment were possible in the Arab states because most suffer from a problem with minorities. It was easy for the fundamentalists to agitate their supporters and sympathizers against two major targets: the state and both religious and ethnic minorities.

This conflict between the state on the one hand and the fundamentalists on the other raises two basic questions:

First What are the major sources of financial and moral support for these fundamentalist groups?

Second How can a certain minority protect itself and maintain its identity?

For the first question, there is a flow of financial transactions from certain Islamic countries as well as Western states to the extremists. Many workers in the Gulf states pay annual alms, giving to the Islamic NGOs which provide basic services for the Muslims. In addition, Arab entrepreneurs contribute money to Islamic organizations all over the world. At the same time, the conflict in Afghanistan involving the former Soviet Union led some states in the West to host many Islamic organizations and provide them with generous banking accounts.

As for the protection of the rights of minorities and nations without states such as the Kurds, there are serious problems. On one hand, nation-states in the Middle East reject the concept of minority and oppose the idea that they suffer from any minority problem, claiming that they have achieved a high level of internal integration and domestic cohesion. Consequently, no calls for self-assertion of separate identities are allowed. On the other hand, some of these minorities, such as the Kurds and the Negroes of southern Sudan, insist on their inalienable right of self-determination. This contention leads to the escalation of violence.

This escalation of extremism as well as radical and/or religious discrimination leads to an endless process of conflict, violence and counter-violence.

It may be useful to indicate here different types of minorities in the Arab countries:

1. Linguistic minorities reach 29.7 million, that is, 12.7 per cent of the total population. These may be Arabs or non-Arabs who speak languages other than the official state language.
2. Religious minorities (non-Muslims) are about 15.7 million, 7.6 per cent of the total population.

3. Islamic sectarian minorities (non-Sunnis) reach 18.6 million, 8.8 per cent of the total population.
4. Islamic minorities (non-Arabs) reach about 5.5 million, that is, 3.7 per cent of the total population. They belong to states outside the realm of Arab states or the Arab world.

This means that minorities represent more than 32 per cent of the total population in the Arab world. This sizeable percentage requires real and fair treatment.

Demographic Causes of Conflicts

It is hard to separate the demographic factors from the socio-economic, ethnic, and religious dimensions in the Middle East. They are so interwoven that it may be difficult to distinguish which conflict relates to which cause. Take Lebanon for example: how can we classify the civil conflict that lasted from 1975-1990; was it religious, ethnic or was it demographic, based on the recent challenge to the distribution of political resources on the assumption that there was a certain demographic balance that characterizes Lebanese society? Between 1943 when the National Covenant was agreed upon, and 1975 when the civil war started, the Muslim population increased to such a degree that it fought for its fair share of power. Other privileged groups resorted to force in order either to defend the *status quo* or divide the state into mini-states on the basis of religious demarcation lines.[4]

In the Maghreb – Morocco and especially in Algeria – ethnic divisions among the population may create opportunities for civil conflicts. The Arabs are the dominant majority while the Berbers still try to preserve their distinct cultural identity. Meanwhile, Arabization has meant not only fighting against French cultural values but also ending any non-Arab cultural identities. This, in itself, represents a challenge to any distinct minority.

If demographic factors play a serious role in conflict escalation in Middle Eastern countries, they may also be a source for future conflict between the Palestinians and Israelis. Table 11.2 distinguishes between different Israeli groups and the Palestinians.

If we assume that the current negotiations between the Palestinians and Israelis will lead to peaceful settlement of their existing conflict over occupied Palestinian territories, one may expect another aspect and perhaps another stage of the Palestinian-Israeli conflict, as demography plays an extremely sensitive role in formulating the perceptions, attitudes and positions of both parties to the conflict.

TABLE 11.2 *Palestinian and Israeli Population**

The Palestinians			The Israelis		
	Total	4,688,000		Total	5,090,000
1	West Bank**	1,000,000	1	Jews	4,175,000
2	Gaza	750,000	2	Arabs	700,000
3	Jordan	1,530,000	3	Others	215,000
4	Syria	300,000			
5	Lebanon	300,000			
6	Saudi Arabia	200,000			
7	UAE	86,000			
8	Iraq	75,000			
9	Egypt	35,000			
10	Kuwait	35,000			
11	Libya	27,000			
12	Others	350,000			

*   *Source:* El milagro de la paz, Revista Espanola De Defensa, October 1993, pp. 60-67.

**   Including East Jerusalem

If the demographic dimension is extended to the Gulf states, we see that we may be faced with conflicts in the future. Nationals in most of the Gulf states do not exceed 20 per cent of the total population, and many of these are naturalized. Expatriates – whether Arabs, Asians or others – form the majority of the population and the main bulk of the labour force in these states. They may not represent a threat to the security and stability of these states now, but their presence puts limitations on the external behaviour of the Gulf states, particularly towards the labour-exporting countries.

These demographic dimensions proved relevant during the Kuwaiti crisis of 1990-1991 and its aftermath. After the liberation of Kuwait, achieved by the forces of international alliance not the Kuwaiti or Gulf forces, Kuwait started to organize the re-entry of expatriate Kuwaitis in order to ensure some domestic balance between the nationals and expatriates.

For the Gulf states, as well as Israel, demographic factors play an extremely important role in future stability and the containment or escalation of regional conflicts.

Arms Race

Arms' sales and arms' acquisitions represent a substantial source of conflict in the Middle East. As a result of the aforementioned causes and lack of confidence among the parties in the region, states compete in acquiring weapons of all kinds. Some states such as Israel, Iraq and Iran are competing in the area of weapons of mass destruction. The Israelis introduced nuclear weapons into a region of very traditional and primitive weapons, and in spite of the 'butter versus guns' dilemma, the Middle East spends huge sums of

TABLE 11.3   *Costs and Casualties Resulting from the Conflicts in the Middle East between 1948-1991*

Type of Conflict	Casualties	Cost in US$ millions	Number of Displaced
1. External			
Arab-Israeli	200,000	300	3,000,000
Iraq-Iran	600,000	300	1,000,000
2nd Gulf War	120,000	650	1,000,000
Others	20,000	50	1,000,000
Total	940,000	1,300	6,000,000
2. Internal			
Sudan	600,000	20	4,000,000
Iraq	300,000	20	1,000,000
Lebanon	180,000	20	1,000,000
N. Yemen	100,000	50	500,000
Syria	30,000	0.5	150,000
Morocco	20,000	3	100,000
W. Sahara	10,000	0.2	5,0000
Somalia	20,000	0.3	200,000
Others	30,000	1	300,000
Total	1,290,000	115	7,255,000
All Conflicts	2,230,000	1,415,000	13,255,000

Source: Saad El-Din Ibrahim, Sects, Ethnicity and Minority Groups in the Arab World. Cairo, Ibn Khaldon Center, 1994, p.16.

money and human resources on arms purchases. Annual arms sales to the Middle East reach US $85 billion, creating, on one hand, economic and social problems and reinforcing distrust among regional actors, and also opening avenues for external powers to intervene and in many cases agitate the regional parties.

I believe that the vicious circle of arms race and distrust leads to conflicts which accelerate arms race and so on ...

The most recent Yemeni internal conflict can be added to these casualties and costs. The economic loss exceeds US$ 10 billion, while the number of deaths is about 40,000, in addition to tens of thousands of wounded persons.

DEVELOPMENT AND REGIONAL COOPERATION: MECHANISMS FOR CONFLICT RESOLUTION

Political and economic development as well as regional cooperation are the counter-forces to conflict and animosity in the area. From the theoretical literature, as well as the European experience of development and regional cooperation after the Second World War, it is understood that animosity, conflict and hatred will be decreased and minimized through the process of joint cooperation and community building.

In the Middle East, the major actors shown in Table 11.4 may be candidates for regional cooperation. In addition, they are the ones in need of both economic and political internal development. It is known that development means the mobilization of national resources, including human resources, for national goals. It also means an equal opportunity for all domestic forces both in the economic sector and in political life. Economic and political development lead a society towards becoming a real community of people. Political development means the institutionalization of the system, the peaceful succession of power and public participation in the decision-making process. The cost of political development is internal: it is the establishment of a domestic consensus regarding the nature of the regime from a non-party or one-party system into a liberal, multi-party system. It also calls for the respect of the rights of minorities and the human rights of all citizens.

As for economic development, it means the reallocation of national resources towards building a modern, advanced and strong economy in order to respond to the expectations and needs of people, especially the young. This process requires the mobilization of national resources, as well as both regional and international aid. For example, the Palestinian-Israeli Declaration of Principles of 13 September 1993 contains appendices concerning mutual development as well as regional cooperation projects. It calls for re-

TABLE 11.4 *Basic Data of Key Players in the Middle East**

Data Actors	Population in millions	GNP per capita**	Economic growth in %	Military in 1000	Life expectancy	Gov. expend. on defence
A. Arab Actors						
Algiers	27,3	1980	3,5	121,7	65,1	n.a.
Egypt	57,9	610	2,8	430,0	60,3	12,7
Iraq	19,7	n.a.	-30,0	382,0	65,0	n.a.
PLO	3,8	1800	n.a.	n.a.	n.a.	n.a.
Saudi Arabia	16,4	7820	4,5	101,0	64,5	n.a.
Sudan	29,1	n.a.	-11,0	72,8	50,8	13,2
Syria	14,5	1160	6,5	408,0	66,1	31,8
B. Non Arab Actors						
Iran	56,0	2170	8,5	473,0	65,0	9,6
Israel***	5,0	11950	6,4	176,0	76,0	22,4
Turkey	56,0	1780	5,5	480,0	67,0	10,4

Sources: Arab Economic Report 1992
            The Military Balance 1992/1993
            World Development Report 1993

*
**   Upper middle income range between $ 2,500 and $ 6,340
*** Including 700,000 Palestinians with Israeli nationality

gional as well as international financial support for the reconstruction of Gaza and the West Bank. The success of this declaration and others depends not only on the good intentions of the signatories, but on the amount of financial aid and transfer of money. What Middle Eastern states need, and especially Arab states, is a well-defined development strategy capable of not only enhancing the standard of living but also improving the quality of life. In this regard, governments need to increase their expenditures on welfare and services rather than on military expenditures.

On the other hand, regional development and joint cooperation in the fields of economics and politics require confidence-building measures in order to bridge the gap between the Arab states and other regional powers.

Table 11.4 shows how Turkey, Iran and Israel are achieving better results in economic growth, life expectancy and other economic and social indicators, yet for the Arabs, regional cooperation means fear of domination and hegemony by neighbouring states, so instead of creating chances for cooperation, regionalism – especially outside the borders of the Arab sub-system – may represent a threat to the already shaky regional balances.

The goal of multilateral negotiations within the framework of the ongoing peace settlement is to build confidence among the actors involved. The negotiations deal with major regional issues such as refugees, regional economic development, arms of mass destruction, water and the environment. Regional cooperation in these five critical areas, all of which could be sources of future conflict, is aimed at creating an environment that is conducive to stable and secure life.

CONCLUSIONS

The shift from an environment of conflict and warrior mentality into peace-oriented attitudes, although important, is extremely difficult to achieve. Besides the requirement for the redistribution of both political and economic resources, there is a dire need for more cooperation and peaceful attitudes from the people in the area. Cooperation and peaceful attitudes can only be formed through the process of socialization of each state, requiring a change in the education curriculum, mass media and other cultural values. It also requires the initiation of exchange programmes and visits between the peoples of the area. Common and joint goals for the region may also help.

One lesson to be learned from the conflicts in the Middle East is that the burden and cost of animosity are hard to bear. They cause disintegration, affect loyalties and national consensus, waste scarce national resources, and lead to deadly wars. The opportunity costs of Middle Eastern conflicts are tremendous and countless.

In the Middle East, people have not yet experienced a life without tensions and conflicts, and they yearn for a better quality of life. This can be achieved through mutual understanding, joint goals and shared interests in the region.

The relationship between conflict and development is not linear. Development does not automatically lead to peace and intimacy. If the goal is to shift from interactions of conflict into cooperation and a peaceful environment, development – both economic and political – should bring with it mechanisms for equal distribution and fair participation. Equal opportunities in each Middle Eastern country, as well as among the states themselves, may represent a safety valve for permanent peace. In this case, development will lead to conflict resolution in the Middle East.

NOTES

1. Bernard Reich, *Israel: Land of Tradition and Conflict* (Boulder, CO: Westview, 1985), p. 53.
2. All literature concerning dependency can be cited here.
3. 'What to do about water', *Jerusalem Post*, 4 January 1991.
4. What added to the domestic sources of conflict are the positions taken by other regional powers, such as Syria, Iraq, Israel and Iran.

12

Conflict, Stability and Development in Central Asia

Shirin Akiner

INTRODUCTION

Three years have elapsed since the disintegration of the Soviet Union and consequent emergence of five independent states in Central Asia – Kazakhstan, Kyrgyzstan, Tadjikistan, Turkmenistan and Uzbekistan[1] – and it is too soon to predict how these new entities will develop. However, although the region has experienced real and fundamental change in the twentieth century, there has also been a significant degree of continuity. Thus, in order to understand the key factors in this period of transition it is necessary to look not only at the configurations that are presently taking shape, but also at the historical background. This paper therefore gives a brief account of the cultural and historical context before attempting to map potential areas of conflict.

HISTORICAL BACKGROUND

The majority of the indigenous peoples of Central Asia are of Turkic origin and almost all are Sunni Muslims. However, beneath this superficial homogeneity lie strong cultural and historical differences. Traditionally, the chief divide was between the predominantly Turkic nomads of the steppe (Kazakhs and Kyrgyz) and the desert (Turkmen), and the settled peoples of the fertile oasis belt, an amalgam of an older Iranian stratum (Tadjiks) and sedentarized nomads (primarily Uzbeks). Despite some economic interaction along the margins of 'the steppe and the sown' and occasional military alliances, the relationship was predominantly one of mutual hostility,[2] reinforced by different attitudes to Islam. The settled peoples, who accepted the new faith within a century or two of the Prophet's death, were orthodox in their beliefs and practices, while the nomads, who were converted over a much longer period (some as late as the nineteenth century), were far more lax. Today,

257

there are few outward differences between the traditionally sedentary peoples and the former nomads, all of whom are now sedentarized (mostly as a result of the collectivization campaign of the 1930s), but undercurrents of suspicion and distrust remain.

For most of its history Central Asia has been divided into a patchwork of independent and semi-independent principalities. Only twice has it been unified: under the Mongols in the thirteenth century (and then but loosely), and under the Russians in the nineteenth century. The main regional powers on the eve of the Russian conquest were the three Kazakh Hordes in the north (the Great, the Little and the Middle), the Khanates of Bukhara, Khiva and Kokand in the centre, and the Turkmen tribes in the south-west. The economic base and internal organization of these formations differed one from the other, but in essence, all were fluid confederations held together by force of arms and the personal authority of the Khan (leader). Among the nomads there was a highly developed system of tribes and sub-sets of tribes (clans, sub-clans, etc); the sedentary peoples had similar, though rather looser, territorially based groupings.

Russian rule was less onerous than that of most other colonial regimes.[3] There was little interference in native institutions; the main changes were in the economic sphere (the production of cotton, for example, was geared to the needs of the Russian textile industry), and the interface between the colonial administration and the local authorities. However, the ultimate source of power, and therefore of authority and patronage, was now no longer the Khan, but the Tsar. This, allied to the growing economic dependence on Russia, destroyed the foundation of the 'tribe states' more effectively and more thoroughly than military defeat.

Soviet power was established in Central Asia in 1918 and consolidated during the next five years. The new regime's policies towards the region were openly interventionist. The avowed aim was, through the Communist Party, 'to help the working masses of the non-Russian peoples to catch up with Russia, which is in the vanguard'.[4] The first, and symbolically most important, step towards the modernization and Sovietization of Central Asia was the National Delimitation of 1924-25, whereby the five republics were created.[5] The borders of these new units were drawn as far as possible along linguistic lines, thereby consolidating within clearly defined territorial limits the speakers of the main indigenous language groups. The philosophical justification for this division was the thesis that language defined the nation,[6] and since the evolution of tribes into nations was, according to Marxist-Leninist-Stalinist theory, part of the historical process of development,[7] the creation of nation-states was a prerequisite for modernization.

Within its own terms of reference the Delimitation was successful, since without any movement of populations some 85 to 95 per cent of the largest Turkic groups (Uzbeks, Kazakhs, Kyrgyz and Turkmen) were encompassed within their respective titular administrative units. The Tadjiks, the only large Persian-speaking group, fared less well. For centuries they had shared a common space and a common bilingual culture with the Uzbeks. There could be no simple territorial division between the two groups and it was the Tadjiks, numerically smaller and less powerful than their Turkic neighbours, who were the losers. Much of the land that they considered to be historically theirs, including the cities of Bukhara and Samarkand, was allocated to Uzbekistan, and only 63 per cent of the Tadjik population was domiciled in Tadjikistan at the time of the first Soviet census in 1926.[8]

The drawing of the new borders provided the physical framework within which traditional societies could be deconstructed and selectively remoulded into Soviet 'nations' or 'nationalities', and the new identities were consolidated in a number of ways. National languages, based on selected regional dialects, were codified and elaborated.[9] Their implementation was facilitated by the rapid development of national literatures, initially consisting of translations of Russian/Soviet works, later extended to include original compositions (which, however, remained faithful to Russian/Soviet models). National histories fashioned the 'creation myths' that gave legitimacy both to the regime and to the new identities. The political socialization of the population was supported by a programme of mass education, aimed at both children and adults.[10] In the early Soviet period literacy rates ranged from some 3 per cent in the south to 7 per cent in the north; by the 1950s, virtually 100 per cent literacy had been achieved throughout the region.[11] Free and compulsory primary and secondary schooling was provided for boys and girls alike. Tertiary education, for which the great majority of students received stipends, was encouraged; within each republic higher educational facilities included at least one university and numerous polytechnics and vocational colleges; each republic also had its national Academy of Sciences, with numerous advanced research institutes, some of which, in the fields of pure and applied science, were of international standing.

Islam, which had governed the social, cultural and intellectual outlook of the region for centuries, was tolerated for the first few years. From the late 1920s, however, it became the focus of a fierce anti-religious campaign. Muslim beliefs and practices were attacked, and the social infrastructure destroyed: Islamic schools, colleges and law courts were closed, the payment of religious taxes prohibited and charitable endowments (*waqf*) confiscated. Almost all mosques were closed. The abolition of the Arabic script, replaced first by the Latin script and then by the Cyrillic, was also, indirectly, an attempt to eliminate the influence of Islam. Soviet institutions and Soviet legal codes, superficially adapted to take account of local conditions, were introduced in place of those of Islam. The manipulation of gender politics was also used as a means of undermining the old order. Women, the 'surrogate proletariat',[12] were given equal rights with men and urged to take up independent careers outside the home. The built environment was likewise Sovietized, with broad streets and multi-storey apartment blocks visually proclaiming the advent of the new era. Western-style ballets, operas and plays, reflecting Soviet taste and ideology, supplanted the traditional performing arts, and together with the socialist realist idiom in paintings and sculpture in the round (prohibited by Islamic law), nurtured a new aesthetic, as well as a new political and social outlook. Collectivization, introduced from 1930 onwards, brought fundamental change both to the organization of labour and to work skills. Traditional forms of farming and animal husbandry, manufacture and trade, were stamped out in order to make way for 'modern' methods. Large-scale communal projects, decreed and organized by the state, robbed the individual of a sense of control and personal responsibility. This facilitated the social transformation of the region, as well as fundamentally altering the economic structure. The 'purges' of the 1930s, which destroyed the intellectual elite of the new republics (including the first wave of communists), completed the moral and spiritual evisceration of Central Asia.

The result of these and other changes was a rapid transformation of the public face of society, although in the private domain there was a high degree of conservatism. Central Asian domestic architecture provides an illuminating metaphor for this process: the furnishings of the outer courtyard (where visitors are received) were modernized, while in the inner courtyard (which is reserved for the family) tradition prevailed. In this private domain, the nature of personal relationships, including those between the generations, between men and women, parents and children, remained almost unchanged. The 'clan culture', an extension of the clan/tribal/regional networks of the past, also retained its vitality. The clans of the Soviet period were more loosely constituted than in traditional society: they were generally based on genealogical ties, but new bonds could be formed through a shared experience or a common professional interest, and these could become almost as powerful as the old tribal connections. The new 'clan leaders' were those who could function most successfully in the Soviet environment; descendants of the old aristocracy had no special privileges, although, on an individual level, within their own circle, they might be held in some esteem. These new networks, despite their somewhat different composition, functioned in a very similar manner to the traditional structures.[13] Central Asians themselves commonly refer to them as 'clans', thus making an explicit link with the previous system. As in the past, client-patron chains of allegiance promoted group solidarity, and this in turn provided a power base from which to carve out covert fiefdoms within the Soviet system. Clan rivalry was intense and generally outweighed loyalty to the national ethnic group. The Soviet regime was not the enemy, but rather provided a new battleground on which, to paraphrase Clausewitz, old hostilities were continued by other means.[14]

Since modernization in Central Asia was imposed from without, not generated from within, some Western observers believed that it would be resented, and would eventually provoke a Muslim backlash, and various 'conflict models' of development were propounded.[15] However, contrary to these expectations, the Central Asians proved to be the most loyal supporters of the Union.[16] There were no secessionist movements in the region and scarcely any opposition to Soviet rule. Several factors contributed to this quiescence. First, Central Asian society – or more accurately – societies, have, throughout history, been exposed to external influences and have developed a high capacity to absorb and adapt to new cultures. Second, the Soviet regime succeeded in coopting the intellectual and leadership elites, who in turn played a crucial role in indigenizing the system. Third, the state created vested interests, not only at the highest level of the bureaucracy, but throughout society, thus providing ordinary individuals with incentives to maintain the system. Fourth, the totalitarian nature of the regime made possible the use of mass terror as well as mass persuasion to coerce the population into compliance; and fifth, there was a genuine perception that life was generally better than it had been under the Khans or the Tsarist administration.

SOVIET INFRASTRUCTURAL LEGACY

Soviet social engineering in Central Asia may not have achieved its original goal, in that the level of development continued to lag behind that of the European republics of the Union, but when viewed in the context of the developing world, it was far from a 'failed transformation'.[17] Today's Central Asian republics have a standard of education that is comparable to that of the developed world. There is a serviceable network of social care, and of cultural facilities. Medical services are well organized, although in some areas chronically under-resourced. Infant mortality is higher than in most European countries, but considerably lower than in countries such as Egypt, Turkey and Iran[18]; life expectancy levels are on a par with those of Latin American countries such as Mexico, Venezuela and Argentina.[19]

Absolute, life-threatening poverty, as exists in many 'Third World' countries, has been eradicated. Society is secular; men and women have equal access to education and employment. Modern (Soviet) state institutions have long been in place and there is a competent body of civil servants. Communication and transport networks span the entire region. There is also some industrialization, mostly, though by no means exclusively, connected with the extraction and primary processing of hydrocarbons and minerals.

On the negative side, Central Asia suffers in full measure from the common shortcomings of the Soviet system: uneven development, inefficiency, inadequate technical maintenance, environmentally harmful technologies, irrational and unsustainable use of resources, lack of familiarity with international institutions, no background in Western-style financial management, and few of the constituent elements of a market economy. Moreover, despite the advances in health care, outside the main cities the provision of sewerage and clean piped water is extremely poor. Most seriously of all, having suffered an even greater degree of rupture with traditional culture than was the case elsewhere in the Soviet Union, the Central Asians are today more disoriented and unsure of their future goals than are their former fellow citizens.

INDEPENDENCE: READJUSTMENT AND LOSS OF SECURITY

The security of Central Asia has, for over a century, been guaranteed by Russia, first through the agency of the Tsarist empire, subsequently the former Soviet Union. The geostrategic importance of the region, traditionally an area of superpower confrontation, ensured that Russia would take whatever measures were needed to secure the external borders against threat and to preserve internal stability. Concomitantly, it was Russia that set the agenda for the region's development. The onus for creating a secure environment has now been shifted to the newly emergent states; likewise, the responsibility for planning and implementing developmental policies. This task has been greatly complicated by the fact that the sudden and unexpected transition from what was, in effect, colonial status to that of *de jure* independence has created an intense sense of exposure, and consequently of insecurity, at every level, from that of the individual to that of the state, in intra-regional relations as in international relations. Each of these levels impacts on one or more of the others, amplifying the general instability and potential for disorder.

Level of the Individual

For the individual, the loss of all the old certainties has brought economic, moral and physical insecurity. Chronic inflation, shortages of basic household commodities, frequent delays in payment of wages and growing unemployment have made daily life a fight for survival. The old Soviet morality – and whether people abided by it or not, the ground rules were at least familiar to all – has been set at naught, while everything that was recently condemned as evil has suddenly become acceptable. The loss of moral direction has created a situation in which the constraints which formerly existed have ceased to operate. On the one hand, this engenders feelings of helplessness and frustration, on the other, it leads to rampant exploitation. The change in society's mores is dramatically underlined by the rise in violent crimes. Five years ago, cases of grievous bodily harm were rare; now they are so common as to cause not only the frail and elderly, but even the young and robust to fear for their personal safety and to circumscribe their activities accordingly.

State Level

Under Soviet rule, the republics were administrative units within a larger state structure. Major policy decisions, in internal and external affairs, were taken by the central authorities, who alone had access to the relevant data. The role of the republican governments was to ensure that directives from the 'centre' were fulfilled as speedily and faithfully as possible. Independence confronted the new states, almost literally overnight, with direct responsibility for a formidable range of problems. This has inevitably created huge stresses and uncertainties, particularly in the vital areas of administration, economy, defence and ideology.

Administration

From a practical point of view, the most urgent need was for the restructuring of the institutions of state management. This entailed such measures as the drafting of new constitutions; the upgrading and expansion of ministries, state committees and other government agencies; the establishment of national banks and other financial institutions; the reorganization of local government, to redefine the relationship between the districts (*rayon*), the provinces (*oblast'*) and the new state capitals. The speed with which these reforms have been initiated is impressive. However, it is inevitable that the process should be disjointed and chaotic. Existing boundaries of competence and responsibility have been blurred, opening the way for power struggles both within the central administrative structures and between the provinces and the central government. There is a high turnover of senior personnel, also frequent changes of the titles and functions of administrative organs. The ceaseless torrent of new edicts, decrees and laws exacerbates the sense of bewilderment.

Economy

The Soviet economy was a highly integrated system, based on specialization, division of labour and extensive inter-republican trade. The aim was not to produce balanced national (that is, republican) economies, but to maximize the economic growth of the Soviet Union as a whole. The Central Asian republics, with their high level of specialization in the production of primary commodities and comparatively low level of industrialization, were more dependent on inter-republican exchanges than were other regions;[20] also on budgetary transfers from the central government (which helped to support the welfare services). Consequently, they have been more severely affected by the economic dislocation that has followed the collapse of the Soviet Union, and are now in the midst of a painful process of restructuring. All the Central Asian governments have expressed commitment to the principles of a free-market economy, but since few of the basic elements are in place there has been little real progress. Indeed, the chief results have been a sharp rise in economic and social tensions. The weakness of the administrative infrastructure, which itself is in a transitional phase, makes it difficult to implement policy decisions. Attempts at privatization have been marred by inadequate preparation and insufficient legal safeguards; this has opened the way to widespread fraud, embezzlement, speculation and other malpractices.[21] Punitive tax reforms have laid a huge burden on private enterprises, forcing even the most honest entrepreneurs to cheat in order to survive.[22] The introduction of national currencies has aggravated inflationary pressures.[23] These and a multitude of other problems create a climate that is hardly conducive to successful domestic economic reform.

Trading relationships between the CIS members are also fraught with difficulties. World prices have been introduced for a number of commodities; problems with transportation, disagreements over terms of trade, frequent delays or defaulting on the payment of debts, as well as political considerations, have made the Central Asians eager to develop non-CIS trade.[24] They are also seeking to attract foreign investment to develop their industrial capacity, particularly for the processing and refining of their natural resources. There were initially high hopes that this would provide a simple solution to the region's economic problems. The reality, however, is proving to be far more complicated. It is unlikely that the Central Asian republics will be able to diversify structures of production in the near future. Consequently, they will be unable to change the commodity composition of their exports and will continue to rely on the production and export of raw materials, and the chronic instability of world prices for these commodities will put them at a grave disadvantage, making it difficult to achieve economic growth. The likelihood is that they will face a period of severe economic decline, during which living standards will fall and it will no longer be possible to maintain the public services that have come to be accepted as a natural entitlement. 'Luxuries' such as advanced research institutes and cultural facilities will inevitably suffer severe cutbacks. This conspicuous regression is already causing deep unease and in the future will undoubtedly have serious political repercussions as people compare current pauperization with former affluence.

Defence

The Central Asian states have no defence concept. Previously, they were protected by, and formed part of, the security arrangements of the Soviet Union. The disintegration of the centralized command structures has left them in a seriously exposed position. They perceive themselves, with considerable justification, to be in a highly volatile environment, ringed as they are by nuclear or threshold nuclear states; with civil wars in progress in Tadjikistan, Transcaucasia and Afghanistan; unstable conditions in Russia; and with the fear of ideological infiltration from Iran and economic infiltration from China. However, they do not as yet have the institutional capability to analyse and assess the nature of these and other threats (including non-military) to their national security. They have inherited contingents of border troops, military bases and training schools, armaments factories, mining and processing plants for strategic materials, and a variety of other installations. In Kazakhstan, these include a sizeable nuclear arsenal,[25] the Semipalatinsk nuclear testing site, and the Baikonur space and missile centre;[26] in Kyrgyzstan, the submarine test range at Lake Issyk-Kul; in Uzbekistan, test centres for biological and chemical weapons; in Tadjikistan, uranium enrichment plants and sophisticated radar stations. Yet although these formidable resources are now under national jurisdiction, they are still almost entirely manned by Slav (mostly Russian) personnel. The Central Asian states are signatories to the CIS collective security agreement of 22 December 1991, which, by ensuring the defence of their external (non-CIS) borders, provides some measure of reassurance. However, given the perception that the chief threat to their territorial integrity is likely to come from Russia, this is an ambiguous solution at best. All the republics have expressed their intention to create national armies, but the cost of such an undertaking is prohibitive.

They have begun to acquire arms,[27] but in the near future are unlikely to be able to support more than symbolic national guard-type formations. Thus it is the CIS, dominated by Russia, that will continue to set the security agenda, thereby prolonging anxieties about the limits of national independence.

Ideology

The collapse of the Soviet system has created a spiritual vacuum: the entire framework within which contemporary Central Asian society functioned has suddenly been discredited, yet it has been internalized to such a degree that it is impossible to ignore it or abandon it. Moreover, there are no ready alternatives: the socio-economic bases of the 'tribe states' of the pre-Tsarist era have been so thoroughly destroyed that there can be no return to that world; supra-national bonds, whether pan-Turkic, pan-Iranian or pan-Islamic, also have little emotional significance for the great majority of the population. Thus, for better or worse, the Soviet national constructs, including languages, histories, territorial boundaries and administrative identities, remain part of the psychological impedimenta of the newly independent states. However, they must be refashioned if they are to answer to the changed circumstances.

As in the Soviet era, it is the state that is brokering the new ideological framework and with it the new national identity. The cultural input differs from one republic to another, but there are three common elements: first, a revision of history, retaining the anachronistic ethno-nationalist interpretations of Soviet historiography, but delineating a new continuity between the pre-Tsarist past and the present, thus providing a relegitimization of the 'nation';[28] second, a limited revival of Islam, to establish a 'national' moral and cultural basis for society in place of that of the Marxist-Leninist ethic; third, the creation of a personality cult around the respective republican leaders, to serve as a focus for personal loyalty and a symbolic guarantee of national integrity.[29]

This current phase of nation-building, which is being undertaken with the same energy and propagated using many of the same tools as in the Soviet period, has already generated a notable degree of national pride and self-confidence. However, there are two problems. First, it addresses only the 'official' level of identity: the underlying, parallel clan/regional identities are as strong and potentially divisive as ever. Second, by elevating the culture of the titular people to the status of official state culture, it has had the effect of marginalizing the non-titular minorities. All these republics are in varying degrees multi-ethnic: in Turkmenistan and Uzbekistan the titular groups account for some 70 per cent of the total population; Kazakhstan is dominated by two large, almost evenly balanced minorities (according to recent reports, Kazakhs 44 per cent, Russians 36 per cent)[30], while in Kyrgyzstan and Tadjikistan the titular groups are in the majority by only a small margin. During the Soviet period there was a tacit acceptance of the privileged position of the titular group. Now there is overt 'ethnocracy'. Non-discriminatory citizenship laws have been enacted in all the republics, but the concept of the state is essentially that of a mono-ethnic nation. Fears that they will, in practice, be treated as second-class citizens have prompted Russians to seek the protection of dual citizenship (this has been granted in Turkmenistan, but is still under discussion in the other republics). Some have already elected to emigrate, either within the CIS or, where the possibility exists, abroad. The non-Russian nationalities (Germans, Greeks, Jews, Tatars, etc.) are also leaving. This is a severe blow to the economies of the new states, since many of those who are leaving are highly skilled technicians. More insidiously, their exodus belies the bright future proclaimed by the new street posters, casting a shadow over those that remain.[31]

Intra-Regional Level

There are two, interlocking, regional contexts: that of Central Asia and that of the CIS. There has never been a strong sense of regional unity in the former. During the Soviet period, links with the European republics were strengthened, but those within Central Asia remained weak. The newly independent states are now attempting to create institutions for regional cooperation and harmonization of policies concerning the economy, defence and internal security, environment, and maintenance of transnational communications and transport networks. Some progress has been made towards the establishment of an economic and defence union between Kazakhstan, Uzbekistan and Kyrgyzstan, but several points of friction remain unresolved. To the latent (and not so latent) rivalries of the past, there have been added new causes for regional competition: there is little complementarity in the economies of these republics and today they are in competition for the same markets; also for the same flows of foreign aid and investment. The two largest republics, Kazakhstan and Uzbekistan, are contenders for political supremacy.

The most immediate threat to regional stability in Central Asia is the civil war in Tadjikistan, which erupted in mid-1992. It has so far shown no signs of spilling over into the neighbouring states, but nevertheless, even if the military threat is not great, there is the risk of on-going influxes of refugees, and of a general increase in smuggling, looting and gang warfare. There is also a very real (although probably groundless) fear that the conflict in

Tadjikistan will open the way to a flood of Islamic fundamentalist insurgency throughout the region. Uzbekistan, Kazakhstan and Kyrgyzstan have joined with Russia to provide a peace-keeping force for the republic. However, their contribution is largely symbolic, since they have extremely limited resources of manpower and equipment.[32] This underscores their impotence in the face of a threat to regional security and is in itself as much a cause for anxiety as is the war.

The Central Asian republics were founder members of the enlarged Commonwealth of Independent States (CIS), formed in Almaty on 22 December 1991. Since then, they have entered into a number of bilateral treaties on trade and economic cooperation with fellow member states, formalizing new, post-Soviet relations. The dominant relationship, however, is with Russia, and is likely to remain so for many years. The Central Asian republics are still intimately bound to the former 'centre' by economic, security and defence ties; by transport and communications networks; by cultural and educational ties; by the large number of expatriate Russian settlers (some 10 million in Central Asia as a whole). These bonds give Russia inordinate influence in the region, yet it is clear, however, that Russia has not yet defined its strategy towards the region. There is a school of thought that holds Central Asia as vital to Russian national interests, both as a buffer against incursions from the south and as a source of strategic raw materials. Yet these arguments are rooted in perceptions shaped by the past: since the days of British India there has been no serious threat from the south; as for strategic materials, Russia has its own supplies of most commodities and could buy what it does not produce, such as cotton, at favourable prices from several other sources. There are also no indications that ethnic Russians in Central Asia are likely to be at risk. Thus it is largely a psychological attachment to the idea of empire that persuades some Russians that control (direct or indirect) of Central Asia is of continuing importance. Meanwhile, others have long considered the region to be an unnecessary encumbrance and an intolerable drain on resources. Russian policy oscillates between these two extremes: the decision to oust the Central Asian republics from the rouble zone, for example, was clearly designed to distance the 'centre' from the periphery, while actions in Tadjikistan indicate a commitment to remain.[33]

There is also an ambivalence in Central Asian attitudes towards Russia. As in most former colonial relationships, admiration and affection for the imperial power is tempered by anger and a desire for retribution. Here, however, there was no liberation struggle, no emotional preparation for independence. The over-riding feeling today is one of inchoate anxiety: there is fear that the Russians will stay, and that this new-found independence will prove to be an illusion, and fear, too, that the Russians will leave, and abandon Central Asia to whatever chaos lies ahead. This dilemma will undoubtedly resolve itself as the newly emerged states redefine their identities and establish links with countries outside the CIS. Russia will certainly continue to be an extremely important trading partner and will retain significant political weight, but as the cultural links are weakened, and the knowledge of Russian language and history becomes less a shared bond, the present instinctive reliance on 'the mother country' will also be reduced. This realignment is only just beginning, but it must inevitably proceed further, since the economic and political foundation of the old relationship no longer exists.

International Level

In January 1992, following the formal dissolution of the Union, the Central Asian republics were pitched headlong into the international arena. A handful of former Soviet diplomats and technical advisers apart, few Central Asians had first-hand knowledge of foreign countries. Moreover, there were almost no direct channels of communication with the outside world. The very first task, therefore, was the creation of a basic technical infrastructure for engagement with the international community. Extraordinarily, within some eighteen months much of this was in place. Tashkent and Almaty are now linked by direct international flights to European and Asian capitals; modern telecommunications systems have been installed; fully functional Ministries of Foreign Affairs and Foreign Trade have been established. The newly independent states were accepted as full members of the UN in March 1992, and have since joined a number of other international organizations (including the WHO, CSCE, NACC, IMF, the World Bank and EBRD). Each republic has established formal relations with a hundred or more foreign countries.

In their incarnation as modern nation-states, the Central Asians have no traditional foreign policy strategies to fall back upon. This gives them a certain intellectual freedom in their approach to international relations, but it also creates a sense of insecurity, as they lack experience in assessing the international environment. Two priority goals have emerged. One is to secure capital investment and technical assistance from abroad. Some progress has been made in this direction, particularly with regard to the development of the oil, gas and gold sectors, although the lack of a modern, Western-style business culture is proving to be a serious hindrance. The other is the need to diversify access routes. At present, the main road, rail and pipeline links lie through Russia, thereby enabling the former 'centre' to retain a stranglehold on foreign trade. The widespread enthusiasm for a modern re-creation of the ancient 'Silk Roads' is not mere nostalgia for past glories, but reflects an urgent concern to secure additional transport outlets. In the east, road, rail and air links between Kazakhstan and China are already in place; in the south-west, a road link exists between Turkmenistan and Iran and a railroad is nearing completion; sea links across the Caspian between Kazakhstan, Turkmenistan and Iran are also operational. The main components of a trans-Asian link, stretching from the Yellow Sea to the Gulf, are thus already in place and could become functional within the next five years.[34] This will bring considerable economic benefits, but equally, by making the region more accessible to external influences, is likely to increase the incidence of political risk.

In the immediate aftermath of independence there was much speculation as to whether the Central Asian states would follow the 'Iranian model' of Islamic fundamentalism, thus moving into the anti-Western camp, or the 'Turkish model' of secular, Western-style democracy. This bipolar method of analysis, a product of the Cold War era, was based on a number of misapprehensions. First, there was an assumption that there was a genuine desire for socio-political reform in Central Asia: in fact, stability, not change, was the chief priority. Second, it was assumed that the help of a 'big brother' to act as protector and guide in the global jungle would be welcome: however, the Central Asians, having finally acquired independence, were determined to establish direct relationships, on terms of mutual equality, with the international community. Third, it was believed that the common linguistic bond between Turkish and the main Central Asian languages would be sufficient motivation to overcome centuries of cultural divergence: in fact, language has not served as a unifying force even within the Central Asian region.

Initially, nevertheless, the Central Asian states did appear to favour a *rapprochement* with Turkey. There was an assumption, at official as well as popular level, that Turkey, as a member of the Western alliance, would be able to provide unlimited aid. It did indeed provide aid (mostly in the form of credits), but far less than had been anticipated. Meanwhile, as more Central Asians began to travel abroad, on fact-finding missions as well as for periods of training, they rapidly modified their original estimates of Turkey's economic potential. Relations have remained cordial and Turkish business interests are well represented in the Central Asian states, but no pan-Turkic 'special relationship' has emerged.

Iran has also not assumed a dominant position, although closer acquaintance has certainly helped to allay some of the anti-Iranian fears and prejudices that the Central Asians inherited from the Soviet period. In the religious sphere, Iran (which is Shiah, unlike Central Asia, which is almost entirely Sunni) has pursued a policy of non-interference, emphasizing instead the need for regional cooperation in trade, exploitation of natural resources, environmental protection, and the development of the Caspian Sea zone.[35] However, like Turkey, Iran does not have the economic resources to provide the hard currency investment required by the Central Asian states. This automatically sets a limit to the extent of its active influence in the region. A number of bilateral agreements have been concluded, particularly with Turkmenistan and Kazakhstan, but for the most part Iran has concentrated on developing a multilateral approach within the framework of the Economic Cooperation Organization (ECO)[36].

The rivalry between Iran and Turkey (denied by official representatives of both countries, but inferred by most observers) is not the only struggle for influence in the region. Other rivalries are also being projected on to all or part of Central Asia. Several Muslim countries are competing for influence, the most active being Saudi Arabia. However, the Middle Eastern country that has had the greatest economic and diplomatic success in the region is arguably Israel.[37] Nevertheless, the Central Asians, especially Kazakhstan, are careful to preserve diplomatic balance by maintaining good relations with the Palestinians.[38] India and Pakistan are also contenders for economic, as well as for political and strategic influence.

The Far Eastern and South-East Asian countries, especially Japan, South Korea and China, represent another block of rival interests, which offset, but also impinge on, the regional ambitions of others. In particular, the growing influence of China, facilitated by better transport links and more relaxed border controls, is a potential security threat to both Russia and India.

The Central Asian leaders have repeatedly stressed their intention to avoid being drawn into any ideological or ethnically based political alliance. Inevitably, however, external leverage over domestic affairs will grow as the Central Asian states are integrated into new trade networks. International aid will also impose its own constraints in internal and external affairs. The various rivalries that are being projected on to the region are already providing Central Asians with the opportunity to play one power off against another, but given their economic weakness and the variety of political pressures to which they are subjected, it will be extremely difficult to maintain the non-aligned stance that they currently espouse. Moreover, it is quite probable that the republics will be drawn in different directions, depending very largely on geographic accessibility and a convergence of economic interests, heightening intra-regional tensions.[39]

POTENTIAL CONFLICT-CAUSING ISSUES

Within the general context of readjustment and loss of security there are a number of specific issues which are potential sources of serious conflict. Whether or not they are activated will depend on variables both within and without the region. These issues are not mutually exclusive and indeed may well interact with one another. Collectively or individually, they are capable of transforming what is currently a reasonably stable environment into one of high risk.

Clan Rivalry

Now that the mediating patronage of the 'centre' has been removed, clan conflicts are resurfacing as different groupings seek to challenge the existing balance of power. The struggle is for wealth and influence, mainly through control of the administrative apparatus, but increasingly, through extended business interests (legitimate and illegitimate). In most cases, the struggle is non-physical, but the case of Tadjikistan, however, clearly illustrates how rapidly clan rivalries can escalate into civil war when ambitions are raised and weapons are freely available.

The most artificial of the Soviet state creations, Tadjikistan was always highly susceptible to factional in-fighting. Nevertheless, in the immediate aftermath of the disintegration of the Soviet Union, Rahmon Nabiyev, the first freely elected President of the republic, appeared to be firmly in control. Precipitate moves against his opponents, however, soon destroyed the delicate coalition of regional interests that had previously existed, and triggered a bitter power struggle. The political labels that the various factions have acquired (neo-communist, Islamic fundamentalist, democratic) have little more than superficial significance. The real contestants are the Khodzhent (Leninabad) clan of the north, the Kulyab clan of the south, and the Badakhshanis of the east; the smaller clans of the central corridor and the Kurgan-Tyube clan of the south-west constantly switch their allegiance from one to the other of the main players, depending on the fortunes of war.[40] No one grouping is strong enough to win control of the entire republic. They therefore need, and are receiving, support from external sponsors, who seek to manipulate the situation to their own advantage.

Although the Tadjik experience will probably not be repeated on the same scale elsewhere, no republic is free of the potential for such conflicts. In Kyrgyzstan, the tension between the northern clans and those of the poorer south are so strong that many Kyrgyz fear they will render the republic ungovernable, possibly leading to partition.[41] There is a revival of Horde rivalry in Kazakhstan, but currently no serious threat to the ascendancy of the Great Horde (who came to prominence under the Bolsheviks and have retained their pre-eminence); however, regional sub-factions are manoeuvring to secure greater autonomy and the outcome may well be that individual local leaders will come to exercise virtual subsidiarity. In Uzbekistan there has always been a rotation of power between the traditional bases of Ferghana, Samarkand and Tashkent; today, there are fierce clan rivalries within the administration, and some regional disaffection, but the incumbent President, Islam Karimov, has secured the support of all the main factions and appears to be in control for the present. Much of the territory of Turkmenistan is the traditional domain of the Ahal-Tekke tribe, who remain the dominant group; however, there are many sub-divisions and friction is rife between these smaller units. There are also rumours that since travel restrictions with Iran have been eased, Turkmen from both sides of the border have been in closer contact, thus increasing tribal tensions as the majority of the Turkmen in Iran are from the Goklen and Yomut tribes, ancient rivals of the Ahal-Tekke.[42]

Political Succession

The four current Central Asian presidents (there is no President in Tadjikistan at the time of writing) all came to power during the Soviet period, having worked their way up through the system. Given that they have only recently acquired independence, it is not surprising that they are more concerned with maintaining social and economic stability than with establishing procedures for handing over power to their successors. Moreover, they are relatively young (the oldest is President Karimov of Uzbekistan, born in 1938; the youngest, President Akayev of Kyrgyzstan, born in 1944) and in passable good health. However, the question of the transfer of power is one that must inevitably be faced.

Throughout the Soviet period it was Moscow that controlled political succession in the Central Asian republics. This was rarely performed through direct intervention, but rather through a long and complex process of sifting, grooming and manipulating choices. Youth organizations (the Young Pioneers, the Communist Youth League) provided the first opportunity for identifying promising individuals; vetting was intensified as their careers progressed, especially once they had joined the ranks of the Communist Party. In the higher echelons, there were always several representatives of the titular nationality of the republic to be found, who had followed parallel career paths, were of similar ability, and had sound political credentials. They were the 'stable' from which senior officials were selected.

Having several potential candidates for such posts provided Moscow with three important advantages: it was an insurance policy against unexpected crises; it strengthened individual bonds with Moscow, since the candidates vied with each other to win the approval of the 'centre'; and it fostered fierce rivalries among the candidates and their supporters, thereby hindering the development of local coalitions.

Nevertheless, the process of selection was by no means wholly governed by Moscow. The clans in each republic played a vital, if, to an outsider, almost invisible role. No individual could attain high office solely on his own merit; he required the support of a powerful network that would, on the one hand, neutralize regional opposition (especially that provided by the clan base of a rival candidate) and, on the other, facilitate his work in such a way as to make his administration a conspicuous success. Thus, the stronger the clan support a candidate was able to attract, the more efficiently he was able to function, and hence the greater his value to Moscow.

There was a further check on the balance of power in the republics: the ethnic segmentation of functions. The post of greatest symbolic significance, that of the First Secretary of the Communist Party of the republic, was generally held by a member of the titular nationality. Functionaries of the second level of seniority, as well as heads of the security services, were Russian, or other 'trusted' nationalities such as Ukrainians or Armenians. This disposition adroitly channelled clan rivalries into particular high-profile areas, while excluding them from other, more sensitive, areas of state control; it also provided Moscow with what was in effect a shadow government.

In recent years, the only significant deviation from this nationalities policy occurred in Kazakhstan with the 'election' in December 1986 of Gennadij Kolbin, a Russian from outside the republic, to the post of First Party Secretary. The move, part of a Moscow-led campaign to root out corruption, provoked an unprecedented public protest from young Kazakhs. The protracted manoeuvrings that followed, which culminated in Kolbin's removal from the Kazakh scene, gave a rare opportunity to trace the power struggles between his prospective successors. Initially, there were three Kazakh candidates for his office: Kamaleddinov, Mendybaev and Nazarbaev. The first of these was soon eliminated, but the other two remained locked in an intricate duel. Mendybaev, who for a while appeared to enjoy Moscow's favour, was, exceptionally, elevated to Second Party Secretary in November 1988; a few months later, however, possibly as a reward for his efficient (according to some Kazakhs, unnecessarily ruthless) suppression of the 1986 demonstration, Nazarbaev secured the premier post, which in late 1990 was converted from that of First Party Secretary to that of President. The two other contenders were demoted and subsequently became political non-entities, leaving Nazarbaev as undisputed leader.

With the collapse of the Soviet Union, the entire context within which this system of political succession in Central Asia had taken place disintegrated. The focus of allegiance has now shifted to the newly independent states. Even though Moscow may continue to exercise covert influence in Central Asia, the mechanisms for ensuring the smooth transfer of political power must be rooted in local institutions. In theory, such mechanisms already exist: all five republics have adopted a presidential system of government and their constitutions stipulate that presidential and parliamentary elections must be held at stated, regular intervals. However, it has become clear from the elections and referendums that have already been held in these republics that the great mass of the population still regards the ballot box in much the same way as it did during the Soviet period, namely, as a device for rubber-stamping the decisions that have been taken, or are going to be taken, by those in power. There are virtually no independent opposition parties in Central Asia (those in Kazakhstan and Kyrgyzstan that might appear to fulfil such a function are, for the most part, concerned with specific ethnic issues). The concept of a 'loyal opposition' does not exist in popular consciousness, and since all channels of mass communication are firmly under government control (and in many cases, censorship) there is little likelihood that an informed public debate on this question will emerge in the near future.

The authoritarian nature of the current regimes, as well as the traditional cultural predilections of the region, favour the re-emergence of dynastic succession. However, during the Soviet period family ties were often a serious liability, and consequently, such relationships were given as little publicity as possible. The biographies of the current presidential incumbents give brief references to the number of their offspring, but little else. None of them appear to have sons waiting in the wings to enter the political arena in the guise of heirs apparent.

The path that this generation of leaders will, in all likelihood, eventually follow is that of adopting a protégé (probably from their own clan, possibly a distant kinsman), who will first serve as a trusted lieutenant, and later will assume the mantle of successor. There is, however, an inherent risk in such a strategy, since it is always possible that the protégé might succeed in building up an independent power base, thus becoming a rival rather than an ally. The Central Asian leaders have had long experience of the dangers of competition from within their own ranks and are therefore highly sensitive to this threat. The desire to pre-empt any attempt to establish a rival camp is no doubt one of the reasons for the very high turnover of senior officials in all these republics. However, this is not a policy that can be maintained indefinitely. As the situation stabilizes, a certain degree of continuity will be introduced and this will permit the rival factions within the ruling circles to regroup. They may well not be able to mount a successful challenge to the current presidents, but when the time comes for a transfer of power, whether for voluntary or involuntary reasons, it is likely that this will trigger internecine struggles within the government itself. The armed forces in these republics are at a very early stage of development and could not represent a significant factor in any such power struggle in the near future.[43] However, the security services (successors to the KGB) might well play a role, giving their loyalty to the candidate most likely to further their own interests. Thus, the process of transition will be prone to dangerous internal stresses until such time as the necessary institutions have been created to ensure an orderly devolution of power.

Inter-Ethnic Conflicts

There is no tradition of inter-ethnic intolerance in Central Asia. However, since the mid-1980s ethnic tensions have been increasing. To date, ethnic physical clashes have been almost wholly restricted to economic rivals, people of very similar ethnic and cultural backgrounds who, aided by their respective clan networks, are competing for the same resources. The most serious incidents have been amongst the middle- to low-income sectors in the densely populated Ferghana Valley. The first major disturbance was between Meskhetian Turks and Uzbeks in June 1989, during which an estimated 300 people were killed, and the second major outbreak of violence, between Uzbeks and Kyrgyz in 1990, was partly triggered by the traditional competition between mountain dwellers and plains people for possession of marginal lands.[44] It is likely that sporadic bouts of low-intensity conflict such as these will continue, but will not get worse unless orchestrated from outside.

There has been no violence or systematic oppression towards those, such as Russians, Germans, Greeks and Koreans, who are perceived to belong to a different cultural and economic sphere, but there has been increasing petty harassment of 'outsiders' in everyday life. It is unlikely, however, that there will be formalized discrimination towards these groups in the foreseeable future. However, in the republics in which the titular people are in the majority, the non-titular groups, if they wish to remain, will have to conform to the cultural and linguistic norms of the titular people, and to accept a certain loss of social status.

In Kazakhstan, the situation is different: the titular people are a minority in their own state; if they are too vociferous in their demands for

'Kazakhification', they will antagonize both the Russian and the smaller ethnic groups (who constitute some 20 per cent of the population). This might lead to bloodshed, and would probably result in the dismemberment of the republic, with the Russians either seeking reunification with Russia, or establishing another independent state. The Kazakh President is attempting to maintain the equilibrium between the different groups, but pressure from Kazakh nationalists (whose position he may well tacitly condone) is forcing him to make ever greater concessions in their favour;[45] at the same time, the Russians, who include within their number armed and highly militant Cossack units, are also adopting a more aggressive stance. They are supported in this by nationalistic Russians in Russia, whose ranks have now been strengthened by the return of Alexander Solzhenitsyn, long a supporter of a partition of Kazakhstan, and the ultra-nationalist Vladimir Zhirinovsky, who spent his youth in Kazakhstan and who is also a firm advocate of Russian rights in the northern tier.

The prospects for ethnic concord in Kazakhstan are thus not encouraging.[46] However, strife is still by no means inevitable. Despite (and perhaps because of) the sabre-rattling of nationalists, there have been no fatal clashes. The example of Tadjikistan has provided a graphic lesson in the horrors of civil war and even those who are convinced that there will be an armed struggle envisage it in the indefinite future rather than the present. In the meantime, there is a growing realization among Kazakh policy-makers that if they were to enter into a conflict with the Russians they would be unlikely to receive any significant assistance from the other Central Asian states. Given that they have no functional armed forces of their own, they would have no option but to seek support from China, Russia's traditional enemy. Military alliance with their eastern neighbour is, however, a strategy that also carries inherent risks, since China still has territorial claims (dating from the nineteenth century) on Kazakhstan. The most likely outcome is that, at state level, the Kazakhs will seek an accommodation with Russia; at grass-roots level, it is probable that there will be intermittent outbreaks of low-intensity conflict, but there will be no escalation into civil war unless there is exogenous pressure on the Kazakh Russian community.

Cross-Border Irredentism

There are two categories of potential cross-border irredentism in Central Asia: that involving CIS members, and that involving 'foreign' states. In both cases there are divided ethnic groups and divided lands. Within the CIS, there are over half a million Uzbeks in Kyrgyzstan (mostly in the Osh region), and over a million in Tadjikistan (in Khodzhent and other border regions); in Uzbekistan there are approximately one million Tadjiks (mostly in the Bukhara and Samarkand regions) and just under a million Kazakhs. All the republican leaders have agreed to honour the existing borders, but the Uzbek populations in Osh (Kyrgyzstan) and Khodzhent (Tadjikistan) are already raising the question of reunification with Uzbekistan. Since this is numerically the largest, and strategically the best situated, republic, it is highly probable that sooner or later these territories, peacefully or not, will be absorbed into Uzbekistan. Tadjikistan's claims on Uzbekistan (Bukhara and Samarkand), however, although they will remain a grievance as long as Tadjikistan survives, are never likely to be realized, since Tadjikistan does not have the human or material resources with which to mount a successful challenge to its larger neighbour (although, as suggested below, the possibility of a Pyrrhic victory, using water as the ultimate weapon, is not entirely to be excluded). Other irredentist claims (for example, that of the Kazakhs on northern parts of Uzbekistan) are also unlikely to be pursued for the same reason.

Outside the CIS, there are over one million Uzbeks in Afghanistan, about one million Kazakhs in China, and some half a million Turkmen each in Afghanistan, Iran, Iraq and Turkey; also two million Tadjiks in Afghanistan (although the term 'Tadjik' used in Afghanistan is much looser in definition than in Tadjikistan). In most cases the historical and cultural links between these groups are too weak to constitute any strong attraction, for example, the Afghan Uzbeks speak different dialects and have a different social structure to the Uzbeks of Uzbekistan. Soviet modernization has further widened the gulf between them. The same is true of the Tadjiks of Tadjikistan compared with those of Afghanistan. The Turkmen outside Turkmenistan mostly belong to different tribes and there is little evidence of a desire to unite (except, possibly, but not very probably, to challenge Ahal-Tekke hegemony). The one group that does espouse strong irredentist sentiments is that of the Uighurs. They number some 250,000 in the CIS (divided between Kazakhstan and Uzbekistan), but over seven million in the Chinese province of Xinjiang. There has long been a movement among Chinese Uighurs to create an independent 'Eastern Turkestan' and there is now open support for this from the Uighurs of Kazakhstan. However, such a state would constitute as great a threat to the integrity of Kazakhstan as to China. Whether or not they laid claim to Kazakh territory, the Uighur secessionists would set a precedent not only for the Russians, but for the Germans (who numbered just under one million in Kazakhstan in 1989) and possibly other ethnic groups who seek autonomy. Rather than encouraging Uighur aspirations in this direction, it is far more likely that the Kazakh government will act in concert with the Chinese to quash them.[47]

Water

Northern Central Asia is relatively well endowed with rivers and lakes, but in the arid south there is a severe water deficit. The main sources of water here are the Amu Darya and the Syr Darya, rivers which rise in the mountains of the south-east and flow diagonally across a number of republics to empty into the Aral Sea. During the Soviet period they were heavily over-exploited in order to support grandiose irrigation schemes for agriculture. Increasing quantities of water were also required for industrial projects and, as the population expanded, so too did the demands for water for domestic use. The cumulative result was that by the 1980s the flow of both rivers had been seriously reduced. This in turn caused a shrinking of the Aral Sea, which has now lost over one-third of its area (currently less than 44,000 square km). The environmental damage is literally incalculable, particularly in the once-fertile delta regions, now reduced to saline deserts and swamps.[48]

The Aral Sea has become a symbol for the Soviet Union's mismanagement of natural resources. International aid is currently being mobilized to help stabilize the level of the water, to prevent further deterioration of the situation. However, the condition of the Sea is part of a much larger problem. Any long-term solution must address the question of water management in the Aral Sea basin as a whole. This will require the active cooperation of all the Central Asian states. Efforts are being made to formulate joint policies, but it is already clear that it will be difficult to translate formal expressions of commitment to the common good into positive action. Upstream, states believe that they have a natural entitlement to the waters that flow across their territories; they are strongly opposed to any limitation of the amount they draw off, for fear of jeopardizing future plans for development. Moreover, they are reluctant to accept curbs on the amount of toxic waste that they discharge into the rivers, since they see this as an infringement of their economic liberty. Unless rational solutions are set in place, there will be a rapid decline in the quantity and quality of water available to the region. The situation is already acute and could eventually become a *casus belli*.

Paradoxically, international aid for the Aral Sea has aggravated the situation: the poorer mountain republics (Kyrgyzstan and Tadjikistan) resent the fact that their richer downstream neighbours are to receive such assistance; there have already been semi-official hints (expressed by senior officials at public meetings) that the mountain dwellers will use the water supply as a bargaining counter to force the people of the plains to agree to share these funds (which have not, in fact, amounted to very much as yet). Tadjiks also speak of using water as an offensive weapon in any territorial dispute with Uzbekistan, and have suggested three ways: poisoning the rivers; restricting the flow; and opening the sluices (or bursting the dams) to flood the plains. It is unlikely that these threats will be realized in the fore-seeable future, not least because they would cause almost as much damage upstream as downstream. However, it is a sobering thought that, with minimal technology, water could be used to inflict almost as much devasta-tion as a nuclear bomb.

At the domestic level water is also likely to become an explosive issue, especially in the desert regions of Uzbekistan and Turkmenistan, as the privatization of land proceeds. At present, the irrigation systems are cen-trally controlled by the regional authorities, and it will be extremely difficult to reorganize these systems so as to cater for individual needs. The situation is complicated by the fact that innumerable illegal private pumps have been set up on the banks of irrigation canals; there is no cost-effective way of monitoring the amount of water that is thus drawn off. When the system is privatized, feuds between neighbours will inevitably arise and not improba-bly lead to violent assaults and attacks on property[49].

Demographic Trends

The Central Asian republics have very high demographic growth rates. They are still in the 'expanding stage' of demographic transition, with high birth rates and low death rates. The rate of natural increase is higher among the main indigenous groups than among the immigrant population, and highest of all in the rural areas, where the majority (and poorest sector) of the indigenous population lives. The lowest rate of increase is in Kazakhstan (which has the largest non-indigenous population), where it is under 20 per 1,000 per annum; the highest is in Tadjikistan, where the average rate is 35 per 1,000, but in rural areas is 39.5 per 1,000. The age structure in these five republics is similar to that in many developing countries; in Uzbekistan, Turkmenistan and Tadjikistan, some 40 per cent of the population are aged under 15 years, in Kazakhstan and Kyrgyzstan, some 35 per cent. The large numbers of people in the fertile age range, and the fact that contraceptive devices are not readily available (and in any case viewed with distaste) mean that it will be difficult to bring about a significant reduction in these growth rates.[50] It is estimated that if present trends continue, the populations of Uzbekistan and Turkmenistan will double in 25 years, Kyrgyzstan in 30 years, Kazakhstan in 45 years; were it not for the ravages of civil war, Tadjikistan's population would probably double in 22 years.

The natural resources of the region are already under severe strain, especially water and productive land. Unless radical improvements are made in the exploitation and conservation of these commodities the environment will be irretrievably damaged. The carrying capacity of the agricultural land has already been stretched almost to the limit. If there is no alleviation of this relentless demographic pressure, the quality of life will eventually diminish to the point where large-scale movements of population, accompanied by social unrest, become inevitable. As yet there has been very little urban migration in Central Asia, but this is beginning to change as young people move to cities in search of work. However, conditions here too are deteriorating. There is rising urban unemployment, an acute shortage of accommodation (the construction industry has been severely affected by the recession), and increasing malfunction of essential social and municipal services, leading to health hazards. The rate of demographic growth was becoming a major burden towards the end of the Soviet period, requiring ever greater investments in education, medical facilities and other basic infrastructural needs. If the economies of these republics can be revitalized, their manpower surplus might yet be turned to advantage. If, however, the decline continues, it will soon become a dangerous liability.[51]

Criminalization of Society

Economic pressures, coupled with the general loss of ethical orientation, have led to a marked rise in personal corruption. The practice of giving and accepting 'presents' is an integral part of Central Asian culture; so, too, is the responsibility to further the interests of friends and relations. However, under normal conditions such obligations are fulfilled within an intuitively perceived and generally accepted scale. Today, that consensus no longer exists: what was previously a stable and 'moral' system has now become a panic-driven free-for-all. This is having a profoundly demoralizing effect on society, sapping people's dignity and self-respect, but at the same time tempting them to indulge in ever greater excesses.

Organized crime has long been entrenched in Central Asia. The anti-corruption campaigns of the 1980s were, from a practical point of view, almost wholly ineffective, but they did reveal the existence, in each of the republics, of vast criminal networks. Based on the clan system, these networks, which came to be known as 'mafias', encompassed the whole of society, from the highest echelons of administration to the lowliest shop-floor workers and collective farmers, not excepting the law enforcement agencies. In some ways they represented the most efficient form of 'international' (in the Soviet sense) cooperation, since despite their strong regional bases they worked closely with similar groups in other parts of the Union, especially in Moscow, the ultimate seat of power. The opportunities for organized crime have rapidly proliferated since independence. The lack of a proper regulatory framework, underpinned by legal safeguards, has opened the way to fraud on a massive scale, particularly in the grey area between state control and the free market. The not infrequent involvement of senior officials in such transactions means that little is being done to remedy the situation. The new private wealth has led to a mushrooming of protection rackets and a consequent rise in physical violence.

The breakdown in law and order is reflected in an explosion of drug-related crimes. Mild narcotics have traditionally been manufactured and ingested in Central Asia. Over the last few years, however, there has been a sudden expansion of the cultivation of opium poppies and cannabis.[52] There has been a sharp rise in drug abuse, especially among the young, yet the most serious aspect of the problem is the ever-increasing volume of drug smuggling. Some opium is produced locally and there are rumours that facilities to manufacture heroin also exist. The main source of narcotics, however, is Afghanistan. It is impossible to seal this long, porous border, especially the remoter sections of the Tadjik stretch. The economy of Badakhshan, the poorest and most isolated region of Tadjikistan, is now wholly dependent on the opium trade. Consignments of drugs are despatched to the neighbouring Central Asian republics and from there to the Middle East, via Iran and Turkey, or to Europe via the Baltic ports.[53] The mafia barons have strengthened their transnational links and are coordinating their activities with partners abroad, including, it is suspected, with cartels in Latin America.

The smuggling of arms is also on the increase. The main destination is Tadjikistan, where a variety of weapons of Israeli, Chinese, US and Soviet manufacture are in circulation.[54] However, there is as yet little outflow of military hardware from the Central Asian republics. The strategic weapons are guarded by highly professional soldiers and it is unlikely that in the near future local mafia groups could have access to these bases, let alone gain operational control of the nuclear warheads. However, if conditions of service continue to deteriorate and morale is weakened, it is not impossible that lapses of security may eventually occur. It would be virtually impossible to acquire the command codes, but even if the warheads were non-operational, they could be dismantled and cannibalized for the construction of simpler (although nevertheless highly destructive) weapons, or used as models for future production. To date there have been no proven cases of the smuggling of strategic materials from military-industrial plants, but this, too, is something that could occur in the future if present security safeguards are relaxed.

The law enforcement agencies in the newly independent republics are chronically under-manned and under-resourced, thus ill-prepared to cope with these problems. All the Central Asian governments have appealed for international help to combat the narcotics-related crimes and, more broadly, all forms of smuggling. However, the power of the mafia networks is so great, and the rewards they are able to offer so tempting, especially in these times of acute economic weakness, that there is a real possibility that in some areas at least, if not in the region as a whole, far from being vanquished, the mafia barons will become the king-makers.

Economic Inequality

During the Soviet period there was marked income inequality between the 'white-collar' elites (political, cultural and professional) and the 'blue-collar' workers. These differences were accepted by society at large; first, because although the system proclaimed equality for all, it was in fact a meritocracy in which high achievers (so long as they abided by the ideological rules of the game) were rewarded with impressive benefits in kind and money; in theory, and to quite a large extent in practice, anyone, whatever their background, could join the ranks of the elite and there was thus hope, as well as belief, that one's children, even if not one's self, could share in this affluence. Second, the most privileged members of society led segregated lives, their wealth hidden from the public gaze; consequently, there was little conscious awareness of the differentials in living standards. Today, the poverty gap is steadily widening as the rich grow richer and the poor poorer. However, whereas before there was a perception that the disparity was justified because it was 'the great and the good' who were being rewarded, now, in popular estimation, wealth is associated with crime and moral degradation. More conspicuous than their Soviet predecessors, the ostentatious lifestyles of the new super-rich present a jarring contrast with the falling standards of living of the majority of the population. There is an increasing sense of alienation as more and more people feel marginalized, unable to share in, or even to comprehend, the economic transformation of society.

The situation is exacerbated by the fact that there is little public debate of such issues. This is partly a legacy of the Soviet period, but it is also a feature of traditional Central Asian culture. In the past, people gave their unquestioning loyalty to the Khan and in return, he ensured their well-being. Today, that habit of communal obedience is still strong, but if the 'new khans', the incumbent regimes, are unable to provide the socio-economic stability that the population has come to expect, they will inevitably lose popular support, leading to social unrest and the possibility of organized insurrection.

Islamic Fundamentalism

There is a schizophrenic attitude towards Islam in post-Soviet Central Asia. On the one hand, there is general agreement among the indigenous population that Islam is an integral part of the national culture; on the other, there is widespread fear of the rise of Islamic fundamentalism. This dichotomy is born from a lack of genuine familiarity with the religion. Since the late 1980s there has been increasing interest in Islamic culture and belief, but for the great majority of the adult population it remains something external to their existence, almost an exotic affectation. This will certainly change: thousands of mosques and hundreds of part-time and full-time Muslim schools and colleges have been opened since 1989, and religious literature is now widely available. Many of the younger generation receive Muslim instruction and attend the mosque regularly. Some girls have voluntarily taken to wearing the *hejab* (headscarf), and a few the entire *paranja* (head-to-toe veil).

However, there are great regional variations. Pockets of devout believers are to be found in the Ferghana Valley, particularly in the vicinity of Namangan, a bastion of Islamic asceticism. This region is the heartland of the Islamic Revival Party and smaller fundamentalist groups such as *Adolat* ('Justice'). The total membership of such movements, all of which are officially proscribed, is probably in the region of 50,000.[55] Elsewhere in Central Asia, active adherence to Islam is much less in evidence. Mosque attendance rose sharply in the immediate aftermath of independence, but has now decreased markedly.

It is not inconceivable that Islam might in time become politicized, a vehicle for expressing the anguish and frustration of those who have lost faith in the ability of the system to provide social justice. Yet it is unlikely that it would affect all the republics and all sectors of the population with equal force. It is highly improbable that, in the foreseeable future, Islamic regimes on the Iranian model would be acceptable to the broad mass of Central Asians. What is more likely is that a series of ongoing confrontations will eventually develop, of greater or lesser intensity depending on the region, analogous to the current situations in Egypt and Algeria. There will be a similar polarization in society, a widening of the gulf between those who advocate secular, Western-style (not excluding neo-Brezhnevian) views, and those who believe in strict adherence to Islamic values. Even with external support, however, neither side is likely to succeed in wholly crushing the other: the clash between two different ethical systems may be contained, but not resolved, by force of arms.

WESTERN AID: A STABILIZING FACTOR?

Most of the aid received by Central Asian states comes from Western governments on a bilateral or multilateral basis, from Western-backed international economic organizations, and from some non-governmental organizations. It takes the form of credits and loans, technical assistance, training and some humanitarian aid. The aim is to help these new states carry through the political and economic restructuring necessary to integrate them into the global community, and to generate prosperity, stability and a friendly (pro-Western) environment. Most programmes have only been operating for two years or less. However, some general characteristics are beginning to emerge which indicate that there are issues that need to be addressed.

First, there is frequently a lack of meaningful dialogue between donors and recipients. Western donors rarely have any knowledge of the region's historical and cultural background, or the current social climate. The aid they offer is thus conceived in a theoretical vacuum. Equally, the potential recipients know almost nothing of the terms of reference within which their interlocutors are operating. The conceptual terminology, even when translated (and it is by no means always easy to ensure competent translation), is opaque for the Central Asians, who until recently had almost no exposure to other systems. The result of this lack of mutual understanding is that the two sides frequently talk past each other, unable (and, more seriously, unaware that they are failing) to engage in constructive communication.

A second obstacle is over-hastiness on the part of both donors and recipients. The former are generally working within the time constraints of their financial year. Often, little action is taken until the very last month; by then, the pressure to disburse the budgetary allocation within the specified period is such that decisions to spend relatively large sums of money are taken on the advice of in-house officials who may assess project proposals from a technical point of view, but have little idea as to whether they are likely to be effective in the target country. The potential recipients, fearful of losing the proffered aid, too often accept such proposals before they have had time to assess relevance to their needs. The result is mutual frustration and disappointment. On the side of the recipients, this is aggravated by astonishment and anger at the vast fees paid to foreign consultants, who proceed to present recommendations that are ill-suited to local conditions, and often impossible to implement.

A third problem is the lack of coordination between donor agencies, leading to an inefficient use of resources, with efforts in some sectors being reduplicated several times over, while other, equally important, areas are neglected. Also, there is a tendency to indulge in 'profligate and irresponsible lending'.[56] The republic that has suffered most in this respect is Kyrgyzstan. Identified by a succession of Western countries as the most deserving Central Asian state because of its apparent devotion to democratic ideas, Kyrgyzstan has been offered, and accepted, so many foreign loans and credits that, after only two years of independence, its external debt is already equivalent to 100 per cent of its GNP.[57] The country is having to borrow yet more this year in order to service interest payments. Kazakhstan, another country favoured by the West, is also deeply mired in debt.[58] Even those Central Asian economists who were originally in favour of market-oriented reforms and integration into the international economy are now beginning to look on the process as a new and more tyrannical form of neo-colonial subjugation.

A fourth area in which there are frequent misunderstandings is that relating to human rights. The Central Asian republics view the conditionality that is attached to many aid programmes as an unwarranted intrusion into their domestic affairs. They feel, and are beginning to insist with increasing vehemence, that they have a different, but equally valid perspective on the relationship between the individual and society. The West's advocacy of political pluralism and freedom of speech appears to many – and by no means only government officials – to be tantamount to a campaign to destabilize the region at a time when it is already precariously balanced on the edge of anarchy.

The eagerness of foreign agencies to work with non-governmental organizations seems similarly subversive in intent. There is no tradition of NGOs in this region. Under Soviet rule only the most innocuous 'informal' non-official associations were permitted. The great majority of those who now put themselves forward as representatives of local NGOs have highly dubious credentials. The gullibility of foreign agencies in their dealings with such individuals is often assumed to be a cover for criminal collusion. The very few who seek to establish genuinely independent organizations are frequently harassed by the authorities, since they are seen as a challenge to the government. In such cases, links with Western organizations, no matter how innocent, immediately become a cause for suspicion.

The image of Western aid agencies has been further compromised by some unfortunate linkages between aid and trade. Again, the country that has been most exposed to such dealings is Kyrgyzstan. The most notorious incident was the murky affair of Canadian involvement in a deal to develop one of the major Kyrgyz gold deposits which, it is alleged, was juxtaposed, if not linked, to a training programme;[59] the revelation that US aid had apparently coincided with the Kyrgyz government's secret agreement to allow the establishment of a US/NATO base in the republic was even more disturbing.[60] To a population that still has many of the prejudices and precon-ceptions of the Soviet era, such revelations have caused a deep sense of anxiety: there is a feeling that 'the enemy' is taking them over by stealth. Against this background it is hardly surprising that the communists have made a stronger come-back in Kyrgyzstan than anywhere else in Central Asia.

There is undoubtedly a real need for Western aid in Central Asia. How-ever, if it is to be used effectively, and to contribute to long-term stabiliza-tion and adjustment, then far greater cultural sensitivity is required and far greater effort must be devoted to the design and implementation of aid programmes. If this is not done, there is a danger that such assistance will come to be seen, as it has in some other parts of the developing world, as a means of furthering Western interests; resentment at being enmeshed in a new, deeper trap of debt and dependence will lead to the rise of anti-Western xenophobia and the very destabilization that donor countries hope to prevent.

OUTLOOK

Despite the social, political and economic upheavals that have followed in the wake of the collapse of the Soviet Union, Central Asia, with the excep-tion of Tadjikistan, has remained relatively stable. The chief reason for this is the highly conservative nature of the social fabric which, especially in the face of external threats, favours consolidation rather than fragmentation. It is underpinned by absolute respect for seniority: each individual is acutely sensitive to, and bound by, the overlapping hierarchies of age, social stand-ing and administrative power. The system is based on allegiance, which in turn stems from confidence in the wisdom of the *aq saqaly* ('whitebeards'). There are two other factors that have helped to preserve stability. One is the low level of political participation: open political debate, based on the concept of loyal opposition, is alien to the indigenous culture. On the surface at least, therefore, there is a high level of consensus. Second, the low inci-dence of urban migration has ensured that the village, and village concerns, remain the primary focus of attention.[61] For the majority of indigenous populations, the state capitals are almost as remote as Moscow, or even as Washington.

Yet the situation is beginning to change. The economic crisis has begun to provoke doubts about the competence of the leadership. Moreover, there has been something of an age revolution as increasing numbers of young people (35 years and younger) assume senior positions owing to their more 'modern' skills. The experience of older age groups is being devalued. The defining role of respect within the societal framework is also beginning to be eroded. Traditionally it encompassed everybody, strangers and members of the community alike. Now, the new 'ethnocracy' is, tacitly, sanctioning the exclusion of 'outsiders' from the hierarchy of esteem. Adolescents no longer feel obliged to behave towards these 'others' with the courtesy that they still reserve for their own. This trend may well spread further, excluding more and more sectors of the population and thus destroying the most stable feature of society. The erosion of traditional norms is also being triggered by the introduction of the 'Coca-Cola culture' (or, as it is called locally, the 'Snickerization of society'). Newly available Western consumer products, films and advertisements are changing the aspirations of the young, especially in urban areas. The increased presence of non-CIS foreigners confronts them daily with examples of a very different lifestyle. The activities of foreign missionaries, not only Muslim, but evangelical Christian, Hare Krishna and others, as well as of political pressure groups working to raise awareness of human rights and democratization issues, are also gradually having an effect.

Society is thus in transition throughout the region. At the same time, the future of the newly independent states is also hanging in the balance. The decolonization of Central Asia, which began in 1924 with the creation of the five republics as administrative entities, has moved into a new phase now that they have acquired political independence. Whether they will be able to achieve economic and military independence remains to be seen, but three outcomes seem likely: reintegration into some form of reconstituted Soviet Union; disintegration into regional enclaves, as in Afghanistan and currently in Tadjikistan; or retention of political independence, but as clients of an extra-regional power. Furthermore, there is the possibility of intra-regional realignments; also, that the republics will not follow identical courses.

The most likely candidate for reintegration, wholly or in part, is Kazakhstan. The catastrophic economic decline of this republic, its inescapable dependence on Russia for transport routes (which can only partially be alleviated by links with China and Iran), its peculiar ethnic composition and strong historical and cultural ties to Russia, will make it almost impossible for Kazakhstan to retain anything but the most symbolic form of independence. There may well be a *de facto* partition of the republic, giving the Kazakhs some degree of autonomy in the south, while the richer industrialized north would remain under Russian control. Such a move would probably have the covert support of the foreign oil and gas companies who were originally tempted by the republic's huge resources, but are increasingly frustrated by the problems of securing export outlets.

It is difficult to see how Kyrgyzstan and Tadjikistan will ever be able to achieve true independence, given not only their social and economic problems, but also their geographic isolation. Tadjikistan will probably continue to be tied to Russia for as long as Russia wishes to accept this responsibility. Kyrgyzstan appears to be on its way to becoming a Western military outpost, a situation which will win it no friends in the region and in the long term may well prove highly unbeneficial to its national interests. Turkmenistan, by contrast, if it is able to avoid internecine clan conflict, could have a prosperous and stable future: with its tiny population (currently some four million), vast hydrocarbon resources, good agricultural potential, and the prospects of access to Gulf ports through Iran, it already exhibits a greater degree of independence than the other Central Asian republics.

The republic that seems likely to have the most problematic future is Uzbekistan. It is here that the demographic pressures and concomitant socio-economic strains are most acute. It also has problems of access and egress. On the other hand, as the successor state to the great sedentary civilizations of the region, and encompassing most of the territory of the three pre-Tsarist Khanates, it sees itself as the natural regional hegemon. Its known resource base is almost as rich as that of its neighbours, but more varied and thus more amenable to diversification. For over a century, Central Asia has been forcibly confined to an existence on the periphery of the Slav world, unhinged from its traditional contacts with Asia. Today, there is great eagerness to redress the balance, but it is Uzbekistan that has gone furthest towards 'regaining the central ground', maintaining its contacts with Russia, but assiduously re-establishing ancient links with the Far East, Middle East, South and South-East Asia. The political and economic influence of the Asian 'Tigers' is likely to be of particular significance: not only do they present a model of economic growth that the Uzbeks would like to emulate, but of more practical importance, they represent a market for Uzbek technical and scientific expertise. Their political authoritarianism and stance on human rights also accords with Uzbek inclinations. However, being at the centre of conflicting influences and interests, especially in a period of transition, creates an environment vulnerable to destabilization. It will need the skills of a consummate statesman to maintain the republic's equilibrium, thereby enabling it to realize its full economic potential.

It is clear that the future of the Central Asian republics – the balance between conflict, stability and development – will be determined by the interaction of local and global forces. The hypothetical permutations of the variables are endless, and today's likelihoods could rapidly become tomorrow's irrelevances. Perhaps the best guide to the future course of events is provided by an Uzbek proverb: 'While there is food on the table and the wife and children are safe in the backyard all will be well; when either is threatened all hell will break loose'.

NOTES

1. In West European languages the term 'Central Asia' has generally been used very loosely to refer to unspecified territories east of the Urals. In Russian, *Srednjaja Azija* (Middle Asia) designated the territory of the four southern republics, Kazakhstan was regarded as a separate unit, while *Tsentral'naja Azija* (Central Asia) referred to territories further to the east (Xinjiang, Mongolia, Tibet, etc.). Since January 1993, however, in popular and official parlance, *Tsentral'naja Azija* (*Orta Asija* in the Turkic languages) has come to be used increasingly as the collective term for the five former Soviet republics, an area of some 4 million square km, with a total population of approximately 60 million.

2. For a good general introduction to the physical geography and early history of the region see D. Sinor (ed.), *The Cambridge History of Early Inner Asia* (Cambridge: Cambridge University Press, 1990).

3. See F.H. Skrine and E. Denison Ross, *The Heart of Asia* (London: Methuen, 1899), which gives an interesting account of the Russian administration in the region, drawing informed parallels with the British administration in India (see especially pp. 408-16).

4. I. Stalin, *Marksism i natsional'nyj vopros* (OGIZ, 1939), pp. 267-70.

5. Only Uzbekistan and Turkmenistan were accorded the status of full Union republics in 1924; the other units acquired this status subsequently, Tadzhikistan in 1929, Kyrgyzstan and Kazakhstan in 1936. Minor boundary adjustments were made at various times during the Soviet period.

6. This was essentially a European concept. In Central Asia, a region where bi- and multilingualism were the norm rather than the exception, language had not previously been a significant marker of identity. A.D. Smith is one of many who trace the history of the identification of nationality with language; see A.D. Smith, *The Ethnic Revival* (Cambridge: Cambridge University Press, 1989), pp. 45-52. See also E. J. Hobsbawm, who sets the question in a broader socio-political framework; see E.J. Hobsbawm, *Nations and Nationalism Since 1780* (Cambridge: Cambridge University Press, 1990), pp. 52-63.

7. I. Stalin, *Marksim i natsionel'nyj vopros*, pp. 9-16.

8. According to the 1926 Soviet Census the percentage of the titular nationality living within their own republic was as follows: Kazakhs 93.6; Kyrgyz 86.7; Tadjiks 63.1; Turkmen 94.2; Uzbeks 84.5. However, it should be borne in mind that there was considerable confusion over the definition of these ethnonyms, which, prior to Soviet rule, had scarcely been used by the indigenous population (the local categories of self-definition were clan, tribe, region and, when confronted by non-Muslims, religion). Political considerations also played some

part in the choice of 'nationality'. Among the Tadjiks, in particular, there was much obfuscation; it is still not uncommon to find, within a single family, one sibling claiming Uzbek identity, another Tadjik. Thus, although the Soviet territorial division was theoretically more successful, in terms of ethnic consolidation, than were similar divisions imposed by other colonial powers, it was nevertheless not quite as consistent as it purported to be.

9. See M. Kirkwood (ed.), *Language Planning in the Soviet Union* (London: Macmillan, 1989); chapters 1-4.

10. As J. Zajda observed, the aims of Soviet education included 'teaching in the spirit of communism and developing a Marxist-Leninist philosophy of life'; J. Zajda, *Education in the Soviet Union* (Oxford: Pergamon, 1980), pp. 108-80. See also J. Morison, 'The Political Content of Education in the USSR', in J. Tomiak (ed.), *Soviet Education in the 1980s* (London: Croom Helm, 1983), pp. 143-71.

11. The speed at which universal basic literacy was achieved is a subject of contention (see Akiner, in Kirkwood, *Language Planning in the Soviet Union*, fn. 10, p. 117, for a brief account of different assessments). Compulsory primary education for children was introduced in 1930; the school programme was extended to seven years in 1949, and ten years in 1952; an eleven-year programme began to be introduced in the 1980s. The entire system of public education was subject to rigid centralized control, with unified curricula, textbooks and marking systems.

12. G. Massell, *The Surrogate Proletariat* (Princeton, NJ: Princeton University Press, 1975).

13. See S. Akiner, 'Ethnicity, Nationality and Citizenship as Expressions of Self-Determination in Central Asia', in D. Clarke (ed.), *Self-Determination: International Perspectives* (London: Macmillan, forthcoming).

14. Crawford Young, *The Politics of Cultural Pluralism* (Madison, WI: University of Wisconsin Press, 1976), p. 11; makes the point that 'neither post-independence Afro-Asian politics nor contemporary political processes in the industrial world permit any other conclusion than a candid recognition that sub-national solidarity is of enduring importance as a political determinant'.

15. See Ajay Patnaik, 'Modernization, Change and Nationality Process in the USSR', in Shams ud Din (ed.), *Perestroika and the Nationality Question in the USSR* (Delhi: Vikas, 1990), pp. 108-15.

16. I had many conversations with members of the so-called 'nationalist' movements that appeared in the Central Asian republics in 1989-91; not only did they not seek secession in their written statements, but even in very private discussions they were not prepared to speculate on the prospects for political independence. Abdurahim Pulatov, the leader of the Uzbek movement *Birlik*, told me that, in his opinion, a premature severing of the links with Russia was undesirable because it would greatly harm the fragile process of democratization. In 1990, along with a number of other republics, the Central Asian governments made declarations of sovereignty (in the Soviet context, the term was not

synonymous with independence, but implied a certain degree of autonomy in the management of domestic affairs). Nevertheless, in the referendum of March 1991 on the future of the Soviet Union, the overwhelming majority of Central Asians voted to retain the Union. Later that year, in the immediate aftermath of the abortive August coup, the four southern republics (led by Uzbekistan) proclaimed their independence; however, the constitutional implications were not clarified and the general impression at the time was that it was a symbolic gesture on the part of the ruling elites to signal their dissatisfaction with the conduct of the central government, rather than a real bid for liberation. There was no public debate of the issue and very little evidence of popular support. Kazakhstan made its declaration of independence on 16 December 1991, thus after the Union had effectively ceased to exist. Today, most Central Asians are proud of their newly acquired independence, but at the same time, nostalgia for the Soviet Union remains strong throughout the region.

17. W. Fierman (ed.), *Soviet Central Asia: The Failed Transformation* (Boulder, CO: Westview, 1991).

18. Infant mortality in 1989 in the first year of life per 1,000 live births was as follows: Kazakhstan 25.8; Kyrgyzstan 32.2; Tadjikistan 43.2; Turkmenistan 54.6; Uzbekistan 37.6. See *Vestnik Statistiki* (Moscow: 1991), no. 7).

19. Life expectancy in 1989 at time of birth for men ranged from 61.8 years in Turkmenistan to 73.1 in Kazakhstan; see *Vestnik Statistiki*, no. 7, p. 75.

20. See M. Kaser and S. Mehrotra, *The Central Asian Economies After Independence* (London: Royal Institute of International Affairs, 1992). The trade/GNP ratios of the four southern republics by far exceed those of sub-Saharan African countries, which are themselves exceptionally high.

21. P. Svoik, the Head of the State Anti-Monopolies Committee in Kazakhstan, took the unusual course of publicly voicing his concerns over the shortcomings of the privatization programme in an article in the national daily *Kazakhstanskaja Pravda*, 19 January 1994, p. 2. He sees the creation of state holdings, which bring together several enterprises, as a covert means of ensuring that the most promising industries remain under the control of bureaucrats. In Kyrgyzstan there have also been major problems at all levels of the privatization process. Better results appear to have been achieved in those republics that adopted a more cautious approach to reform.

22. See an article by Zh. Kulambetov, *Slovo Kyrgyzstana*, 13 April 1994, p. 3. According to him, some 80 per cent of the profits of a commercial enterprise are taken in tax (some sources suggest an even higher rate), and 'mad interest rates' are charged on bank loans. The situation is similar in Kazakhstan.

23. Kyrgyzstan, Turkmenistan and Kazakhstan launched their own currencies in 1993; Uzbekistan used a transitional coupon currency until June 1994; Tadjikistan is still (late 1994) teetering on the brink of the rouble zone. The value of these new currencies against the dollar continues to fall. The Kazakh *tenge* has suffered the most, falling from 4.7 to the dollar in December 1993 to 41.25 in June 1994.

24. Turkmenistan, which relies heavily on its gas exports to CIS members, has been especially badly hit. In February 1994, Ukraine alone owed US$ 700 million. Turkmenistan is now taking a tougher line and insisting on repayment in kind (barter) or hard currency; *Izvestija*, 22 February 1994.

25. Kazakhstan has finally agreed to cede jurisdiction over the nuclear arsenal that is located on its soil to Russia; it is anticipated (perhaps over-optimistically) that the strategic missiles will be withdrawn within the next few months, leaving Kazakhstan nuclear-free by 1995; *Panorama*, 7 May 1994. Tactical weapons have already been withdrawn.

26. The Kazakhs have reached an agreement with the Russians whereby the latter will pay for most of the maintenance costs of Baikonur, and in return be allowed to continue to use it; *Kazakhstanskaja Pravda*, 10 February 1994, p. 1.

27. *Komsomol'skaja Pravda*, Moscow, 24 November 1993, claimed that Kyrgyzstan had acquired a sizeable arsenal of weapons from Israel.

28. At the first International Congress on Cultural and Scientific Cooperation in Central Asia, organized by UNESCO and the Islamic Republic of Iran in Tehran, 14-18 November 1992, senior academic representatives of all five republics made an urgent request to UNESCO for financial and material help for the rewriting of their national histories.

29. This trend is most pronounced in Turkmenistan, where the President has been given the official title of *Turkmenbashi* 'Leader of the Turkmen'; many streets and buildings have been renamed after him, also the port of Krasnovodsk on the Caspian Sea and the Kara Kum canal. These displays of homage may seem excessive to foreigners, but it must be said that most of the local population seem to be genuinely in favour of them. See, for example, the report by P. Conradi in *The European*, 1-7 July 1994, p. 5. In the other republics the sentiments are as strong, but expressed with slightly more discretion. Such overt adulation is part of the indigenous culture (a feature that was strengthened during the Soviet period when extravagant praise for the leadership was the norm). In addition, in these times of crisis and transition a tough, autocratic ruler is felt to be a necessary precondition for stability; this phenomenon is by no means confined to the developing world. See R. Emerson, *From Empire to Nation* (Cambridge, MA: Harvard University Press, 1967), p. 290.

30. *Panorama*, 16 July 1994, no. 28, p. 11.

31. The republic from which there has been the greatest outflow is Tadjikistan (the Russian population has been reduced by almost three-quarters, to approximately 100,000); large numbers of Slavs are also reported to be leaving Kyrgyzstan (some 100,000 this year alone, out of a total Russian population in 1989 of 840,000). There is a steady exodus from Uzbekistan, and some Russians are said to be leaving southern Kazakhstan and the republic's capital, Almaty. Turkmenistan, however, claims that it is experiencing an inflow of other nationalities. See *Central Asia Newsfile*, December 1993, vol. 1, no. 14, p. 11.

32. There are frequent complaints in the Russian press that the Central Asian republics are not fulfilling their treaty obligations to provide troops and equip-

ment. See, for example, the reports in *Segodnja*, 23 February 1994; and *Izvestija*, 3 March 1994.

33. K. Eggert, writing in *Izvestija*, 11 July 1993, summarizes the arguments as to why Russia cannot abandon Tadjikistan; his primary conclusion is that it would open the way to 'Muslim extremism' in Central Asia.

34. Iran and China are equally enthusiastic about the prospects for this route. Dr Velayati has made frequent references to it; Premier Li Peng, when he visited Central Asia in spring 1994, also spoke of the need for a 'new Silk Road' (*International Herald Tribune*, 20 April 1994). In the *Beijing Review*, 5-11 October 1992, pp. 16-8, an even more ambitious 'Eurasian transport corridor' is projected, stretching from the port of Rotterdam to that of Lianyungang, a distance of 10,900 km. The main rail links are already in place, but multiple tracks are currently being constructed in some parts of China so as to meet the expected increase in demand towards the end of the century. Trans-shipment yards have already been built at the border stations of Alatau and Druzhba to enable trains to change their wheels, since CIS railway gauges are wider than those used by China (and internationally).

35. The Caspian Sea Cooperation Zone was created, on Iran's initiative, in February 1992; it brings together the five littoral states of the Caspian Sea. It is primarily concerned with the protection and sustainable exploitation of the resources of the Sea.

36. The Economic Cooperation Organization developed out of a series of previous regional alliances, dating from 1955, between Iran, Pakistan, Turkey and, briefly, Iraq. In 1984 Iran attempted to revitalize the alliance with Turkey and Pakistan, but it was only in February 1992, when the first summit meeting of Heads of State of ECO members was held in Tehran, that the organization embarked on a sustained programme of activities. The five Central Asian republics, as well as Azerbaijan and Afghanistan, have now also become ECO members.

37. See R. Freedman, 'Israel and Central Asia: A Preliminary Analysis', *Central Asia Monitor*, 1993, no. 2, pp. 16-20; and A. Nedvetsky, 'Israel's Policy: The Post-Soviet Moslem Republics', *Middle East Monitor*, September 1993, vol. 2, no. 2, pp. 28-36.

38. Yassir Arafat was given a warm reception by government officials when he visited Kazakhstan in September 1993. Links between Kazakhstan and the PLO date back to the Soviet period, when Palestinian students were encouraged to pursue their studies in Almaty. Some 100 Palestinian postgraduates are currently studying there.

39. Turkmenistan's growing links with Iran are already a cause for concern to the Uzbek President, who fears that they might eventually pose a threat to the region's stability; see interview with President Karimov by Vitalij Portnikov in *Nezavisimaja Gazeta*, 21 June 1993, p. 3.

40. As in Afghanistan, alliances are highly fluid and it is impossible to analyse the situation from a rational point of view. The report by Igor' Rotar', in the

Russian newspaper *Nezavisimaja Gazeta*, 16 April 1994, describes the kaleidoscopic nature of the situation. It is impossible to be certain how many deaths and displaced persons have resulted from this conflict, but the number of dead is probably over 100,000; the total number of refugees has been estimated at between 100,000 and 350,000.

41. See *Kyrgyzstan Chronicle*, 21 December 1993, no. 4, p. 4, which, under the provocative title, 'The North-South Axis: What is Shattering It?' presents the results of a recent survey of public opinion on the subject.

42. The question of YomutÁhal-Tekke rivalry was raised in articles in *Izvestija* (20 May 1994) and *Segodnja* (12 May 1994); they evoked an angry rebuttal from a group of eminent Turkmen in *Izvestija*, 9 June 1994.

43. The armed forces were created from units of the Soviet army, together with all their equipment and property, that were stationed on the republic's territory at the time of the collapse of the Soviet Union. Subsequently many of Slav origin, particularly the officers, have elected to return to their own republics, so these armies are already below strength. Moreover, they represent but small parts of what was a much larger, unified complex and so at present are unbalanced and lacking in cohesion, with major shortfalls in many vital areas. It will take a considerable amount of time, money and planned effort to create viable national forces. See Shirin Akiner, 'Soviet Military Legacy in Kazakhstan', in *Jane's Intelligence Review*, vol. 6, no. 12, pp. 552-5.

44. Estimates of casualties in both these conflicts vary wildly, depending on the personal bias of the source. Partisans of the groups that were involved have confused the situation still further by producing video films of the events, at least some of which appear to have been faked. It is unlikely that more than 500 people were killed in the first sequence of clashes in 1989, and more than 200 in the second in 1990.

45. In the run-up to the March 1994 Parliamentary elections there were several instances of administrative discrimination against Russian candidates. In the event, 49 Russian deputies were elected, a slightly lower percentage than in the previous Parliament (27.7 per cent instead of 28.6 per cent). The percentage share of the Kazakh deputies rose from 54.5 per cent to 58.2 per cent. The share of other nationalities fell.

46. See S. Suslikov, *Izvestija*, 26 January 1994.

47. Kazakh policy-makers favour a 'united China', according to a report by S. Vankevich in *Panorama*, 30 April 1994, p. 2.

48. B. Z. Rumer, *Soviet Central Asia: 'A Tragic Experiment'* (Boston, MA: Unwin Hyman, 1989), pp. 76-104.

49. Visitors to Turkmenistan, including members of the Moscow Institute of Geography, have long been aware of clashes between Uzbeks and Turkmen over the latter's plans to extend the irrigation network system. The Uzbeks believe that it will seriously deplete their own water supply.

50. There was a slight fall in fertility rates in the mid 1970s, but they then began to rise again. See data in *Naselenije SSSR 1987* (Moscow: Finansy i Statistika, 1988).

51. According to the demographer V. Perevedentsev, in Uzbekistan and Tadjikistan in the near future, for every ten people who leave working age, another 35 will enter it. See 'Evrazia', *Moskovskije Novosti*, 11 October 1992.

52. In Uzbekistan, the Ministry of Internal Affairs has announced that in the course of its annual anti-narcotics campaign in June 1994 (code-named 'Operation Poppy') it destroyed 60 hectares of high-grade opium; over 3,000 people were arrested; and prosecutions are to be brought against over 200 local administrators for failing to take action to prevent the illegal cultivation of narcotic substances. The Kyrgyz State Commission for Drug Control announced an increase of six to seven times the amount of opium smuggled into the republic in the period April to July 1994. In southern Kazakhstan alone, some 5,000 tonnes of marijuana are now produced annually. Most of it is smuggled out of the republic but there is a growing domestic demand. See the reports by E. Denisenko in *Nezavisimaja Gazeta*, 21 July 1994; *Panorama*, 11 June 1994, no. 23; and *Nezavisimaja Gazeta*, 22 June 1994, p. 13.

53. *Moskovskije Novosti*, 12 September 1993, describes routes and prices.

54. G. Khaidarov and M. Inomov, *Tadjikistan: Tragedy and Anguish of the Nation* (LINKO, 1993), p. 42.

55. Estimates given by local Muslims in spring 1994.

56. M. Williams, *International Economic Organizations* (New York: Harvester Wheatsheaf, 1994), p. 83.

57. The sum that was owed in early 1994 was $400 million; this is not large by international standards, but given that a large proportion of the loans appears to have been frittered away on imports of consumer goods and foreign travel for officials, also that debt repayments are set to rise sharply over the next couple of years, the anxiety of many Kyrgyz economists and policy advisers is understandable; see *Slovo Kyrgyzstana*, 22 April 1994, p. 3.

58. *Panorama*, 30 April 1994, p. 3.

59. In 1993 the Kyrgyz Parliament set up a special Commission to investigate irregularities in the government's dealings with Seabeco, a Swiss-Canadian brokerage firm that had been involved in the development of the Kyrgyz gold industry. The Commission catalogued an extraordinary saga of mismanagement and loss of millions of US dollars of state funds (see *Komsomol'skaja Pravda*, 24 November 1993). In March 1994 the Kyrgyz press began to investigate the terms of the government's agreement with the Canadian firm Cameco for the development of the Kumtor gold deposit. No wrongdoing on the part of Cameco has emerged, but there is a strong body of opinion in the republic that the Canadians have been given terms that are not in Kyrgyzstan's best interests.

60. *Nezavisimaja Gazeta*, 21 January 1994, based on an article in the Kyrgyz daily *Vechernyj Bishkek* of 20 January 1994, reported that high-level talks were underway regarding the establishment of a US military base in Kyrgyzstan

within the framework of NATO; the Kyrgyz Ministry of Defence declined to comment on the matter. There are also reports that the United States may be in the process of establishing a naval base in the Caspian Sea, in the Kazakh port of Aktau; see *Panorama*, 2 April 1994, p. 1.

61. Between 75 and 85 per cent of the indigenous peoples of the region were rural dwellers, according to the 1970 Soviet census. The level of migration within each republic was low (less than 5 per cent) and movement out of each republic lower still. See Shirin Akiner, *Islamic Peoples of the Soviet Union* (London: Kegan Paul, 1983). Full data have not been released since then, but there is not likely to have been much change in the ratio of urban to rural dwellers.

13

Conflict Resolution in South Asia*

Kingsley M. de Silva

SOURCES OF CONFLICT

The South Asian region has some of the most intractable political conflicts of any part of the world and at three levels: international, national and subnational. Yet it has not attracted the attention of conflict resolution theorists as much as the various regions of Africa have. This chapter is not meant to fill this gap in theoretical or political analysis, but rather to raise some relevant issues; identify some of the specific points of conflict and the sources of such conflicts; assess these in the light of the changes in the world situation especially in the context of the revolutionary changes that have occurred in Central and Eastern Europe with the simultaneous collapse of communist regimes there; and to indicate potential changes in the nature of South Asia's conflicts in the late 1990s. In doing so it will seek to identify some common themes in South Asian conflicts, their similarities and diversities, and attempt some broad conclusions on the prospects for their management if not resolution.

The reality of internal struggle, the potential for external conflict and the prospect of bloodshed on an enormous scale are greater in South Asia than in most other parts of Asia, with the possible exception of the Middle East. No ethnic and or religious conflict in recent times has resulted in greater carnage and destruction than the Hindu-Muslim rivalry that led to the partition of the British *raj* in 1947. It caused between 500,000 and one million deaths on that occasion, and resulted in nearly 15 million refugees – an enormous number given the population of the *raj* at that time.

---

* This is a revised version of a paper presented at the second South Asian Dialogue held in Kandy, Sri Lanka, in November 1992, and has been previously published in the *International Journal on Group Rights*, 1, 1994, pp. 247-67. Reprinted by permission of Kluwer Publishers.

Few regions in any part of the world are dominated by a single state – in population, in armed might and in the size of the economy – as India dominates South Asia. Thus the very vastness of India is a central feature of any study of conflict resolution in South Asia. To complicate matters even further, each of India's neighbours has minority groups with linguistic, religious or cultural ties with groups in India, or aspires to establish such ties with them. India has been, and is in, a position to exploit these links to its advantage, or the disadvantage of its neighbours, whenever it wants.[1]

Just as South Asia is a geographical oddity because of the overwhelming dominance of India, it is also an oddity because of the virtual impossibility of demarcating a distinct boundary on two of the four sides of this large subcontinental landmass. To the north lies the Himalayan frontier and beyond it China and, up to very recently, the Soviet Union and now the various 'istans', the Islamic states of Central Asia. To the north and northwest lies the Islamic world. To the north-east and east is Burma/Myanmar, in part a buffer and in part a link between South and South-East Asia. Burma/Myanmar appears prominently in this article because it was part of the *raj*, and many of its present problems have their roots in its colonial past, just as some of India's problems in the north-east stem from the conquest and absorption of Burma. It also illustrates one significant feature of the evolution of the *raj*, the use of its resources for purposes of imperial penetration into what is now part of South-East Asia. Only in the south, where the subcontinental landmass tapers down into a triangular form, do we find a distinct and undisputed boundary – the sea around South Asia. The Himalayas are an unmistakable geographic boundary, but politically they are an indistinct one, and very much in dispute.

Many of the conflicts in South Asia – international, national and subnational – have their roots in the region's colonial past or in the manner in which independence was attained such as, for instance, the problems between India and Pakistan stemming from the partition of the *raj*. India, Pakistan and Bangladesh (not to mention Burma/Myanmar) were all part of the *raj*. Of the other four SAARC countries, two were peripherally linked to the *raj*: Nepal and Bhutan. Sri Lanka, like the Maldives, was independent of the *raj* and was controlled by the Colonial Office. The Maldives had a tutelary relationship with Whitehall through the Governor of Ceylon (Sri Lanka). All the successor states of the *raj* have inherited border problems from the *raj*, which bring them into conflict with neighbouring states (India and China, for instance, and to a lesser extent in terms of the violence it has generated, Pakistan and Afghanistan) or with each other (India and Pakistan, and Bangladesh and Burma). Post-independence definition or redefinition of boundaries also brings these states into disputes with neighbours (India and

China) or over resources such as irrigation works (India and Pakistan) and river waters (India and Bangladesh not to mention India and Pakistan).

Migration of population from the *raj* and within it, some of it voluntary and some of it involuntary, has contributed and still contributes to tensions among and within the states of South Asia, and among their neighbours. The voluntary demographic shifts could be divided into two chronologically distinct categories; some go back to colonial times and others are post-independence. The *raj* was treated as a vast reservoir of labour which the British despatched to colonies as far away as Guyana in the Caribbean, Fiji in the Pacific, Natal in South Africa, and to Mauritius in the Indian ocean region, and closer home, to Sri Lanka, Burma and Malaya, wherever there was a shortage of labour – an early form of transnational transfer of popula-tion.[2] These Indian groups have remained in the receiving colonies and questions relating to their political status have led to prolonged and acrimoni-ous disputes between the governments of the *raj* and the host territories, with Ceylon (Sri Lanka) and Burma being the most prominent examples in South Asia. At the present time voluntary population shifts *within* India are far more significant, for the tensions they generate, than issues relating to the political status of the Indian community in neighbouring states.[3] In north-east India, for instance, Bengali-speaking groups, both Hindu and Muslim, have moved from densely populated parts of eastern India and from the former East Pakistan (now Bangladesh) into the relatively under-populated Assam and neighbouring regions. These movements continued after independence in the form of illicit or illegal migration and have contributed to an upsurge of separatist agitation in Assam and the north-east, an agitation provoked by opposition to outsiders from India and Pakistan before 1971, and thereafter from Bangladesh as well. In one of the most densely populated parts of the world it is natural for people to move out of their own regions or countries in search of living space if not a better life. Some of the comparatively under-populated parts of South Asia have thus acted as a magnet for illegal migrants. Bhutan, which is host to a large migrant population from Nepal, is one example, and the other was the illicit immigration to Sri Lanka from the coasts of Tamil Nadu and Andrapradesh. This latter has now stopped, but only because the conditions of virtual civil war in the north of Sri Lanka make migration there a singularly dangerous proposition.

The involuntary movements of population – refugees or displaced persons – are associated with cataclysmic political events such as the parti-tion of the *raj* in 1947; the Chinese government clamping down on Tibet's autonomy and Buddhist culture in the late 1940s and early 1950s; and the creation of Bangladesh in 1971; or ethnic conflict as in the case of Tamils from Sri Lanka after 1983; and the civil war in Afghanistan. The consequences that stem from these movements of refugees are familiar, but the point in the South Asian context is that they are historically conditioned. In most instances the response of the host society is ambivalent at best, and in some instances, such as with the Biharis in Bangladesh, they are treated as a burden on the host society while they themselves yearn for a home in Pakistan. The government of Pakistan has so far been reluctant to bring the Biharis stranded in Bangladesh into Pakistan, but in contrast Pakistan has provided a haven for nearly 5 million Afghan refugees, about one-third of the population of Afghanistan, one of the largest refugee flows into a single country in recent times. Unlike the refugees displaced by the partition of the *raj* in 1947 and accommodated in both India and Pakistan, these refugees regard themselves as temporary sojourners who have every intention of going back to Afghanistan whenever the situation there permits them to do so.[4]

The fact that the hostility between India and Pakistan looms so large in the South Asian political landscape should not divert attention from the domestic tensions, which are, in fact, more significant as threats to the political stability of many countries in the region. All too often these domestic tensions spill over borders into neighbouring states and trigger inter-state conflicts: the conflict between India and Pakistan which led to the creation of Bangladesh; the Kashmir imbroglio which has resulted in three wars between Pakistan and India; and the problems of Sri Lanka's north and east which attracted Indian intervention. In the mid- and late 1940s these internal tensions had resulted in the partition of the *raj* and the establishment of Pakistan – the triumph of nationalism linked with religion – and less than 24 years later Bangladesh was created – the triumph of linguistic nationalism. With the current salience of Hindu fundamentalism in India, with its insistence that being a Hindu is the defining principle of being an Indian, the interplay of religion and nationalism has come full circle. Hindu 'fundamentalism' is now a mass movement in India, and given the size of Hindu India – *Hindutva* – its demands and claims have in turn provoked similar reactions from Muslims, Sikhs, and to a lesser extent from Buddhists and Christians.[5] As the recent events in Ayodhya demonstrate, the communal violence set in motion in so many parts of the country poses a grave threat to the stability of the Indian polity, both through further rounds of violence between Hindus and Muslims, and in the alienation of Indian Muslims.

The recrudescence of politicized religion in the contemporary public life of India is an appropriate point of departure for a brief reference to an aspect of religion that deserves more publicity and attention from South Asian scholars and politicians than it has received so far – the threat to the survival of Buddhism in the Himalayan region. The parlous state of Buddhism in

Tibet is, of course, the core of the problem. Many Buddhist monasteries, and other sites of religious significance to Buddhists, have been destroyed by the Chinese, and even those that survive do so under severe restrictions. The Chinese see Tibetan Buddhist monasteries as centres of resistance to their control over Tibet. Tibet's problems are beyond the scope of South Asian conflict resolution, but many aspects of the survival of Himalayan Buddhism are very much within its scope, beginning with the threats to the survival of Buddhism in Ladakh, and the decline of Buddhism in Sikkim under Indian rule. Bhutan, of course, remains a Buddhist kingdom, but one aspect of the present conflict between the Bhutanese and the Nepali minority is, of course, the perceived threat to Bhutan's Buddhist society from an influx of Hindus. Beyond the Himalayas and on to the Chittagong hill tracts of Bangladesh we confront the threatened position of Bangladesh's Buddhist minority.[6] And finally there is the current renewed threat to Buddhist holy places in Buddha Gaya from politicized Hinduism.

How does one resolve these conflicts, distil and develop proposals that could help to ameliorate them, and promote political, economic and social conditions that enhance the prospects for regional and global stability? If appropriate conflict resolution policies are to be developed, we need to understand the complex nature of most of these conflicts and to analyse them in their multiple contexts. It is first necessary to understand the underlying factors that produce ethnic conflict and above all armed separatist movements in general, which is hard enough. But the situation is rendered all the more difficult because South Asian separatism now draws inspiration, and on occasion support, from similar movements elsewhere in the world. The crumbling of the former Yugoslavia and the breakup of the former Soviet Union gave fresh hope to South Asian separatist groups operating in other parts of the world, especially some *diaspora* associations of dissident South Asian ethnic minorities living in Western countries. The so-called Sikh Council of Khalistan in Washington DC – among the most vocal advocates of a would-be Sikh state – responded to the declaration of independence by Slovenia and Croatia in July 1991 by conferring its own somewhat presumptuous 'recognition' on the new republics. The ludicrousness of this gesture should not divert attention from the fact that representatives of separatist groups living far away from their own homeland were delighted at the unravelling of a multi-ethnic state and its disintegration into its component elements, and were seeking to exploit this to their own advantage. They were hoping that these developments outside India would strengthen their own efforts to establish a Sikh state on the border between India and Pakistan.

Kashmiri separatists living in the United Kingdom and the United States reacted in much the same way to the restoration of independence of the three

Baltic republics of Estonia, Latvia and Lithuania, as their Sikh counterparts did to the declaration of independence by Slovenia and Croatia. What mattered to them was the fact that the United States had never recognized the absorption of these states into the Soviet Union under the terms of the Hitler-Stalin pact. They pointed out that the absorption of Kashmir into the Indian union in 1947 had not been recognized by the UN. The unstated assumption was that the UN should reopen the question of self-determination for Kashmir. Indeed, the breakup of the former Soviet Union is seen by some of these expatriate communities as a welcome harbinger of a similar process in India, and as the means to satisfy their separatist aspirations.

The Soviet Union was the world's largest multi-ethnic state in the extent of territory controlled, a huge transcontinental empire. India is, and always has been, the world's largest multi-ethnic state in terms of population. What lessons can be drawn for the future of India, and indeed of South Asia, from the collapse of the Tsarist-Stalinist empire? If one today needs clues to the points of potential ethnic tension in Russia and other states that were once part of the Soviet Union – and there are many such points – one needs to go back in history to identify the various stages by which the Tsars and their communist successors expanded their empire, in particular the stages by which the Tsars absorbed various non-Russian ethnic groups into the empire. Each of these various stages of expansion is today like a fault-line in the Russian state, and all of them are potentially explosive. While the situation in the two countries is substantially different, India also has many fault-lines – too many – based on the stages in building the *raj*, for any complacent dismissal of the view that the collapse of the Soviet empire does have a message for the rulers of other large multi-ethnic states. Besides, not all of India's fault-lines date back to the *raj*; some of the most dangerous of them all – the Hindu-Muslim discord – are pre-colonial.

The current situation, with several major trouble spots in South Asia associated with separatist agitation, makes the situation even more dangerous for regional and global political stability. The principal separatist trouble spots in India, Kashmir, the Punjab and Assam are all border states, and this adds to the volatility of the situation. The north and east of Sri Lanka, Sind, Baluchistan and the North-West Frontier Province of Pakistan are also, in their own way, border regions, if not states. Many, or all, of these have had or have potential for cross-border tensions.

THE COLONIAL ROOTS OF SOUTH ASIAN CONFLICTS

If the British decision to dismantle the *raj* was a confession that it was no longer possible to resist the nationalist upsurge directed by the Indian National Congress, the partition of the *raj* demonstrated the strength of ethnicity, in combination with religion, as the principal source of internal tensions and conflicts in societies striving to free themselves from the bonds of colonial rule. The creation of the state of Pakistan in 1947 was expected to have settled at least some of these problems, since the larger segment of the Muslim minorities of the *raj* were brought within the boundaries of the new state through one of the most terrible cataclysms of modern times. But within 24 years the state of Pakistan was divided, the birth of Bangladesh demonstrating the superior strength of language and culture as points of identity in a state that was constructed on the basis that religion was the principal bond of identity of its people.

Even in its current more cohesive form, Pakistan illustrates the problems that post-colonial states confront from national and internal boundaries devised by colonial rulers for their own purposes. Where such frontiers separate people of the same ethnic group, they are often challenged. The Durand Line, devised by the British government in 1893, which left the Baluchis and Pushtuns divided between Afghanistan and the British *raj*, is an example. The Afghans never recognized the validity of this line, and after the partition of the *raj* into India and Pakistan, the latter inherited the British-imposed boundary. Disputes over this boundary have remained a source of discord between Afghanistan and Pakistan since 1947. Pushtun merchants who had great influence with the government in Kabul have long aspired for an outlet to the sea to facilitate their trade, and have supported the rights of self-determination to Pushtu and Baluchi citizens in Pakistan's frontier regions. It is no exaggeration to say that the ramifications of this hostility between Pakistan and Afghanistan have had a disturbing impact on the Afghan polity, as well as a crucial influence on the external relations of these two countries.

The Durand Line, in fact, illustrates one of the key features of the administration of the government of India under the *raj*, the point made by Guy Wint, a British publicist, in 1947:

> that the true frontiers of the Empire delineated not the lands it administered but the lands it protected.

Bhutan and Nepal were among the lands so protected. Through timely seizures of territory, the construction of alliances, and the exercise of influence, the Indian government [of the *raj*] turned South Asia into a political unit knit together for defence.[7]

Apart from 'annexing territory, the Indian government, with the British government behind it, built for their defences an outwork of alliances and spheres of influence'. The central feature of the defence plan of British India was, of course, the Himalayas. Then as now the Himalayas were more distinctive geographically than politically, but any ambiguity on the latter level was settled in favour of the *raj* by the deft exercise of a combination of military power, clever diplomacy and sheer bluff.

The defence thinking of the *raj* lives on, a lively presence in Delhi, and by no means a ghostly one. It has drawn India into conflict with many of its South Asian neighbours, and more importantly with China. India's war with China of 1962 will not be discussed in this chapter, but the point is made that since 1959 relations between the two Asian giants have been seriously affected by conflicting interpretations on the 'true frontiers' of the *raj* in the Himalayan region.

The following extracts from a recent book by an American scholar, Steven A. Hoffman, provide a succinct summary of the issues in the conflict. Hoffman drew a contrast between the Indian and British viewpoints on this.

> Underpinning them all was the fervent belief that an Indian nation had existed through time – defined by culture, common experience, custom and geography – long before the British had created and imposed their own state structure on the subcontinent ... Crucial to the British view had been the belief that India existed as a viable political unit only because of British military and administrative power.[8]

And more specific to the issue of national boundaries was the Indian assumption that:

> India's traditional and customary boundaries had long existed and had evolved naturally, since they were based on the activities of populations and cultures and on geographical features such as mountain ridges and watersheds. The British had chosen to reinforce these boundaries, or to deviate from them, for strategic reasons and because their knowledge of Indian geography was not complete. More important, however, was that when acting as definers of borders, the British were not basing their thinking on historical evidence. That was why they could wittingly or unwittingly sacrifice Indian interests when formulating frontier and border decisions.[9]

The Kashmir region is part of this same Himalayan frontier, and the key to the most long-standing of the disputes between India and Pakistan. In the north-east there is every possibility that disputes over this same frontier will bring India and Bangladesh into conflict with Burma, whenever that country becomes strong enough to assert its rights on the international scene again.[10] The roots of the Kashmir conflict go back to the imperial conflicts of the nineteenth century as the *raj* contrived to build a buffer zone between British India and the Tsarist empire. Although the British established control over Kashmir they did not make it part of British India. They sought to establish boundaries with China and with Afghanistan in the Kashmir region, but these were never clearly or fully demarcated. Today the same uncertainty prevails over demarcation of the actual line of control between the Indian- and Pakistani-held parts of Kashmir, resulting in conflict over the Siachin Glacier in the high Himalayas. To make matters even more complex, Pakistan and China have reached agreement over part of the border of Kashmir, but that part of the border is contested by India.

Disputed political boundaries are not the only points of disharmony in these post-colonial states. Political establishments in all of South Asia are embroiled in protracted conflicts with ethnic and religious minorities which seek to resist the expanding powers and demands of the state. Often the pluralist reality of ethnic and cultural configurations is overshadowed by assertions of a homogenetic identity within the boundaries of these post-colonial states. The post-independence states of the region bear the marks of their colonial origins through the processes of pre-colonial consolidation and expansion, and of state-building, which they have inherited. The new rulers, as legatees of their colonialist predecessors, often disregard indigenous forces such as language, culture, religion and ethnicity with the same insouciance. As a result, conflicts over identity are a major, if not the principal, source of internal tensions in India, Sri Lanka, and Pakistan, in that order.

The current reality in South Asia is that language, culture, religion and ethnicity stemming from pre-colonial times, and acting separately or in combination, have assumed the proportions of explosive forces threatening the stability of the post-independence political settlement. The successor states, which are intent on preserving their inheritance unchanged, confront separatist forces immanent in these powerful but contradictory processes of state-building on the foundation of colonial and pre-colonial structures. The minority ethnic resistance takes the form, more often than not, of separatist movements seeking the creation of new states in which the minority could convert itself into a majority. Thus separatism is as much the result of the processes of imposing colonial rule in these regions, as it is a result of the re-emergence of powerful pre-colonial forces seeking a political identity coincident with language and culture, and/or with religion.

While separatism appears to be endemic in South Asia and could be, and is, a powerful destabilizing force, it has generally been held at bay by an even more powerful force: Asian nationalism embodied in the post-colonial state-system of Asia. It would be true to say that up to very recently the great obstacle that separatist movements in the 'Third World' faced was a general hostility to disturbing the *status quo*. Because practically everyone is vulnerable to the pull of indigenous and often external forces, it was seen to be in everyone's interest to help existing post-colonial nation-states resist threats to their integrity from indigenous and external separatist forces.

A general reluctance to disturb the *status quo* embodied in the boundaries of the post-colonial state system, however, did not prevent or even inhibit involvements in ethnic conflicts in neighbouring states. India's intervention in Sri Lanka's ethnic conflicts, Pakistan's covert involvement in the affairs of the Punjab, or India's in Sind, are examples. And of course there was the classic case of a regional power's successful exploitation of ethnic conflict in a neighbouring state to its own strategic advantage, the events that led to the dismemberment of Pakistan – in its original political manifestation – in 1971.[11]

Conventional wisdom has it that there have been very few successful separatist movements in the post-colonial societies of the 'Third World'. Bangladesh is generally seen as the product of the only successful separatist movement in post-independence South Asia and therefore a unique development. This is at best a half truth. There is another way of looking at the emergence of Bangladesh - as the second phase of the most successful separatist agitation in South Asia in recent decades, part of a process by which the British *raj* was torn apart before and at the time of the transfer of power through the Muslim insistence on separation from Hindu. Those who 'invented' Pakistan were not very anxious to incorporate Bengal within such a state. But Kashmir was always seen to be an integral part of it; to that extent one more item in the separatist's agenda in South Asia remains unfulfilled, and remains the source of the greatest danger to the peace of the region. Again we need to remember that other successful but very peaceful separatist movement under the *raj*: Burma, securing a separate, if still colonial, status after 1935, separate from the *raj* of which it had been made a part in the process of being swallowed up in three gulps: 1824, 1852, and 1886.

In the current international environment of the end of the Cold War, this tolerance of the sanctity of boundaries, even when they are seen to be manifestly disputed boundaries, and the general reluctance to countenance sepa-

ratism or to treat it as a legitimate force, which formed such important
features of political behaviour at an international level for so long, are likely
to fade away. The enormity of these changes has already resulted in a greater
willingness to tolerate separatism. A world which accepts the dismemberment of the former Yugoslavia – a Balkanization of the Balkans – is hardly
likely to give as much thought as in the past to changes in international
boundaries in the post-colonial world. The rulers of most post colonial states
will have to learn to live with that.

TWO CASE STUDIES IN THE COLONIAL ROOTS OF POLITICAL CONFLICT

The two case studies chosen here to illustrate the contemporary significance
of the colonial roots of political conflict in South Asia are Sri Lanka and
Burma, the first of which was independent of the *raj* and the second very
much a part of the *raj* for over a century. Both states confront powerful
separatist movements. In both instances separatism arose, in part at least,
from the processes of constructing the colonial state. We begin first of all
with Burma. The British in India were, in the first instance, the successors
of the last of the great Muslim dynasties which dominated northern India for
about 1,000 years - the last of whom were the Mughals who ruled for 300 of
them. But the empire constructed by the British was much larger than anything the Mughals had ever controlled. It was unique in Indian history as the
empire which controlled the whole of the Indian subcontinent. But in building it, in welding it and consolidating it, the empire builders of the *raj*
incorporated within it peoples and territories which Indian rulers had seldom
been able to control. The north-east and north-west frontier territories of the
raj, acquired through the conquest of Burma and the subjugation of the
Sikhs, are examples of these. From them spring some of contemporary
India's most troublesome separatist movements.

The subjugation of the Punjab is more familiar to us than the conquest of
Burma. By a curious coincidence one of the principal figures in both was
Lord Dalhousie, and in confronting the problems of the Punjab and Assam
the rulers of modern India are his heirs. In their determination to protect this
inheritance they remain faithful to the Dalhousie tradition. The clash between the forces of the British East India Company and those of the Burmese
kingdom in the early nineteenth century was a conflict between two expanding and dynamic empires. The Burmese had already routed their Thai rivals,
and were expanding westwards and southwards in the direction of Bengal.
That expansion was seen to threaten the British East India Company's main

centre of activity, Bengal and Calcutta, and therefore the Burmese had to be stopped, and stopped they were through the conquest of part of Burma.

The absorption of parts of the present north-east frontier of modern India, including Assam, thus stemmed from the East India Company's conflict with the Burmese kingdom. Assam, which had remained independent of the Mughal empire, became part of the *raj*. And not the Assamese alone, but other peoples of Sino-Tibetan or Tibeto-Burmese stock were absorbed into the rapidly expanding British *raj*. Special administrative arrangements were made to keep them apart from the major ethnic group of the north-east, the Bengalis, but with the end of empire and the partition of the *raj* these arrangements have broken down, and these people have been under enormous pressure from the Bengali-speaking Hindus and Muslims, to the point where the Assamese feel that their identity is seriously threatened.[12]

As for Burma, after the first Anglo-Burmese war of 1824, and the treaty of 1826, relations between the British and the Burmese were generally strained. It was a matter of time before their conflicting interests resulted in another clash. The second Anglo-Burmese war brought another part of Burmese territory into the British *raj*, and this time - in 1852 - it included Rangoon, which Dalhousie had great ambitions of converting into another Singapore. The third Anglo-Burmese war brought upper Burma within the *raj*. The Burmese had been unfortunate in their kings who never matched their Thai counterparts in statecraft and political skills. They gave the British every possible excuse to make conquest seem justified.

Burma was ruled as part of the *raj* with, what seems in retrospect, disastrous consequences for the Burmese. For one thing, absorption in the *raj* permitted very easy entry of Indians to Burma as traders, labourers, technicians and money-lenders. The economic development of Burma became a process of exploitation of resources for the benefit of British trading houses and Indian traders and money-lenders. Indeed the imposition and consolidation of British rule in Burma was a joint enterprise, British and Indian.

In 1931 there were over one million Indians resident in Burma. Until 1920 or so, the presence of this large minority presented fewer problems than they did after 1920, when the spread of Indian land ownership changed the picture completely. By then Indians owned more than half the rice lands of Burma, a good part of which had come their way through a process of foreclosing on mortgages. As a result there was mounting friction between the Burmese and Indians, brought to a head by the impact of the great depression of 1929 which had resulted in large-scale foreclosures of land by the Indian Chettyar community and widespread unemployment. The 1930s saw several anti-Indian riots, especially, but not exclusively, in Rangoon. The principal motivating factor in these riots was the economic one.[13] The bitterness these caused strengthened the desire of the Burmese for separation from India, a separation which came in 1937.[14] In a recent article two Burmese scholars point out that 'Rangoon became an overseas suburb of Madras, and the average Burmese citizen no longer felt at home in his own house'.[15]

Thus one stream of political evolution emphasized Burma's distinct identity and its separation from the *raj*, while the second strengthened the forces of ethnic separateness within Burma, between the Burmese majority (generally the more advanced people of the plains and the Irrawaddy delta) and the minority peoples, the Karens, the Shans, the Kachins and others. The Burmese 'empire' had been on the crest of a wave since the late eighteenth century when the Burmese had inflicted a humiliating defeat on their Thai rivals. But their defeat and conquest by the British meant that Burmese rulers did not have time to consolidate their conquests, and to get the various ethnic groups living within their territories to acknowledge their position as subjects of the Burmese kings. Indeed, conquest by the British served to emphasize the differences between these people - and the Karens in particular - and the Burmese majority.

British conquest and rule in Burma and Sri Lanka are a study in contrasts. In Sri Lanka a very early attempt at rule through the Madras administration of the British East India Company led to a major rebellion in 1797-98. Thereafter, whenever officials in London were tempted to treat Sri Lanka as a unit of the British *raj* in India, the memory of this rebellion served as a warning against the perils involved. Thus Sri Lanka was administered through the Colonial Office. But although the patterns of absorption in the colonial system were different in Burma and Sri Lanka, they had much the same consequences. In both a sense of separation from India was strengthened.

Between 1796 and 1818 the British had achieved what the Dutch and Portuguese before them had failed to do - to bring the whole of Sri Lanka under their control. In doing so the British realized the objectives and aspirations of Sinhalese rulers of the past, objectives and aspirations which these latter had failed, for the most part, to achieve since the early part of the fifteenth century. The British proceeded to weld together an island polity by merging the Kandyan kingdom with those parts of the littoral which they had conquered from the Dutch. Between 1832 and 1889 they redrew the internal boundaries of the island, a process which at every stage had purely political objectives. The nine provinces that emerged were merely administrative units bereft of any traditional historical identity, with the single exception perhaps of the Central Province. At the time of independence Sri Lanka had been a cohesive political entity for over a century, a nation-state but also a state-nation created by the British.

British policy in Burma had kept peoples and territories apart in matters of administration, but in Sri Lanka people were brought into closer contact, and the island's administration, as we have seen, was made more cohesive. Ironically, both policies led to much the same problems for the post-colonial legatees of the British. The second feature – and here there was greater similarity in the policies pursued in the two colonial territories – was an increase in the elements of ethnic and religious diversity in the colonial political structure. Bringing the Sinhalese areas of the littoral (not to mention the Tamil areas) within the island polity thus meant the introduction of a large and powerful Christian minority into a Buddhist society; bringing the Tamil dominated Jaffna peninsula and its peripheral regions in the northern province into the unified colonial structure contributed another significant element to its ethnic diversity, as did the entry of large numbers of Indians who were mostly Tamils from the southern parts of the *raj*.

Indian traders and money-lenders were an influential element in Sri Lanka's colonial economy, but not on the same scale as in Burma. The crucial issue in Sri Lanka was the political status of the Indians in Sri Lanka, and this arose as early as 1928 when the pathbreaking report of the Donoughmore Commissioners recommended the introduction of universal suffrage, a recommendation that was implemented as early as 1931. Controversies over the political status and voting rights of the Indians brought the two colonial governments – the *raj* and the government of Ceylon – into prolonged and eventually unsuccessful negotiations over the next 15 years or so. In the early 1940s the colonial administrators in the island's colonial administration served as *mediators* between Sri Lankan politicians and the government of the *raj*.

This process of colonial consolidation and integration left behind the legacy of an over-centralized state, a legacy which accounts, in part at least, for the difficulties experienced by post-independence governments in introducing measures for the devolution of power to regional units of administration. In this regard the pattern of colonial administration is a contrast to that of most parts of the British *raj* in the Indian subcontinent, where there was a much greater tolerance of regional and local identities.

The close proximity of the Jaffna region – the core area of Tamil settlement in Sri Lanka – to Tamil Nadu aggravates the difficulties involved in granting any substantial measure of autonomy to the Tamil areas of the north and east of the island, for the Sinhalese in general fear that such autonomy would strengthen separatist sentiment, rather than act as an effective check to it. The close links that were established between Tamil groups, ranging from the moderate Tamil United Liberation Front (TULF) to various separatist groups including the Liberation Tigers of Tamil Eelam (LTTE), and the government and opposition in Tamil Nadu have naturally aggravated the situation, the more so because of the establishment of training camps and bases for Tamil separatist activists from Sri Lanka in Tamil Nadu from the early 1980s. Devolution of power has thus taken on a cross-national dimension in which India's role in Sri Lankan affairs in the 1980s became an acutely divisive one within the country. It explains why the presence of the Indian peace-keeping force in the island during the years 1987 to 1990 proved to be the catalyst of an upsurge of national sentiment directed against India. Memories of invasions from south India in centuries past were invoked to strengthen anti-Indian feeling.

In looking so much into the roots of their history, Sri Lanka's people have been compelled, as recent events have demonstrated so tragically, to relive some of the agonies of that tormented past. This tendency to cherish the past and to yearn for its restoration is not confined to the Sinhalese. It has affected the Tamil minority as well, and forms the basis of their claim to a 'traditional homeland',[16] the successor as they see it of the Jaffna kingdom. But the historical evidence provided by the Tamil advocates of a 'traditional homeland' in support of their claims is so flimsy that only 'true believers' can accept them. Thus the Sinhalese and Tamils (or large and influential numbers of them) meet in the dark recesses of their respective pasts and fight once more the battles of long ago.

CONFLICT RESOLUTION

South Asian conflict resolution has three unusual features. The first is the fact that the Sino-Indian dispute over their common border along the Himalayas is *sui generis*. It is a major international dispute, and one that has led to war once (in 1962) and brought the two countries to the brink of hostilities on other occasions. Over the years conflict management has been a matter of bilateral negotiations, and very seldom one of third-party mediation. In the wake of the 1962 war between India and China, a group from the non-aligned nations movement gathered in Colombo under the then Sri Lankan Prime Minister Mrs Bandaranaike's leadership in an effort at mediation. It did not meet with much success. The pattern of conflict management on the Sino-Indian conflict will continue to be bilateral rather than multilateral. The Sino-Indian dispute over the Himalayan border has links with other disputes. One that is purely South Asian is between India and Pakistan over Kashmir.

The other has the potential to bring India and Bangladesh into disputes with Burma.

Second, the principal asymmetrical feature of the South Asian political system, the overwhelming dominance of India, makes multilateral negotiation over issues that involve India's interests and concerns virtually impossible. The negotiating process is essentially bilateral, and where India's interests are involved, intrinsically unequal. The exception, of course, is the critically important South Asian conflict, that between India and Pakistan over Kashmir. It has led to war between the two countries on three separate occasions, and remains a potentially dangerous flashpoint that could disturb not merely the peace of the region but of the world. This dispute, above all, keeps arms spending in India and Pakistan at enormously high levels, and commits both to the development of nuclear weapons and the maintenance of massive defence establishments, all of which consume resources which could be put to better use in programmes of poverty alleviation in both countries. It also prevents the development of a common South Asian defence policy.

Mediation and conflict management in this dispute have been attempted at three levels, beginning first of all with the United Nations. Indeed, the capacity for conflict resolution of the newly created UN was put to the test as early as 1947-48 in the dispute between India and Pakistan in Kashmir. Since then there have been numerous Security Council resolutions on Kashmir, and even today the UN maintains a peace-keeping presence on the cease-fire line. There have been third-party mediations, especially by the Soviet Union in 1965, as well as bilateral negotiations between the two countries since 1971-2. But none of these have brought the conflict anywhere near resolution.

The policy of benign (or not so benign) neglect which India has pursued since the early 1970s now faces a severe test in a changed situation in Kashmir through a new development, the stirrings of a national self-determination movement among Kashmiri Muslims. It is a movement that has within it the potential to undermine the territorial integrity of both India and Pakistan. This crucially important new development has two facets: the Kashmir Muslims have begun to look beyond Pakistan, to Afghanistan, Iran and the Middle East; second, the forces of democracy and nationalism that led to the collapse of the Soviet Union and the communist states of Central and Eastern Europe are at work in Kashmir. *Diaspora* Kashmiri groups in the West, especially in the United States, have succeeded in internationalizing this issue, as they struggle to win influence in the US House of Representatives and the Senate.

The end of the Cold War would normally have made it easier to evolve a satisfactory set of proposals, bilaterally, to begin a resolution of this conflict, but the new factor of Kashmiri nationalism makes such a resolution less likely today. The problem, in fact, has a new manifestation, a combination of ethnicity and nationalism which makes resolution more difficult than ever before.

We turn next to the third important feature of South Asian conflict resolution: the internal conflicts, the ethnic and religious conflicts of South Asia, especially those in India, Sri Lanka and Pakistan, and we confront one of the crucial issues in the theory and practice of conflict resolution, the difficulties inherent in the resolution of conflicts involving ethnicity and politicized religion. In many of these conflicts, responses and reactions to colonial rule have affected the thinking and behaviour of ethnic and religious groups in their rivalries and, after independence, in their tensions, as some sought redress of historic grievances, and others to protect hard-won advantages from erosion by new policies. The extent, duration and the levels of violence and impact of these on the political structures and institutions in these countries during the course of these conflicts have varied greatly. All these countries have endured very high levels of violence ranging from sporadic but deadly terrorist attacks to virtual civil war, or sustained guerrilla warfare in parts of each country.

Problems of identity, national and/or ethnic, appear in high relief in all these disputes. Indeed the issue of conflicting identities is the central theme.

Many of the conflicts have been internationalized to a greater or lesser degree either by affected minority groups within the country, by *diaspora* elements living in voluntary or involuntary exile and working in association with representatives of the minority at home, or by interested external agencies ranging from neighbouring states to prestigious international non-governmental organizations. India insists that the Punjab dispute is an internal problem and has resisted all efforts on the part of the Sikh minority to internationalize it. Even so, the Indian government has conceded – for instance in its well-known *White Paper* on the Punjab crisis published in 1984 – that 'external forces, with deep-rooted interest in the disintegration of India ...' had a role in exacerbating the tensions within Punjab. Although the 'external forces' officially identified are the Sikh *diaspora* groups in North America and Western Europe and especially the separatist groups among them, Pakistan is often seen and criticized as the principal source of external support for Sikh separatist groups operating in Punjab.

As in other conflict situations in other parts of the world, there are two approaches to the management of social conflict: structural and cultural. The first of these emphasizes the importance of political and/or institutional change as the means of resolving conflict, and its principal underlying assumption is that change and progress are facilitated best by devising new political structures and institutions or revitalizing existing ones to serve this new purpose.[17] At the political level the structural approach emphasizes negotiations and a search for compromise between political representatives of the groups in conflict. In contrast the cultural approach emphasizes the need for reconciliation between communities in conflict, through mutual understanding and shared responsibility. It operates at the level of the community, concentrates on relationships between communities in conflict and emphasizes the importance of non-governmental community relations' organizations in the processes of reconciliation.[18]

This disjunction in practical approaches to conflict resolution has its parallel in two clear strands of thought in conflict resolution theory: one which emphasizes the need for negotiation, bargaining on the sharing of power and emphasizing the need for compromise; and the other which concentrates on communication, relationships and mutual problem-solving as the basis for long-lasting resolution.

It would be true to say that the first of these, the structural approach, has been preferred to the cultural approach in the resolution of South Asian ethnic conflicts. But a review of the peace accords that Rajiv Gandhi negotiated in the Punjab, Assam and Sri Lanka leaves us in little doubt about the formidable difficulties that confront mediators seeking to resolve ethnic conflicts, especially where these have persisted over long periods of time.[19] Indeed, ethnic conflict is less amenable to meditation than other conflicts, including conflicts between states.[20] In many cases – Punjab and Sri Lanka are good examples – there is a multiplicity of interested and conflicting parties, as well as divided authority on one or more sides, all of which make it difficult to reach agreement, or to make an agreement stick once it has been reached. Besides, leaders of extremist groups – including some of the factions of the Akali Dal in Punjab or the LTTE and many of its rivals in Sri Lanka – see few gains in a peaceful outcome, and have little or no interest in the give and take of mediation. External forces with a stake in the outcome – India in the case of Sri Lanka – are complicating factors. Generally the principal sources of intractability in South Asia's ethnic conflicts have been indigenous forces rather than external allies and mentors.

There is also the 'mediation-with-muscle' aspect of the structural approach of resolution theory and practice. In Sri Lanka, as in Punjab, the Indian army was used in a calculated demonstration of military power to impose the will of the Indian government in support of what were seen to be India's national and strategic interests. The difference was that in Sri Lanka the use of the Indian army followed the signing of an accord and flowed from its clauses, while in Punjab the accord itself had to deal with the consequences that flowed from the army's intervention. In both instances the use of the army did little to resolve the conflict; on the contrary, the consequences were well-nigh disastrous for India's own national interests, and not least for the two leaders who ordered the resort to force. Mrs Gandhi was assassinated by her Sikh bodyguards within a few months of Operation Blue Star, as the army assault on Amritsar's Golden Temple was called; Rajiv Gandhi was assassinated nearly four years after he sent the Indian army to the north and east of Sri Lanka, an assassination which was carried out by the LTTE to avenge the deaths caused by the Indian army in Jaffna and elsewhere in the north and east of the island.

The use of the Indian army in Punjab on that fateful occasion was a purely internal matter for the Indian state; and for which there were some precedents in India's recent history. There were very few precedents in international politics for the decision to use an army in an attempt to resolve an ethnic conflict in a neighbouring state. One such precedent was the Indian intervention in East Pakistan which led to the creation of Bangladesh, and the other was the Turkish intervention in Cyprus. These were unilateral decisions of the two governments, India and Turkey. In contrast, the use of the Indian army in the north and east of Sri Lanka had the support of the Sri Lankan government and of its president at that time, J.R. Jayewardene.

The structuralist facet of conflict resolution has very little to show in its endeavour to resolve South Asian conflicts. The cultural facet, in contrast, has not been given much chance. It may not be of much use in the resolution of the Ayodhya temple crisis,[21] now that it has been transformed by recent events into a major cleavage in the Indian polity, but it has its uses in handling the simmering conflict at Buddha Gaya. There does seem to be little prospect of the structural facet of conflict resolution being able to cope with such a problem. Indeed such quintessentially identity-related issues are best handled through the cultural approach. The only way to address such a problem is through a process of negotiation and bargaining, realistically aiming at a compromise solution. Here political skills have to be reinforced by an overt recognition of the salience of cultural factors in conflicting assertions of identity.

We turn now to a brief analysis of two significant themes that need to be given high priority in any forward planning by South Asian political leaders and administrators, the first of which are potential conflicts over the sharing of scarce natural resources, and the second, a framework of policy or an identification of policy options on the problem of refugees and displaced persons.

We begin with negotiations over the use of scarce natural resources – water and irrigation facilities. In the context of a massive increase of population in most countries of South Asia, pressure on scare water resources is almost certain to become as combustible an issue here as it is in the Tigris-Euphrates basins. In fact the situation could become more dangerous here because of the scale of the population problem. Bangladesh, for instance, with twice Sri Lanka's land area has six times Sri Lanka's population. Thus, in the last decade of the twentieth century and in the early years of the twenty-first, disputes over the sharing or use of natural resources, river waters for instance, can be as contentious an issue as disputes over purely strategic considerations. Indeed the two – natural resources and strategic considerations – are often linked. With regard to this there is a major achievement, the Indus valley treaty of 1960 between India and Pakistan, negotiated through the good offices of the World Bank.

What is essential today after more than three decades of the treaty is a fresh examination of the issues it was designed to handle, keeping in mind population increase in both countries and the need to conserve water resources for the benefit of users in both. In the east, the sharing of water resources of the Ganges and the Brahmaputra is even more complex because three countries are involved: Nepal, India and Bangladesh. One needs to add a fourth if the generation and efficient transmission of hydro-electric power is considered: Bhutan. The negotiation of a multilateral treaty between India, Bangladesh, Nepal and Bhutan over the use of the waters of the Ganges-Brahmaputra basin and its power resources for the benefit of all these countries should be placed high on the list of priorities for South Asian politicians and administrators.[22] This region contains over 400 million desperately poor people. By the early twenty-first century water is certain to become a scarcer resource than it is today because the population will have more than doubled. Disputes over the sharing of water could lead to acute political tensions unless measures are taken now on a multilateral basis to resolve the problem before it becomes any worse.

The current situation in the former Yugoslavia and Central and Eastern Europe has focused attention on a phenomenon that has long been familiar in South Asia, the question of refugees. Refugee flows stem from a number of factors, the most obvious being some calamitous political event, a civil war or invasion; second, the possibility, indeed the near certainty given the population explosion in many parts of South Asia, of illicit or illegal immigration to neighbouring states, such as for example Bangladeshis to India, and Nepalis to India and Bhutan. Since most countries in South Asia have yet to take adequate measures to contain population growth, the enormous pressure on an already inadequate labour market will drive people to take their chances through migration. Third, there is also the recent appearance of Muslims from the Arakan region of Burma/Myanmar in Bangladesh. People who are threatened on account of their religious or political beliefs, or even their ethnic identity, have fled since time immemorial. The situation in South Asia, most parts of which are already overcrowded, calls for long-range efforts to contain such potential movements of refugees or illegal immigrants. Once they have entered, policies have to be devised to protect and assist refugees and illegal immigrants, and to prepare them for one of three options: repatriation, absorption through a policy of integration with the local community, or where possible resettlement in a third country. With regard to this problem, conflict resolution calls for regional harmonization of policies, through bilateral as well as multilateral processes of negotiation, in short an urgent task for SAARC.

NOTES

1. See Partha S. Ghosh, *Cooperation and Conflict in South Asia* (New Delhi: Manohar, and Urmila: Phadnis, 1989); and *Ethnicity and Nation-Building in South Asia* (New Delhi: Sage, 1989).
2. The other source of supply was, of course, Chinese labour from southern China.
3. In both countries this problem is now a minor issue. The Burmese took a much tougher stand against their Indian minority than Sri Lanka, where a settlement was reached after long drawn-out negotiations.
4. On the effects of the Afghan conflict on Pakistan, see M. Isphani, 'Pakistan: Dimensions of Insecurity', *Adelphi Papers*, 246 (London: Brassey's for the International Institute for Strategic Studies, 1990); and Tom Rogers, 'Harbouring Instability: Pakistan and the Displacement of Afghans', in K.M. de Silva and R.J. May (eds), *The Internationalization of Ethnic Conflict* (London: Pinter for the ICES, 1991), pp. 58-75.
5. For discussion of this important theme, see Prasenjit Duara, 'The New Politics of Hinduism', *The Wilson Quarterly* XV, 3, 1991, pp. 42-52; Ainslee T. Embree, *Utopias in Conflict: Religion and Nationalism in Modern India* (Berkeley, CA: University of California Press, 1990); R.E. Frykenberg, 'The Emergence of Modern Hinduism, as a Concept and as Institution', in Gunther D. Sontheimer and Herman Kulke (eds), *Hinduism Reconsidered* (Delhi: Manohar, 1989), pp. 29-49; Bruce D. Graham, *Hindu Nationalism and Indian Politics: The Origin and Development of the Bharatiya Jana Sangh* (Cambridge: Cambridge University Press, 1990); Romila Tharpar, 'Imagined Religious Communities? Ancient India and the Modern Search for Hindu Identities', *Modern Asian Studies*, vol. 23, 2, 1989, pp. 209-31; and Romila Tharpar, 'Syndicated Moksha', *Seminar*, 313, September 1985, pp. 14-22.

6. See B. Chaudhuri, 'Ethnic Conflict in the Chittagong Hill Tracts of Bangladesh', in S.W.R. de A. Samarasinghe and R. Coughlan, *Economic Dimensions of Ethnic Conflict* (London: Pinter for the ICES, 1991), pp. 135-55.
7. Guy Wint, *The British in Asia* (London: Faber, 1947), p. 22.
8. Steven A. Hoffman, *India and the China Crisis* (Berkeley, CA: University of California Press, 1990), p. 25.
9. Steven A. Hoffman, *India and the China Crisis*, pp. 25-6.
10. See Alistair Lamb, *Kashmir: A Disputed Legacy, 1846-1990* (Hertfordshire: Roxford Books, 1991); and R.G.C. Thomas (ed.), *Perspective on Kashmir* (Boulder, CO: Westview, 1992).
11. See Richard Sisson and Leo E. Rose, *War and Secession: India, Pakistan and the Creation of Bangladesh* (Berkeley, CA: University of California Press, 1990).
12. On the problems of Assam, see Myron Weiner, *Sons of the Soil: Migration and Ethnic Conflict in India* (Princeton, NJ: Princeton University Press, 1978); and Myron Weiner, 'Assam: Coming of Age', *India Today*, 15 January 1986, pp. 22-35.
13. Michael Adas, *The Burma Delta: Economic Development and Social Change in an Asian Rice Frontier, 1852-1914* (Madison, WI: University of Wisconsin Press, 1974); and Guy Wint, *The British in Asia*, pp. 95-103.
14. The fate of the Indians in Burma in the 1940s is discussed in H. Tinker, *Separate and Unequal: India and the Indians in the British Commonwealth, 1920-1950* (London: Hurst, 1976), pp. 340-2, 359-67.
15. See Maureen Aung-Thwin and Thant Myint-U, 'The Burmese Ways to Socialism', *Third World Quarterly*, 13, 1, 1972, pp. 67-75.
16. For discussion of this, see K.M. de Silva, 'Separatism in Sri Lanka: "Traditional Homelands" of the Tamils', in Ralph R. Premdas, *et al.*, *Secessionist Movements in Comparative Perspective* (London: Pinter for the ICES, 1990), pp. 32-47.
17. For a statement of the views of this school see I.W. Zartman, *Ripe for Resolution: Conflict and Intervention in Africa* (New York: Oxford University Press, 1989); and I.W. Zartman and Maureen Berman, *The Practical Negotiator* (New Haven, CT: Yale University Press, 1982).
18. See E. Azar, *The Management of Protracted Social Conflict* (Aldershot, Hants: Dartmouth, 1989); E. Azar and John W. Burton (eds), *International Conflict Resolution* (Sussex: Wheatsheaf, 1986); and John W. Burton, *Resolving Deep-Rooted Conflict: A Handbook* (Lanham, MD: University Press of America, 1987).
19. See K.M. de Silva and S.W.R. de A. Samarasinghe, 'Introduction', in *Peace Accords and Ethnic Conflict* (London: Pinter for ICES, 1993), pp. 1-15.
20. For a somewhat different perspective on this, see Marc Howard Ross, 'Ethnic Conflict and Dispute Management', in Austin Sarat and Susan Silbey (eds), *Studies in Law, Politics and Society*, vol. 12 (Greenwich, CT: JAI Press, 1992).

21. On this dispute see S. Gopal (ed.), *The Anatomy of a Confrontation: The Babri Masjid Ramjanmabhumi Issue* (Delhi: Vikas, 1990); and Prasenjith Duara, 'The New Politics of Hinduism', *Wilson Quarterly*, XV, 3, 1991, p. 42.

22. For a stimulating discussion of these issues see B.G. Verghese, *Waters of Hope: Himalaya-Ganga Development and Cooperation for a Billion People* (New Delhi: IBH, 1990).

14

The Regional Dimensions of the Causes of Conflicts: Latin America

Makram Haluani

INTRODUCTION

Latin America, like any other geographic and cultural region of the planet, has its share of domestic and inter-state conflicts,[1] but a general review of the frequency and intensity of both domestic and inter-state conflagrations in Latin America show that it is less beset by the phenomenon than other parts of the world, including the highly industrialized North. By certain standards, Latin America seems to have less widespread domestic strife and international conflicts, with their predictable results, as detailed below.

According to a recent study of international conflicts that occurred between 1945 and 1985, only 23 out of 269 of those occurring throughout the world took place in Latin America.[2] Of the 14 countries and regions around the world where the United Nations' peace-keeping forces are active, El Salvador is the only Latin America country that is hosting these forces (530 observers).[3] The international relief group *Médecins sans Frontières* has mentioned ten areas around the world in which entire populations are at 'immediate risk' from war, famine, disease and displacement, yet Peru is the only Latin American country mentioned in this report.[4] Of the estimated 18 million refugees and displaced persons world-wide, Latin America accounts for fewer than 1 million, basically from the Central American region.[5] The Human Development Index (HDI), created by the United Nations Development Programme, defines the average deprivation index on the basis of a 1000-point scale. Countries such as Japan and Canada have an average of 0.983 and 0.982 respectively, whereas Sierra Leone shows an HDI of 0.065 and Guinea 0.045. In so far as the Latin American countries are concerned, the HDI ranges between 0.864 (Chile) and 0.489 (Guatemala).[6] The figures for the estimated presence of land-mines in all the regions of the world range from 67 to 110 million. Latin America (Central America, Colombia, Peru and the Malvinas/Falkland Islands) contains between 300,000 and one million land-mines.[7] Latin American countries have fewer incentives to import weapons than other regions in the world, as shown in Table 14.1.[8]

TABLE 14.1   *Number of Major Weapon Systems per Region*

	1975-1976	1982-1983	1988-1989
Middle East and North Africa	29,291	50,637	58,840
Sub-Saharan Africa	3,803	10,627	13,511
South Asia	6,257	8,352	10,465
East Asia	13,735	24,193	31,726
Latin America and the Caribbean	5,091	8,935	12,087

According to Herbert K. Tillema, Latin America experienced few overt foreign military interventions (34 out of a world-wide total of 591) between 1945 and 1985, mainly from the United States.[9] Moreover, having gained their political independence starting in 1824, Latin American conflicts have strong ingredients of domestic causes and motives for both their internal and inter-state conflicts.[10] Colonialism does appear as a historically important factor in the *modus operandi* of their political systems, but as a powerful remnant of the past that has yet to be overcome.

Another set of causes of conflict has its origins in the presence and actions of the United States, its commercial and geopolitical interests in the Latin American region, and in its hegemonic designs.[11]

The aim of this chapter is to study the nature and scope of conflicts currently occurring in Latin America. It also aims to provide a typology of conflicts in and between Latin American countries in order to clarify the nature of these conflicts and the potential for escalation or settlement. The conclusions attempt to offer a variety of possible remedies for each kind of conflict in contemporary Latin America.

The typology is mainly based on the theme of conflicts, and not on a country-by-country basis. Latin American countries, in spite of conspicuous, national-specific and individual political system-related differences, have far more similarities than differences in their domestic conflagrations. From a conceptual point of view it is, therefore, quite feasible and empirically practical to speak of Latin American problems as a phenomenon generally applicable to single countries and regions. The common cultural and histori-cal heritage that all Latin American nations share is strongly influenced by their colonial history and makes such a typology methodologically feasible and didactically desirable.

POLITICS AND POLITICAL SYSTEM: MOTHER OF ALL CONFLICTS

The very historic nature and contemporary conditions and functions of current Latin American political systems lend themselves to create sources of various societal tensions among the different domestic actors. The historically based deficiencies of Latin American political systems are entrenched in the lack of institutionally raised and protected, truly democratic, political and social values.[12] Personal traits in government, whether local or national, are clearly felt in every Latin American system, and the strong presidential systems owe their dominance of the executive over parliamentary and judicial branches to these personal and *caudillista* characteristics of political life in Latin America, where institutions and values are more subordinated to the personal will and interests of the powerful political, socio-economic and/or military elites than to the general will of society, thus weakening state-building and governance processes. Perhaps this political idiosyncrasy can be traced to the very origins of the system of political authority first established by the Spanish conquistadors. Unlike the first immigrants to the North American region, the Spanish conquistadors came to South, and later Central America on a military mission, with horses, arms, armour and gunpowder, to set up authority based on military prowess in order to further the material interests of the Spanish crown. Their mission was not to find a new home far away from religious persecution, as was the case of the English immigrants in North America. Spanish rule in Latin America was based, from the very beginning, on the principle of exploitation of the mineral wealth which was thought (and later found) to be present in the South American El Dorado. The civilian, family-based and new-home-finding orientation in North America created a different political system. In Central and South America, Spanish rule emphasized the military-dominance aspect in and of national politics, making it an omnipresent factor in shaping the destinies of the Latin American countries.[13]

In the wars of independence, the military once again played a dominant role in fostering and winning them. All Latin American countries, with the exception of Brazil, experienced the process of independence from Spain as a traumatic, military engagement and cruel conflict, marking the various national identities with the legacy of disputes, competition and armed conflict as a viable and reliable means of asserting their own interests and political will. Hence, the *caudillista* and militarist/personalist traits in Latin American political systems were created by both the Spanish rule and by the wars of independence, in which there were relatively few civilian leaders and heroes.

Aside from the individual aspect in politics and the dominance of the military elite, Latin American political systems suffered from the lack of a systematic and effective use of political accountability by those holding office, whether imposed or elected, towards the general public or other institutions. In spite of the division-of-powers' (checks-and-balances') system inspired by the North American example, the presidential/executive branch has been blessed from the beginning with extraordinary powers, despite the fact that almost all constitutions call for an equal division of powers among the executive, parliamentary and judicial branches of government. The president-centred power came about more from practice than from the theory and spirit of the constitutions, and the way in which presidents have exercised their powers has helped enhance them at the expense of the other two branches.[14] It seems that the main purpose of entrenching the presidential powers was to ensure a feeble state, making it a tool in the hands of the elites, who never had to fear the state as an obstacle to their rule.

This explains the loss of parliamentary and judicial authority *vis-à-vis* the power of the president which, over the years, helped weaken any institutionalized accountability mechanisms. Even the political parties that began emerging earlier this century, in the 1920s and 1930s, opted to side with the presidential branch and mostly neglected their initial role as correctors of public policy. The combination of the lack of institutionalized, widely accepted, respected and protected values, plus the lack of strong and reliable accountability mechanisms, left a vacuum in society over which forces would act as a counterweight to the presidential, often autocratic, system of government in Latin American countries. These personal traits, and the weakness of control mechanisms, left a clear stamp on the political system in Latin America: the vested interests of influential elites seem to prevail over rational, public interest-oriented policies, and inefficient management of government affairs are fixtures of these political systems.

Very little guidance was expected and actually came from the United States in the way of orientation on democratic pluralistic systems. The numerous tensions and rivalries between Latin American countries moved the region even farther away from Simon Bolivar's dream of a 'United States of Latin America', paving the way for the United States' hegemonic control over foreign policies, especially in Central America.[15]

The multiple problems that beset contemporary Latin American societies have not only highlighted the inefficiencies of political systems and a style of politics both inherited from the last century and reinforced by the contemporary ruling elites, but they have been compounded by gradual and considerable population growth and a subsequent increase in this population's ideal and material expectations. The traditional power elites, comprised of conservative oligarchies, the Church and the even more conservative military, began facing a changing society more aware of its rights and its capacity to influence public policy in its favour.

The 1930s saw the rise of non-traditional political forces such as the leftist political parties and unions, the emergence of the paternalistic states, a less conservative and more socially aware Catholic Church, and a more professional military that was aware of the changing political environment in Latin America.[16] The economy was now viewed as the main driving force behind the desired societal progress, and as industrialization and modernization coincided with the elites' interests, they became the official and popularly accepted national goals. Work and material prosperity were now more important than ideal values. Ethnicity was not a pressing issue for the native and indigenous Latin Americans or for the growing number of immigrants from a Europe ravaged by the Second World War.

The 1950s and 1960s witnessed the surge in Marxist thought and doctrines. The Cuban revolution and the creation of communist parties, coupled with the Cold War and East-West confrontation, turned Latin America into another arena where the United States and the former Soviet Union were each offering development models. Because of the problems and inefficiencies of their political and economic systems, the Latin American countries now began facing armed, leftist insurgences in rural areas, specifically in Mexico, Central America, Colombia, Venezuela, Peru, Ecuador, Bolivia, Brazil and Chile.[17] The insurgency's aims, although slightly different in each of these countries, pursued one same general objective: more equitable distribution of wealth and land. The fault-lines in the political systems often became actual armed conflicts, of civil-war magnitude, as was the case in Guatemala and, later, Nicaragua.

The crushing of the rural guerrillas, aided by technical assistance from the United States, provided through the School of the Americas in Fort Gulick, Panama, gave way to the rise of urban guerrillas, also with leftist tendencies and the same objective, in Uruguay, Argentina, Brazil and, to a lesser extent, Colombia and Chile. The conflicts that the Latin American countries now faced proved to be less ideological in substance than claimed by the governments being challenged. The instability and problems that the governments claimed were caused by the insurgencies persisted even after the revolutionary rebels were subdued, proving that these problems were inherent in the system itself and not a product of leftist agitation.[18] The rise of the urban guerrillas paved the way for military dictatorships that proved ruthless in 'pacifying' their respective countries. The systematic and outrageous violation of the most fundamental of human rights in Latin America began in the name of national and state security. Somehow, the government-leftist guerrilla conflicts overshadowed the deeper problems and inadequacies of the political systems in Latin America. It gave the governments an opportunity to sidestep development projects and claim greater legitimacy in order to combat 'destabilizing' factors.[19] The actions of the right-wing death squads in Central America, Uruguay and Argentina only intensified the domestic conflict and underlined the urgency of human rights as a political issue.

The gradual return of all Latin American countries to democratic rule was achieved by a set of both internal and external factors. On one hand, the domestic scene included the necessity for the military regimes to give up power because their capability to govern effectively was coming to an end. The mounting problems and the military's inability to solve them made their retreat from power inevitable. Moreover, pressure from the Roman Catholic Church and human rights groups, as well as from moderate political parties, set the stage for the withdrawal of the military from active politics. On the other hand, the United States applied diplomatic and economic pressure to accelerate the democratization process.[20] The Central American oligarchies were the last of the Latin American elites to accept democratization, and they did so at a time when leftist opposition to their rule had been virtually decimated by right-wing death-squad activities. Yet the inflexibility of Central American 'ruling families' when it came to implementing a more equitable distribution of land and wealth is the main source of domestic political friction, with great potential for full-fledged and renewed armed conflict. The political system, still responding primarily to the interests of the economic and political elites, is proving inept at accommodating the legitimate interests of the burgeoning middle class, let alone those of the larger lower class.[21]

The end of the Cold War era left a huge vacuum in the friend-or-foe black-or-white mentality of many Latin American regimes, especially the military elites. This took place while the 'lost decade' was approaching its end in Latin America. The 1980s were known as the 'lost decade' because of the financial burden caused by the rolling back of debt negotiations and the painful toll they took on the subsidy policies of almost all Latin American governments.[22]

Neo-liberal economic policies and privatization of state-run enterprises are now the slogan of the 1990s. The rapid growth of the urban population in all Latin American countries and the rise in their material aspirations have put tremendous pressure on their respective governments to improve public services, economic efficiency and output, day-to-day and long-term management of public administration and funds. Themes like administrative efficiency and integrity, corruption, human rights, decentralization of the national administration and strengthening of municipal authority, and better social welfare programmes, among others, are the main and most pressing concerns of the vast majority in Latin America.[23] The fault-lines that contemporary democracies cannot and/or will not be able to cure have considerable potential to turn into socially explosive issues. Ideologies no longer matter in Latin America. No society, except for Cuba, questions the neo-liberal and market economy as the main and only tenet of the nation. But 'civil society' in Latin America has become strong and gained awareness of its ability to influence public policies. Aside from ethnicity and unresolved military-civilian issues, social discontent is the one issue that may challenge the democratization process and turn into violent conflictual confrontation between the general populace, be it middle or lower class, and its government.[24]

TYPOLOGY OF CONFLICTS IN LATIN AMERICA

Noting that Latin American countries have more similarities than differences in the spirit and *modus operandi* of their respective political systems, it is quite feasible to draw up a general typology of the conflicts that are currently present in their domestic domain, on the governmental as well as the societal basis.

Domestic Conflicts

This sphere of tensions can be either a people-versus-government or a societal sector-versus-societal sector confrontation, or a specific elite's challenge to the regime. The domestic conflict area is basically a politically motivated confrontation, possibly with an ideological undertone. The roots of political, domestic conflicts lie in the organization of the government, public policies, the state and how they function. In this respect, the efficiency of state policies, the degree to which they fulfil the demands of society, the transparency of the decision-making process ('black box') and how responsive they are to new demands, all determine the state's legitimacy and credibility in the eyes of the population and, hence, the integrity and functionality of the regime.[25] The extremely complex nature of contemporary Latin American societies is characterized by the following aspects: the growing power of the middle class and its social movements as a limited alternative to the discredited political parties; the changing political role of the military in domestic politics; the influence of the private sector and the labour unions on economic policies; the reintroduction of the Catholic

Church into domestic politics; the increasingly sophisticated nature of democratization; and the fact that the lower classes (now between 26 per cent and 42 per cent of the population of any Latin American country) can exercise a certain degree of power on the outcome of voting. Moreover, the fact that the informal economy is the backbone of the lower classes in Latin America implies that any policy that infringes on the benefits of this parallel economy would literally mean a violent social explosion. The very nature, function and legitimacy of the regime determines the kind of political relationships that exist among the various societal forces and between the government and those forces.

We can divide the domestic conflict map into three different spheres:

Political Dissidence
In view of the multiple fault-lines and deficiencies in the current democratic regimes throughout Latin America (the only exceptions being Cuba and Haiti), the possibility that public policies will be conceived and carried out in a way that is unbalanced, and thus unsatisfactory for one societal group or another, is quite high.

We can argue that all armed conflicts, especially active insurgencies and military *coups d'état*, arise from political dissidence on the part of one specific, mobilized and sufficiently conflict-empowered group, whether organized or not, against the regime.

In contemporary Latin America, we can list four aspects that offer sufficient basis for dissidence and for potentially violent political conflicts. First, military-civilian relations have improved greatly during the last decade, but budgetary allocation policies and arms procurement decisions can still cause a great deal of tension and friction between financially hard-pressed civilian governments and a military high command that is eager to protect the corporate sense of mission and professional price of their high- and mid-level officers and troops. It cannot be argued that the Latin American military are institutionally armed right-wing societal forces that follow orders from Washington to quell leftist sentiments and policies in the region. Actually, the Latin American military's patriotic and nationalistic sense of mission has been put to the test often enough against the US's 'big stick' approach to the region. The modern, professional military's appraisal of the political landscape is one of discontent with civilian politicians who have corrupted the system and with it the top-ranking officers, while they continue to use the country's resources as their private cheque-book.[26] The military's record for doing just that, and for flagrant disregard of human rights, helps to lower the military's sense of being on moral high ground. Yet the indignation felt by the military at the civilian politician's inept handling of the nation's affairs and fiscal policies may well give way to violent action against a given democratic regime. Venezuela's two attempted *coups* in 1992 are good examples of this type of conflictual situation.

Second, the faulty democratic practices are tarnishing the image of democracy as a viable political system and way of life. Electoral frauds and frequent as well as unpunished human rights' violations are undermining the legitimacy and the practical functions of democratic regimes, especially the newly installed ones in Latin America. The 'old democracies', such as those in Mexico, Colombia and Venezuela, have perfected the mechanisms for defending and entrenching themselves. Meanwhile, the new democracies have a more difficult mission to accomplish, in that they have to erase the vices of both the past and the present at the same time. They must successfully cope with the maze of problems they face and build a good, lasting name for democracy.[27] Faulty democracies have a strong potential to cause severe social tensions that can quickly turn into violent, widespread actions against governments. Latin Americans do not question the wisdom and practical necessity of living in a democracy. But they do question the specific kind of democracy to which they are subjected. The missing mechanisms for accountability and the ease with which important politicians or members of socio-economic elites commit illegal actions cause a sort of collective anger that may well be channelled into violent actions against the regime. Still, the impeachment of Brazilian President Fernando Collor de Mello in 1992, and the charges of corruption against Venezuela's former Presidents Jaime Lusinchi and Carlos Andres Perez in 1993, prove that Latin American democracies have self-correcting mechanisms and do use them.

Third, political and administrative corruption is an omnipresent theme and issue in all Latin American societies. As for faulty, deficient democracies, corruption is a problem that affects the welfare and the integrity of the system as a whole, but unlike corruption in highly industrialized countries, this process in Latin America, much like other regions of the developing world, thrives on public funds.[28] Individual officials dip into public funds to finance private projects or to achieve illicit private wealth. The funds are usually transferred abroad, causing a secondary harmful phenomenon: capital flight. In the developed world, private (industry) funds are used to assure legislative compliance by political parties, thus securing an almost 'healthy' recycling of surplus financial assets, since the funds stay in the country and are somehow put back into the national system of economic circulation. Meanwhile, corruption in Latin America drains public funds with no favourable effect whatsoever on the national economy. It involves funds that are taken out of national circulation to benefit just one individual or family, usually abroad. Moreover, little accountability is possible since the beneficiaries of this kind of corruption manage to say out of reach of the affected country's judicial system. The accumulation of corruption scandals and the constant reminder that a considerable part of the fiscal misery that Latin American countries experience stems from uncontrolled and unpunished corruption, provides a strong potential for social unrest and even violent, conflictual mass behaviour.

Fourth, necessary but ineptly implemented economic policies represent another potential for extremist political polarization as a first step towards a conflict situation. The costs of structural adjustments cannot be entirely eliminated but they can be limited in scope and duration. The 'lost decade' of the 1980s was burdened by a monstrous collective debt of US $330 billion by 1982. In 1993, the debt stood at $420 billion, yet it is not quite so much of a problem. Creditors accepted a scheme to ease interest payments and most debtor nations are back in the international financial community. The debt payment plans are forcing all Latin American countries to apply fiscal austerity measures, to cut back on state subsidies for public services and to offer state-run money-losing enterprises for privatization.[29] This switch from paternalistic, protectionist, state-interventionist policies in the economy is opening up the Latin American markets for world trade and for international competition, making investments and private-sector projects more likely. Still, government policies affect the vast majority of the population because the national, as well as the regional and international private sectors active in Latin America cannot absorb the growing number of job seekers crowding the employment markets. How government regulates inflation, US dollar exchange rates, control of banking and financial systems, and distribution of products (especially food and basic needs), will decide how the majority of the population, mainly the middle and lower classes, will judge the government's legitimacy and efficiency. The informal economy provides income for an estimated 47 per cent of the Latin America population,[30] and governments that take their responsibilities lightly may well face popular discontent, leading to violent actions such as rioting and looting.

Armed Insurgency

Latin American political history is one of armed insurgencies against both legitimate and illegitimate regimes. The rural and urban guerrilla movements of the 1960s and 1970s have, in some cases, been either crushed, co-opted into the mainstream political establishment or have moved on to form leftist political parties. Not even democratization has brought the traditional oligarchies, especially in El Salvador and Guatemala, to give in to the insurgents' agenda.[31] Unlike Nicaragua, where the Sandinista insurgency's victory in

1979 provided it with the opportunity to implement the policies for which it had fought, the Salvadorean, Guatemalan and, to some extent, the Honduran elites are still resisting domestic and external (US) pressure to accommodate domestic policies for former insurgents. The fact that the traditional elites, including the ultra-conservative military, are reneging on their promises to open up the system and adopt reformist land policies, has convinced the former insurgents that armed conflict is the only viable instrument for imposing their demands on the national agenda. The rekindling of right-wing death squad activities in El Salvador is a strong indication of the elite's unwillingness to accept moderate political players in the national decision-making process,[32] although another cause of this situation is the ongoing extremist bi-polarization of society and the gradual weakening of political and social forces that could assume the role of credible mediators between the antagonists.

In the case of Colombia, the armed insurgency has a long tradition of violence. Yet the high electoral abstention in Colombia, and the meagre popular support for the various, and not at all united, rural guerrilla groups, highlight the Colombians' dissatisfaction with both guerillas and government.[33] It is the relatively ideological undertone that some Colombian insurgents have, especially the National Liberation Army (ELN) and the Armed Forces of the Colombian Revolution (FARC), that keeps them functioning as an ideological platform opposing the system. Four out of five Colombian leftist insurgent groups have laid down their arms and joined the democratic process since 1989. For the enemies of the system, the guerrillas represent an effective way of venting their dissatisfaction. On the other hand, however, Colombian guerrillas have tarnished their reputation for ideological purity by helping the illegal drug cartels protect the processing plants, smuggling routes and airstrips;[34] moreover, Colombian guerrilla activities along the border with Venezuela have been limited to kidnapping wealthy farmers and demanding ransom for their release. Such activities have had a negative effect on their recruiting efforts, which explains the lack of any change in their paramilitary conflict capabilities over the last eight years.

The third active insurgency in Latin America is the *Sendero Luminoso* (Shining Path) in Peru. This movement began in 1980, which means that it is a relatively new phenomenon in the country, and *Sendero's* activities are quite country-specific and have both ideological and ethnic undercurrents. Its charismatic, now captured, leader, Abimael Guzman, combined Maoist doctrine with indigenous elements to form a new type of insurgency in Latin America. The fanaticism of the *Senderistas* can only be explained by the attraction of its ideals and Guzman's charisma and disciplined leadership. So far, *Sendero Luminoso* has cost Peru more than 25,000 lives and $22 billion in material damage. Its members believe that all non-indigenous white Peruvians are foreigners who must be expelled in order to build a new civilization based on indigenous and Maoist-communist values.[35] Hard-core *Senderista* members number between 20,000 and 25,000, most of whom are highly motivated and disciplined, despite the absence of their captured leader. The urban population has little, if any, sympathy for the *Senderistas* or their urban counterparts, the *Tupac Amarus* – the atrocities committed by both the rebels and the Peruvian security forces are alienating them – whereas loyalties are divided among the rural population. *Senderistas* are known to levy taxes on coca leaf growers in the Upper Huallaga Valley region, and to own the coca-processing plants, earning around $50 million a year. Regardless of the fact that some sectors of Peruvian society, especially the rural indigenous population, are attracted by *Sendero*'s ideals, its violent, repressive tactics have been deterring new recruits. It is still capable of disrupting communications and public services, but has proven not to be effective in challenging the standing among Peruvians of the popular president, Alberto Fujimori, who applaud his handling of the legislative branch (suspending the Constitution in April 1992), but are still reeling from the impact of his neo-liberal economic policies: austerity and an end to subsidies. The *Sendero* movement will not be crushed easily. The causes behind its mobilization are too deeply rooted in ethnic and idealistic values to be neutralized by repressive action on the part of the police or army.

Ethnicity-Based Conflicts

It is estimated that there are 675 indigenous groups living in Latin America, either in their own cultural environment or semi-assimilated into contemporary Latin American societies, and 472 of these tribes are known to live in the South American region, while the rest live in Central America and Mexico. Despite popular belief, indigenous groups are not very present in the conflict map of Latin America. They have either been forced to live in areas assigned to them or to semi-integrate into the society around them.[36] However, they do have grievances, and strong ones at that.

Their knowledge of how society works is limited and made use of by those who are integrated. Indians, specifically the Mapuches in Chile, Mayas in Central America and Mexico, and Incas in Peru, take part in social movements to protest and demand better living conditions for themselves. The *Sendero Luminoso* guerrilla group in Peru has a very strong indigenous element. The uprising in the Mexican state of Chiapas in January 1994, spearheaded by the Tzeltal, Tojolaval and Chol Indians, has clearly shown that Indian passivity is a myth. Centuries of neglect, both benign and malevolent, have not subdued the Indians; on the contrary, it has sharpened their sense of social injustice suffered at the hands of the new masters of the continent.[37]

Ethnicity-based conflicts are present because Indians participate in anti-regime revolts or insurgency movements, such as the Guatemalan Revolutionary Organization of the People in Arms (ORPA) or the Chiapas Zapatista Army of National Liberation, and because they live in disputed areas or in regions coveted for their mineral and agricultural wealth. Cases such as those of the Brazilian-Venezuelan Yanomamis, whose territory has been invaded by illegal Brazilian miners (*garimpeiros*), who even maimed as many as 15 Indians in order to frighten them away, are well documented. The Chiapas uprising proved successful because Mexico was extremely sensitive to world public opinion on the eve of its entry into the North American Free Trade Agreement with the United States and Canada. Mexico's vulnerability worked in favour of the Indian insurgents, but not every indigenous group in Latin America has the same advantages as the Chiapas Indians.

Ethnicity-based conflicts would only come about if the ethnic groups' strength and conflict capability were to be enhanced, either from support from other national groups, strong regional and international support, or the sudden weakening of the state. Ethnicity-based movements in Latin America have always been noted for their demands for ethnic corporatism and autonomy to secure their cultural rights, and their participation in sub-national conflicts is conditioned by their numerical and qualitative strength and by the degree of expected success.

Inter-State Conflicts

In the case of inter-state conflicts, Latin America has seen a number of border and territorial disputes that led either to border clashes or full-fledged wars. Examples of border clashes include the Quesada incident between Nicaragua and Costa Rica in 1948, the Mocoran occupation between Honduras and Nicaragua in 1957 (two more incidents of the same kind in 1962 and 1968), and the Qualquiza raids between Ecuador and Peru in 1978, among at least twenty others that occurred between 1945 and 1985.[38] Territorial disputes that ended in wars include the Triple Alliance war of 1864-70 between Paraguay, on one side, and Brazil, Argentina and Uruguay on the other; the Pacific War of 1879-84 between Peru and Bolivia, on one side, and Chile on the other; the Chaco War between Bolivia and Paraguay from 1932-35; and the Soccer War between Honduras and El Salvador in 1969. All Latin American countries have border disputes with their neighbours, whether Latin American or not:[39] Guatemala and Belize, and Venezuela and

Guyana, are two examples of Latin American/non-Latin American border tensions. This issue has a considerable potential for conflictual bellicose behaviour, especially on the part of the Latin American countries involved.

It should be noted in this regard that Latin American countries are no different from others, where governments that are being criticized turn border disputes into issues of national pride in order to rally popular support behind the embattled regime and distract attention for a while from other, pressing domestic problems such as economic hardship or sub-national uprisings. The Snipe Island and Beagle Canal dispute between Argentina and Chile has been used for this purpose. Furthermore, it can be argued that the Argentine military junta's decision to invade the Malvinas/Falkland Islands in 1982 was partly an effort to help the military regain the prestige and legitimacy it had lost in the eyes of the Argentine public with the 'Dirty War' against both real and imagined opponents of their regime. Nevertheless, border disputes, even used to distract attention from the government's ineptitude in dealing with domestic political and/or economic problems, can still ignite conflicts that may lead to military-type confrontations. One deterrent in this case would be the military's unwillingness to become involved in such a conflict in order not to risk losing equipment that may never be replaced because of lack of funds. Military high commands may not be eager for this type of conflict because it could reveal possible technical-professional inadequacies (the Argentines in the Malvinas conflict in 1982) in performing duties for which they claim so much of the national budget. Moreover, some officers view their equipment as a necessary instrument for intimidating civilian politicians or dissidents, or both, and are unwilling to risk losing these tools, which could weaken their position in domestic politics, much less a possible military defeat and the ensuing loss of prestige.

Another possible scenario of inter-state conflicts are spillover effects from domestic strife. Tensions and war-like activities came about between Honduras and El Salvador in 1982 because of Salvadorean guerrilla operations in the border area between the two countries, and the Central American peace process (Contadora Group) was developed in order to contain the civil strife occurring in every country and to prevent it from spilling over into neighbouring countries.[40] This situation reinforces the hypothesis that the Latin American military is mainly viewed as an internal security apparatus that is only capable of containing and controlling national/domestic security challenges, not external ones. On the other hand, inter-state conflicts may arise from natural growth situations, such as unwanted immigration and cross-border population movements, forcing the respective governments to resort to a military solution, concentrating troops in the border areas, and a military face-off that may end up in an actual shooting war.

Transnational Conflictual Issues

The liberalization of the economy has brought about a continental block of nations whose economies no longer recognize borders. All border areas between Latin American countries have developed an economic life of their own, and this economic dynamism has been necessary, considering the extremely central identity and administrative nature of all Latin American countries. The border areas are among the most neglected regions of the countries: the vast areas and the difficult topographic features (rain forests or mountainous regions) lend themselves to a certain degree of physical isolation, especially in the case of the larger countries on the continent. On the other hand, remarkable demographic changes, basically a great increase in the population, compounded by predictably higher economic and material expectations, have pushed the border areas to develop their own economic life with little, if any, guidance from the central authorities. The tendencies for administrative decentralization in Latin American nations derive precisely from their respective governments' acknowledgement of the fact that they can no longer rule from the centre, much less do so effectively, but they still cling to the territories in order to assert sovereignty. Consequently, separatist and autonomy-seeking regions are a potential source for inter-state conflicts since they involve the countries where these movements are active. The emancipation of border regions is a slowly, but vigorously growing process that may cause friction, not only with the respective nation, but with the neighbouring ones as well.

The drug cartels are another example of sources of both domestic and inter-state conflicts. The illegal drug industry (growing, processing, smuggling and marketing) has grown into a vast empire worth billions of US dollars, providing income that would otherwise be unattainable to thousands of peasants in Peru, Bolivia and Colombia, as well as to thousands of other involved in the day-to-day illegal operations.[41] The laundering of illegal drug revenues is becoming another booming financial service industry throughout Latin America, Europe and the United States. Venezuela is known to be a favourite place for laundering money; according to Drug Enforcement Agency (DEA) estimates, some $2 billion were laundered there in 1993. The drug revenues are viewed as a threat to the national security of the Latin American countries involved, because they provide a source of wealth that is not accountable to the state. This wealth can 'buy' the loyalties of individuals that are supposed to serve the country. Drug money is known to have infiltrated all walks of political life: election campaigns; members of parliament; politicians; and state-run institutions. Drug cartels in Colombia provide select social and public services that the government should, but cannot. The cartels are thus operating in competition with the state, making it a structure that is virtually useless for a considerable part of the population. Yet, from a pragmatic viewpoint, governments are somewhat relieved to find that the cartels are providing some of the services that they cannot. Instead of resenting the competition, they regard the cartels as a necessary and somewhat useful nuisance, although they recognize the cartels' potential as a force that can take away their legitimacy. The easing of their burden is the kind of pay-off they are willing to accept despite the price they are paying: loss of legitimacy.

As a source of conflict, illegal drug cartels are an issue, not so much between Latin American governments, but rather between the cartels and the US government. The United States regards drugs as a menace to its society and its national security, so it has therefore been providing financial, technical and intelligence aid to several Latin American governments, specifically the Peruvian, Colombia, Bolivian and Venezuelan authorities. The drug issue was the official motive for the US invasion of Panama in December 1989, and it will certainly be the reason for another confrontation between the US and, possibly, Haiti and Cuba. The United States fears that the cartels are creating impressive financial empires that are not connected with the traditional elites in Latin America, whose fortunes are already tied in with the American financial system. This fear of 'counter-elites', unaccountable to US political and financial power, raises the spectre of political resistance to US influence in the region, backed by the independent economic resources of the cartels. *Dependista* scholars in Latin America point out another reason for US hostility to the cartels: they account for approximately 20 per cent of the US national deficit, as this is the amount that leaves the United States every year to pay for the drugs. The *dependistas* call the cartels 'Latin America's answer to the debt crunch' and the 'only Catholic-Hispanic transnational company in the world'.

CONCLUSIONS

Considering the great complexity of conflict-related issues and factors in all Latin America countries, it would be a daunting task to conceptualize remedies for all of them. Country-specific problems call for country-specific answers. Yet we will attempt to formulate some ideas, in general terms, for the problems addressed in this chapter. At the same time, these suggestions involve areas of Latin American political life that lend themselves to future academic research on the subjects:

a. Better designed and implemented economic policies that aim to ensure more equitable distribution of public goods. Higher and fairer salaries that help reduce the level of administrative corruption.

b. More effective grass-roots organizations within both the middle and lower classes. This will help create stronger and more sensitive public opinion to counter deficient formulation and implementation of public policies and will thus strengthen the democratization process. Public opinion would then function as a complementary judicial system, to ensure public awareness and adherence to the spirit of the constitution by officials, both elected and appointed.

c. More effective judicial instruments to enforce political accountability and improve protection of public goods.

d. More pressure from international, informed and sensitized public opinion on the perpetrators of unjust practices against human rights. This would help reduce or even put an end to such practices.

e. Better functioning of law enforcement institutions and mechanisms, whose members are trained to adhere to the spirit of the constitution, fundamental human rights and their professional obligations.

f. A gradual demobilization of the armed forces would also help reduce the military's influence in politics. Reductions in arms purchases would help stabilize the national budget in favour of more urgent civilian needs such as education and health.

g. More professional training for the security forces, whether police, national guard or armed forces. Latin American security personnel need to be more conscious of their true mission: protecting the lives and property of their fellow countrymen.

h. More awareness of human rights and environmental issues at all societal levels. Respect for human rights, especially those of minorities, will help reduce the level of potential conflict, as there will be fewer cases involving abuse of human rights.

i. Less Messianism and populism in politics and society. Pragmatic politicians and honest public servants are needed to solve a country's problems, not those who offer themselves as 'prophets of salvation'. Such populist and demagogic tactics only heighten expectations of their fellow countrymen which probably cannot be met.

j. Fewer personalized and *caudillista* traits in politics. More institutionalized values and policies that are not subject to personalized processes and systems, built around a single leader.

k. More cooperation between the international banking system and Latin American nations to help stem the flow of embezzled public funds to the industrialized countries.

Finally, some remarks on the main regional mechanisms for inter-state conflicts in Latin America. The most important of such mechanisms is the Organization of American States (OAS), founded in April 1948, one year after the Rio Pact was signed as a collective security organ between Latin American countries and the United States. Both the Rio Pact and the OAS are conceived as systems that seek to assure continental American sovereignty in solving their own regional crises with a minimum, if any, of foreign intervention. The OAS has been successful in peacefully resolving some fifteen cases of disputes between Latin American countries since its creation, yet it must be noted that the OAS includes English-speaking Caribbean nations as well as Canada, Surinam and the Bahamas, making it more a multicultural continental body than merely a Latin American and US organization. Nevertheless, the omnipresent US dominance within the OAS structure is a political fact that none of the OAS members can afford to ignore. The Monroe Doctrine, declared in 1823, sought to assure the absence of foreign, that was, European, influence in inter-American relations, leaving the United States a free hand in imposing its will on the weaker nations in the region, very much in accordance with its interests.

The OAS proved instrumental in resolving the Dominican crisis in 1965 by putting together an inter-American intervention force to end it. But the US attitude during the Falklands/Malvinas war of 1982 underscored its dominance of the OAS and its selective approach in dealing with inter-American problems. The decisive US tilt towards the United Kingdom during that crisis caused serious internal rifts within the OAS. Most Latin American countries recognized the obvious: the OAS is permitted to act decisively only when it serves US interests.

The Central American crisis during the 1980s gave rise to another set of regional mechanisms for solving inter-state disputes: political groups of Latin American countries that act as intermediaries. The awareness among these countries that some sort of unity among them could help counterbalance the hegemonic US position led them to form the first of such groups in January 1983: the Contadora Group. Mexico, Colombia, Panama and Venezuela joined forces to seek a peaceful and negotiated settlement of the crisis originating from Nicaragua's confrontation with its Central American neighbours.The fact that the United Nations was not allowed to play a significant role in that crisis led the Contadora Group to ask for and receive the European Community's support in convincing five Central American countries to sign the Guatemala Act in August 1987, the Process for Solid and Lasting Peace in Central America. These efforts paved the way for the signing of the Esquipulas Acts, strengthening the peace process and underscoring Central American resolve to negotiate its own peace accords, even in the face of US objections. It should be noted here that the gradual softening of the Sandinistas in Nicaragua, a process brought about by US pressure, was a main factor in achieving peace in Central America.

The regional mechanisms for conflict resolution in Latin America are currently experiencing the interaction of political as well as economic and commercial interests. In the wake of Mexico's entry into the North American Free Trade Agreement and the proliferation of neo-liberal domestic economic policies within the region, groups such as the G-3 (Mexico, Colombia and Venezuela), MERCOSUR (Argentina, Brazil, Paraguay and Uruguay), and the Central American Common Market are showing a strong tendency to integrate Latin American countries through commercial links, leading to the assumption that such links would weaken the potential for armed inter-American conflicts in the near future. The preoccupation with economic issues of all Latin American countries, and their inherent weakness in this respect, represents a strong incentive for them to assign top priority to economic integration, making political conflicts with possible armed outcomes less desirable. The regional economic integration mechanisms are thus slowly but surely taking the place of political crisis-solving functions.

NOTES

1. In this context, Latin America refers only to the Spanish- and Portuguese-speaking regions of the continent, including the Caribbean islands of Cuba, Haiti and the Dominican Republic. It does not include the English- and French-speaking countries and dependencies in the Caribbean, Central America and the north-eastern area of South America, nor Aruba and the Netherlands Antilles.

2. Herbert K. Tillema, 'Foreign Overt Military Intervention in the Nuclear Age', *Journal of Peace Research*, vol. 2, no. 26, 1989, pp. 179-96.

3. *Time* magazine, 18 January 1993, p. 14 (Latin American edition).

4. *The World Paper*, November 1993, p. 4.

5. *Time* magazine, 24 June 1991, pp. 18-24 (Latin American edition).

6. *The World Paper*, March 1994, p. 5.

7. *Time* magazine, 20 July 1992, pp. 17-20 (Latin American edition).

8. Keith Krause, 'Arms Imports, Arms Production and the Quest for Security in the Third World', in Brian L. Job (ed.), *The Insecurity Dilemma: National*

Security of Third World States, (Boulder, CO: Lynne Rienner, 1992), pp. 121-42.

9. Herbert K. Tillema, 'Foreign Overt Military Intervention in the Nuclear Age'.

10. Bradford E. Burns, *The Poverty of Progress: Latin America in the Nineteenth Century* (Berkeley, CA: University of California Press, 1980); Maria del Carmen Velasquez, *La Vida Politica en Hispanoamerica* (Caracas: Academia Nacional de la Historia de Venezuela, 1986); and Donald M. Dozer, *Latin America: An Interpretative History* (New York: McGraw-Hill, 1962).

11. Michael C. Desch, *When the Third World Matters: Latin America and the United States' Grand Strategy* (Baltimore, MD: Johns Hopkins University Press, 1993); Tom J. Farer, *The Grand Strategy of the United States in Latin America* (New Brunswick, NJ: Transaction Books, 1988); and Manuel Ugarte, *El Destino de un Continente* (Buenos Aires: Ediciones de la Patria Grande, 1962).

12. Robert Kern (ed.), *The Caciques: Oligarchical Politics and the System of Caciquismo in the Luso-Hispanic World* (Albuquerque, NM: University of New Mexico Press, 1973); Fernando Muro Romero, *Las Presidencias-gobernaciones en Indias: Siglo XVI* (Sevilla: Escuela de Estudios Hispano-Americanos, 1975); and Carlos A. Montaner, *La Agonia de America* (Barcelona: Plaza & Janes, 1989).

13. Lorenzo Meyer and Jose L. Reyna, *Los Sistemas Politicos en America Latina* (Mexico, DF: Siglo Veintiuno Editores, 1989); Louis K. Harris and Victor Alba, *The Political Culture and Behavior of Latin America* (Kent, OH: Ohio State University Press, 1974); Virgilio R. Beltran, *El Papel Politico y Social de las Fuerzas Armadas en America Latina* (Caracas: Monte Avila Editores, 1970); and John Lynch, *Caudillos in Spanish America, 1800-1850* (Oxford: Clarendon Press, 1992).

14. Dieter Nohlen and Mario Fernandez (eds), *Presidencialismo versus Parlamentarismo: America Latina* (Caracas: Editorial Nueva Sociedad, 1991); Alain Rouquie, *et al.*, *Dictaduras y Dictadores* (Mexico, DF: Siglo Veintiuno, 1986); John Lynch, *Caudillos in Spanish America*; and Maria del Carmen Velasquez, *La Vida Politica en Hispoanoamerica*.

15. Mario S. Hernandez, *Las Tensiones Historicas Hispanoamericanas en el Siglo XX* (Madrid: Ediciones Guadarrama, 1961); David Bushnell and Neill Macauly, *The Emergence of Latin America in the Nineteenth Century* (New York: Oxford University Press, 1988); and Magnus Morner, *Region and State in Latin America's Past* (Baltimore, MD: Johns Hopkins University Press, 1993).

16. Oscar Waiss, *Nacionalismo y Socialismo en America Latina* (Buenos Aires: Ediciones Ignaz, 1961); Fernando Mires, *La Rebelion Permanente: Las Revoluciones Sociales en America Latina* (Mexico, DF: Siglo Veintiuno, 1989); John Johnson, *Political Change in Latin America: The Emergence of the Middle Sectors* (Stanford, CA: Stanford University Press, 1958); and Eduardo M. Frei, *America Latina: Opcion y Esperanza* (Barcelona: Editorial Pomaire, 1977).

17. Timothy P. Wickham-Crowly, *Guerrillas and Revolution in Latin America: A Comparative Study of Insurgents and Regimes since 1956* (Princeton, NJ: Princeton University Press, 1993); Wilbur A. Chaffee Jr, *The Economics of Violence in Latin America: A Theory of Political Competition* (New York: Praeger Publishers, 1992); Luis Mercier Vega, *Guerrillas in Latin America: The Technique of Counter-State* (New York: Praeger Publishers, 1969); and Regis Debray, *The Long March in Latin American Guerrilla Movements: Theory and Practice* (Boston, MA: New England Free Press, 1966).

18. James Kohl and John Litt (eds), *Urban Guerrilla Warfare in Latin America* (Cambridge, MA: MIT Press, 1974); and Michael Radu and Vladimir Tismaneanu, *Latin American Revolutionaries: Groups, Goals and Methods* (Washington, DC: Pergamon and Brassey's International Defence Publishers, 1990).

19. Robert Wesson (ed.), *The Latin American Military Institution* (New York: Praeger, 1986); Brian Loveman and Thomas M. Davies Jr (eds), *The Politics of Anti-Politics: The Military in Latin America* (Lincoln, NB: University of Nebraska Press, 1989); Jaime Pinzen Lopez, *et al.*, *America Latina: Militarismo 1940-1975* (Bogota: Editorial Oveja Negra, 1983); and Alberto V. Rocha, *La Militarizacion del Estado: America Latina 1960-1980* (Lima: Instituto de Investigaciones Economicas y Sociales, 1988).

20. Philip O'Brien and Paul Cammack (eds), *Generals in Retreat: The Crisis of Military Rule in Latin America* (Manchester, NH: Manchester University Press, 1985); Alain Rouquie, *The Military and State in Latin America* (Berkeley, CA: University of California Press, 1987); Augusto Varas, *La Autonomia Militar en America Latina* (Caracas: Nueva Sociedad, 1988); and Robert A. Pastor (ed.), *Democracy in the Americas: Stopping the Pendulum* (New York: Holmes & Meier, 1989).

21. David Collier (ed.), *The Authoritarianism in Latin America* (Princeton, NJ: Princeton University Press, 1979); Douglas A. Chalmers, *et al.*, *The Right and Democracy in Latin America* (New York: Praeger, 1992); and Lawrence S. Graham, *The State and Policy Outcomes in the Latin American Vortex: Politics in Latin America* (New York: Praeger, 1990).

22. Jeffry A. Frieden, *Debt, Development and Democracy: Modern Political Economy and Latin America* (Princeton, NJ: Princeton University Press, 1992); James L. Dietz and Dilmus D. James (eds), *Progress Toward Development in Latin America: From Prebisch to Technological Autonomy* (Boulder, CO: Lynne Rienner, 1990); and Barbara Stallings and Robert Kaufman (eds), *Debt and Democracy in Latin America* (Boulder, CO: Westview, 1989).

23. Arthur Harris and Stella Lowder (eds), *Decentralization in Latin America: An Evaluation* (New York: Praeger, 1982); Elsa Laurelli and Alejandro Rofman, *Descentralizacion del Estado: Requerimientos y Politicas en la Crisis* (Buenos Aires: Ediciones CEUR, 1989); George A. Lopez and Michael Stohl (eds), *Liberalization and Redemocratization in Latin America* (New York: Greenwood Press, 1987); Margaret E. Crahan (ed.), *Human Rights and Basic Needs in the*

Americas (Washington, DC: Georgetown University Press, 1982); and Peter M. Ward (ed.), *Corruption, Development and Inequality: Soft Touch or Hard Graft?* (London: Routledge, 1989).

24. Susan Eckstein (ed.), *Power and Popular Protest: Latin American Social Movements* (Berkeley, CA: University of California Press, 1989); Arturo Escobar and Sonia Alvarez (eds), *The Making of Social Movements in Latin America: Identity, Strategy and Democracy* (Boulder, CO: Westview, 1992); and David Slater (ed.), *New Social Movements and the State in Latin America* (Cinnaminson, NJ: FORIS, 1985).

25. Barry Ames, *Political Survival: Politicians and Public Policy in Latin America* (Berkeley, CA: University of California Press, 1987); Steven W. Hughes and S.G. Mijeski, with case studies by S.G. Bunker *et al.*, *Politics and Public Policy in Latin America* (Boulder, CO: Westview, 1984); Enrique Krauze (ed.), *America Latina: Desventuras de la Democracia* (Mexico, DF: J. Moritz, 1984); Carlos A. Montaner, *La Agonia de America*; and Howard J. Wiarda (ed.), *Politics and Social Change in Latin America: Still a Distinct Tradition?* (Boulder, CO: Westview, 1992).

26. Paul W. Zagorski, *Democracy versus National Security: Civil-Military Relations in Latin America* (Boulder, CO: Westview, 1991); Augusto Varas (ed.), *Check on Democracy: New Military Power* (Westport, CT: Greenwood, 1989); and Louis Goodman, *et al.*, *The Military and Democracy: The Future of Civil-Military Relations in Latin America* (Lexington, MA: Lexington Books, 1990).

27. Pablo C. Gonzalez, *El Estado en America Latina: Teoria y Practica* (Mexico, DF: Siglo Veintiuno/Universidad de las Naciones Unidas, 1990); John A. Booth and Mitchell A. Seligson (eds), *Political Participation in Latin America* (New York: Holmes & Meier, 1979); David Collier (ed.), *The Authoritarianism in Latin America*; and Larry Diamond, *et al.*, *Democracy in Developing Countries: Latin America*, vol. 4 (Boulder, CO: Lynne Rienner, 1989).

28. Robin Theobald, *Corruption, Development and Underdevelopment* (Durham, NC: Duke University Press, 1990); Robert E. Kitgaard, *Controlling Corruption* (Berkeley, CA: University of California Press, 1988); and Peter M. Ward (ed.), *Corruption, Development and Inequality*.

29. Howard Handelman and Werner Baer (eds), *Paying the Costs of Austerity in Latin America* (Boulder, CO: Westview, 1989); Robert Bottome, *el al.*, *In the Shadow of the Debt: Emerging Issues in Latin America* (New York: Twentieth Century Fund Press, 1992); Barbara Stallings and Robert Kaufman, *Debt and Democracy in Latin America*; Guillermo O'Donnell, *et al.*, *Transitions from Authoritarian Rule: Latin America* (Baltimore, MD: Johns Hopkins University Press, 1986); and Howard J. Wiarda and Harvey F. Kline (eds), *Latin American Politics and Development* (Boulder, CO: Westview, 1990).

30. Victor E. Tokman, 'El Imperativo de Actuar: El Sector Informal Hoy', in *Nueva Sociedad*, no. 90, 1987, pp. 93-105.

31. Saul Landau, *The Guerrilla Wars of Central America: Nicaragua, El Salvador and Guatemala* (New York: St Martin's Press, 1993); Joseph S. Tulchin and Gary Bland (eds), *Is there a Transition to Democracy in El Salvador?* (Boulder, CO: Lynne Rienner, 1992); and Robert H. Trudeau, *Guatemalan Politics: The Popular Struggle for Democracy* (Boulder, CO: Lynne Rienner, 1993).

32. Martha K. Huggins (ed.), *Vigilantism and the State in Modern Latin America: Essays on Extra-legal Violence* (New York: Praeger, 1991); and Edelberto Torres-Rivas, *Repression and Resistance: The Struggle for Democracy in Central America* (Boulder, CO: Westview, 1989).

33. Enrique Santos Calderon, *La Guerra por la Paz* (Bogota: Fondo Editorial CEREC, 1985); and Jenny Pearce, *Colombia: Inside the Labyrinth* (London: Latin American Bureau, 1990).

34. Enrique Santos Calderon, *Fuego Cruzado: Guerrilla, Narcotrafico y Paramilitares en la Colombia de los Ochenta* (Bogota: Fondo Editorial CEREC, 1988); and Diana Duque Gomez, *Una Guerra Irregular entre dos Ideologias: Colombia 1982-1990: Un Enfoque Liberal* (Bogota: Intermedio Editores, 1991).

35. William A. Hazleton and Sandra Woy-Hazleton, 'Terrorism and the Marxist Left: Peru's Struggle against *Sendero Luminoso*', *Terrorism: An International Journal*, vol. 11, no. 6, 1988, pp. 471-90; and James Anderson, *Sendero Luminoso: A New Revolutionary Model?* (London: Institute for the Study of Terrorism, 1987).

36. Richard Graham (ed.), *The Idea of Race in Latin America: 1870-1940* (Austin, TX: University of Texas Press, 1990); and Michael D. Olien, *Latin Americans: Contemporary Peoples and their Cultural Traditions* (New York: Holt, Rinehart & Winston, 1973).

37. John E. Kicza (ed.), *The Indian in Latin American History: Resistance, Resilience, and Acculturation* (Wilmington, DE: Scholarly Resources, 1993); Mauricio Solaun, *et al.*, *Discrimination without Violence: Miscegenation and Racial Conflict in Latin America* (New York: Wiley, 1973); and Robert B. Toplin (ed.), *Slavery and Race Relations in Latin America* (Westport, CT: Greenwood, 1974).

38. Herbert K. Tillema, *International Armed Conflicts since 1945* (Boulder, CO: Westview, 1991), pp. 22-44.

39. Alan J. Day (ed.), *Border and International Disputes* (Harlow, Essex: Longman, 1987), pp. 377-428, 435-42.

40. Jack Child, *Geopolitics and Conflict in South America: Quarrels among Neighbours* (Stanford, CA: Hoover Institution, 1985); Michael A. Morris and Victor Millan (eds), *Controlling Latin American Conflicts: Ten Approaches* (Boulder, CO: Westview, 1983); James Petras and Morris Morley, *Latin America in the Time of Cholera: Electoral Politics, Market Economies and Permanent Crisis* (New York: Routledge, 1992); Jack Child, *The Central American Peace Process 1983-1991: Sheathing Swords, Building Confidence* (Boulder, CO: Lynne Rienner, 1992).

41. James Painter, *Bolivia and Coca: A Study in Dependency* (Boulder, CO: Lynne Rienner, 1994); Peter Smith (ed.), *Drug Policy in the Americas* (Boulder, CO: Westview, 1992); Felipe MacGregor (ed.), *Coca and Cocaine: An Andean Perspective* (Westport, CT: Greenwood, 1993); and Jaime Malamud-Gofi, *Smoke and Mirrors: The Paradox of Drug Wars* (Boulder, CO: Westview, 1992).

Part VII

POLICY PERSPECTIVES

15

Conflict and Development: Causes, Effects and Remedies

Jan Eliasson

INTRODUCTION

There is a Dutch metaphor about a little boy at a dike, who did not have enough fingers to put in the dike's holes, yet the ocean was pressing from the other side. This metaphor reflects the acute current situation for the United Nations, struck by an explosion of crises and enormous demands on peace-keeping, peace-making and peace-building. The urgent task for the UN now is to deal, much more than we have done up until now, with root causes instead of symptoms. Moreover, the 'growth industries' of the UN are peace-keeping and humanitarian action, obviously areas that deal with the symptoms, not with the causes. This gives rise for concern.

The conventional wisdom about the relationship between conflict and development is that conflict undermines development. But what we should look at more deeply is how development and humanitarian action can prevent or diminish conflict. Three major themes shall be dealt with here: first, the changing international environment, focusing especially on what these changes have meant for the United Nations; second, the relationship between peace-keeping, peace-making and peace-building (in the form of humanitarian action and assistance); and third, the imperative of prevention.

CHANGING INTERNATIONAL ENVIRONMENT

As to changes in the international environment, two factors should be underlined. One is the end of the Cold War, which in UN terms meant the virtual end of the veto in the Security Council and the vitalization of the Council as a body responsible for international peace and security. Today the Security Council deals with practically all serious conflicts around the world. During the 1960s, the Security Council, for instance, never dealt with the Vietnam war, and the veto was frequent from the Soviet side in the 1950s and later

347

from the Western countries on issues about the Middle East and Southern Africa, becoming a sad feature of the work of the United Nations.

We now live in a different situation: Chapter VII of the UN Charter is used to an extent that was never the case before. The UN has 'muscles', which it was criticized for not having in the past. Actually, the two types of criticism the UN is receiving these days is that it either has too many muscles, as in Somalia, or too little, as in Bosnia.

A cautionary note on this first change though: the debate on Bosnia in early 1994 showed that we cannot take for granted that the veto will not be used in critical situations. The combination of the NATO ultimatum and Russian pressure on the Serbs created a situation in which the veto issue was avoided. But we do not know what would have happened if the matter had been brought to the Security Council at the beginning of that threatening confrontation.

The second change in the international environment is the explosion of civil wars. We are now, in a way, paying the price for the Cold War, as ethnic and religious forces inside nations are bursting into action, not least because the blanket of the Cold War has been lifted. This ethnic conflict has been likened to a historical pendulum. The Security Council of the United Nations, responsible for international peace and security, has since 1992 dealt with more civil wars or civil war-like situations than international conflicts, and a realistic forecast is that this will be the case for a number of years to come. Therefore, it is extremely important that the UN adapts and is prepared to deal with problems and crises within borders at as early a stage as possible.

In political and moral terms, this means that solidarity does not automatically stop at the border, as was the case with Pol Pot's genocide in Cambodia. A balance now has to be struck between sovereignty and non-interference on the one hand, and solidarity with people in need on the other. At the end of the Cold War we should learn that nations are not pawns in a geopolitical chess game, but rather societies with human beings who have a right not only to political freedom, but also to economic and social justice. Borders are now crossed when it comes to providing humanitarian relief. We have the right of access to people in need, we have governments' commitment to the well-being of their own people, as laid down in General Assembly Resolution 46/182, adopted in December 1991. This was of use in the negotiations with, for example, Sudan, which resulted in humanitarian corridors from Kenya in order to reach people in desperate need in southern Sudan.

A reflection on ethnicity: it should not automatically be seen as a negative phenomenon, as is sometimes the case in the debate today. Ethnicity is also a positive force, something that was repressed for many years in many countries. The fact that it now explodes is often the result of the breakthrough of democratic forces, and the danger is that we see these forces being used for fragmentation, micro-nationalism, so that many nations around the world are threatened by disintegration into smaller and smaller parts. The sad choice that we often face is breaking up a nation into smaller entities, or asking people to live side by side after terrible atrocities, as in Bosnia.

What, then, have these two major changes, the end of the Cold War and the explosion of civil wars, meant for the United Nations? First of all, the UN has become more active. It does not any longer stop acting at national borders. Second, the UN's role has become more comprehensive. The UN is not only at the borderline in an observer function, but is crossing into the country, performing political tasks such as reconciliation in Somalia or monitoring elections in Mozambique, as well as humanitarian work. The third change is that the United Nations' role has become more exposed, both in a physical and political sense. The UN is losing people by the week, where we earlier lost them by the month. One of my most difficult tasks as Under-Secretary-General was to send off cables which allowed aid workers to go to Sudan, Somalia, Afghanistan, Angola and Mozambique and then see several of these young men and women being killed. This was a terrible moral burden to carry.

By exposed, though, not only physical dangers but also political dangers are implied. When the UN enters sensitive civil war situations with strong ethnic and religious components, it automatically becomes more controversial. It will have to take a position against a Khmer Rouge faction in Cambodia, against Mr Karadzic in Bosnia and it may have to take a position against 'the war-lords' in Somalia. This means that the Secretary-General of the United Nations these days represents an organization that is inherently more controversial than before. However, we have to accept that role because we have a commitment to the people in need, to human beings in danger. This is, to me, the most civilized conclusion of the end of the Cold War and we have to respond to this moral imperative. If we do not accept that role for the United Nations, who else will perform it?

PEACE-KEEPING

Now to the second theme: peace-keeping and its relationship to peace-making and humanitarian action. During my years as Under-Secretary-General, one of my strongest personal experiences was what

I saw when I visited Somalia in September 1992. This humanitarian night-mare made me realize that the United Nations needed to have a stronger military presence to turn the tide, but also to do humanitarian action, peace-keeping and peace-making at the same time. We must not think in terms of first doing military action, then reconciliation, and then humanitar-ian action or development. There is an enormously important gain to be made by doing peace-making, peace-keeping and peace-building simulta-neously.

There is a dynamic relationship between these three activities. For example, if there was a massive humanitarian programme in Somalia, jobs would be created for young men who would otherwise brandish weapons from their vans, health clinics and schools could be opened, and mines could be removed - about one million mines have been laid all over Somalia. This would not only be the right thing to do from the human perspective but also from the point of security, since such action would immediately affect the conflict level. Such a substantial humanitarian programme would have an immediate effect on the level of conflict as well as on security. It would also promote peace efforts and reconciliation.

In the case of Somalia, I found it depressing that for every dollar the United Nations was to spend on humanitarian assistance we had to spend ten dollars on military protection in 1993 (US $166 million compared to $1.5 billion). This fact clouded the very purpose of the operation. I realized the need for the UN to have military muscle, but I also feared the risk that military activities could become not a means but an end in itself, and that we would risk becoming part of the conflict. This eventually happened: the confrontation, which peaked in October 1993 with 18 American deaths, led to the decision by the United States and some other countries to leave Soma-lia.

Another outcome of this confrontation was that general support for the United Nations diminished considerably in the United States and elsewhere, limiting willingness to take action for peace enforcement. It is clear that the preparedness among member states to risk the lives of their young men and women in civil wars has diminished. Multilateral varnish can turn out to be rather thin in such situations, both when it comes to human sacrifices and money.

It is crucial that humanitarian action is carried out even under difficult circumstances, and that we do not fall into the trap of divorcing humanitarian action completely from the United Nations. I have the greatest respect for the non-governmental organizations, and the Red Cross, and they should be supported massively. But it is also important for the United Nations to show, in situations like Somalia, that it has three potential roles to play: the peace-keeping role (the military dimension), the peace-making role (the political dimension), and the peace-building role (the humanitarian dimension). If we separate away humanitarian action and resort to playing only military or political roles, we risk selling the soul of the United Nations. This world organization must always attempt to bring relief, impartially, to people in need.

PREVENTION

The third theme is the imperative of prevention. During these intensive years at the UN dealing with humanitarian crises, I felt very much like a fireman who had to work both day shift and night shift, growing ever more frustrated at not catching the people who set the buildings on fire. When I travelled around the world to places like Somalia, Mozambique and Sudan, I was struck to see the terrible price that had to be paid for this 'fireman syndrome'. We deal with fires, not with finding the arsonists before they put the match to the house. We pay an enormous price for acting too late, in terms of human lives and financial burdens.

Early warning must be translated into early action. For instance, two years ago a drought in Southern Africa was threatening ten countries and was going to be the worst disaster in the region's history. The UN system mobilized $700 million from donor nations in cooperation with SADC, Southern Africa's regional organization. The World Food Programme (WFP) did all the logistical work. The United Nations negotiated with South Africa to open the ports – this was before sanctions were lifted – and rains in some areas helped, but still the water level in Bulawayo, Zimbabwe's second city, was only eight per cent of its normal level in September 1992. If that level had decreased further, there would have been hundreds of thousands of people on the roads in that area alone. It is impossible to tell what effects such a social upheaval could have had.

Fortunately, this emergency programme prevented the looming disaster from turning into massive famine. But there are no heroes for early action, no Nobel Prizes for prevention. Instead, we tend to make heroes of the person who comes out of the burning building with the child in his arms, not the person who tried to prevent the fire. We must start to consider much more what can be done to stop a conflict from developing.

A wide range of measures can be applied at early stages before the use of force comes into play, from early warning and information gathering, to fact-finding missions, to applying Chapter VI of the UN Charter with measures like mediation and arbitration, to peace-keeping operations, to action under Chapter VII to deal with threats against international peace and security. It should be realized here that sanctions today are a rather blunt instrument. Sanctions almost always have to be balanced by large-scale humanitarian programmes to countervail their negative humanitarian effects. Sanctions should hence be more precise, if they are to lead effectively to peaceful solutions.

A range of measures can consequently be applied to prevent a conflict, and this potential should be used, because once the genie – the war – gets out of the bottle, it is tremendously difficult to get it back in. I was mediating for a long time between Iran and Iraq, and I am currently negotiating in the Nagorno-Karabakh conflict. It is my deep frustration how solutions become more and more difficult for every month of war that passes.

POSSIBLE SOLUTIONS

A more reasonable and realistic international division of labour needs to be discussed. The expectations on the United Nations today are simply too high; the organization is overburdened and we risk a short-circuit situation. The UN is overworked and, in some regards, not able to cope with the crises in the peace-keeping and humanitarian areas. If the demands and expectations continue to rise, we risk a situation where multilateralism and the United Nations are blamed more and more. There should be concern about this crisis of expectations. Few seem to realize that the world organization is made up of its member states and of the citizens of the member states.

Under this pressure, we need to emphasize the roles of regional and non-governmental organizations and offer them greater responsibility. We need to think about the democratization of international cooperation and action. We also need to get the practitioners to meet more often with the theoreticians and ask 'who, when and how?' in early warning, prevention, mediation and conflict resolution. We should, for instance, try to achieve better coordination between all those doing monitoring and conflict resolution in order to mobilize the capacity and talent that exists.

UN reform efforts must continue to be enforced - there is still a lot to do. First, the relationship between the Security Council and the General Assembly must improve. Article 29 in the UN Charter permits the creation of subsidiary organs to the Security Council. This article may be used, for instance, to create a committee comprising those countries that contribute to peace-keeping forces, thereby building links between the Security Council and the General Assembly. These new links between members of the UN should be built, for if they are not, the distance between these two major organs might grow too large. Second, the Economic and Social Council needs to be reformed – something substantial has to be done to incorporate economic and social factors and make a broader security analysis a reality. Third, the Secretariat needs to be reformed. One way of doing this could be to create a clearer relationship between headquarters, specialized agencies and UN programmes. Better coordination of UN activities in the field is also badly needed.

The third conclusion is more of a concept: new creative ways to analyse crisis situations should be found. These crises should be viewed from the perspective of institutions and mandates, but from the perspective of problems. Currently, many people do not seem to accept a problem if there is no mandate or institution responsible to deal with it. So let us put the problems in the centre.

The fourth conclusion: an action programme for prevention should be developed, both in the economic, social and political arenas. We need to work out, in an inter-disciplinary way, conflict resolution mechanisms for civil wars, not least by analysing more deeply the patterns and causes of conflict.

All this boils down to something very basic. The effectiveness of international cooperation through the United Nations is fundamentally a question of the respect for its moral and ethical force. We have recently seen an outbreak of the law of the jungle, and should recall that the best method of preventing conflicts is by living up to the UN Charter, to international law and to the principles and rules of humanitarian law. There must be no slackening of this respect, which is our common first line of defence. We must go back to basics and let the moral and ethical forces guide international relations.

The idea of the founding fathers of the United Nations was that the world organization was to stand for peace, development and a life in dignity for all. Looking at the map today, we can see that we are not heading in this direction. But we must not lose sight of the vision. If we grasp this opportunity at the end of the Cold War, the idea of the United Nations, of international cooperation and of multilateralism, will prevail, not only because of the classical reasons that guide most of us – justice and solidarity – but also for reasons of survival, security and, indeed, enlightened self-interest. These could create a tremendously strong coalition and foundation of support for the United Nations.

16

A Dutch Policy Perspective

Jan Pronk and Paul Sciarone

INTRODUCTION

Conflict and development are closely linked in various ways. Wars have not infrequently seriously disrupted societies and pushed their development back by decades. There is also, however, a reverse relationship: that the development process goes hand in hand with conflict.

This may be seen from the definition of development employed here: development is improvement in the chances of survival of individual people, particularly in the length and quality of their lives. It is a process of social change with economic, social, cultural and ecological dimensions which are all interrelated. These various dimensions do not all develop in the same direction in the process of social change. At times they are in opposition and this causes tension and friction. Not all processes of social change may be seen as development. This depends on what the people within the societies concerned think of them. But there will always be people who think that their chances of survival have been reduced as a consequence of change, which implies, in principle, a social conflict.

Conflicts are unavoidable. This does not, however, make them desirable. In any case, the escalation of conflict beyond a certain level of violence should be prevented. Violence is bad for two reasons: for many people it leads to the reduction of their chances of survival, which is the opposite intention of development; and above all, violence contains the risk of uncontrollability.

Conflict is inherent to development, yet the escalation of conflict into violence is not inescapable. It makes little sense to aim for an improvement in the chances of survival through development aid, unless an effort is made at the same time to control conflicts and either prevent or limit violence.

Large-scale poverty combined with scarcity of resources provokes conflict over the division, possession and use of land, water and energy. Where the state is in the hands of privileged groups and propertied classes, conflicts over the division of resources can degenerate into an armed struggle for political power. The past few decades have seen a number of outstanding examples of this, mainly in Asia and Latin America, and in a number of these cases the local conflicts were part of the global power struggle between the former Soviet Union and the United States.

Since the end of the Cold War, the relationship between development and conflict has assumed a new dimension. On one hand, the change in international relationships has led to the resolution of a number of long-running conflicts. The examples of Afghanistan, Cambodia, Angola and Mozambique, however, show that this is a very fragile process, easily breaking out into renewed violence. On the other hand, the end of the Cold War has provided an opportunity for new outbreaks of violence. Some of these conflicts are new, but others have existed for a long time with little or no opportunity to break out during the period of East/West tensions. Be they new or already existing, dormant and now bursting into life, many of these conflicts are very complex, because they are not only an expression of political differences, or of economic opposition, but are to a large extent also cultural, being ethnic or religious in origin.

Now that the danger of global warfare has receded and the desire on the part of the West and the East to carve up the South in spheres of influence is reduced, the development conflicts in the South are no longer seen as an ideological or power struggle between East and West. As a result, countries or parties now see a greater opportunity to move towards aggression, as both Iraq and Yugoslavia have demonstrated. The huge amount of arms that was manufactured during the Cold War, part of which was delivered to 'Third World' countries, acts as a match to dry straw in such volatile situations. Unstable relations in a number of developing countries and in the former Soviet Union have led to the current peatland fire situation, with some parts smouldering and others bursting into conflict. And it is not yet over, as every day conflicts may burst out violently, as happened in Rwanda and Chechnya.

COLLECTIVE SECURITY AND DEVELOPMENT AID

Is it possible to manage the current conflicts, which differ in so many ways from pre-1989 conflicts? The United Nations has undertaken more peace-keeping operations during the last four years than in the previous 45, and the results of these peace-keeping operations are a clear indication that international cooperation in the context of the United Nations is gravely inadequate.

During the Cold War, West European states concentrated on the prevention of armed conflict between East and West. There were also, however, armed conflicts taking place in other parts of the world which were predominantly internal in nature. Since the disappearance of the opposing blocs, the number of inter-state wars has dramatically reduced, but of the 30 major armed conflicts in 1993, 28 were internal in nature. This has focused attention on the overwhelming importance of intra-state violence.

Intra-state violence may take one of two forms. The first is violence which occurs in phases where the formation of a state – in the sense of the establishment of the monopoly of violence – is as yet incomplete. This is referred to as anomic violence, occurring as a result of the denial of, or lack of respect for, legal standards and authority. It is also therefore inherent to the development process. Second is the violence practised by the state – or rather the governing regime – against its own people. This type of violence is also characteristic of a certain stage of the development process of almost every society.

These three forms of violence and threat of violence are related to differing sorts of armaments. In inter-state wars (wars between states) large weapon systems are deployed, and it is only the more developed countries that deploy advanced weaponry. Smaller, lighter weaponry is deployed in anomic violence as well as in regimes of terror.

The various types of violence are obviously connected, and only terrorism may occasionally be a response to anomic violence. Both forms of developmental violence could lead to inter-state conflict or similar conflicts elsewhere. Cross-border minorities belonging to a stateless people or world religion, for example, could cause geographical or horizontal escalation. International economic interests, including those of third parties, can also fan the flames with money, arms and means of communication. All of the above render the management of new conflicts a never-ending task for our system of law.

THE INTERNATIONAL COLLECTIVE SECURITY SYSTEM

International law, as laid down in the United Nations Charter, provides for a collective security system that in fact is only intended for intra-state relationships. The founders of the Charter had obviously not envisaged the situation with which we are currently faced, in which almost all of the major conflicts occur within states. It is therefore understandable that the UN does not provide an effective security structure. Nor can the judicial instruments offered within the Charter be applied to inter-state relationships and in particular armed conflicts within states, without some legal manoeuvring. In opposition to the principle of sovereignty and non-interference on which the international collective security systems are based, it would appear that the permanent members of the Security Council are willing to expand their numbers in order to be in a position to act collectively in internal conflicts. But in order to do so, it is at least formally required that these conflicts be shown as a threat to international peace and security. In practice this can lead to lack of evenhandedness in dealing with similar cases, which is in opposition to the notion of a system of law.

A second reason for the failure of peace-keeping operations has to do with the function of the UN itself. The UN, and especially the permanent members of the Security Council, refuse to act decisively in many cases. The UN organization is also not well equipped to deal with the new tasks, its management and internal coordination being inadequate. The implementation of peace missions is hampered by the fact that most member states are not providing sufficient personnel and are not carrying their share of the financial burdens. The result is that the 'blue berets' are only sent in when enmity rages on a large scale, and then with an ambiguous mandate that on the one hand demands neutrality – such as in the provision of humanitarian aid or the separation of warring factions – and on the other hand demands that they assume a position in favour of one of the parties – such as in the protection of specific areas. The blue berets are also as a rule badly prepared and too lightly armed.[1]

The Secretary-General, in his report *An Agenda for Peace* of June 1992, made a number of recommendations to increase the UN capacity to strengthen the international collective security system. In addition, there is currently a debate on the composition of the Security Council and the authority of the Secretary-General. One application of this discussion would be to ensure that representation on the Security Council matched the current international power balance, and in so doing increase the legitimacy of its decisions, without nonetheless harming the decisiveness of the Security Council. The Netherlands is a supporter of an altered composition of the Security Council, with Germany and Japan receiving permanent seats and regional superpowers from other continents being offered Security Council seats on a semi-permanent basis. India, Nigeria and Brazil come to mind as examples. The Netherlands argues, above all, for strengthening the Secretary-General's position, by increasing his room for manoeuvre and right of initiative in his relationship with the Security Council on the one hand, and by increasing his executive authority on the other, predominantly with reference to peace initiatives.

In *An Agenda for Peace* the Secretary-General points to the relationship between peace and security on one side and all aspects of development on the other. The poor economic and social circumstances of many groups of population may lie at the root of armed conflict and vice versa. Political stability is not an end in itself but is a precondition to social and economic development. According to the Secretary-General, efforts directed at promoting peace and security should go hand in hand with development aid and they should each support the other. A similar integrated approach to preventative diplomacy, 'expanded peace-keeping' and 'post-conflict peace-building', are also examined in *An Agenda for Peace*. It is vital that potential armed conflicts are not only flagged at as early a stage as possible, but that adequate international action is also undertaken in order to prevent escalation. It is also important that an international effort is made to restore order and authority and to rebuild the economy after resolution of an armed conflict.

CAUSES OF CONFLICT IN DEVELOPING COUNTRIES

Formation of the State

The process of state formation is not complete in many developing countries. The means of violence are not fully centralized in the hands of leaders and the legitimacy of the central government leaves a lot to be desired. Traditional structures, which often enjoy greater legitimacy in the eyes of the people, are still in place. The official institutions are weak. The result is a fragmentation of power along the lines of the loyalties of the population. In the process of diversified economic development and modernization, the social middle classes, which have an interest in stability as well as freedom, are not yet fully developed.

Governments in such weak states, with little legitimacy and weak institutional capacities, can only partially manage social development. In reaction to this, the interests of the state are often equated with those of the government. They can barely hold their own through the use of violence.

This has consequences for security. The weak state is not only a threat to internal security, but is also far more vulnerable to external threats than strong states. Afghanistan, Angola, Lebanon, Liberia and Somalia are examples of this. A factor of great influence in this extreme vulnerability, especially in Africa, is the manner in which ethnicities, religions or languages are spread across arbitrarily drawn borders.

Are violent conflicts in developing countries an indication of political decline or are they just a step on the way to the formation of a stronger state? By examining the historical process of formation of states in Europe, some researchers have deduced that violence goes together with the first phases of the formation of states, and once a certain degree of monopoly of violence within a state has been achieved, the nation begins to take shape, enabling the state to suppress further violence within the nation. A large number of developing countries, particularly following decolonization, are undergoing a more or less similar process. But there are also examples of regimes which resort quickly to the use of violence to protect their own positions and interests and do everything possible to maintain their power by violent means. This hinders development, both in the economic and socio-political sense. When this is combined with the violent repression of those who are opposed to the governing regime, not only for political or ideological reasons, but also on the grounds of ethnicity, religion or differing nationalities, the result is not a strong state with a recognized monopoly of violence, which in turn leads to less violence, rather it is a contrived state and fragmented nation and eternally spiralling violence.

Ethnicity

The importance of questions of race and ethnicity for the durability of a society has been neglected for a long time. Research into violence is directed at states. Whatever happens in terms of ethnicity, culture or religion within a state is perceived as being of marginal importance. The phenomenon of ethnicity in social conflicts is recognized but is insufficiently understood.

It would appear that more and more people in an increasing number of countries in the East, West and South do not wish to live in a multi-racial, or even a multi-cultural society. This is not just applicable to the prosperous majorities in these countries, but also for the minorities concerned. They demand their own place to settle, if not their own territory or country. Modern social conflicts in the West, during the construction of a mixed economy, the welfare state and a representative democracy, are primarily about the equality of rights within a culturally heterogenous society. This would appear to be just as much the case in the development process following decolonization in the South. Movements striving for culturally homogenous societies have been gaining in power and influence since the 1980s. This call for homogeneity, coupled with the attendant marginalization and exclusion of minorities, is a backwards step on the way to a civilized global society.

The conflicts that result from this new call for separation and protection are spreading like wildfire across the globe. More and more countries are confronted with strident demands for separate status from a variety of groups. In the 'Third World', but not only there, ethnic differences are being used as a weapon against social civil rights. In some places this process is aggravated by fundamentalism, which implies that belonging to a certain group confers an extraordinary, often quasi-religious significance. Fundamentalism is gaining ground, even in Europe.[2]

There is no unequivocal answer to the question of whether ethnicity is a historic fact or human invention. Some tend to the idea that there is a sort of fundamental link between members of an ethnic group, by means of which a sort of natural society forms with its own characteristic myths, memories, values and symbols. This ethnic identity generally exists subliminally, but is, according to this version, constantly present and offers an explanation for the 'us' as opposed to 'them' feeling. Others, particularly leaders, see ethnicity as a means, an instrument, to form groups in order to achieve political ends. Whichever meaning it has, ethnicity is in itself not a sufficient condition for conflict. Differences of race and culture must be made socially relevant and ultimately politicized in order to result in conflict. Ethnicity therefore is not a cause of conflict. Indeed the opposite may be the case, that war strengthens ethnicity. This can be seen in the outbreak of armed struggle in the former Yugoslavia, which led to a greater emphasis of the differences between Serbs and Croats.[3]

People may force themselves, or sometimes even be forced, to value, to choose one group as opposed to another. Ethnic elites play an important role in this process. They mobilize the members of an ethnic group on the basis of a circumscribed cultural heritage. This leads to the politicizing and purification of that heritage. The emphasis on one's own identity sometimes goes hand in hand with the mobilization of fear of others, or hate of others, and thus leads to a purification not only of the cultural heritage but also of the group itself and of its territory. The bloody consequences of this are well known. These are conflicts connected to the process of social change, state and nation formation, and are seldom without destructive consequences. In addition there are trans-frontier effects that the international community can, in no small measure, destabilize.

Economic Causes of Conflict

Owing to their nature, ethnic conflicts are more intense that social ones. The latter lend themselves sooner to compromise, because it is possible to reach a win-win solution. On the contrary, ethnic oppositions often carry a zero-sum implication and are only available for resolution when irreparable damage and suffering has been inflicted. This mutual suffering is often borne only by the members of the group, not by the leaders, who maintain their position of being 'right'. There are also other, more personal, goals that the leaders are endeavouring to reach by this manipulation of cultural opposition.

Apart from that, there is also a socio-economic dimension to ethnic conflicts, just as in conflicts inherent to the formation of states. When one ethnic group, for example the Tutsis in Rwanda, allow another (the Hutus) less room for economic manoeuvre, there is yet another reason for conflict. On the other hand this implies that the removal of economic opposition between groups could help to prevent the escalation of conflict. It would be a necessary part of, although not the entire, condition. Is that it, or is there always an aspect of inequality in conflict? Or is it that socio-economic inequality is a necessary precondition to conflict?

Internationally speaking, integration in the economic system is important for developing countries, although it carries its attendant problems. As a consequence of their weak economic development and weak state structures, developing countries are very vulnerable to developments in the international economy. This vulnerability is expressed in the dependence on a limited number of export goods, which means that fluctuations in the world-market prices of these products can have major consequences. In addition, the debt crisis, and the predominantly painful accommodations that have to be made to relieve this crisis, world-wide inflationary developments and trade barriers which cut off access to markets for 'Third World' products, are major problems for developing countries. These problems are seldom without consequences for the social relationships within the countries themselves. Sudden reductions in income, unemployment and a continued reduction in living circumstances can lead to insurrection and opposition.

Economic inequality within countries is a second cause of concern. Theories about poverty and economic inequality on a macro-scale do not provide a clear picture in relation to armed conflict. Various research findings indicate that economic inequality is at the most a necessary precondition to armed conflicts. For that matter, it would appear that expressions of violent opposition only manifest themselves after the first changes have occurred and not in situations of apparently unalterable misery and inequality.

Would rapid social and economic development lead to less resentment and political opposition? Or should economic and political development be regarded as independent goals, in that economic progress does not necessarily result in political stability? There does not seem to be a generally applicable theory on this point. Cultural factors play a role, just as do the history of the relevant nation, the international context, the formation of the state, the preferred economic model and the political system.

The economic structure and relationships, and the division of wealth, are strongly influenced by the political structure in developing countries. The division of wealth is done more on the grounds of political considerations than on economic ones, often resulting in corruption and economic misman-agement which in turn offers an additional reason for the flaring of conflict.

THE NEED FOR MORE RESEARCH

There are three important domains that offer cause for conflict in the 'Third World': the formation of the state, cultural opposition and economic inequal-ity. This tends to indicate that as yet the questions raised have no answers. The relationship between the possible causes and factors that play a role in this are extraordinarily complex. On the other hand, the international situa-tion has seldom been as uncertain as it is today. In order for the world to anticipate potential conflicts, with the intention of prevention, management and resolution, better research of another sort is essential.

It is obvious that the formation of the state (including the issue of ethnic-ity), socio-economic development and inequality, as well as armament issues in various regions, have differing effects on conflict. It is for this reason that a Dutch government-financed research programme in cooperation with the Institute of International Relations 'Clingendael' and local researchers is being carried out to examine these relationships in West Africa, Southern Asia and Central America. The intellectual contribution of 'Third World' researchers to the field of polemology (conflict studies) has been extremely limited to date. This must change, given that it is these very researchers who are often far better informed as to the effects of the interrelationship of the various causes of conflict.

No matter how important such research is, however, conflict manage-ment cannot afford to await its results. A start has to be made now on a programme which makes the connections between the economic, political and cultural factors in conflict.

DEVELOPMENT AND CONFLICT PREVENTION

The first component of a programme to limit violence and to manage conflict in the 1990s is socio-economic in nature. It is essential that development aid policy assigns priority to a reduction of inequality and poverty within and between countries. This implies a concentration on the necessities of life, questions of distribution of wealth and employment issues, in order to prevent an increase in the numbers of frustrated unemployed who offer a ready breeding ground for ideas propagated by both populist and fundamentalist politicians. Economic growth as a macro-economic aim takes second place as a priority. This is the opposite to what is currently generally accepted. Nonetheless, if we wish seriously to reduce violence and prevent escalation, the aim of economic growth, at least as far as it results in greater inequality, which is inevitably the case in certain stages of economic development or in the choice of a particular rate of growth and production structure, must be subordinate to the aims of an equal distribution. The socio-economic element of a policy programme directed at reducing violence must offer people a better life than that of their parents and promise that their children shall have a yet better one than they themselves have. This requires a socio-economic policy that is characterized by what the United Nations refers to as 'human development': development of, by and for people. For this reason the emphasis must lie in fighting poverty from the bottom up, with the participation of the population not only in the implementation but also in the formulation of the policy.

THE POLITICAL DIMENSION OF DEVELOPMENT: GOOD GOVERNANCE

The socio-economic element cannot be viewed as separate from the political. The goal of less inequality is not only economic but also political in nature. The past has demonstrated that a purely economic approach does not work. It would appear that there is no such thing as a 'trickle down' effect.

Therefore the second element of a broad programme must be directed at the political dimension of development: 'good governance' or building up or strengthening democratic institutions. Incorrect state formation is an important cause of armed conflict in developing countries.

This is pre-eminently about the growth and distribution of power, with both internal and external aspects. Since decolonization, the emphasis in most African countries has been placed on receiving international legitimacy and having solidarity with other developing countries.

Owing to the changes in international relations since the end of the Cold War, the internal aspect of state formation has assumed the greatest importance. The one-party state is often an instrument of internal repression of the rural population and a victim of the pursuit of profit and consumerism, which benefits the elite. After having impoverished the rural population, and now the urban population as well, most African countries find that they can barely maintain their place in the world market and are confronted with the exhaustion of their environment by a high rate of population growth. Democratization movements are now asking for a new policy, new leaders and other means of redistribution.

If developing countries wish to take control of their fate, then it is absolutely essential that they set their houses in order. This implies structural alterations and 'good governance', not imposed from outside but given form and content from within.

Maintainable state formation demands political-social coalitions that place the state above group interests and at the service of security and justice. 'Good governance' means that leaders and governments must be accountable to and responsible for the people, in such a way that scare resources are not wasted by corruption and extravagant or unnecessary military expenditure, for example. 'Good governance' is part of the democratic legitimacy of policy and is necessary to keep the aforementioned perspective on progress and welfare open. Where this does not or only partially occurs, certainly in cases where ethnic or religious discrimination is an issue, the risk of armed conflict and the disintegration of the state increases.

African countries have to cope with a major obstacle. The formation of states is a process which is inherently one of conflict, something we have learned from European history. This means that methods of resolving these and other potential conflicts in as 'civilized' a manner as possible, so that they do not escalate into violence, must be afforded particular attention. This implies that the promotion of economic development must be undertaken together with the building or strengthening of democratic institutions that are suitable to the circumstance of the country concerned. Consideration of the local situation is necessary: permitting various political parties and holding national elections do not necessarily imply democracy.

In introducing democratic parties in multinational societies, the relationships between the various groups must be borne in mind. If this does not occur, or only partially occurs, what was intended as a solution to a number of problems would more readily lead to a growth of opposition and conflicts. 'Good Governance' therefore refers also to fundamental processes of national reconciliation, a social contract and 'civil society'.

MILITARY EXPENDITURE

There is a particular element of 'good governance' that deserves further attention: military expenditure in developing countries and the international arms trade.

One of the great dilemmas of security is that the purchase and manufacture of weapons in one country is perceived in the neighbouring countries as a threat. This can lead to a counteraction which in turn leads to an arms race. Apart from the threat, or perception of a threat, of armed conflict in immediate or close proximity, there are other reasons for purchasing arms. A second reason for arming may be found in the desire for greater political influence in the region and the protection of a sphere of influence. A third motive may be found in the process of state formation: arming may be seen as a measure of independence by political elites – that the government can stand on its own feet. This may at a certain juncture lead to arming against one's own citizens who may be seen by the government not as the essence of the nation but as a threat to the state.

Military expenditure in many developing countries is high to very high in relation to expenditure on social development. By reducing military expenditure and reallocating the available money to development goals, the governments of these countries could demonstrate their dedication to development. Despite the fact that a decrease in military tensions since the mid-1980s has been ascertained in many developing countries, this decrease is not so much the result of a changed political view of security and military questions but is simply the consequence of a shortage of financial means. Various donor countries and international financial institutions are exerting pressure for greater economies in non-productive expenditures, which include military expenditure.[4]

Such economies prompted by financial and economic reasons are in themselves useful, but are not in themselves structural. Political and diplomatic initiatives are necessary in order to improve the security situation in the 'Third World'. In order to reach a constant decrease in military expenditure, a number of proposals would need to be worked out along the following lines:

— In regions in which countries feel threatened by their neighbours a regional policy dialogue needs to be introduced or strengthened. Cooperation on security and economic issues between neighbouring countries must be pursued in order to prevent regional arms races and to manage conflicts over natural resources or as a result of regional economic inequalities.

— Greater openness or transparency in relation to information on military expenditure could be seen as a measure of trustworthiness and would therefore have a beneficial effect on the security situation. Without this openness it is much easier for those who have interests in military expenditure in both importing and exporting countries to convince the policy-makers that more arms are necessary. The opportunity for interest groups, lobbies and corrupt practice to manipulate policy would be seriously reduced through such openness.

— As long as there is a large supply of arms available on the world market it will be very difficult to prevent excessive military expenditure in a number of countries. A funding policy based on the diversification and conversion of the military industry could go hand in hand with the imposition of a tax on arms exports. By using the UN Arms Register it would be possible to supervise the raising of such a tax as far as it involved the export of large weapons.

— Specific aid programmes directed towards the demobilization of soldiers and military conversion could provide the means to reduce the military sector.

— Finally, in cases of exorbitant military expenditure in developing countries, other countries and international organizations could impose conditions on the granting of aid with regard to the amount of money spent on specific areas such as military expenditure. Ultimately, aid could be reduced should the conditions not be complied with.

Effective tackling of exorbitant military efforts goes beyond the reach of development aid. In addition to political and diplomatic initiatives to increase regional security, coherence in arms exports policy in donor countries is very important. It goes without saying that for the Netherlands this should be carried out within the European Union. The credibility of efforts to decrease military expenditure in a given developing country by linking this to development aid is seriously undermined if a coordinated and careful arms export policy is not implemented at the same time. Such an arms export policy should be under the primacy of the Ministry of Foreign Affairs, given that arms export trade interests should weigh less heavily than considerations of war and peace, international stability and a global system of law.

SMALL ARMS

The international debate on military expenditure seems to bypass the proliferation of small-calibre arms.[5] This is, for example, why the discussions on a new regime to succeed CoCom have made practically no progress on the issue of export control for conventional weapons. An exception to this should be made in respect of land-mines, which, thanks mainly to American NGOs, are now in the public eye. This has led to the United States, France and Belgium proclaiming export moratoria. The Netherlands has also announced the intention to destroy all anti-personnel mines.

Small arms deserve special attention, given that the numerous internal armed conflicts in developing countries are fought predominantly with this type of weapon. These conflicts last longer and in doing so claim more victims, and aid workers attempt to alleviate the suffering of these victims with great courage in Somalia, southern Sudan, Angola, Afghanistan, former Yugoslavia and Rwanda.

Since the end of the Cold War, groups which are active below the level of the state – such as nationalist separatist movements, ethnic liberation organizations, political extremists and terrorists – are the most destabilizing arms' purchasers. Those involved in trade with these groups keep their distance from the current policy instruments for controlling trade in conventional weapons.

Small-calibre arms may be taken to mean machine guns, automatic weapons, mortars, land-mines and raw explosives, the technology for which is between 40 to 100 years old. Even the more complicated of these types of weapons, such as portable anti-aircraft guns and anti-tank rockets, are not registered in the UN Arms Register. Statistics on the transfer of arms are of little use with regard to small arms, given that trading with these groups operating below the level of the state (sub-state groups) is not included, and the UN Arms Register only covers large-weapon systems. The financial scale of small-arms' trade cannot be compared with that of the larger weapon systems. Nonetheless, it can be ascertained that of the 30 major armed conflicts in the world in 1993, 26 were fought almost completely with small and light arms.

Fighting groups which have the *de facto* control over a territory find it relatively easy to come by small arms. This territorial control enables the groups to command an income by raising taxes or extorting money from citizens, and control over the region makes the transfer of arms physically feasible. For those groups which do not command sizeable financial resources or regular external military support, conquest or capture are the most reliable ways of getting arms. Theft from stores is another very common way in which terrorists obtain weapons. Although most armed forces have to contend with the theft of arms, this problem is far smaller in the West that in the former Soviet Union. The immense armouries of the Red Army are an important source of weapons for armed resistance groups such as the Armenians and Azerbaijanis. Not all weapons claimed to be stolen are in fact obtained by theft: theft may be a useful cover to conceal the actual origin of the weapons. It has been more or less proved that the tanks and artillery claimed by the Khmer Rouge to be stolen, were, in fact, supplied by the Chinese.

The private arms trade has, generally speaking, little interest in supplying sub-state groups, unless the government of the exporting country endorses this action. Most arms dealers abide by the permit policy and the export regulations of their government. The major exceptions to this are dealers in countries where there is no clear arms export policy, such as the countries of the former Soviet Union and in Central and Eastern Europe.

Contrary to expectation, it would appear that illegal arms' dealing only plays a marginal role in arming insurgents. Illegal dealers and insurgents prefer not to do business with each other. Most sub-state groups have difficulty in complying with the terms imposed by illegal dealers such as cash payments, exorbitant prices and arranging for shipping themselves. The black market is more appropriate to the delivery of small amounts of armaments, weapon system components and know-how to states that are isolated because of trade embargoes. South Africa and Iraq are examples of states that have built up a high-grade arms industry by using the black market. In addition there is a large grey area between official and illegal arms dealing. This context includes illegal shipments via transit countries and what could be referred to as 'silent trade', 'covert operations' from more or less autonomous regions within a country which bypass the rules of the official arms export policy.

Stolen or captured weapons put sub-state groups in a position to fight at a low-intensity level and to survive, but are not sufficient for victory. States play a decisive role as the only source of large weapons and advanced equipment, by supplying arms to sub-state groups. The Vietnam War is a good example. It was only after North Vietnam had supplied the Vietcong with heavy arms that the power balance in the fight with the South Vietnamese army altered, which in turn led to direct American involvement. The PLO was only able to build up a vast stockpile of weapons with the support of the former Soviet Union. Libya supported the IRA with SA-7 rockets and Semtex, among others. The apparently spontaneous outbreak of the Zulu struggle in South Africa in the early 1990s was only made possible with the lavish support of the South African army and police. Rebel groups lacking support from other states barely survive and many are forced to give up the struggle. The Nicaraguan Contras were barely interested in continuing their struggle after American support had been withdrawn. When the rebels in El Salvador had to manage without Russian support, the peace negotiations made rapid progress.

In order to prevent the proliferation of small weapons in sub-state groups it is essential that adequate international and multilateral measures are taken in the near future. Even taking into account that the available knowledge on the dimensions and nature of this problem is patchy, it is still possible to point to a few directions in which solutions may be sought. These are as follows:

— In general: more effective supervision of compliance with the regulations and laws against illegal arms trading. In particular the efforts to improve the controls over arms' exports in the former Soviet Union and Central and Eastern Europe should be directed more towards small and light weaponry.

— The establishment and reinforcement of specific export control systems for certain small and light arms. The universality of the Conventional Weapons Treaty aimed at limiting the use of mines must be improved and its scope widened to include internal conflicts. Mines which do not have a self-destruct mechanism must be completely prohibited. The possibility of setting up an international fund for mine clearing must be examined.

— The support that states provide to sub-state groups must be more closely examined. This important aspect of the arms trade is difficult to tackle given that states consider this an extremely sensitive part of their foreign policy. Both the United States and Russia have decreased or stopped their support to terrorists and rebels since the end of the Cold War. This is obviously not true of other important states such as Iran, Syria, China and North Korea. A set of formal instructions based on international consensus needs to be pursued in order to limit the support of states to sub-state groups.

— The insertion of small and light arms into the agenda of international regimes and registers that concern the transfer of arms.

— Reinforcing the effectiveness of the United Nations Arms Register by extending the categories of registered weapons and lowering the thresholds. In addition, in the longer term, altering the juridical basis of the Arms Register to make it a treaty with compulsory registration and verification needs to be considered.

— Finally, the establishment of international standards to determine when the transfer of small and light arms is permissible and in which situations it must be prevented at all costs.

CONCLUSIONS

The 1990s are marked by many violent conflicts, and it is of the utmost importance to develop an international capacity that may assist in the control of these conflicts. By so doing it will be possible to prevent more people falling victim, the escalation of the use of arms, their misuse by third parties and the geographical spreading of conflicts. Reform of the international system of law is needed in order to achieve this: new meanings need to be given to terms such as national sovereignty and humanitarian intervention, as well as giving greater authority to the organizations of the international community.

This is particularly applicable to the United Nations. The increased powers must be seen as linked to the prevention of escalation by means of early warning, monitoring, conciliation procedures and preventative diplomacy. The earlier a legitimate international political intervention in a conflict occurs, the less need exists for international military intervention at a later stage. Military intervention often comes too late and is generally too limited, and should be an exception. Those who realize this will want to spend more money and thought on prevention. Nonetheless, prevention is not a side issue that can be undertaken piecemeal in an amateurish fashion and postponed at will. On the one hand, the cost of prevention is of great benefit: prevention by economic and political means costs far less than military intervention; and on the other hand, prevention can be costly – money, human resources, politicians' attention, development of professional expertise – especially for the communities in which the conflicts occur. Neglecting conflict prevention, which is what appears to be the case at the moment, can only cost the world even more.

NOTES

1. Jan Geert Siccama, 'Het Einde der Vredesmachten?', *Socialisme en Democratie*, 12, 1993, pp. 532-5; and Mats R. Bernal, 'Whither UN Peacekeeping?', *Adelphi Paper*, 281, (London: International Institute for Strategic Studies, October 1993).
2. Ralph Dahrendorf, 'The Modern Social Conflict' (London: Weidenfeld & Nicolson, 1988), pp. 154-7.
3. This was written by Bart Tromp in an article in *Het Parool* towards the end of 1993.
4. Daniel Hewitt, 'Military Expenditures 1972-1990: The Reasons behind the Post-1985 Fall in World Military Spending', a paper prepared for the OESO seminar held in February 1993; and C.M. Shano, 'Developments in Military Hardware

and Personnel in Africa, 1985-1992', a research note prepared for the Clingendael Institute, March 1994.
5. Aaron Karp, 'Arming Ethnic Conflict', *Arms Control Today*, September 1993.

Concluding Remarks

To conclude this book, the editors would like to make a few remarks regarding the research project into the causes of conflict in developing countries, of which this volume is a first landmark. Since the Dutch Minister for Development Cooperation, Jan Pronk, commisioned this research project from the Netherlands Institute of International Relations 'Clingendael' in 1993, and the international seminar in 1994, the project has proceeded in the direction indicated in the policy conclusions by Jan Pronk and Paul Sciarone. They referred to three important domains that offer cause for conflict in developing countries: the processes of state-formation and nation-building; identity and cultural issues; and economic inequality. These domains are also at the centre of the next phase of the project. This phase, on which Clingendael Institute has recently embarked, consists of in-depth studies of regional conflict configurations. They are:

1. The processes involved in the formation of states and nations and the role therein of 'good governance', democratization, human rights, minorities and ethnic-cultural factors.
2. Socio-economic factors, specifically: (a) the effects of poverty and economic inequality; (b) the influence of environmental factors on conflicts; and (c) globalization, in particular the consequences of the integration of developing countries into the world market.
3. Armaments, with special reference to the role of small arms in internal conflicts, the trade in such weapons, and the implications for conflict of arms races between countries or regions.

The study has two aims, the first being to add to the overall store of knowledge. The development of theory relating to the origins of conflicts requires further refinement, and the project should help to explain why some countries are more susceptible to the escalation of conflicts to the level of large-scale armed hostilities. It is of importance in this context to study the interrelationship of the above-mentioned three configurations contributing to the causes of armed conflict in and between developing countries. Second, the study should be policy-oriented, and the findings can be made available for policy recommendations in both the North and the South. More detailed knowledge of processes leading to armed conflict can also result in specific recommendations for the development of early warning indicators. The research of this second stage will be conducted by researchers in developing countries, the regions involved being Central America, South Asia and West Africa.

Index